Java Programming with the SAP® Web Application Server

 PRESS

SAP PRESS and SAP NetWeaver ESSENTIALS are issued by
Bernhard Hochlehnert, SAP AG

SAP PRESS is a joint initiative of SAP and Galileo Press. The know-how offered by SAP specialists combined with the expertise of the publishing house
Galileo Press offers the reader expert books in the field. SAP PRESS features
first-hand information and expert advice, and provides useful skills for professional decision-making.

SAP PRESS offers a variety of books on technical and business related topics
for the SAP user. For further information, please visit our website:
www.sap-press.com.

Jens Stumpe, Joachim Orb
SAP Exchange Infrastructure
Learn everything about Routings, Mappings, Proxies, and
Business Process Monitoring
2005, 270 pp., ISBN 1–59229–037-X

Chris Whealy
Inside Web Dynpro for Java
A guide to the principles of programming in SAP's Web Dynpro
2005, 356 pp., ISBN 1–59229–038–8

Steffen Karch, Loren Heilig
SAP NetWeaver Roadmap
2005, 312 pp., ISBN 1–59229–041–8

Jo Weilbach, Mario Herger
SAP xApps and the Composite Application Framework
2005, approx. 270 pp., ISBN 1–59229–048–5

Andreas Schneider-Neureither (Ed.)
The ABAP Developer's Guide to Java
Leverage your ABAP skills to climb up the Java learning curve
2005, 495 pp., ISBN 1–59229–027–2

Karl Kessler, Peter Tillert, Panayot Dobrikov

Java Programming with the SAP® Web Application Server

 PRESS

Translation SAP AG
Copy Editor Nancy Etscovitz, UCG, Inc.,
Boston, MA
Cover Design department, Cologne, Germany
Printed in Germany

ISBN 1-59229-020-5

Contents

6 Web Dynpro: Developing User Interfaces 213

9   SAP NetWeaver Java Development Infrastructure: Step by Step to the Example Application   371

10   SAP NetWeaver Java Development Infrastructure: Configuration and Administration   393

11 The Architecture of the SAP Web Application Server — 439

12 Supportability of SAP Web Application Server — 483

Preface

SAP NetWeaver is based on the SAP Web Application Server—the technological basis of all modern SAP solutions. Without the SAP Web Application Server (SAP Web AS), no Enterprise Portal, Exchange Infrastructure, Business Information Warehouse, or SAP enterprise software would be able to run. SAP Web AS is the platform on which applications can be developed and operated. The success of SAP's software depends largely on the efficiency and robustness of SAP Web AS.

As we reflect over the past decades, SAP's implementation of the application server at the end of the 1980s and the beginning of the 1990s was revolutionary. SAP's competitors—in so far as they existed at the time—were building two-tier applications. Some competitors moved the entire business logic to the frontend, creating the extremely cost-intensive *fat client*. This was difficult to scale as numbers of users increased, since every user process was assigned to a shadow process in the database. Other SAP competitors moved the business logic to stored procedures running directly in the database, but soon learned that with stored procedures an application couldn't be run on a database platform without recoding the entire application.

SAP's solution to this problem was to insert a separate tier between the frontend and the database: the *application tier*. This was when the application server—as we know it today—was born—even outside the context of SAP.

The application server from the days of R/3 still had all the features of a modern application server. It abstracted data from the underlying operating system and database platform, and optimized access to database resources using a sophisticated transaction and update concept. It provided a platform-independent programming language (ABAP) that was tailored to meet the requirements of professional enterprise software.

Many ideas from the world of Java, such as generating bytecode interpreted by a virtual machine, have been state of the art in the ABAP world for a long time. Another advantage of Java was that the development and runtime environments were interlinked. There's probably no other system in which you can perform all development work without ever having to leave the system. As the system compiles itself incrementally after changes, you no longer have the long generation times that were standard for classic C and Java development.

The swift success of the R/3 System on the market led to the application server being widely distributed. At the same time, the Internet and the World Wide Web (WWW) took off at an incredible speed. Proprietary worlds were no longer in demand; instead, people wanted open standards that were adopted by the Internet community. And the primary standard was the Java programming language. Even though its core wasn't designed for business applications, it was popular because it was simple and platform-independent. Consequently, Java became quickly widespread (largely because of the Internet).

But not all concepts from those early years had any chance of success: Downloading entire applications on request from the Internet onto simple devices still remains an illusion. Endeavors to define a Java-based application server that different software providers could implement were taken more seriously, although it wasn't until well-known providers (including SAP) actually began to implement the J2EE standard that Java had any real opportunity for success in the field of enterprise software.

However, implementing the standard came at a price. You had to implement many functions that were not imperative for business applications. Conversely, the J2EE standard could not sufficiently define many requirements essential for a business application, primarily the user interface, which is fundamental for business applications because an application's acceptance by end users depends largely on the user interface. This is where SAP's many years of experience with enterprise software came into play. Even in the earliest versions of SAP's software, the user dialog was the focal point. This tradition is currently supported by Web Dynpro for SAP Web AS. Web Dynpro represents an application's user interface running in the SAP Enterprise Portal and, as such, is often the starting point for a development project. Powerful tools such as the SAP NetWeaver Developer Studio (NWDS) help you to design your applications as prototypes, while Web Dynpro supports a highly declarative, model-oriented approach.

In addition to the user interface, elements and issues such as business logic, service-orientation, persistence, scalability, and maintainability are vitally important for the success of an application. A comprehensive chapter is therefore dedicated to each of these issues, starting with **Chapter 1**, which focuses on SAP Web Application Server's positioning within SAP NetWeaver and introduces the most important SAP NetWeaver components.

Chapter 2 focuses on the SAP NetWeaver Developer Studio, while **Chapter 3** demonstrates the development and deployment of a simple application using the J2EE programming model. This chapter does not discuss J2EE comprehensively (after all, several books are already available on this subject); instead, it focuses on how the J2EE model is supported by the different perspectives of the NWDS. **Chapter 4** presents the different procedures that are supported by SAP for Java persistence. The discussion includes relational models as well as object persistence, which is frequently used in Java circles. **Chapter 5** introduces the world of Web services from SAP's perspective. Web services form the technological basis for the anticipated Enterprise Services Architecture (ESA). Because of the central importance of the user interface, **Chapters 6** and **7** are dedicated to Web Dynpro. The Java development process and the infrastructure provided by SAP cover three chapters. **Chapter 8** introduces the component model that is necessary for the infrastructure and the infrastructure elements that build on it. The J2EE example introduced in Chapter 3 is expanded upon in **Chapter 9**, which further clarifies the use of the infrastructure. **Chapter 10** then describes how you set up and operate the Java development infrastructure.

In **Chapter 11**, we discuss the architecture, scalability, and high availability of the SAP Web Application Server (SAP Web AS). In **Chapter 12**, we address the subject of supportability, which is indispensable if applications are to be operated successfully.

This book includes a voucher that you can use to order a DVD free of charge. The DVD contains a test and evaluation version of SAP Web AS Java 6.40 and the SAP NWDS. The Developer Studio Workspace already contains the examples and samples described in the various chapters. The test version also includes components of the SAP NetWeaver Java Development Infrastructure (JDI). See the DVD's root directory for details on the installation and configuration of these applications.

In conclusion, I would like to express my gratitude to all colleagues who have contributed to this project. My special thanks goes to the team of authors: Alfred Barzewski (Chapter 2, *SAP NetWeaver Developer Studio: Features, Tools, and Perspectives*, and Chapter 3, *SAP NetWeaver Developer Studio: Step by Step Example Application*), Jürgen Opgenorth and Markus Küfer (Chapter 4, *Java Persistence in the SAP Web Application Server*), Dominik Schlund, Anne Lanfermann, and Martin Huvar (Chapter 5, *Web Services in the SAP Web Application Server*), Peter Tillert (Chapter 6, *Web Dynpro: Developing User Interfaces*), Bertram Ganz (Chapter 7, *Web Dyn-*

pro: *Developing Business Applications*), Wolf Hengevoß (Chapter 8, *SAP NetWeaver Java Development Infrastructure: Component Model and Services*, and Chapter 9, *SAP NetWeaver Java Development Infrastructure: Step by Step Example Application*), Yu-Nong Zhang (Chapter 10, *SAP NetWeaver Java Development Infrastructure: Configuration and Administration*), Panayot Dobrikov (Chapter 11, *The Architecture of the SAP Web Application Server*), and Miroslav Petrov (Chapter 12, *Supportability of the SAP Web Application Server*).

I would also like to acknowledge the following translators for their contribution to the German and English versions of this book: Joanne Parker, Gabriele Erfurth, Jan Hakemeyer, Jack Primrose, Michele Coghlan, and Oliver Stiehl. Special thanks also goes to Thomas Hübner and Michael Neumaier who provided the installation on the accompanying DVD. Finally, I would like to thank editors Florian Zimniak, Inken Kiupel, and Nancy Etscovitz at SAP PRESS very much for their teamwork.

Karl Kessler
Product Manager SAP NetWeaver Foundation
Walldorf, May 2005

1 SAP NetWeaver

This book focuses on the SAP Web Application Server (SAP Web AS) Java application platform. To clarify the position of SAP Web AS, this chapter provides a short overview of SAP's application and integration platform—SAP NetWeaver.

1.1 The Necessity of a Platform for Enterprise Software

1.1.1 Motivation for Introducing a Technological Platform

SAP has been producing enterprise software successfully for more than 30 years. SAP's enterprise software controls all business processes in the company and is therefore an important factor in the company's success. However, SAP does not only develop business applications such as software for maintaining customer relationships (Customer Relationship Management—CRM), software for optimizing production (Supply Chain Management—SCM), or software for maintaining supplier relationships (Supplier Relationship Management—SRM). With each generation of its business applications, SAP also provides a technology platform that abstracts from the underlying hardware and system software (operating systems, database systems, networks), and also provides appropriate tools, frameworks, and services for developing applications.

1.1.2 SAP Basis as an Example of a Successful Technology Platform

SAP Basis is a prime example of a technology platform. It was the basis for the R/3 System and the mySAP Business Suite, and was instrumental in the success of these SAP solutions. SAP Basis has been integrated into the SAP NetWeaver application platform. Nevertheless, it is worth examining the SAP Basis architecture to determine which features have been used in the context of SAP NetWeaver, and to pinpoint those areas where SAP NetWeaver goes beyond the SAP Basis architecture.

1.1.3 Architectural Features of SAP Basis

One outstanding feature of the SAP Basis platform is the use of a platform-neutral programming language (ABAP) that was optimized for developing business applications. In addition to elementary language

ABAP Programming Language

constructs and data types, ABAP has a sophisticated technology for accessing table-type data structures (internal tables) in the main memory. Database tables are accessed using a portable SQL subset that is embedded in the language in terms of syntax and semantics. ABAP supports both procedural and object-oriented (OO) programming styles and can be used easily to implement GUI-oriented or browser-based user interfaces (Business Server Pages, Web Dynpro for ABAP). The runtime environment for ABAP programs has been optimized for high scalability. ABAP programs are generated in an intermediate code and are executed concurrently in large caches on the application server by several work processes that are assigned to users for the duration of a dialog step (see Figure 1.1). A dispatcher ensures that free work processes are assigned correctly to active user sessions. The division into dialog steps results in balanced transaction behavior, as database resources (locks, open cursors, and so on) can be held only during a dialog step.

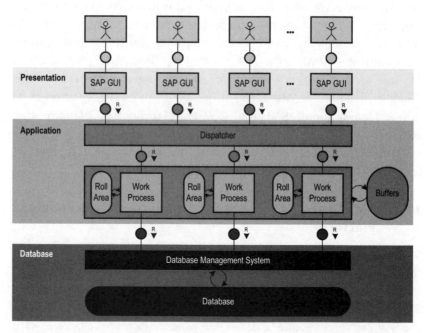

Figure 1.1 SAP Basis Architecture

SAP Basis Tools, Frameworks, and Services

Another important feature of the SAP Basis platform is its integrated development environment, which can be used to define database structures such as tables and views. These ABAP Dictionary definitions can then serve as the basis for many data structures that are used in programs. All dependencies between development objects are managed actively, which means that if an object changes, all dependent objects are regenerated as required. Changes to development objects can be transported from one system to another. This creates a development and production landscape that enables development to be distributed to large teams.

SAP Basis provides numerous services and frameworks, although only Business Workflow is cited as an example. This framework offers tools and an Application Programming Interface (API) so that applications are compatible with workflows.

What are the advantages of the SAP Basis technology platform? Because of its lack of dependence on the underlying hardware and software system, SAP solutions were available on all popular platform combinations and, consequently, they could be used by all customers. The effort required for porting was restricted to the system kernel. And since application developers didn't have to be familiar with a platform's special features, they were free to focus on the business know-how.

Advantages of a Technology Platform

The use of tools and frameworks enabled the standardization of applications in terms of usability, which, in turn, promoted performance optimization. A uniform application that uses shared services and frameworks such as workflow is easier to implement at the customer site and is therefore more likely to gain acceptance.

The great success of the R/3 System contributed directly to SAP Basis being widely distributed. SAP Basis is undoubtedly a robust and highly scalable application platform that can be used to develop business applications of any size. In addition to being an application platform, SAP NetWeaver is also an integration platform and, as such, far exceeds SAP Basis in its integration potential.

1.2 SAP NetWeaver as an Integration Platform

1.2.1 Integration within a System

Traditionally, enterprise software has always optimized selected processes or process sections in the company. The R/3 System is another excellent example of this enterprise software. The R/3 System optimizes sales order processing integrated within a single system and, in doing so, considers all aspects of this essential process. All process steps are logged in the system—from the receipt of the order to the availability check and production scheduling right through to invoicing. All relevant data is transferred in the background to financial accounting and prepared for cost accounting. From a technical point of view, the consistency of the business data is ensured by a shared database, a comprehensive Dictionary, and appropriate function interfaces. However, this approach is no longer optimal when data can't be saved in a shared database for technical or organizational reasons, for example:

▶ Heterogeneous landscapes generally develop following acquisitions and mergers.

▶ Innovative applications such as CRM and SRM provide their own database.

▶ Business processes exceed corporate limits (for example, Company A: procurement—Company B: order processing), see Figure 1.2.

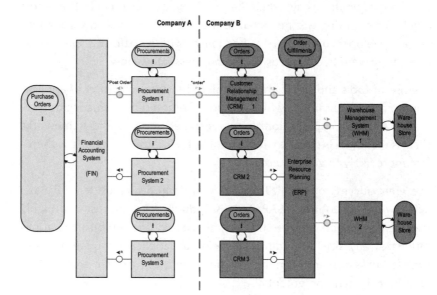

Figure 1.2 B2B Integration: Procurement—Order Processing

It is therefore not enough to simply optimize the processes within a system. Rather, it is precisely those processes between several involved systems—possibly belonging to different companies—that must be coordinated with each other so that as many steps as possible can be automated.

1.2.2 Standards Enable Integration

Web Services   Internet technology and standardization are important requirements for leveraging the integration potential. Standards support a shared language that is accepted and adapted by all those involved. One example of these standards is Web services, which enables a service to be called over the

Internet. Determining which technological basis called the service, or which technological basis is available to it, is irrelevant. Web services are therefore an important technological module for implementing integration scenarios. Other examples include the use of platform-neutral programming languages such as Java, which is being further developed (language, tools, and frameworks) by many companies.

1.2.3 Example of an Integration Scenario: Invoice Verification

The problem of integration can be explained by using a simple yet business-critical process, namely, invoice verification. Invoice verification is a process with objectives that are easily formulated:

▶ A company wants to pay for only those goods and services that it actually ordered and received.

▶ Invoices should be paid only once.

In the simplest case, all necessary information is stored in a system. In this case, we need only check whether a corresponding correct purchase order has been entered in the system for the invoice. Things become more complicated when several systems are involved, however. This is always the case if:

▶ Historically, divisions developed simultaneously

▶ The company resulted from a merger between other companies

▶ Procurement is decentralized but financial accounting is organized centrally, and a service provider may even have been outsourced

1.2.4 Component Architecture of Invoice Verification

Figure 1.3 shows the structure of the solution.

So that the invoices can be verified in a standard format, incoming invoices are standardized by the unifier component and saved in the invoice pool. Invoices can be received in many different ways. In addition to the familiar paper format, electronic exchange formats such as Electronic Data Interchange (EDI) or Extensible Markup Language (XML) are used increasingly to automate invoice processing. For smaller suppliers, our solution also supports a supplier portal where suppliers can log on directly. Once the incoming invoices have been standardized, it is important to provide as much context information as possible for verifying the invoice—this is the Context Builder component's responsibility.

Electronic Exchange Formats

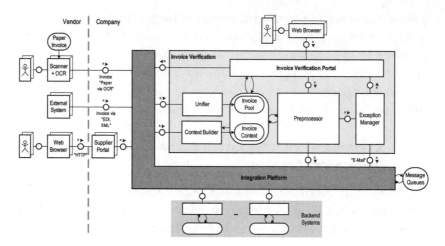

Figure 1.3 Invoice Verification Architecture

If the invoice is assigned a reference to a purchase order number, you can compare the invoice directly with the purchase order. If not, we have to find the open purchase orders for the suppliers involved and assign the invoice accordingly. Invoice duplicates are filtered out during preprocessing (by the preprocessor component) and exception management is triggered where necessary. Once the invoice has been verified successfully, it is passed to the back-end system for further processing. The user interface for invoice verification is represented by the portal, which gives the user a complete overview of the process steps that are connected with invoice verification.

1.2.5　Requirements for an Integration Platform

Features　This simple example shows the minimum features that an integration platform must provide:

▶ Portal technology for creating role-based central access to relevant information for users (invoice verifiers)

▶ Exchange infrastructure for connecting back-end systems (A2A integration) and for integrating business partner systems (B2B integration)

▶ Application platform for implementing invoice verification.

The relevant components are all included in SAP NetWeaver 04. An overview of the most important NetWeaver components is provided in the following section.

1.3   SAP NetWeaver Components

Figure 1.4 presents a classic overview of the SAP NetWeaver components.

Components for
the Integration

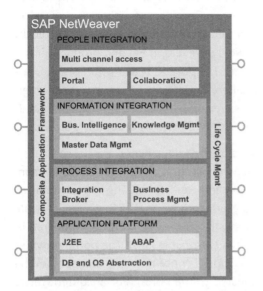

Figure 1.4 SAP NetWeaver Component View

The application platform includes the ABAP stack (formerly SAP Basis)
and the Java stack that supports J2EE standard 1.3. The three upper levels
represent the SAP NetWeaver integration layers: "People Integration,"
"Information Integration," and "Process Integration." All integration layers are based on the application platform and use the functions of both
the ABAP and the Java stack. From the diagram, one could infer that the
integration layers are hierarchically based on each other, although this is
not the case. The integration layers were created independently of each
other, but have grown together and share functions, so that in subsequent releases one refers to the NetWeaver Services, and not to the components provided by SAP NetWeaver. The component view is useful as an
initial reference, and the representation in layers (known as the *fridge*) has
quickly become accepted.

1.3.1   People and Information Integration

In the context of SAP NetWeaver, People Integration refers to the user
interface and access to the system. The integration aspect is based on all
users having standardized, role-based access to all systems that they need
for their job using the Web browser and the Enterprise Portal. Alternative

User Interface

frontends are therefore no longer necessary because the portal doesn't require you to log on to back-end systems (single sign-on, SSO). In a typical SAP environment, a user must access a range of different systems. For example, a manager needs access to an HR system where all HR-related information—such as applications, performance feedbacks, and salary data and so on—is stored. The current business development is typically created in a financial system, however. Development and production are, in turn, controlled by other systems. The portal's task now consists of harmonizing access to these very different systems, which may even originate from different manufacturers, meaning that the user no longer needs to know in detail in which systems the different information is stored.

Portal Content Portal integration is made possible by the role concept. Every user plays a role in the company, such as an administrator, a manager, a salesperson, a purchaser, an invoice verification clerk, and so on. The role contains all functions and information that a user needs to be able to access. The role concept in the Enterprise Portal has been created so that the degree of administration required remains at a reasonable level. The portal provides the external framework; the actual portal content usually comes from the back-end systems that are connected to the portal. Portal content refers not only to static Web content, but also to real, interactive applications in SAP. The Java platform was therefore implemented in SAP NetWeaver so that content conforming to the standard could be developed for the Enterprise Portal. The main content of this book discusses the actual technologies used for this implementation.

iViews The primary unit for content in the portal is known as an *iView* (integrated view). An iView represents a self-contained application in the portal that can be referenced with other iViews in various manners. iViews can be implemented technically in very different ways. The more prominent examples include Web Dynpro applications, HTMLB-based applications, and BSP applications; however, even SAP transactions that are started by the Internet Transaction Server (ITS) and SAP Business Information Warehouse (SAP BW) reports represent iViews.

If different iViews are semantically related, they can be summarized on a portal page. The portal infrastructure supports the exchange of information between different iViews using portal eventing at the frontend. iViews and pages are the modules for worksets, which, in turn, are the modules for portal roles. Both worksets and roles are represented by folder structures that are also used in the portal for navigation (top level and detailed navigation). Each individual user in the portal is given individual access to various applications in very different systems as a result of the assignment of roles to portal users.

The issues of knowledge management and collaboration are closely related to portal technology. In its early phase, the Web was primarily used for easy access to documents. In addition to the structured information provided by portal applications and BW reports, companies have a large amount of unstructured information (all types of documents) that is critical for their success. It is therefore essential that every user in the portal can access documents. Knowledge Management (KM) in NetWeaver is not a document management system (in the same way that the portal is not an application system); rather, it is a pair of brackets around the existing document and content management systems that are integrated in KM using generic interfaces. This enables full-text indexing and searching (Enterprise Search) and a comprehensive classification and taxonomy system as well as feedback functions.

Knowledge Management and Collaboration

Because documents are used mainly for exchanging information, you may also want to access shared documents, for which SAP NetWeaver provides a series of collaboration technologies. The communication takes place in so-called *Collaboration Rooms*, based on Internet forums. Technically, a *room* is a document container that can integrate project-specific data such as calendars, task lists, and so on. The room's (browser-based) interface is completely embedded in the portal. An invitation mail gives you access to a room. Room templates help you define a new room and support different usage scenarios. A room can also be the starting point for Real-Time Collaboration (such as WebEx). The objective of collaboration is not restricted to static documents; typically, users may want to exchange the results of a BW report or a portal application. In cross-NetWeaver scenarios (such as information broadcasting), the Enterprise Portal and Business Information Warehouse "NetWeaver components" are closely linked.

In addition to the ABAP stack, Business Intelligence (BI) is the most mature component in SAP NetWeaver. This is not surprising if you consider that reporting is integral for making strategic decisions, such as:

Business Intelligence

▶ Identifying customer and market potential

▶ Optimizing warehouse stock

▶ Selecting and optimizing procurement

Because company data was distributed over several systems and represented in different ways, SAP started building a Business Information

Warehouse in the 1990s. Unlike the systems in which data is mainly entered—for example, Online Transaction Processing (OLTP) systems such as mySAP ERP or mySAP CRM—the data in BI is available exclusively for analysis and assessment; for example, Online Analytical Processing (OLAP) systems.

To design the analysis and assessment as flexibly and comprehensively as possible, and to achieve optimal performance for reporting, data is extracted from the OLTP systems, refined (information that is not required in reporting is hidden), and physically saved in data structures that are suitable for OLAP applications (known as InfoCubes) in SAP BW (see Figure 1.5).

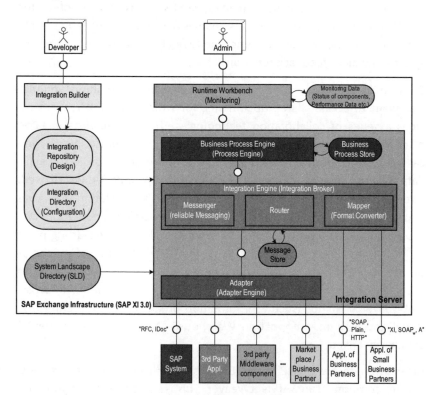

Figure 1.5 Basic Structure of Business Intelligence

The backend of BW is based technically on the ABAP stack, into which the additional BI content is inserted. Frontends are usually the Web browser for displaying reports—Microsoft Excel for defining queries and reports and for processing report data, and the classic SAP GUI is used for administrative purposes. Within SAP NetWeaver, BI is closely integrated with other NetWeaver components. The Enterprise Portal enables central, role-based access to reports and analyses, and the collaboration technologies help to facilitate working in teams.

There are several reasons why an OLTP system is not usually suitable for analysis and reporting:

▶ The data in the OLTP system is often highly normalized. For reporting purposes, this normalization reduces performance considerably as the data has to be aggregated with expensive join operations.

▶ OLTP applications have been brought into line with established business processes. Ad-hoc queries and analyses are difficult to perform.

▶ OLTP systems don't usually support universal, multi-dimensional reporting. Conversely, OLAP's universal data structure of InfoCubes enables data to be consolidated according to different categories. For example, revenues can be analyzed according to region, division, and customer group, for example. Combinations of data in different categories can also be mapped easily.

OLAP systems fall into different categories depending on how the data is saved. With relational OLAP (ROLAP), the InfoCubes are saved in tables in a relational database. Alternatively, you can use tree-type structures (MOLAP) to create multidimensional data. Although this type of access can be implemented very efficiently, it also has disadvantages if the data structure has to be set up again. OLAP Systems

For the ROLAP model, the star model is frequently used to represent the data. At the center of the star model is a *fact table* containing the primary facts (atomic, aggregated information that can be summarized in general), with *dimension tables* clustered around it. In the example above, the fact table contains the revenue data, whereas the dimension tables contain detailed data about customers, regions, and divisions. The fact table is linked to the dimension tables using foreign key dependencies. A multi-dimensional query searches first for suitable records in the dimension tables. The suitable facts are then filtered out using the foreign key dependency. To nullify the disadvantages of the star model caused by the lack of normalization, a series of other models are used that combine the star model with the normalized view.

Unlike Business Intelligence, Master Data Management (MDM) is a very recent SAP NetWeaver component. MDM is used primarily to consolidate the master data (customers, suppliers, employees, and material) that plays an important role in companies. Starting with MDM, master data Master Data Management can usually be distributed to other components and systems using Process Integration functions.

1.3.2 Process Integration

To integrate processes across systems, you must define them in a design time tool and then execute them in a designated engine. A series of typical tasks and problem areas occur that must be addressed and resolved by the Process Integration infrastructure. The SAP Exchange Infrastructure (SAP XI) is available in the SAP NetWeaver architecture specifically for this purpose. The previous functions of business process management, which concentrated on workflows with user interaction, were enhanced with cross-system integration processes in SAP NetWeaver.

Basic Requirements for the Infrastructure The following requirements must be met by the infrastructure in order for successful Process Integration to occur:

▶ **Messaging**
This includes the fundamental task of transmitting a message (typically an XML document) reliably from the sender to the recipient. Generally, this involves a certain quality of service, such as asynchronous linking with the assurance of delivering messages in the correct sequence only once. Asynchronicity ensures that the recipient does not necessarily have to be available at the time when the sender wants to send the message.

▶ **Routing**
Here it is decided to which recipient a message should be transmitted.

▶ **Mapping**
If the sending and receiving formats are not the same, then mapping enables the message to be mapped and transformed so that the receiving side can process the message successfully.

▶ **Business Process Management (BPM)**
Routing alone will suffice as long as messages can be forwarded independently of each other. To coordinate logical dependencies in the flow of messages that applications want to exchange—in addition to coordinating the time flow and subsequent steps—you need an executable process description that models the flow of communication between the relevant systems. The process is executed in the Business Process Engine, whose class business workflow functions were enhanced with cross-system process control. You can only adapt company processes flexibly to changed outline conditions via business process management.

The infrastructure must comprise the following components:

▶ Design and configuration tools for defining processes and configuring the landscape

▶ Integration Server that is responsible for the messaging, routing, and mapping tasks

▶ Process engine for executing the BPM

▶ Adapter for adapting the relevant systems (such as protocol adapting)

▶ Monitoring tools for monitoring the smooth operation in the exchange infrastructure

The architecture of the SAP Exchange Infrastructure (SAP XI) becomes clearer if you consider the aspects of design, configuration and integration server separately (see Figure 1.6).

Exchange Infrastructure Architecture

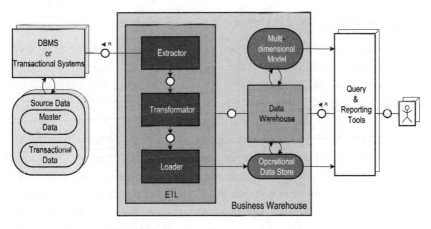

Figure 1.6 SAP XI Architecture

The Integration Builder is the central tool for defining XI content (message interface, mappings, and so on). All definitions are saved in the Integration Repository. The Integration Repository accesses structural information (such as software components) that is managed in the SAP System Landscape Directory (SLD). The SLD describes centrally the system landscape that is installed and also plays an important part in the Java Development Infrastructure.

Design Environment

Message interfaces are defined for the XI centrally in the Integration Builder based on XSD (data types) and WSDL (message types) and they are therefore compatible with Web services. However, it is clear that XI provides considerably more benefits via routing and mapping than does a Web service infrastructure. Proxies can then be generated from the message interface definition for the ABAP stack and the Java stack that the application can use. The application is therefore clearly separated from the technical implementation of XI.

The actual configuration for the SAP Exchange Infrastructure is saved in the Integration Directory. This includes rules that define how messages are routed correctly in a given landscape, as well as information about associated systems from business partners in what are called *collaboration profiles*, which are required for Business-to-Business (B2B) communication.

The runtime environment is implemented by the Integration Server, which is responsible for delivering messages and executing the integration processes in the Business Process Engine. The Integration Server is monitored in the Runtime Workbench.

1.3.3 Application Platform

The SAP NetWeaver application platform is based on two pillars, the Java and the ABAP stack. The ABAP stack represents the continuous advances in development of SAP Basis. Important technological innovations such as Web Dynpro and Web services were implemented on both the Java stack and the ABAP stack (Web Dynpro for ABAP is delivered with NetWeaver 05). This is not remarkable when you consider that ABAP remains the principal code basis for SAP's enterprise software. Of course, there is the question whether both stacks will be developed concurrently in the future, or whether the use of stacks will be optimized for certain usage scenarios. As we already mentioned, the strengths of the ABAP stack lie in its scalability and its integrated development landscape. It is precisely in these two areas that the Java stack has since made up time. The Java stack is even ahead in user interface development, because the Enterprise Portal and Web Dynpro technology are implemented in Java. The penetration by the Enterprise Services Architecture (ESA) will influence the orientation of the language stack considerably, although there is still a ways to go until that time (see the following section). There's still some basic homework to be done: Reintegrating the industry solutions into mySAP ERP is a good example of the work to be completed. The code bases must be consolidated on the ABAP side before anyone can even think about a service-based architecture.

If you are asked about the Java stack architecture, the answer is easy: The Java stack complies with standard J2EE 1.3. This is just one aspect, however. SAP has implemented the standard in the Java stack, although the standard doesn't cover all of the aspects that are necessary for successful business applications based on Java.

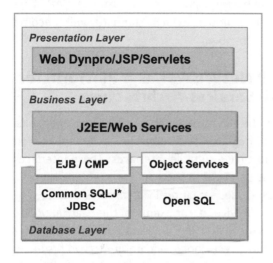

Figure 1.7 Java Stack

Figure 1.7 outlines the J2EE model. Applications can be divided roughly into three layers. Technologies such as Java Server Pages (JSPs) and servlets are available for the user interface. The business logic is mapped by Enterprise JavaBeans (EJBs); the database layer is mapped using Java persistence technologies.

JSPs and servlets can be used to implement very simple, usually platform-dependent user interfaces. SAP's Web Dynpro technology goes much further than the standard here. Web Dynpro is a model-oriented user interface and is supported by a wide range of graphical tools.

The application level (EJBs) is distinguished by comprehensive Web service support. This includes defining and calling services (proxy generation) as well as registering services based on Universal Description, Discovery, and Integration (UDDI).

Persistence is integral to Java programming. Even if the majority of SAP applications continue to be based on ABAP persistence, important system layers for NetWeaver (Portal, Java Development Infrastructure) are based on Java persistence. More recent frameworks such as the Composite Application Framework (CAF) also use the SAP Web Application Server's Java persistence. Like ABAP, the basic requirement for Java persistence was database independence. Unfortunately, SQL cannot be embedded syntactically in Java because of standardization. In this case, you have to

Persistence

rely on a precompiler (SQL/J), or access JDBC directly but without support at design time. Previously, attempts were made in the Java community to overcome the language barrier using object persistence. SAP offers several models (CMP, JDO), although which standard will become accepted in the interim is still unknown.

1.4 Prospects: SAP NetWeaver as a Platform for the Enterprise Services Architecture

In this chapter, we have seen the extent to which SAP NetWeaver enables enterprise applications to be integrated at different levels. An application that should be integrated must have suitable interfaces. These interfaces are also known as "Enterprise Services" in the context of enterprise software. An Enterprise Service includes semantically all aspects that have to be considered for the use of a service. If, for example, the "Cancel order" Enterprise Service is called, simply deleting the data record in the database where the purchase order was originally entered won't suffice. Actions have to be triggered in all associated systems in parallel to this. For example, a connected supplier system must be informed about this change. If data was transferred from the purchase order to an associated reporting system, the cancellation must also be considered.

Enterprise Services Architecture
The more comprehensive and extensive the range of Enterprise Services, the more real the image of the Enterprise Services Architecture (ESA) becomes. It is not enough to simply provide a technological platform with which Web services can be implemented. SAP has announced the ESA with the goal of providing a technological platform (SAP NetWeaver) and adding Enterprise Services incrementally to its enterprise software (ERP, CRM, SCM, and so on). The platform has already been introduced to the market (with the successful ramp-up of NetWeaver '04); the transition to a service-based architecture of enterprise solutions will naturally require more time and, for this sole purpose, SAP's roadmap has set aside the next three years. Simultaneously, customers and partners have to make their solution compatible with services to benefit from the advantages of a service-oriented architecture.

Advantages of a Service-Oriented Architecture
The advantages of a service-oriented architecture for enterprise software are obvious. A new generation of applications can be built on the basis of Enterprise Services: composite applications. Composite applications use services from several underlying systems and, in this respect, generate added value. Composite applications can combine the services of SAP solutions and partner solutions. This develops the technology platform into an application platform.

Traditionally, SAP's user interfaces were designed with professional users in mind and were equipped with a number of functions and features. The available user interface technologies permit a high degree of dynamism. Consequently, the use of the technology remains within a small circle of highly specialized experts with relevant programming knowledge (such as the readers of this book). To tap into additional user circles, it is therefore imperative that the user interface is simplified and normalized. Furthermore, business experts even without programming knowledge must be able to configure schematic user interfaces from standardized UI patterns. This configuration is only possible if the application has normalized interfaces so that generic UI patterns can be defined with actual application services. Of course, the nature of these services serves the needs of user interfaces, and their granularity differs from the SAP Exchange Infrastructure's message-oriented services. Both service types have a lot in common (such as data types used, implementation aspects), however, which is why SAP is consistently pushing the development of the Integration Repository as the Enterprise Services Repository in future releases.

Pattern-Based User Interfaces

2   SAP NetWeaver Developer Studio: Features, Tools, and Perspectives

This chapter introduces you to the SAP NetWeaver Developer Studio (NWDS). First, you'll learn about the most important features and design concepts on which SAP's Java development environment is based. This is followed by an overview of the perspectives and functions that are provided by an extensive range of utilities and tools.

The SAP NetWeaver Developer Studio (also known as the Developer Studio) is SAP's own development environment for developing Java-based, multilayered business applications. The new development environment is based on Eclipse, an open source product whose architecture is a suitable platform for integrating specific functions. Although Eclipse provides extensive, built-in Integrated Development Environment (IDE) functions, these functions are mostly generic. Developing large-scale business applications involves specific requirements that can be met only by making far-reaching enhancements to the Eclipse platform. For example, you could enable large teams of developers who are distributed across geographical locations and working on the same components to cooperate efficiently. The optimal way to use the support from additionally required project types and object types—as well as logical views of the projects and their development objects (instead of a file and directory-based view, which is typical in Eclipse)—is to enhance the infrastructure so it can implement new tools. Eclipse therefore provides a platform that can seamlessly incorporate any number of additional functional enhancements according to a standardized mechanism.

Eclipse Platform

2.1   User Interface

Before we examine the functions, let's look at the Developer Studio's user interface.

The basic modules of the user interface are based on the Eclipse user interface paradigm; the IDE user interface comprises perspectives, views, and editors. All of the components that are visible at any one time are represented by a *window*. A window therefore represents the Developer Studio's actual user interface and usually provides users with several perspectives, of which only one is visible at any one time. Figure 2.1 shows a window with a section of the J2EE perspective.

Window

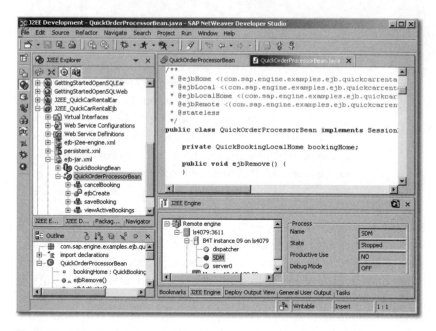

Figure 2.1 User Interface for the SAP NetWeaver Developer Studio

Perspectives A *perspective* always has a toolbar and a set of views and editors that are combined according to task-specific aspects. Users can open different perspectives with a mouse click to perform additional tasks within the development environment. Each perspective initially provides a set and an array of views and editors, although users can easily combine them, thereby adapting them to their individual requirements. In addition to the basic perspectives already included in the Eclipse standard, the Developer Studio provides a series of additional perspectives for various application development requirements. These additional perspectives are discussed in detail in Section 2.5.

Editors *Editors* are required to process development objects. They enable users to open, process, and save development objects. The changes made by users in an editor are not saved automatically, but follow the *open-save-close sequence* that is typical for files. In addition to the standard editors for texts and Java source texts, the Developer Studio provides additional editors for processing special development objects. These editors help Enterprise JavaBean (EJB) developers to better organize their activities. For example, the EJB editor in Figure 2.2 is connected to the Enterprise JavaBean. The EJB does not represent a file but a logical object, which, in addition to the bean class, also combines the corresponding component and the home interfaces. The EJB editor is also a central point of entry for working with EJBs. You use pushbuttons to navigate to the individual parts of the EJB and individual tabs provide different views of the EJB.

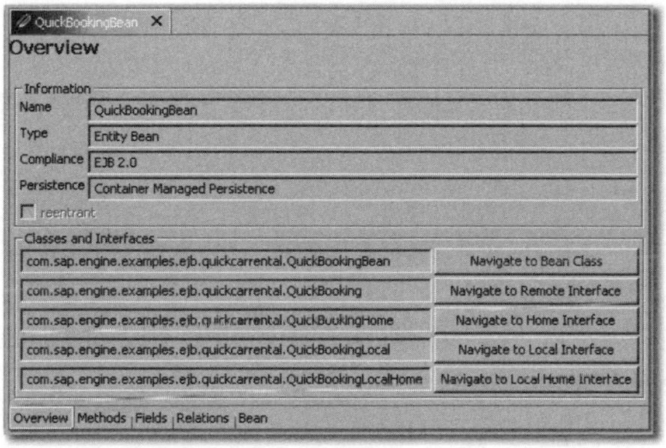

Figure 2.2 Different Views of the EJB: General Properties, Methods, Fields, Relationships, Bean Classes

Typically, *views* are used to represent a tree of structured data and are therefore suitable for visually displaying projects or other internal structures of XML files, for example. Figure 2.4 in the following section shows the Web Dynpro Explorer as an example of a view providing a logical view of a certain project structure. Views and editors are also often closely connected. Editors are often started from a view to open an object for processing from the tree structure. In many cases, certain information is required about an object that is currently being processed. This is a typical area where the *property view* is used. This chapter, along with Chapter 3, describes a number of additional views. **Views**

2.2 Workspace, Projects, and Development Objects

The Eclipse *workspace* is a central concept[1] for managing all resources locally. The workspace is not only the physical directory where project resources are locally saved; it is also the place where metadata is stored for managing information about projects, and, alternatively, for managing information about user-specific IDE settings. This workspace concept therefore abstracts from the physical file storage location and enables local resources to be organized flexibly under the IDE's control.

---

1 This workspace concept is fundamentally important for organizing any resources controlled by the local IDE. It should not be confused with the Design Time Repository (DTR) workspace, which will be discussed in a later chapter dealing with the SAP development infrastructure.

Workspace Combines a User's Projects

All development resources can be used as a workspace component in the Developer Studio. A workspace consists largely of one or more projects, where each project is mapped to the corresponding user-specific directory in the file system. This is displayed in Figure 2.3: In any given workspace, two projects can be linked to different directories, even on different drives. Each workspace has a default directory where metadata is saved in a separate file. This means that the metadata can be stored in a different location than the one with the actual project resources. Such a workspace directory can also be used as a physical storage for project resources.

Experience shows that it is best to decide between the workspace and the physical representation of the project data. They are separated particularly when the Design Time Repository (DTR) is used as a global storage location of project resources. In this case, all resources are available in the local DTR directory, which is automatically referenced from the default workspace. This mapping mechanism can therefore ensure that the external DTR files are handled as project resources in the Developer Studio.

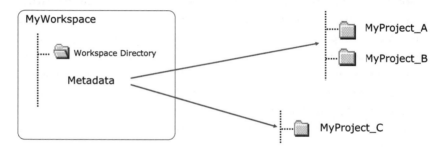

Figure 2.3 Mapping User-Specific Project Directories Using the Workspace Metadata

Projects as Containers for Development Objects

As with many other development environments, the Developer Studio groups related resources. In principle, a project can contain any number of files and directories. A special feature of projects is that they cannot contain additional projects. In this way, resources can be encapsulated optimally in a project. The group of development resources within a project is oriented according to clearly defined task areas. For example, EJBs cannot be created in the Web module project; conversely, EJB module projects do not allow developers to include Web resources such as servlets or Java Server Pages (JSPs).

In summary, projects are containers in which the related development objects are controlled at design time by the development environment. A workspace can contain any number of projects, which are displayed in the *navigator view*. The resources for the individual projects are shown here as files that are also displayed hierarchically in the form of a tree structure.

Unlike a file and directory-based arrangement, all SAP-specific projects offer a logical view of the resources that are also displayed here as a tree structure. Starting with the project structure, developers can start different context-specific actions, such as creating a new object, opening the editor, and so on.

Logical Views of Development Objects

By default, several views of a project type are available, each of which emphasizes different aspects of a project. Figure 2.4 shows the structure of the Web Dynpro project in the Web Dynpro Explorer.

Figure 2.4 Logical View in the Web Dynpro Explorer of the Development Objects in a Web Dynpro Project

2.3 Features

The Developer Studio provides full support for developing large-scale Java projects as well as standard technologies (J2SE, J2EE, XML, Web services, and so on) and SAP technologies (Web Dynpro, Java Dictionary, and so on). The Developer Studio gives application developers a central point for developing presentation logic as well as business logic, including data retrieval and persistence.

Developer Studio as an Integration Platform

2.3.1 Integrating the Java Development Infrastructure

The special feature of the SAP NetWeaver Developer Studio is that—in addition to providing toolsets for different Java development requirements based on corresponding SAP project types—it is integrated consistently into a robust SAP development infrastructure. The combination of both aspects makes the Developer Studio a highly productive and comprehensive development environment that spans the whole development cycle of Java projects, including configuration and transport management. This solution is particularly advantageous when you create extensive server-based business applications requiring large teams of developers.

Development Processes in the Team
Large development requirements make it necessary to divide the work into a number of projects sharing clearly defined dependencies. The development tasks are then frequently distributed among several teams. The development process therefore has to support teamwork so that the resources used by many team members can be synchronized, for example.

Local Development Processes
The Developer Studio also supports a local development process where Java Development Infrastructure (JDI) is not used. In this scenario, a developer processes a somewhat limited task with his or her projects, and will usually want to execute the application on only one PC. Generally speaking, the developer will not define any external references either to make his or her functions available to other projects. The project resources are saved on a local PC unless a central repository is used. Such local projects are typically used for test and demo scenarios, or even example applications, which is why they are best suited for developers with little experience of the environment.

Design Time Repository (DTR)
The Java Development Infrastructure includes a range of services (see also Figure 2.5). The Design Time Repository (DTR) is a repository for saving and versioning Java source texts and other design time objects centrally. The DTR has mechanisms that efficiently coordinate comprehensive projects that can be distributed across geographical locations if there are multiple users. The DTR is integrated in the Developer Studio using the DTR client. The main developer activities such as checking in and out are already available in all project types. Furthermore, special tools are available to developers in the development configuration perspective.

Component Build Service (CBS)
An important part of the infrastructure is the central build on which the SAP component model is based. The Component Build Service (CBS) keeps the build results as well as the environment required for the build (for compiling required libraries, generators, and build scripts) ready in a central archive pool. Developers can download these archives from the Developer Studio to their local environment. For each configuration that is used, the CBS then keeps the appropriate versions of the archive ready.

Code lines are created, consolidated, validated, and deployed in central systems on the basis of defined software logistics processes. The Change Management System (CMS) manages the transportation of software changes within an SAP Java development landscape. The CMS is represented in the Developer Studio by the transport view; the transport view releases the software changes so they can be transported further by the development and consolidation landscape.

Change Management System (CMS)

Transporting software packages requires a description of the system landscape, for which the SAP System Landscape Directory (SLD) provides a solution. All descriptions of the system and transport landscape are saved centrally in the SLD. As a central check instance for names of development objects, the name service is also part of the SLD. To avoid naming conflicts, the name reservation service makes it possible to reserve unique names globally.

System Landscape Directory (SLD)

In general, the central development process can be described as follows: The development environment has to be configured first so that it can use the JDI. Developers therefore must have corresponding authorizations in order to log on as JDI users. In addition to accessing the components of the infrastructure (DTR, CBS, or SLD server), developers also require a suitable view of the JDI environment, which is why they have to import a predefined *development configuration*[2] from the SLD into the Developer Studio beforehand. The development configuration then provides its local development environment with all the necessary information for addressing the infrastructure services. Even the components and libraries that are required for the development are identified in this configuration step. Each development configuration generally consists of a set of software components, which are, in turn, assigned to a set of development components.

Configuring the Development Environment

Considered from a slightly different angle, the development process is represented as shown in Figure 2.5.

Steps in the Development Process

❶ If the developer opens a project[3] in the Developer Studio, the required components and libraries—as well as the relevant Java source texts— will be available on his or her local PC.

---

2 A development configuration can best be compared with an R/3 development system in ABAP development. Here too, developers have to log on to a system before they can create, edit, and change the status of their development objects within a defined package hierarchy.

3 Each development component is identified by exactly one project in the SAP NetWeaver Developer Studio. Projects are created in the Developer Studio with the appropriate project type based on the DC data from the repository.

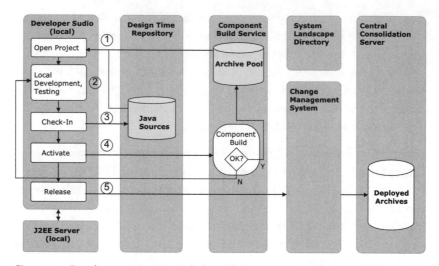

Figure 2.5 Development Process Including All Components of the Java Development Infrastructure

❷ Developers can make the required changes to the project, performing a local build[4] and then testing these changes in their local environment. To access a test server, only the corresponding J2EE server from the LAN has to be entered in the Developer Studio settings.

❸ When checking the objects back in, the developer saves the changed sources in the central repository, the DTR.

❹ The Developer Studio enables developers to activate their changed objects. The development objects that were previously inactive now become active. Activation always requires a successful central build process. The build request is passed to the CBS. The build service works in the background, checks all dependencies for the changed source texts, and triggers the central build process. The main advantage of this activation is that a build can take place promptly at the developer's request, resulting in less troubleshooting time compared with a *nightly build*. Only those components that could be successfully built by the CBS become active. In other words, the build service makes the relevant archive available to other developers in the team only if the build was successful. The team is therefore provided with error-free components and libraries. However, if an error occurred during the build

---

4   Beginning with a project, the component build can be started locally to check the changes that were made. Unlike the Eclipse standard build, the component build not only triggers the compilation of the project resources; it checks their consistency with the component model as well. This build operation is the same as the one performed following central activation in the Component Build Service (CBS).

operation, then a corresponding error message is displayed immediately. The developer can either make the necessary changes to his or her local environment and test them straight away, or debug it first.

⑤ Once all tests and the activation are successful, the changes can be released for transport. The developer can also control the transport release from the Developer Studio; only then is the CMS responsible for controlling the transport using a defined transport landscape. The CBS processes the release request and then incorporates the changes in the assigned consolidation system's import queue. The changes from the queue are imported into the consolidation system at established intervals. Once the import into the consolidation system is successful, the archives that are created by the build server are summarized as a new version and deployed on a J2EE server. Consequently, the new archive is forwarded to a central consolidation server.

Once the test run has been successful as part of quality management measures, the new software version is released for productive use.

2.3.2 Server Integration in the Developer Studio

So that the development process can be supported efficiently, it must be easy to access a deployment and test environment. The current state of a project can be deployed on a J2EE server in the LAN with little administrative effort, and the application can be executed on this server for test purposes. Another important requirement is that debugging can be initiated from the development environment and controlled centrally in all steps. The Developer Studio provides an optimum infrastructure for doing this as well as relevant tools.

Server Operation Support in Run and Debug Mode

Depending on how the SAP Web Application Server (SAP Web AS) is installed, the Developer Studio supports different scenarios for server operation.

With the Developer Workplace installation, the simplest case is where the SAP Web AS is installed on the same local developer PC as the Developer Studio. This simple standalone version is based on a single server configuration. In this case, the SAP Web AS consists of only one instance (shown in Figure 2.6 as *00*), which, in turn, includes a few central processes. These processes consist of a Java Dispatcher, the Software Deployment Manager (SDM), and a node that represents the actual server process (*Server0*). With the server node, you can toggle between

Developer Workplace Installation

run and debug modes. If debugging has been activated, the server is stopped and the connection to the server is reserved completely for the debug session.

Single Server Configuration

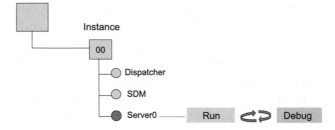

Figure 2.6 Process Nodes for the Single Server Configuration

LAN Scenario In general, developers access a Web AS from the Developer Studio, which is installed on any computer in the LAN. The simple Developer Workplace installation can be used even in a LAN scenario. The Developer Studio and the server (including the database) are distributed to different computers, however. Nevertheless, a single server configuration should be the exception rather than the rule in developer teams; rather, you will usually find a cluster configuration in these circumstances.

A typical SAP Web AS cluster configuration groups together several Java instances (shown in Figure 2.7 as *00, 03,* and *07*). Each of these instances consists of a dispatcher and one node or several nodes that represent the actual server processes (*Server0, Server1, ..., ServerN*). Furthermore, a Java instance is assigned to an SDM node. In such a cluster configuration, one or possibly even several server nodes can be reserved for debugging. Once debugging has been activated, the reserved server is removed from the cluster configuration by the message server and it is then reserved solely for debugging. For that reason, incoming requests are no longer forwarded to the reserved nodes. A debug session can take place using the debug port of the reserved debug node without influencing the remaining server nodes in the cluster.

In a production system, most nodes are reserved for operating the SAP Web AS and therefore have a **productive** status. Such productive server nodes cannot be used for debugging.

WAN Scenario In the WAN scenario, the SAP Web AS runs outside of the firewall. An important example of the use of this scenario is remote debugging in a customer system. SAP provides special services for accessing applications on the customer side using HTTP and debugging the corresponding projects. The server connection is made using the SAP router technology through firewalls.

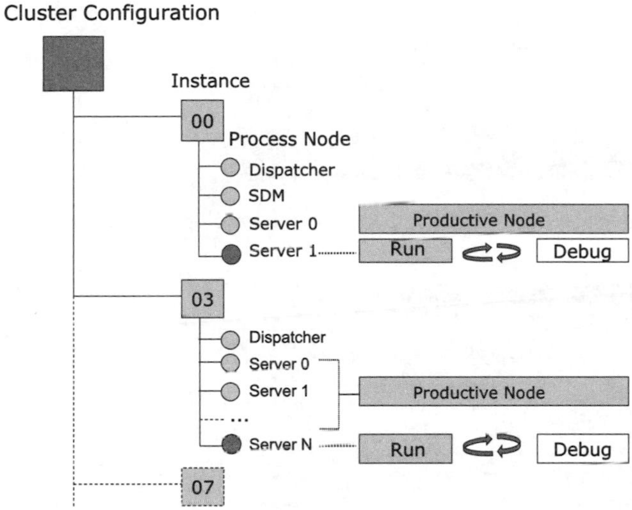

Cluster Configuration

Figure 2.7 Cluster Configuration

Tool Support

The J2EE Engine view gives developers a tool that not only provides them with information about the status of the assigned server, but also enables them to control individual process nodes from within the Developer Studio. The view is divided into two windows (see Figure 2.8): The left part of the window in this view contains a tree display of the individual instances and process nodes. Figure 2.8 displays a single server configuration, to which the process nodes for the dispatcher, the SDM, and the actual server process belong. You can use the context menu for the individual tree nodes to perform operations such as starting or stopping a process, switching to debug mode, and so on. The right part of the window displays the status information for the selected node; for example, whether it is a productive node, the current status of that node, or whether the user is in debug mode.

J2EE Engine View

The appropriate server settings are entered in the Developer Studio on the Preferences page. In Figure 2.9, the **Preferences** page displays two different settings depending on the installation option. Whether the assigned server is installed on the local developer PC or on any address in the LAN, you must select the options appropriate for the remote or the local installation.

Preferences

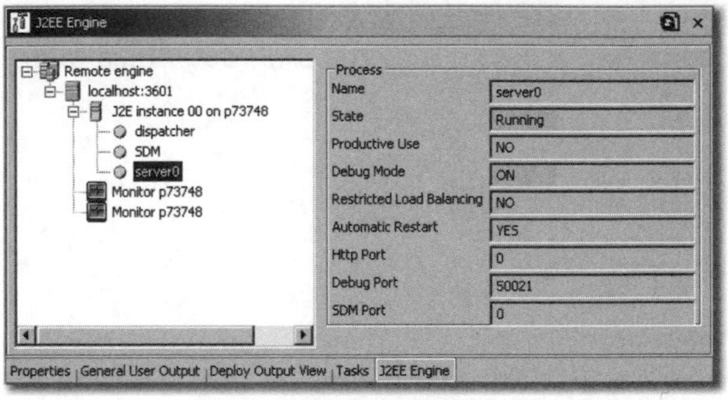

Figure 2.8 J2EE Engine View as a Fixed Component in the Developer Studio

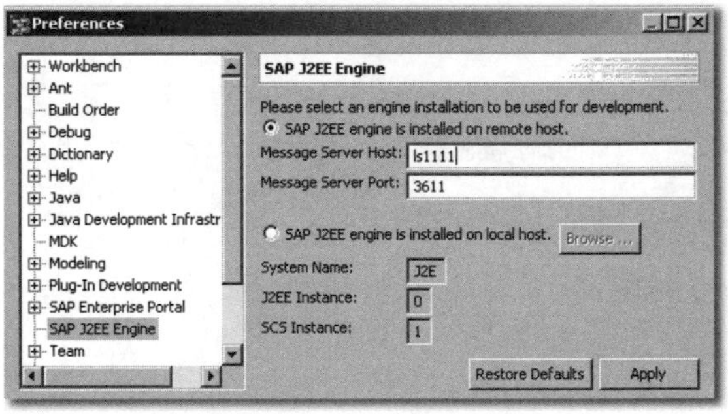

Figure 2.9 Server Settings on the Windows Preferences Page

Start and Debug Configuration with Server Access

Whether an application should be started from the Developer Studio on the J2EE server, or if debugging is required, an appropriate start configuration is required. In addition to the standard configurations, the Developer Studio provides additional start configurations, particularly for J2EE Web applications (for JSPs and for servlets) and for Web Dynpro applications. A start or a debug configuration can be created in the Developer Studio, whether the application in question is executed or debugging is performed for project resources. As Figure 2.10 shows, a configuration is fixed to a server node on which the application is started in run or debug mode. The developer needs to assign only the required instance to the configuration. An important advantage of such a reusable configuration is its link to the respective application: All additional environment data that is required to execute or debug an application is defined once and can be reused as often as needed. The start or debug configuration uses the server nodes that are assigned and generates the start or debug URL without any further action.

The developer assigns those instances of the SAP Web AS in which a Web application is started in debug mode on the **J2EE Engine** tab.

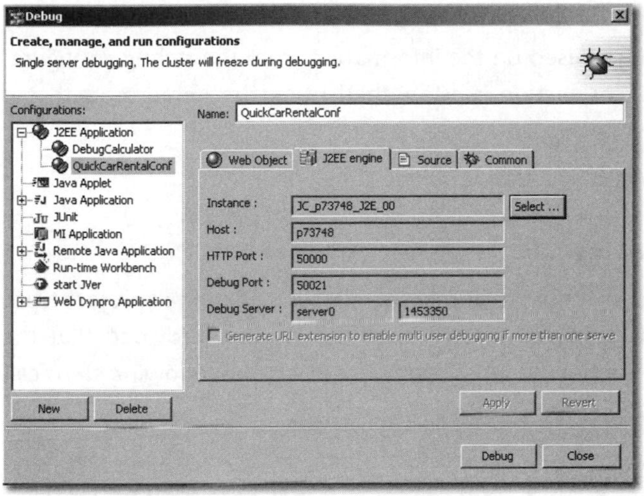

Figure 2.10 Example of a Start Configuration for Debugging a J2EE Web Application

Debugging Process

The server integration in the Developer Studio results in the following steps for the general debugging process:

1. Check the general requirements for debugging: Only server nodes that are not determined for productive use can be switched to debug mode. In a cluster configuration, the relevant node also must have the status **Restricted Load Balancing**. Only such server processes can be isolated from a cluster.

2. Enter the server connection in the Windows **Preferences** page in the Developer Studio.

3. Activate debugging from the J2EE Engine view:
   Note that in a cluster configuration, a debug mode remains integrated in the cluster until a debug session is activated for it. **Activate remote debugging** means that the relevant debug node is isolated from the cluster. The message server then removes the nodes from the list of its destinations so that incoming requests can no longer reach the activated debug node. From the time of the activation, the debug node is no longer involved in the cluster communication and will have to be restarted after the debug session.

   In a single server configuration (Developer Workplace installation), the server is stopped when debugging is activated and it is reserved only for the debug session.

4. Set the breakpoints at the required point in the Java source code.

5. Create a debug configuration.

6. Start debugging: Based on the information from the debug configuration, a server connection is established using the debug port that is entered, and a debug URL is generated.

7. Stop debugging in the debug view.

Process for Deployment

The general process for deploying archives is the same for all project types using the means provided in the Developer Studio. Provided that the SDM can run as part of the SAP Web AS instance, the following steps can be distinguished:

1. Update the project data within the Developer Studio project: The data is generated on the basis of the project metadata (**Rebuild Project**).

2. Generate a transportable archive from the project metadata (**Create Archive**).

3. Deploy the archive from the project view (**Deploy**).

2.4   Architecture

Before we examine the specific functions of the individual tools in more detail, let's look behind the scenes at the architecture on which the SAP NetWeaver Developer Studio is based.

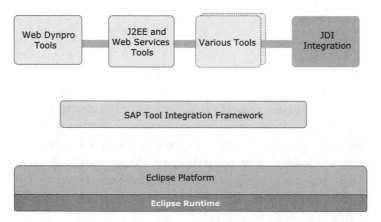

Figure 2.11 Architecture of the SAP NetWeaver Developer Studio

As shown in Figure 2.11, there is a difference between the following three software levels in the Developer Studio from an implementation point of view:

- ▶ Eclipse as an integration platform for plug-ins
- ▶ The SAP tool integration framework
- ▶ Various toolsets for developing applications and integrating the JDI

The Eclipse platform controls the IDE core functions and conversely provides a powerful infrastructure for extending it. This platform therefore
provides a type of basic development environment where a large part of
its functions is rather generic. This corresponds exactly to the objective of
Eclipse, however, which consists of providing a robust and universal infrastructure whenever possible for developing highly integrated tools. Tools
and utilities are implemented for the actual requirements of application
development. The objective here is to be able to process almost any contents and types (Java, C, JSP, XML, HTML, and so on) and enable different
tools—that can also originate from different manufacturers—to be integrated seamlessly. It is possible to implement such a concept thanks to
well defined Java APIs, which are open to tool manufacturers for their
own IDE extensions.

Eclipse—the Platform for IDE Extensions

New functions (tools) are made available using the platform's *plug-in
technology*. A plug-in is the smallest unit with which a function can be
developed and delivered separately. A small tool can be implemented
with a single plug-in, although more complex tools may have to be distributed using several plug-ins. Eclipse uses the concept of *extension
points* for its extensions. Extension points are a set of well-defined entry
points in the platform, with which new plug-ins can use existing platform
functions. In turn, new plug-ins can define their own extension points for
a possible connection and therefore present themselves as a service provider.

Plug-Ins as Technical Modules for IDE Extensions

The Eclipse platform consists of a platform runtime and several subsystems, which are implemented via one or more plug-ins. The main
Eclipse infrastructure is provided by some of these basic plug-ins. Examples of these plug-ins are the resource management system and the
Eclipse Workbench itself. The Developer Studio implies all these standard
components and features of the Eclipse Workbench and expands them
with a range of tools and services that are grouped in corresponding SAP
views depending on the task.

The SAP NetWeaver Developer Studio is based on the Eclipse platform
with a separate framework layer that is intended for integrating tools. This
forms the actual basis for integrating SAP tools. The reasons why such a
lot of effort is made here are explained in the following points in particu-

SAP Tool Integration Framework

lar. On the one hand, a generic approach is required to create a connection between the pure file and directory-based view that is typical in Eclipse, and the logical view of development objects in SAP projects.

Another important reason is to make developing plug-ins more efficient in SAP and to standardize the tools. For example, all DC project types should be based on a metadata concept. In addition, from a logical point of view, the same DTR developer operations (sync, checking out, checking in DTR activities) should be offered in various toolsets and project types that have a similar look and feel. Even the provision of generic components, for example, for tree displays of projects or for multi-page editors for processing XML files, originates from this objective. Furthermore, the underlying steps for creating plug-in user interfaces using a further abstraction layer in the UI programming model should be standardized and simplified.

The SAP Tool Integration Framework essentially contains two different layers—one for the model abstraction and one for the tool service.

The *model abstraction* is a generic layer that is used as the basis of the graphics connection, as well as to display design time objects at a logical level. This layer is therefore an abstraction of the physical file and directory nature of the objects. The *tool service layer* is based on the model layer as well as directly on Eclipse, and provides different services for integrating tools uniformly and consistently. Special APIs are also integrated in the tool service layer, such as those for archiving or logging and tracing. All tools can be uniformly connected to a tracing configuration with little effort.

The Developer Studio provides a range of tools for all aspects of developing applications. The special feature of these development tools is that they integrate seamlessly with the Java Development Infrastructure. In this way, all development objects that are created can be saved and managed in a central repository (the DTR), in a central build process using the CBS, forwarded to change management, and then distributed using a defined software logistics process.

2.5   Tools and Perspectives

The Developer Studio provides a range of tools for various aspects and tasks in developing applications. Connected tools are summarized according to task-specific requirements in what are called *perspectives*. The following section is an overview of the functions of the most common developer perspectives and toolsets.

2.5.1 Development Configuration Perspective

The development configuration perspective is used as a starting point for working with the Java Development Infrastructure and also for developing projects on an SAP component basis. When a developer is working in online mode in this perspective and wants to use central services, the first step is that he or she must log on to the Java Development Infrastructure. You need a development configuration to configure the Developer Studio for the JDI connection. Importing a development configuration automatically sets up the access paths for the services that are used in the development environment, such as the URI belonging to the DTR that is used, the CBS that is assigned, and the name service.

Starting Point for Working in the JDI

To display the development configuration perspective in the Developer Studio, choose **Window Open Perspective** and then select **Development Configurations**.

The main components of the development configuration perspective include views for browsing repository contents and a list of the open DTR activities.

The two repository views—**Active DCs** and **Inactive DCs**—provide a hierarchical view of components at a logical level. Each development configuration defines a section of the contents to be displayed, thereby defining the server view for the respective user. By default, a development configuration has several software components, and a set of development components is assigned to each of these. The corresponding tree structure is represented by two different views, one for the development components that were already activated, and another one for those that are still inactive. Developers use these views as a starting point for various activities, including importing development configurations, checking out DCs, or creating new DCs.

Server View

Furthermore, the perspective gives a local view of development objects with the **Local DCs** view. This lists only those DCs whose development objects are also saved in the developer's local file system. Just like the two repository views, this local view provides access to the activities that are assigned to the objects.

Local View

Once changes have been made to project resources, access to all underlying DTR operations makes available a view that lists all of a user's current activities. The DTR activities contain all changes to the project resources. The **Open Activities** view lists the user's open activities with each individual change.

List of DTR Activities

The **Activation View** enables developers to activate changes, and therefore transfer the relevant DCs from an inactive to an active state.

Figure 2.12 shows a section of the development configuration perspective. The view in the upper left part of the window lists the repository's content. In the example shown, this predefined, logical view of the server contents is provided by a development configuration ("6.30 SP7 REL Playground"). The upper middle part of the window displays the local view and shows all projects once they have been checked out to the local file system. The two views in the top right part of the window display a list of all of the developer's DTR activities. The **Property view** (bottom left) displays the properties of the selected object from any of the previous views. The DTR console displays important status information or confirms the operations that were completed during the session.

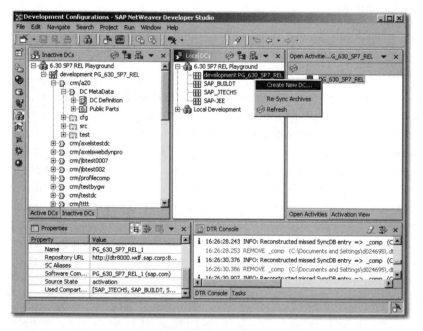

Figure 2.12 Development Configuration Perspective

The Development Configuration perspective's services include the following tasks:

▶ Import development configurations

▶ Browse component contents in the central repository and in the local file system

▶ Check out entire DC projects and individual project resources

- Create new DC-based projects for different project types (Web Dynpro DC project, Dictionary DC project, and so on)

- Integrate all basic DTR operations, such as creating new activities, assigning changes to activities, displaying changes, checking into the repository, or undoing changes

- Integrate the build and the deploy function

- Activate development components

- Display the properties of any objects (development configuration, software component, DC, development object, activity)

2.5.2 Dictionary Perspective

Developing portable and high-performance database applications requires not only a powerful persistence framework, but also tools that enable the platform-independent definition of database objects at design time. For this purpose, all tables in a central Java Dictionary[5] are defined for multiple platforms. The Developer Studio provides the necessary design time tools in the dictionary perspective. The dictionary perspective has various tools for defining database objects such as tables and indexes independently of the platform, as well as defining global data types known as *simple types* and *structures*.

The Java Dictionary's Design Time Tools

With the Dictionary Explorer, the perspective shows the logical structure of the dictionary projects. This view is used as the starting point for the relevant development activities, such as creating or processing dictionary data types and tables. The procedure here is the same as it is for many other types of projects: To create a new development object starting with an initial project frame, the developer selects the required category from the context menu at the required node in the project structure and starts the creation wizard. In this way, global data type definitions (simple types and structures), as well as tables and indexes, can be created as database objects based on XML metadata descriptions.

Dictionary Explorer

User-defined, global data types are specified in a designated editor. This helps developers define *simple types* as well as *structured types*, which consist of several elements. When defining data types, you can record semantic information about a type. You can also link UI text information

Editor for Global Data Types

---

5 With the Java Dictionary, the SAP Web Application Server provides a framework for the platform-independent definition and the central storage and management of database objects and global data types. The objects in the Java Dictionary are used for multiple applications in the field of Java-based projects. The dictionary perspective provides the Java Dictionary's most important design time tools.

to a data type, and centrally store texts to be used as input help, field labels, column headers, or quick info. Later, you can display these texts when you use the data type in the layout of Web Dynpro applications, for example. The value ranges of the new data types are derived from the predefined (built-in) types[6] that are automatically mapped to the standard Java Database Connector (JDBC) data types.

Editor for Tables and Indexes
The table editor from the dictionary perspective enables the database-independent definition of tables. A table definition is mainly specified by table fields (table columns) and key fields. Furthermore, table indexes can be defined for selected fields and the technical settings can be used to buffer the table and determine the type of buffering. A table definition that is saved in the Java Dictionary in this way is created as a physical table definition in the database when the table is deployed, and is translated into a representation of the respective database.

Figure 2.13 shows an example of a dictionary project with the project structure displayed in the Dictionary Explorer. You can also see the table editor where the table fields are created. A compressed XML description of the tables that are currently selected is shown in the outline view.

The Dictionary perspective's services include the following tasks:

▶ Generate a project framework for dictionary projects, both for local projects and projects based on the SAP component model

▶ Create platform-independent database objects (tables, indexes) as part of the Java Dictionary

▶ Create user-defined, global data types (simple types, structures) as part of the Java Dictionary

▶ Automatically map predefined dictionary types and simple types to appropriate JDBC data types

▶ Create transportable archives

▶ Deploy archives

▶ Rename tables and table fields

▶ Delete tables

---

6 The Java Dictionary provides a set of predefined data types (built-in types), which are either used directly or when user-defined data types are created. Examples of predefined types are string, short, time, and timestamp. Both the predefined and the derived simple types are portable data types that are converted to standard JDBC types without any additional effort and can therefore run on all DBMS platforms that are supported.

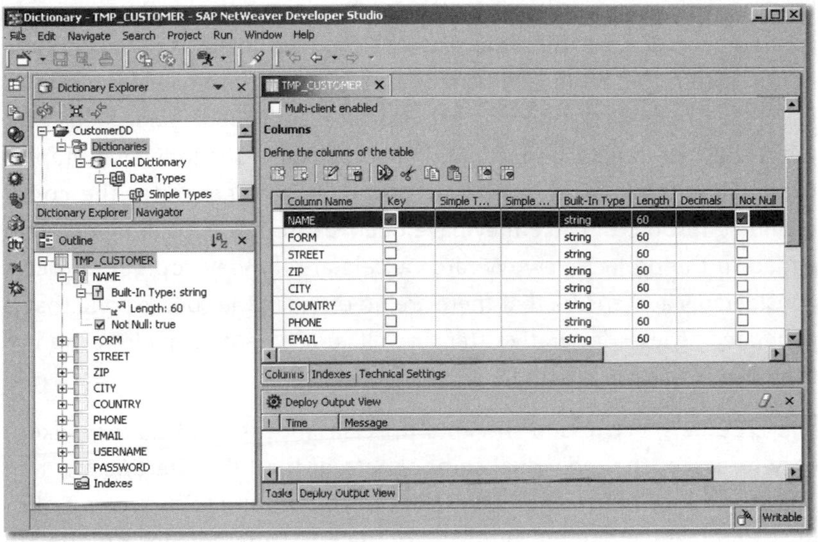

Figure 2.13 Table Definition in the Dictionary Perspective

2.5.3 J2EE Perspective

The J2EE development perspective (or J2EE perspective) offers uniform access to the development resources within different J2EE project types. Three different project types are available for distributing J2EE application resources:

▶ The *EJB module project* is used as a container for Enterprise JavaBeans at design time. Finally, all these resources are combined into a Java archive (JAR) along with the deployment descriptors.

▶ All Web resources are managed in a separate project, the *Web module project*, and create the Web archive (WAR) with the relevant deployment descriptors.

▶ An *enterprise application project* combines all J2EE resources in a J2EE application. The resulting archive is the EAR, which is the transportable unit of a J2EE application in the Developer Studio.

The J2EE perspective presents views that can be used to visualize J2EE projects in the J2EE Explorer, or the J2EE DC Explorer for DC-based projects in the Java Development Infrastructure. They provide a logical view of the relevant project structure and are available as a starting point for the main development activities such as creating or editing development objects.

J2EE Explorer

Wizards	Starting with a given project structure, development objects are always created according to the same pattern: The user selects the appropriate nodes within the project hierarchy and calls the first page of a wizard using the Create operation. This processes the individual dialog steps with which the new object is specified. The sequence of the individual steps is fixed in the wizard and, in the last step, the user generates the corresponding resources. Once they have been created, the resulting object is added to the project view. Wizards accelerate the development process considerably and ensure that there are no errors in the source code that is generated. These declarative steps result in a type of default version of the objects that are created.
EJB Editor	The J2EE perspective and the Enterprise JavaBeans (EJB) Editor make it easy to access the individual components of the EJBs. Starting from an overview page, you can navigate to the bean class and to the corresponding component and home interfaces of the EJB. Different views of the EJB enable developers to focus their work on clearly-defined tasks.
JSP Editor	The Java Server Pages (JSPs) and HTML editors make it easy to create and edit Web resources. In addition to syntax highlighting, pretty-printer, and code-completion, these editors are also equipped with a preview function.
Deployment Descriptors	All deployment descriptors are implemented as multi-page editors and provide developers with efficient support when configuring the J2EE application without having to change the XML source text.
Diagram View	As an alternative to project structure-based work, the J2EE perspective enables all declarative steps to be performed using graphical editing tools. Diagram views should be particularly useful if they are used in extensive projects to display components and their relationships to each other.

To display the J2EE perspective in the Developer Studio, choose **Window · Open Perspective** and then select **J2EE Development**. Figure 2.14 shows a section of the J2EE perspective with the J2EE Explorer (left), the **Overview** page of the EJB editor for an Entity Bean (top right), and the J2EE Engine view (bottom right).

The J2EE perspective's services include the following tasks:

▶ Create J2EE projects with and without a connection to the SAP component model

▶ Wizard support for creating and defining Enterprise JavaBeans (session beans, entity beans, message-driven beans)

▶ Wizard support for creating and defining Web resources for the J2EE standard (HTML pages, JSPs, servlets, filters, listeners)

▶ Configure the J2EE applications using deployment descriptors

▶ Create archives (JAR, WAR, EAR)

▶ Support declarative steps within projects using graphical tools

▶ Option to create a DataSource alias for addressing the database resource within a project

▶ Deploy EAR archives

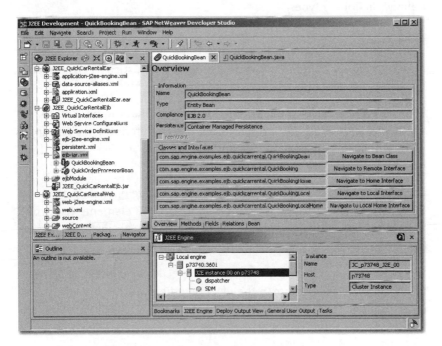

Figure 2.14 A Section of the J2EE Perspective

2.5.4 Web Dynpro Perspective

Web Dynpro introduces a new generation of browser-based applications for creating professional user interfaces as part of SAP Web AS. In addition to the necessary runtime services and the metadata model, the Web Dynpro technology also provides a range of design time tools. The tools that are relevant to Java developers are included as part of the Developer Studio in the Web Dynpro perspective. They support developers during the entire development cycle of Web Dynpro applications, starting with generating project components and implementing controllers to deploying and testing the finished application. Most of a Web Dynpro application is usually generated declaratively. The objects in a Web Dynpro application are usually created using wizards or graphical tools, thereby keeping the work based on manual programming to a minimum.

Web Dynpro Explorer The Web Dynpro Explorer is a central component of the Web Dynpro perspective. It provides a logical view of local and DC-based Web Dynpro projects within the Java Development Infrastructure (JDI). You can use the project structure shown in the Web Dynpro Explorer to access all Web Dynpro entities and source texts. Furthermore, each Web Dynpro project provides a local Java Dictionary that can be used to create user-defined dictionary types.

Data Modeler The Data Modeler maps relationships between the entities of a Web Dynpro project using graphical means. The Data Modeler is also suitable for creating different parts of the Web Dynpro project, such as custom controllers and model objects.

Navigation Modeler The Navigation Modeler is another graphical tool that can be used to create individual modules of user interfaces, views, determine their arrangement within the view set, and define the application's navigation structure declaratively.

View Designer To design the layout of the individual views, the developer starts the View Designer, which provides several predefined view elements (controls). View elements can then easily be added to the layout panel using drag & drop.

Context Editor Developers can use the Context Editor to specify the context assignment to a view controller, and map the view data fields to the model data, to dictionary data types, or even to the context of a different view controller.

Model Tools Web Dynpro tools also ensure that the back-end logic is integrated seamlessly. According to the Model View Controller (MVC) paradigm, persistent data is provided in the Web Dynpro by a model layer of the entire application. There are relevant model types for the various back-end scenarios. This is how the business functions that are encapsulated with BAPIs are accessed using the *adaptive RFC model*. A model is provided declaratively within the Web Dynpro project. Powerful wizards and generation tools are available that assist developers.

Local Dictionary User-defined data types and UI service information (text and value services) can be created using a local Java Dictionary.

Figure 2.15 shows a section of the Web Dynpro perspective with the Web Dynpro Explorer (left), the Data Modeler (top right), and the View Designer (bottom right).

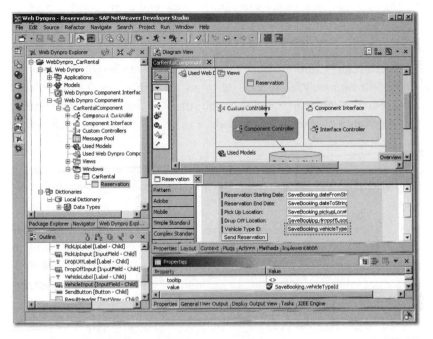

Figure 2.15 A Section of the Web Dynpro Perspective

The Web Dynpro's perspective's services include the following tasks:

▶ Generate a Web Dynpro project framework with and without a connection to the SAP component model

▶ Create Web Dynpro components as reusable and structuring units in the application

▶ Design the application with graphical support in the Data Modeler and Application Modeler

   ▶ Define relationships between components of a Web Dynpro project

   ▶ Create views and view sets

   ▶ Define the view sequence using navigation links

▶ Design the view layout with the graphical View Designer

▶ Define view contexts to store local view controller data and its references (to model data, dictionary types, or to other view contexts)

▶ Integrate a project-related Java Dictionary in which user-defined data types (simple types and structures) as well as UI information can be entered and managed

▶ Import model descriptions to achieve back-end connection

2.5.5 Web Service Perspective

The Developer Studio provides Java developers with ongoing assistance when defining new Web service providers, or in case Web service clients are used. The server integration within the IDE provides a comfortable test environment. All associated tools and other utilities are included in the Web service perspective.

To display the Web service configuration perspective in the Developer Studio, choose **Window · Open Perspective** and then select **Web Services**.

EJB and Java Explorer

The Web service endpoints—as well as all remaining development objects that are required when a Web service is created—are displayed in the relevant projects in the EJB and Java Explorer. That means in particular, virtual interfaces, Web service definitions, and deployment descriptors are organized in the EJB module projects.

Client Explorer

Client proxies that were generated for a Web service can be organized in relevant projects in the Client Explorer. The development environment helps developers to create relevant projects (deployable/standalone proxy project).

Web Service Navigator

The Web Service Navigator is used to display the Web services that were deployed on any server.

Figure 2.16 shows a section of the Web service perspective with the EJB Explorer, the Java Explorer, the Client Explorer, the Web Service Navigator, and the integrated test environment for Web services.

The Web Service tools include the following functions:

Support for Web Service providers

▶ Create Web services for Session Beans and Java classes as Web service endpoints:

  ▶ Web service creation wizard for defining the properties of the Web service with a predefined profile

  ▶ User-controlled, explicit definition of components of Web services (virtual interfaces, Web service definition, service configuration)

- ▶ Option of deploying Web services on the J2EE server
- ▶ Integrated UDDI publishing
- ▶ Integrated test environment

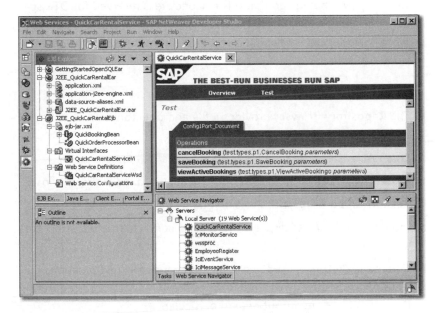

Figure 2.16 A Section of the Web Service Perspective

Support for Web Service clients

- ▶ Integration of the UDDI client browser: All Web services that were published on a dedicated server according to the UDDI specification can be identified by a UDDI client browser.

- ▶ Create Web service client proxies: The Developer Studio enables you to generate platform-specific client proxies based on the WSDL definition and manage them in specific client projects.

2.5.6 DTR Perspective

With the DTR perspective, the Developer Studio provides expert tools that are used in special cases such as solving version conflicts or during repository administration. The DTR perspective is available only in online mode, therefore, the user must be logged on to the DTR server at all times. Unlike the Development Configuration perspective, the Repository Browser offers a pure file and directory-based view of the DTR contents. The logical view—with a predefined structure for the DCs and their development objects as they are offered in the development configura-

Tools for DTR Experts

tion perspective—is missing here. For that reason, the Repository Browser is used by only those users who are most familiar with the repository's directory structure.

In summary, we should add that this perspective is reserved for DTR specialists who can perform more complex operations on the DTR server in order to solve special conflicting cases or to carry out certain DTR administration tasks.

The DTR perspective groups several views:

▶ The **Repository Browser** provides a file and directory-based display of DTR contents.

▶ **Open Activities** displays a list of all activities that are still open.

▶ **Closed Activities** displays a list of the activities that are already closed.

▶ **Version Graph** displays the version graphs for the required resource.

▶ **Integration Conflicts** displays the version conflicts that occurred during integration.

▶ **Command Output** is used to output commands for the operations that were performed by users. The errors and failures that occurred during DTR operations are output here in particular.

Figure 2.17 shows a section of the DTR perspective with the Repository Browser (top left in the window) and two views for the DTR activities and the command output (at the bottom of the screen).

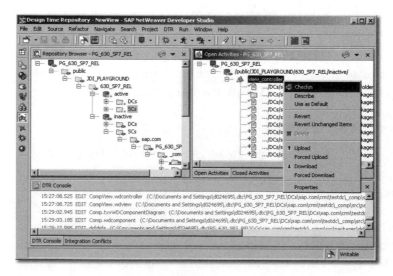

Figure 2.17 A Section of the DTR Perspective

The range of functions of the DTR perspective include all underlying DTR operations (such as adding changes to activities, creating new activities, viewing changes, checking into the repository, and so on) as well as extended operations for solving version conflicts. Lastly, this perspective also enables you to access different administration tasks, such as managing files within DTR workspaces or configuring the DTR server.

3   SAP NetWeaver Developer Studio: Step by Step to the Example Application

Based on an actual example, this chapter will provide you with information on the practical work of the development environment. On this "guided tour," you will set up— step by step—a simple employee application using J2EE standard tools. Then, you will deploy and execute the application on the J2EE server. You'll have the opportunity to become familiar with the close relationships that exist between various Developer Studio tools.

For optimal use of this chapter, you should be wholly familiar with the Java programming language and also have had experience with the J2EE programming model. To be able to perform all the steps, you'll require the SAP NetWeaver Developer Studio (SAP NWDS) and need access to the J2EE server. The Developer Workplace Version for Release 6.40 that you have received with the DVD, which accompanies this book, is suitable for this purpose. We recommend that you install this version before you begin the first exercise.

Prerequisites

In the example application, which we will develop step by step, we'll pay more attention to instructive aspects than to implementing a realistic application scenario. Therefore, we won't be creating a bank application or a complex department store scenario. Rather, our objective is to present—using an easy to understand example—the options that the Developer Studio provides as a development environment for enterprise applications. In the forefront, therefore, we'll focus on the interaction between different toolsets and on the connection to services that efficiently support the application process and simplify the daily work of the developer. You can view this chapter as an introduction to the work with the Developer Studio. After working through all the steps in this chapter, you'll be in a position to organize the basic processes and development steps (UI and EJB development, data model design, and so on) within the framework of the Developer Studio using suitable tools. You will also be able to tailor the appropriate tasks to your projects and their respective development objects (see Figure 3.1).

Target

Local Development Process

All the steps involved are described solely from the point of view of a local development process. This means that all project resources are stored and managed on the local hard disk. Contrary to what occurs when using the Java Development Infrastructure (JDI), these projects are not development components. However, in Chapter 9, you'll learn how to implement this example application in the JDI context in the form of component development.

3.1 Employee Example Application

Data Model

We will begin the development of our example application by creating the underlying data model. Here we create database-independent table definitions as part of the Java Dictionary. Starting from the Dictionary project, we'll create an appropriate archive and deploy it on the J2EE server.

Persistence Layer and Business Logic

We will use *Container Managed Persistence* (CMP) entity beans to access data records. The business logic of the application (creating new employees, displaying employee data) is implemented by a stateless session bean. At design time, the *Enterprise JavaBeans* (EJB) module project serves as a container for all enterprise Java beans. All these resources must, in the long run, be grouped into a Java archive (JAR) along with the appropriate deployment descriptors.

Presentation Layer

A simple Java Server Page (JSP) is provided to implement the Web client. This JSP should also be able to transfer the data to the session bean. All the Web resources are managed in a separate project, the Web module project, and—together with the appropriate deployment descriptors—form the Web archive (WAR).

In an enterprise application project, we then group all the resources together to create a type of J2EE overall application. But first we need to deploy the resulting archive (EAR) before we can initially call our employee application.

Web Service

From the session bean, we will define a Web service and thus provide the business functions of our example application to other, external applications (Web service clients) as well.

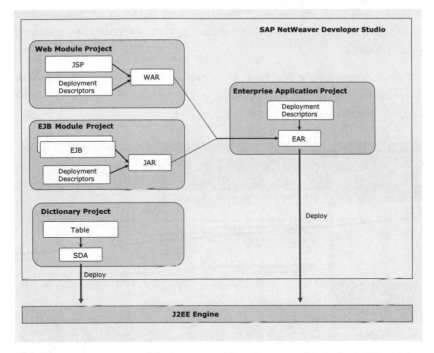

Figure 3.1 Project Types and Organization of Development Objects for the Employee Application in the Developer Studio

3.2 First Steps in the SAP NetWeaver Developer Studio

3.2.1 Starting the Developer Studio

To start the Developer Studio, the activated platform runtime requires— **Start Parameters** in addition to having access to a Java Virtual Machine (JVM)—a path specification for storage of all metadata for project information and user-specific settings. A standard JVM is typically assigned when the Developer Studio is installed and entered as the start parameter.

If you're starting the Developer Studio for the first time after its installation,[1] you usually have to specify the default workspace. The start procedure is interrupted in this case and a dialog box for selecting the workspace directory is displayed. You must then either adopt the default value or choose another directory for the workspace in order to continue the

---

1 In general, you start the Developer Studio using the desktop shortcut, or you start from the Windows **Start** menu. An alternative and very pliable option is to use batch files. Several batch files can be used as configuration files in order to start the Developer Studio with different start parameters, depending on requirements.

start procedure. When you start the Developer Studio again, the assigned workspace is used. The start procedure is then executed without any interruption.

When accessed for the first time, the development environment provides a welcome page. If the workspace is still empty, this page will look roughly like the page displayed in Figure 3.2.

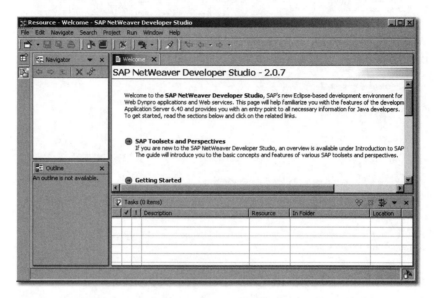

Figure 3.2 SAP NetWeaver Developer Studio—First Call

3.2.2 Settings Under Windows Preferences

At this point we recommend that you familiarize yourself with the standard settings for the Developer Studio and that—where required—you supplement them with additional entries. You can access the corresponding **Preferences** page via the menu path **Windows · Preferences**. When working through the steps in this chapter, you will need, in particular, a connection to a J2EE server. Therefore, there should be a corresponding entry under **SAP J2EE Engine**. In Chapter 9, we'll look at other settings that are required for using the Java Development Infrastructure (JDI).

3.3 Defining the Data Model

Before we begin with the development of our employee application, we must first define a suitable data model that will be the basis for this application. For the purpose of instruction, we are not overly interested in a sophisticated data model with many interrelated complex tables. Instead, the data model should be kept simple and we should be able to make do with a single table that can handle the management of persistent employee data.

In this practical step, we will create a new table in the Java Dictionary and then add the required columns in the appropriate editor. Then, we'll create a corresponding archive for this table definition. From the Developer Studio, we will then be in a position to deploy this archive on the J2EE server. In this way, we ensure that the table definition—initially available only locally—is also converted into a physical representation on the database instance.

3.3.1 Creating a Dictionary Project

To create tables, we first need a suitable project in the Developer Studio. For this very purpose, Dictionary projects are provided which, at design time, serve as containers both for Dictionary data types and structures as well as tables. With the help of a wizard, we create an initial project framework for the new Dictionary project.

We start the Create wizard via the menu path **File · New Project**. In the displayed wizard window, we select the category **Dictionary** in the left window section and then select the entry **Dictionary Project** in the right window section (see Figure 3.3). To get to the next dialog step, we click on **Next**.

New Project Wizard

Figure 3.3 Selecting the Dictionary Project in the New Project Wizard

In the Wizard window displayed, the system prompts us to assign some general project properties. We enter the name **EmployeeDic** in the corresponding input field for our Dictionary project, but we leave the standard settings for **Project contents** and **Project language** unchanged (see Figure 3.4).

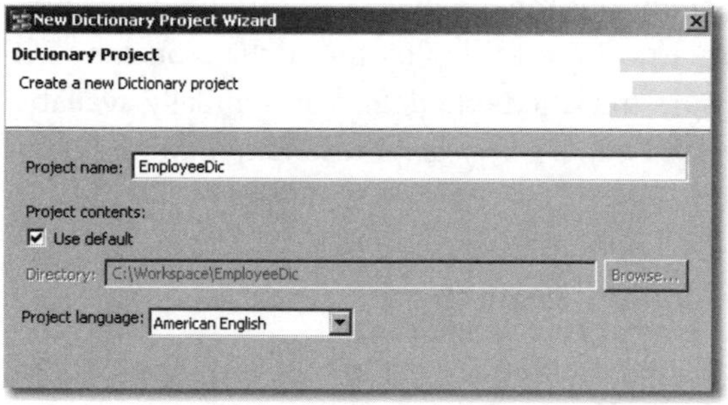

Figure 3.4 General Specifications for Dictionary Project

Now all we need to do is click on **Finish** and leave the remaining work for the Create wizard. This generates a standard structure for the new Dictionary project and also creates the project folder with the name **Employee-Dic** in the appropriate workspace directory. When we open the Dictionary perspective now, a project node with the same name is visible in the Dictionary Explorer.

In exactly the same manner, you can have other project types created in the Developer Studio using a suitable wizard; for example, a Web Dynpro project or different J2EE project types.

3.3.2 Defining the Employee Table

In the first work step, we will create a table for the employee data as part of the project just created and then we will add the required table fields as columns.

To create a table, you should display the project **EmployeeDic** in the Dictionary Explorer. There we will expand the project structure and open the context menu for the node **Database Tables**. To start the corresponding Create wizard, we simply choose the menu option **Create Table** from the context menu (see Figure 3.5). In the dialog box that appears, we are prompted to enter a name for the table.

Name
Conventions for
Database Objects

Remember that, generally, a standard prefix is already specified in the input field for the table name. As you can easily see, this prefix is derived from the presetting that is entered for the Dictionary objects under **Windows · Preferences · Dictionary · Nameserver Prefix**. This name prefix is based on the name convention for database tables and enables a clear separation of development objects that are created at customer sites, partner sites, and at SAP with the purpose of avoiding name conflicts.[2] The two namespaces TMP_* and TEST_* are of a special nature. They can generally be used for test objects and prototypes.

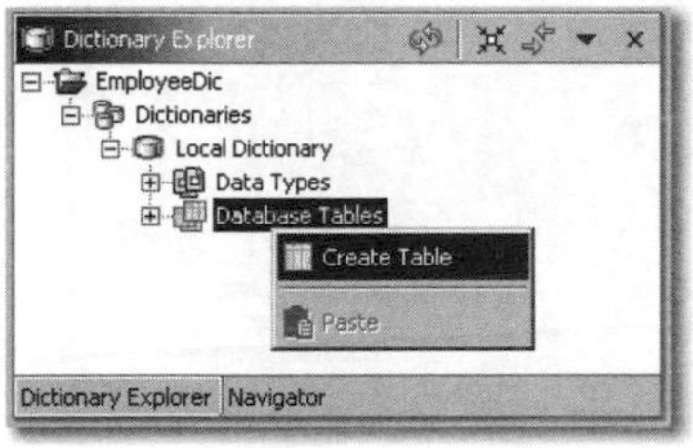

Figure 3.5 Creating a Table in the Dictionary Project

For our table, we enter the name TMP_EMPLOYEES and then click on **Finish**. As a result, a corresponding entry for the new table in the project structure will be available under the node **Database Tables**. By double-clicking on the table name, we can open the table editor and add the individual table fields.

The first field is to have the name **ID** and we enter this under **Column Name** in the first line of the table matrix. Since this column is to contain the primary key of the table, we also select the field **Key**. Under **Built-In Type,** we choose the data type **long**, and under **Description,** we enter the short description "Employee's ID." In the standard version, the property **Not NULL** is set for each new field. We use this opportunity to assign initial values for each field in the database table. The second table name is given the name **LASTNAME**. In addition, a **String** of length **30** is assigned as data type[3] and "Employee's last name" as the short text. **FIRSTNAME** and **DEPARTMENT** are added and defined accordingly (see Figure 3.6).

Table Fields

In this way, the basic properties of our employee table are set. However, we want to include two additional steps and mention something that you should keep in mind. We'll show you how to set up an index for a table column and, in addition, how to activate the table buffering in the table

---

2 Under *http://service.sap.com/namespaces*, these customers and partners of SAP can reserve a name prefix for database objects.

3 From the specifications for **Built-In Type** and **Length**, you get the assignment to the JDBC Type. This is automatically converted by the wizard.

editor. Here we follow the basic principle: Make as many decisions as possible at design time!

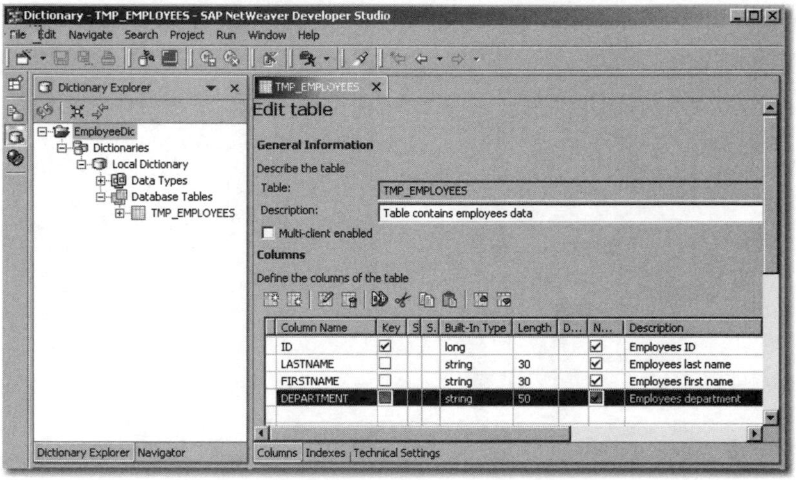

Figure 3.6 Defining Columns for the Table TMP_EMPLOYEES in the Table Editor

Secondary Index

To be really precise, the index is actually a secondary index. As a rule, there is a distinction between the primary and the secondary index with tables. The primary index is defined through the key fields of the table and is automatically created on the database, along with the physical table itself. Normally, data records are sorted according to the value in the primary key. However, if you expect data records in an application to be searched frequently for another field, we recommend setting up a secondary index for this field.

To create an index of the field LASTNAME, for example, we simply select the tab page **Indexes** in the table editor and then click on the pushbutton **New ...** in the left window section. For the index name,[4] we enter TMP_EMPLOYEES_I1. Then, we select the required table field in the right window section by clicking on **New ...** (see Figure 3.7).

Technical Settings

To activate a table buffer, we need only a few mouse clicks. We click on the tab **Technical Settings** in the table editor, select the appropriate checkbox, and then assign the granularity[5] to the buffering as it appears in Figure 3.8.

---

4 As with table names, the standard prefix flows into the index name. Like table names, index names are limited to 18 characters.

5 You can use the granularity to define whether the table should be loaded with all data records (fully buffered), or loaded only partially into the buffer as soon as the first data record is accessed.

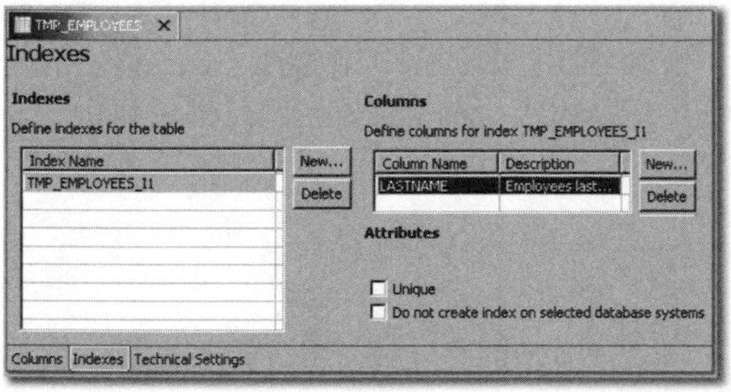

Figure 3.7 Defining an Index in the Table Editor

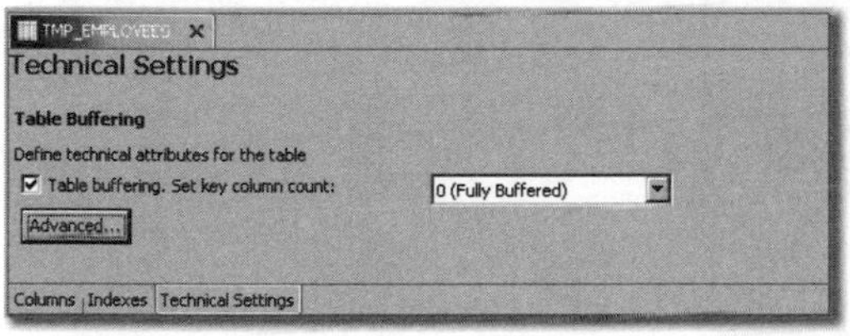

Figure 3.8 Activating the Table Buffer in the Table Editor

Certain metadata was generated for our project during the previous procedure. We therefore save the entire result of our efforts to-date with **Save All Metadata** by clicking on the 🗃 icon from the toolbar.

Thus, our table is completely defined and is available so far as a local project resource in the form of an XML file. One important result worth looking at is that our table—as part of the Java Dictionary—has a database-independent definition.

3.3.3 Deploying the Table

So that we can transfer the table definition from the current Dictionary project to a database instance, we need an archive file. This kind of Dictionary archive represents a transportable unit of the Dictionary project and groups all the Dictionary definitions of the project from the generated metadata. Only when we deploy the created archive on the J2EE server will the physical representation of the table in the database instance also be generated on the assigned database using **Create Table**.

Dictionary Archive

Before we begin with this step, we should ensure that the J2EE server and the respective Software Deployment Manager (SDM) server process[6]

Preparing the Deployment

---

6 The Software Deployment Manager (SDM) is generally started, as part of a server instance of the SAP Web AS, together with the other server processes of the instance.

have also been started and that the database is online. Only then do we choose the project node in the Dictionary Explorer, open the context menu, and select **Create Archive**. Afterwards we select **Deploy** from the context menu of the project node (see Figure 3.9).

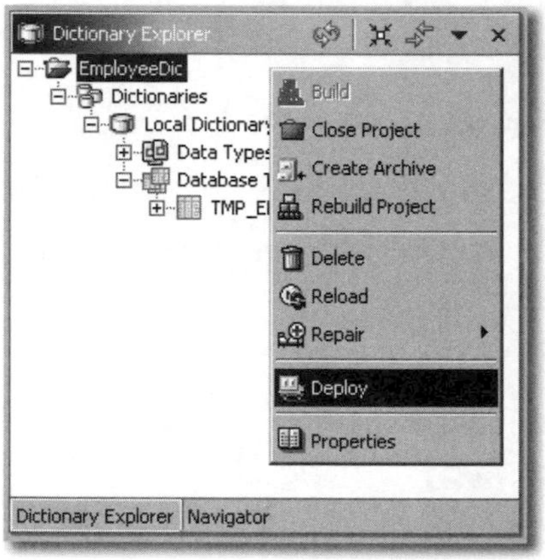

Figure 3.9 Deploying the Table from the Dictionary Project

In the **Deploy Output View** (see Figure 3.10), we immediately get a confirmation as to whether the deployment process has run successfully. From this view, we can also directly look at the respective log file.

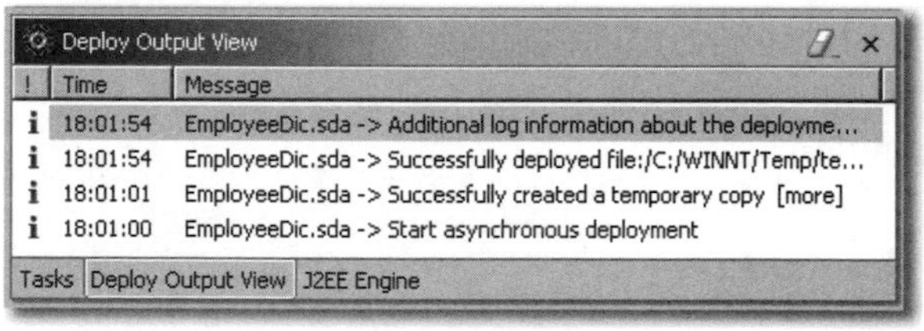

Figure 3.10 Display in Deploy Output View After Successful Deployment

SQL Studio If you are using the SAP DB as a database system and have installed SQL studio, you can verify that the table was correctly created on the database instance. For this verification, all you need to do is register on the database server via SQL studio and then do a search for TMP_EMPLOYEES in the list of all tables deployed on the current server. Provided you have SQL knowledge, you could also create a few data records for the new SQL studio.[7]

---

7 Direct data maintenance for the table—for example, using a simple input template—is not possible in the Developer Studio.

3.4   Accessing Table Data

Now we must decide how we want to enable access to table data records   **CMP Entity Bean**
in our J2EE application. Admittedly, there are several options that all have
their special traits and strengths. In our example application, we'll use
Container-Managed Persistence (CMP) and will defer the discussion
regarding different persistence types in the context of SAP Web AS until
Chapter 4, which deals explicitly with the topic of persistence. By using
CMP entity beans,[8] we can use to our advantage lesser implementation
effort and optimum tool support, and leave the responsibility of data
acquisition and storage to the EJB container. In order to execute CMP, the
EJB container requires exact specifications at runtime as to which persistent attributes of the entity beans should be mapped onto which database tables and columns. Therefore, in the following step, we will create
a CMP entity bean and link it with the TMP_EMPLOYEES table created
previously. This entity bean will model an employee entity and contain
the four fields ID, LASTNAME, FIRSTNAME, and DEPARTMENT. For each
column of the table, therefore, we will create a corresponding CMP field.
With the help of appropriate access methods to the CMP fields, new data
records will be created in our employee application. Finally, during the
implementation of the method `ejbCreate()`, we will consider with
which ID a new table data record is to be created.

3.4.1   Creating an EJB Module Project

To create and implement entity beans, we first need a new EJB module
project. For this purpose, we again start the **New Project Wizard** via the
menu option **File · New Project**. In the displayed wizard window, we
choose the **J2EE** category in the left section, and then choose **EJB Module Project** in the right section. By choosing **Next**, we get to the next wizard window, where we enter "EmployeeEjb" as the name for the new
project. With regard to the other values, we simply adopt the default settings and close the procedure by clicking on **Finish**. The wizard generates
an initial project frame for the new J2EE project, creates a project folder
in the assigned workspace directory, and automatically opens the J2EE
perspective (see Figure 3.11). The *J2EE Explorer* now serves as a central
starting point for further activities regarding EJB development.

---

8 With entity beans, there are two options for storing persistent data. With CMP
   entity beans, the task of data acquisition and storage is delegated to the EJB container. Conversely, an entity bean of the type Bean-Managed Persistence (BMP)
   must handle the database connection, the instantiation, and the deletion of
   objects.

Figure 3.11 Initial Structure of an EJB Module Structure of an EJB Module Project

The initial project structure already contains two deployment descriptors: the standard descriptor *ejb-jar.xml* and a server-specific descriptor named *ejb-j2ee-engine.xml*. In the next step, we add an entity bean to this project.

3.4.2 Defining the Employee Entity Bean

General Properties of the Entity Bean

New EJB Wizard We open the context menu on the project node **EmployeeEjb** in the J2EE Explorer and choose the option **New · EJB ...** to start the EJB wizard. In the displayed dialog window, we assign certain elementary properties as shown in Table 3.1.

Field Description	Assigned Value
EJB Name	Employee
EJB Project	EmployeeEjb
Bean Type	Entity Bean
Default EJB Package	com.sap.demo
Generate default interfaces	Checkbox selected

Table 3.1 General Properties of the Employee Entity Bean

We navigate to the next definition step **Add Interfaces and Superclasses**. In our case, no other interfaces and superclasses are required. We therefore continue with the procedure by again clicking on **Next**. In the displayed wizard window, we choose **Container Managed Persistence** as **Persistence type** and create the required persistence fields in the following, also referred to as *CMP Fields*.

Specifying the Primary Key and Other CMP Fields

Each instance of an entity bean is identified by a unique key. For this purpose, we will first create a field with the name **ID** and specify it as the primary key. Each instance of the employee entity bean is uniquely identified with this key field. Subsequently, we add further CMP fields that will incorporate the corresponding data records of the table TMP_EMPLOYEES.

To create a CMP field, we click **Persistent Fields** in the left window section and then choose **Add**. To the right, an input template is displayed in which the name of the CMP field and the appropriate type can be assigned.

To create another field, we click in the left section of the wizard on the node **Persistent Fields** and choose **Add**. The fields are defined in accordance with the list in Table 3.2.

Name	Type (Fully Qualified Name)
id	java.lang.Long
firstname	java.lang.String
lastname	java.lang.String
department	java.lang.String

Table 3.2 CMP Fields of Entity Bean

To specify the already existing field named **ID** as primary key, we click on the entry **PrimaryKey** in the left window section. Using the option **Simple**, we select the required CMP field (see Figure 3.12). By clicking on **Next**, we get to the next dialog step and will add another Finder method to the standard set of methods for the entity bean.[9]

Finder Method ejbFindAllEmployees()

Each entity bean always contains the standard Finder method `ejbFindByPrimaryKey()` that is used to pass a primary key value as a parameter for the required object. However, besides this mandatory method, an additional application-specific, multi-object Finder method named `ejbFindAllEmployees` is to be added. It should return a reference to all existing employee objects and later be used to supply a client with all employee data.

---

9 CMP entity beans can define so-called *Finder Methods*. These are query methods for finding one (single-object Finder method) or several entity objects (multi-object finder method). Finder methods are declared only in the home interface. Their behavior, in contrast to standard methods, is not specified using Java code, but through query statements. The description of the search query is entered using the declarative query language EJB QL. We will formulate an appropriate statement for our example in the *ejb-jar.xml* at deployment time. The search criterion is defined by the method parameter. The home interface provides Finder methods to clients.

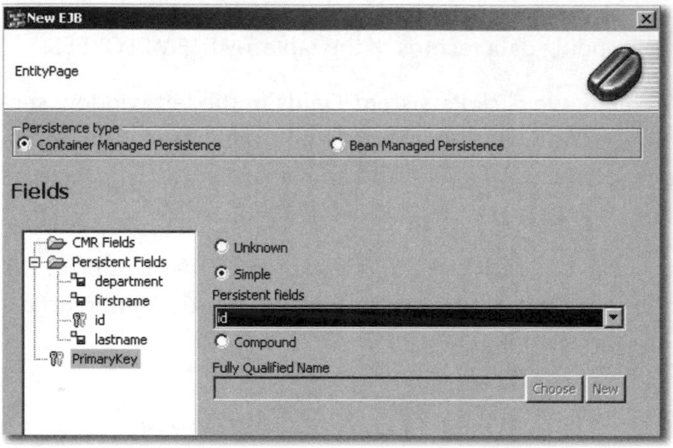

Figure 3.12 Defining a Primary Key for an Entity Bean of the Type Container Managed Persistence

To create a Finder method, we select the node **Finder Methods** in the tree display (left) and choose **Add**. To the right, an input template appears. Here we can enter the required method name and the return type. Since, in this case, we are dealing with a multi-object Find method, we assign *java.util.Collection* as return type. Using **Finish** we close the Create procedure.

Bean Class, Component Interface, Home Interface

The wizard generates the bean class EmployeeBean as well as the local interface EmployeeLocal, the remote interface Employee, the local home interface EmployeeLocalHome, and the home interface EmployeeHome with the appropriate Get, Set, and Find methods.

In addition, you have *persistent.xml* as another deployment descriptor for the project. It is created automatically as soon as we have created the first entity bean of the type Container Managed Persistence in the EJB module project. We will need this descriptor later when we enter the appropriate description at the time of deployment to map the entity bean and its CMP fields onto the database table and the corresponding table fields.

EJB Editor

If we now expand the project structure in the J2EE Explorer (see Figure 3.13) and double click on the bean node **EmployeeBean**, the respective bean editor will be opened. From the **Overview**, we can navigate to all components of the EJB using the appropriate pushbuttons and tab pages.

Implementing the Entity Bean Class

If we click the pushbutton **Navigate to Bean Class** in the **Overview**, the generated source code of the bean class is displayed in the Java editor.

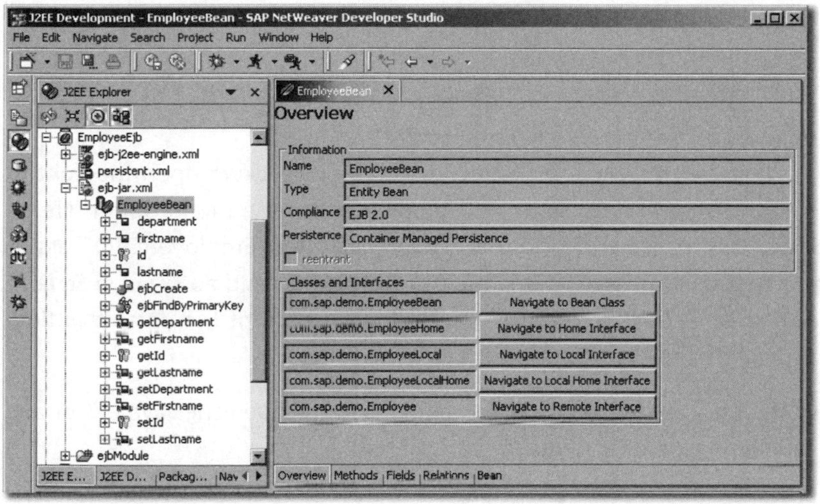

Figure 3.13 Employee Entity Bean

The implementation of this class will require adding only a few lines of Java code in the method `ejbCreate()`. Here we will ensure that, whenever a data record is created for an employee object, an employee ID is generated using a time stamp. Of course, we don't wish to offer a sample solution at this point for generating an ID. With the example in Listing 3.1, we merely simulate the creation of an ID. In a productive system, on the other hand, a real ID generation procedure should be used.

```
public Long ejbCreate() throws CreateException {
    long id = System.currentTimeMillis();
    Long temp = new Long(id);
    setId(temp);
    return null;
}
```

Listing 3.1 Method ejbCreate of the Entity Bean Class

3.4.3 Creating a Data Transfer Object Class

At this point, we're already including data exchange with possible clients—in particular, Web service clients—in our planning. For this purpose, instances are required and these instances will serve as a type of capsule for data to be transferred across various layers. However, this is the typical application area for so-called *Data Transfer Object* (DTO) *Classes*. Clients cannot directly access data records in the database, but

DTO Class as Instance

only through instances of DTO classes.[10] Therefore, in the next step, we'll create a new Java class that can be serialized. Principally, this class will declare the suitable attributes and provide the appropriate Set and Get methods.

New Class Wizard To create such a class for the EJB module project, we open the context menu for the project node, and simply choose the menu option **New · Java Class.** As a name for the new class, we enter "EmployeeDTO", assign the package *com.sap.demo*, which already exists, and add *java.io.Serializable* as the interface. For the other values, we adopt the default settings and create the class by clicking on **Finish**.

When the creation procedure is complete, we open the Java editor and add some field definitions to the class body:

```java
private String lastname;
private String firstname;
private String department;
private long employeeId;
```

Then, in the editor, we select all the lines with the attributes just added and choose **Source · Generate Getter and Setter** from the context menu. In the displayed selection box, we click on **Select All**. In this way, the respective Set and Get methods are generated for all attributes (see Listing 3.2). Finally, we save the current editor content using the corresponding icon in the toolbar.

```java
public class EmployeeDTO implements Serializable {
        private String lastname;
        private String firstname;
        private String department;
        private long employeeId;

        public String getDepartment() {
                return department;
        }
        public void setDepartment(String string) {
                department = string;
        }
        public long getEmployeeId() {
```

---

10 This approach is based on the situation that the persistence schema is hidden from the client and its view of the business data is based on the methods from the component interface.

```
        return employeeId;
    }
    ...
}
```

Listing 3.2 Implementation of the DTO Class

3.5   Defining the Business Logic

In the previous section, we set up data access using a CMP-supported entity bean. Now we will devote ourselves to the business logic. Since we have decided to use EJBs, session beans[11] are usually the optimal way to encapsulate the business logic.

For this purpose, we will create a stateless session bean named `Emplo-yeeServices`, and then add and implement the required business methods. Using the business methods, arbitrary clients should be in the position to accept registration data entered by the user and finally pass it to the entity bean `Employee` for storage. In addition, it should be possible to pass all existing data records on all existing employees to clients.

Stateless Session Bean

3.5.1   Creating Session Bean EmployeeServices

To create a session bean, we start the same wizard that we used when creating the entity bean.

Thus, we open the context menu on the project node **EmployeeEjb** in the J2EE Explorer and again choose the menu option **New · EJB ...** In the displayed dialog box, we assign certain elementary attributes, as displayed in the list in Table 3.3.

Field Description	Assigned Value
EJB Name	EmployeeServices
EJB Project	EmployeeEjb
Bean Type	Stateless Session Bean

Table 3.3 General Attributes of the EmployeeServices Session Bean

---

11 In distributed applications, session beans implement the application-relevant processes and tasks, perform transaction management, and enable accesses to low-level components, such as entity beans or other data access components, as well as auxiliary classes. This implementation of session beans adheres to the Session Façade Design Pattern, and serves as an example of the clear separation of the different layers (data accesses and business logic) with the goal of increasing performance at runtime.

Field Description	Assigned Value
Default EJB Package	com.sap.demo
Generate default interfaces	Checkbox selected

Table 3.3 General Attributes of the EmployeeServices Session Bean (cont.)

By clicking on **Next,** we navigate to the dialog box **Add Interfaces and Superclasses**. However, because we don't need any other interfaces and superclasses, we leave this window by choosing **Next**.

Even if adding session bean methods is possible at every other development time, here we use the opportunity in the next dialog step to create all the business methods that will be required from now on.

To create a new method, we select the node **Business Methods** in the tree display (left) and click on **Add**. To the right of this, an input template will appear. Here we enter the required method name `registerEmployee` and assign `java.lang.Long` as return type. In addition, we add the parameters `firstname`, `lastname`, and `department`, and assign the type `java.lang.String` to each of them.

In the same way, we also create the second method named `getAllEmployees`. Here we enter our specifications as we did in Figure 3.14, we click on **Finish** and trigger the generation procedure (see Figure 3.14).

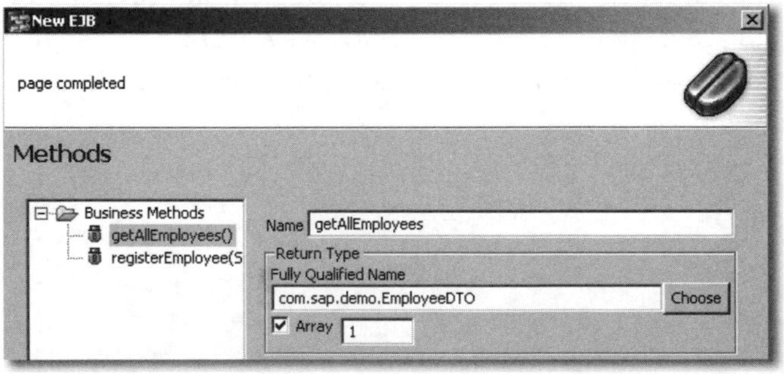

Figure 3.14 Creating the Business Method getAllEmployees

As displayed in Figure 3.15, the wizard creates an appropriate bean class, the corresponding interfaces (the local interface, the remote interface, the local home interface, and the home interface), and the subsequent EJB standard methods and both business methods.

Figure 3.15 The Session Bean EmployeeServices

3.5.2 Implementing the Bean Class

The procedure so far has been mostly of a declarative nature. We will now devote ourselves to the implementation of the specific service functions of our example application. Using the business methods of the session bean, we will implement those functions that will be provided for the client applications.

The business methods of the session bean are always implemented in the bean class. In addition, the bean class contains a number of other methods that particularly serve to implement the life-cycle activities of the session bean. These methods are called *callback methods* and can be divided into methods that create and delete objects, and methods that perform state management. Here, it will suffice if we implement the callback method `setSessionContext()` in addition to the two business methods `registerEmployee()` and `getAllEmployees()`.

To get to the source code of the bean class, we double-click the entry **EmployeeServiceBean** in the J2EE Explorer and thus open the EJB editor, which—together with the **Overview** page—is displayed on the screen. Using the pushbutton **Navigate to Bean Class**, we open the Java editor and can now add some fragments of source code to the session bean class.

Reference to Entity Bean

First, we define a new instance attribute with the name `employeeHome` of the type `EmployeeLocalHome`. The session bean can use this Local Home object to reference the entity bean. To get the reference to the entity bean, we perform the Java Naming and Directory Interface (JNDI) lookup[12] with the context variables jndiContext and store the reference, after successful casting, in the Local Home object employeeHome. This implementation is performed in the method setSessionContext() (see Listing 3.3).

Remember that the name ejb/Employee is used in the Lookup method as a reference for the entity bean. We will refer to this again later when we get to the *ejb-jar.xml* deployment descriptor.

```
private EmployeeLocalHome employeeHome = null;

public void setSessionContext(SessionContext context) {
    myContext = context;
    try {
    Context jndiContext = new InitialContext();
    employeeHome = (EmployeeLocalHome)
    jndiContext.lookup("java:comp/env/ejb/Employee");
    } catch (NamingException ex) {
    throw new EJBException(ex.getMessage(), ex);
    }
}
```

Listing 3.3 Declaration of the Local Home Object and Implementation of the Method setSessionContext()

Business Methods of the Session Bean

The first business method registerEmployee() serves to be able to create a new employee entity on the database. The data required for specification of an employee is passed via method parameters. To access the entity bean, the session bean (as client) calls the method create() through the Local Home interface.[13] The EJB container passes this call at runtime to the bean instance method ejbcreate(). The accesses to the persistent fields are performed with the help of Set methods. Consequently, the business method returns an ID of the type long. You will find the full implementation of this method in Listing 3.4.

---

12 JNDI (Java Naming and Directory Interface) allows clients to find EJBs and to access them without having to know their real names and the physical storage place in the network.

13 In a remote interface, the method create() would be called in the same way as it would for the remote home interface.

```java
public long registerEmployee(String lastname, String firs
tname, String department) {
   long result = 0;
   try {
      EmployeeLocal employee = employeeHome.create();
      employee.setFirstname(firstname);
      employee.setLastname(lastname);
      employee.setDepartment(department);
      result = employee.getId().longValue();
   } catch (CreateException ex) {
      throw new EJBException(ex.getMessage(), ex);
   }
   return result;
}
```

Listing 3.4 Business Method registerEmployee()

With the second business method getAllEmployees(), it should be possible to return all available data on a client to all existing employees.[14] You will find the full implementation of this method in Listing 3.5.

To implement the data transfer between the entity bean and the client, we now use the DTO class EmployeeDTO. To find the entity bean, the Find method findAllEmployees() is called through the Local Home interface. The result of this call is stored in an object of the type Collection and corresponds exactly to the return type of a multi-object Find method. As soon as the searched for entity objects have been found, we store the result in an array whose length matches the number of entity objects exactly. To determine the contents of the individual array fields, appropriate Set methods of the DTO class are used and the complete array is returned as a return parameter.

```java
public EmployeeDTO[] getAllEmployees() {

EmployeeDTO[] result = new EmployeeDTO[0];
   try {
      Collection col = employeeHome.findAllEmployees();
      Object[] obj = col.toArray();
      result = new EmployeeDTO[obj.length];
      for (int i = 0; i < obj.length; i++) {
```

---

14 The client can be a JSP, a servlet, a Java class, or another EJB; or, it can be a Web service client.

```
        EmployeeLocal employee = (EmployeeLocal) obj[i];
        EmployeeDTO temp = new EmployeeDTO();
        temp.setFirstname(employee.getFirstname());
        temp.setLastname(employee.getLastname());
        temp.setDepartment(employee.getDepartment());
        temp.setEmployeeId(employee.getId().longValue());
        result[i] = temp;
      }
    } catch (FinderException ex) {
        throw new EJBException(ex.getMessage(), ex);
      }
    return result;
}
```

Listing 3.5 Business Method getAllEmployees()

We now add to the bean class those imports that are still missing, provided this has not already been done. To do so, we click anywhere in the
Java editor and choose **Source · Organize Imports** from the context
menu. The missing import lines are then included; now, there shouldn't
be any errors displayed in the source code of the bean class. Finally, we
simply need to adapt the format of the new lines by choosing **Source ·
Format** from the editor's context menu. Then, we save the editor content
by selecting the appropriate icon from the toolbar.

3.6   Creating Deployment Descriptions

After we have created the two EJBs and the required declarations in the
home and component interfaces, and fully implemented the appropriate
bean classes, we will prepare the deployment of all components on the
J2EE server in the next step. As a result of the EJP module project, we will
create a corresponding Java archive, the JAR. However, before we combine all the resources of the project in this archive file, we must enter
additional information specific to how EJBs should be configured and
then used in the target environment. Certain properties of EJBs and their
special requirements that pertain to the runtime environment are stored
in declarations in deployment descriptors and can be interpreted by the
EJB container. All the required deployment descriptors are contained in
the EJB module project and already have some predefined descriptions.

In the following sections, we will specify other EJB properties. However,
here we don't need to write the new entries directly into the XML source;

instead, we'll utilize easy-to-use input templates that are supplied in the multi-page editors.[15]

In addition to the predefined entries, you'll now enter a certain amount of deployment information for the two beans `Employee` and `Employee-Services` for *ejb-jar.xml* and *persistent.xml*. The deployment descriptor *ejb-j2ee-engine.xml* serves to enter server-specific information and is not required in our example application.

3.6.1 Creating Descriptions in the ejb-jar.xml

Local Reference to the Entity Bean

When we implemented the session bean class, we accessed the entity bean using a symbolic name during the JNDI lookup. This type of EJB access has advantages over using real names to access entity beans. For example, if the real name of the entity bean changes over time, we would then no longer need to make any modifications in the source code. In our case, the entity bean and the calling session bean are to be managed in the same EJB container. Therefore, local references[16] are appropriate. So that the use of local references is possible, the referenced EJB must implement a local interface.

Symbolic Names for Local EJBs

To define a local reference, we open the deployment descriptor by double-clicking the appropriate node *ejb-jar.xml* in the J2EE Explorer. In the displayed multi-page editor, we select the **Enterprise Beans** tab and expand the node **session beans · EmployeeServicesBean**. Then we select the **ejb-local-ref** node beneath it and click on **Add**. A dialog box with the list of all the EJB module projects in the workspace is displayed. After we have selected the entity bean `EmployeeBean` from the appropriate project, a suitable input template is displayed. Here an entry for the reference name is proposed. In accordance with the specifications in Figure 3.16, we change the name to "ejb/Employee" so that it matches the reference in the JNDI lookup (see Listing 3.3) and is defined in relation to the context **java:comp/env**.

---

15 The Developer Studio provides a high level of flexibility for all J2EE project types for working with deployment descriptors. It enables the user to work as a multi-page editor where direct editing of the XML files can be omitted. For the same reason, direct editing of the XML source is also possible for the expert.

16 With EJB 2.0, references to other EJBs can be either local or remote. Defining symbolic names to support remote interfaces is also possible. Here we refer to them simply as references. They are displayed in the XML source by the element `<ejb-ref>`.

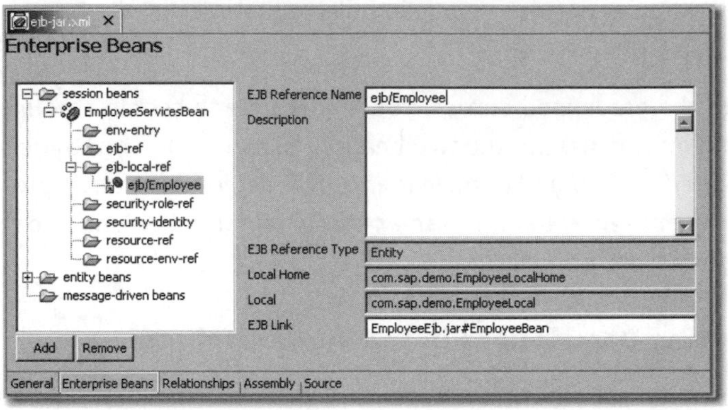

Figure 3.16 Creating a Symbolic Name for the Local EJB Reference to the Entity Bean

The new entries are added to the XML source within the element `<ejb-local-ref>`. To verify this, select the **Source** tab. As you can see from Listing 3.6, the value for `<ejb-link>` is identical with the value for `<ejb-name>` for the referenced entity bean, provided it comes from the same JAR. In the standard version, the name of the JAR file is added to the EJB link here.

```
<ejb-jar>
...
    <enterprise-beans>
        <session>
        ...
            <ejb-local-ref>
            <ejb-ref-name>ejb/Employee</ejb-ref-name>
            <ejb-ref-type>Entity</ejb-ref-type>
            ...
            <ejb-link>
                EmployeeEjb.jar#EmployeeBean
            </ejb-link>
            </ejb-local-ref>
        </session>
        <entity>
            <ejb-name>EmployeeBean</ejb-name>
...
</ejb-jar>
```

Listing 3.6 Generated XML Source for Local Reference in the ejb-jar.xml

Formulating a Query Using an EJB QL Statement

Search Queries in Find Methods

You will remember that we created an additional Find method named ejbFindAllEmployees when we created the entity bean Employee-Bean. However, the behavior of this query method has so far not been specified anywhere. As is typical for Find methods, this specification is not done using Java code, but using EJB-QL statements.[17] With this kind of statement, you can formulate suitable search queries. This is precisely what we want to do—formulate the required EJB-QL statement in the deployment descriptor *ejb-jar.xml*. To do this, we expand the node **entity beans · EmployeeBean · query** in the appropriate multi-page editor. Then we select the node directly beneath it for the Find method find-dAllEmployees. Then, in the displayed input template, we enter the EJB QL statement Select object (p) from EmployeeBean p under **EJB QL Statement** (see Figure 3.17).

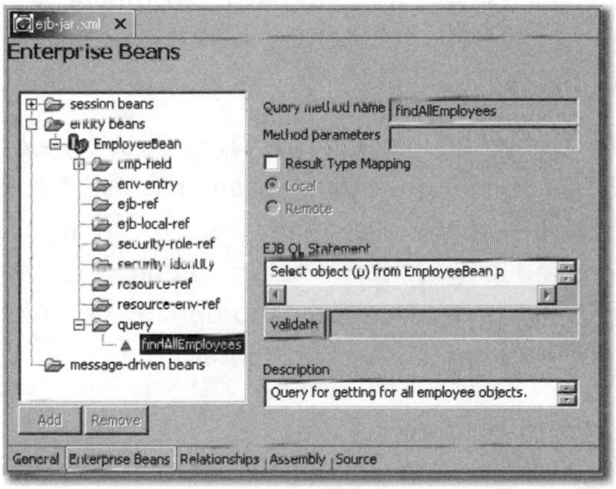

Figure 3.17 Creating a Query Using a Select Statement in the ejb-jar.xml

The new entries are added to the XML source within the ⟨query⟩ element in accordance with Listing 3.7.

```
<query>
  <description>Query for getting for all employee objects.
  </description>
  <query-method>
    <method-name>findAllEmployees</method-name>
```

---

17 EJB QL is a standardized query language based on EJB 2.0. With it, you can describe—in declarations in the deployment descriptor—the behavior of Find methods, independently of the database used. EJB QL statements are similar to SQL statements. Among others, we find here the SELECT statement.

```
    <method-params/>
  </query-method>
  <ejb-ql>Select object (p) from EmployeeBean p
  </ejb-ql>
</query>
```

Listing 3.7 Generated XML Source with Query

Defining Transaction Control

Transaction Attributes So far, we have not made any specifications anywhere regarding the transaction behavior of our example application. In fact, with EJBS, you can usually implement the transaction logic under program control in the bean class itself or leave it entirely up to the EJB container. With entity beans, the decision regarding transaction behavior—based on the container-supported approach—has already been made. For the session bean, too, we use the container-supported approach. We define the transaction behavior using the transaction attributes, which we select in the deployment descriptor.

To do this, we select the **Assembly** tab in the multi-page editor for *ejb-jar.xml*, and then choose the entry **container-transaction**, and lastly click on **Add**. In the displayed dialog box, we select the two EJBs. In accordance with the specifications in Figure 3.18, we select **Required** as the **Transaction attribute** and thus define that the appropriate business methods will always be executed in the transaction context.

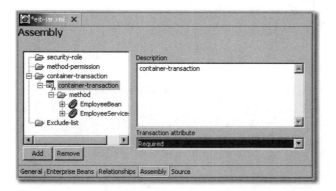

Figure 3.18 Assignment of Transaction Attribute in ejb-jar.xml

In our last step, we now save the new contents in the *ejb-jar.xml* using the appropriate icon in the toolbar and display the XML source. The entries for transaction control are shown within the element `<container-transaction>` (see Listing 3.8).

```
<container-transaction>
  <description>container-transaction</description>
  <method>
    <ejb-name>EmployeeBean</ejb-name>
    <method-name>*</method-name>
  </method>
  <method>
    <ejb-name>EmployeeServicesBean</ejb-name>
    <method-name>*</method-name>
  </method>
  <trans-attribute>Required</trans-attribute>
</container-transaction>
```

Listing 3.8 Generated XML Source for Transaction Behavior

3.6.2 Creating Server-Specific Deployment Descriptions

In order for the EJB container to handle the database accesses at all, it must know the data source as well as adhere to the rule that dictates which entity beans are mapped onto tables and which bean attributes are mapped onto the respective table fields. We now need to supply this information exactly as it appears. The container-managed persistence is configured in a special, server-specific deployment descriptor, the *persistent.xml*.

Database Accesses and the Data Source Alias—Motivation

To enable communication with the database for table access from within the application, we use a Data Source alias. This is a symbolic name for addressing a database resource server-side. We will assign such a name in a J2EE project at design time and can link it in its entirety with our employee application. The database connection pool[18] has knowledge about the path for the physical database resource on the J2EE server. In general, several Data Source aliases can be assigned to each connection pool from the start. A Data Source alias, on the other hand, is assigned on an application-specific basis. The system data source plays a special role in the use of aliases. It is automatically created when the J2EE server is installed. The system data source is provided for use by several applications. When we create the Data Source alias later on in the enterprise application project, it is automatically assigned to the system data source.

Data Source Alias: Connector Between Application and Database

---

18 A *DB connection pool* is a predefined data source on the J2EE server, which is responsible for caching and managing open database connections to any arbitrary database instance.

The use of an alias in this case has several advantages. First, the developer doesn't need to specify the path name for the physical data source. Also, the administrative task that is otherwise demanded of the developer is no longer needed. It would have had to have been performed with a separate administration tool. Lastly, this use of the data source enables you to keep the entire application portable.

You must not forget that once an application is deployed, it will run on any database instance.

Addressing the Data Source in the Deployment Descriptor

We must now ensure that an appropriate entry for addressing the data source is maintained in the server-specific deployment descriptor. To do this, we open the corresponding multi-page editor by double-clicking the node **persistent.xml** in the J2EE Explorer. There we enter the name "TMP_EMPLOYEES_DATA" for the Data Source alias (see Figure 3.19). Otherwise, we adopt the default values on this page and save the new contents.

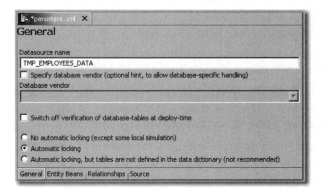

Figure 3.19 Entry for the Data Source Alias in the Deployment Descriptor persistent.xml

Remember that with this step we have only entered a name for the data source in the deployment descriptor. We will create the Data Source alias with this same name only later as part of the enterprise application project.

Mapping CMP Fields to Table Fields

Now we select the **Entity Beans** tab and then the **Employee** entity bean, and assign the table TMP_EMPLOYEES as shown in Figure 3.20. The selection is done via the icon to the right next to the field for the table name. We expand the **cmp-field** entry in the tree display and check the mapping of the CMP fields in the entity bean to the table fields. Only if this assignment has not been performed correctly do we make any changes (see Figure 3.21).

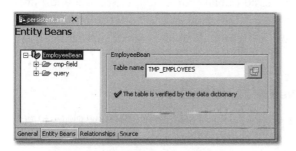

Figure 3.20 Assignment of Employee Entity Bean to Table TMP_EMPLOYEES in the Deployment Descriptor persistent.xml

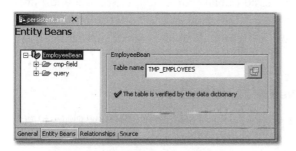

Figure 3.21 Checking the CMP Mappings

3.6.3 Creating the Java Archive

We have now created all the elements of the EJB module project. Only the EJB JAR archive is missing. The JAR archive groups all the elements of the project. To create the JAR, all that is required is a single mouse click. Simply click on the EJB module project **EmployeeEjb** and choose the menu option **Build EJB Archive** from the context menu.

3.7 Creating a JSP-Based Web Application

The Developer Studio provides—at design time—a special container for managing Web resources such as JSPs, servlets, static HTML pages, custom tag libraries, and screen and graphic files. To provide a container of this type, we will create an appropriate project at the start—a Web module project. To keep the Web application as straightforward as possible, we will add a JSP to the project as a single resource and implement it via the user interface of the Web client.[19] In addition to the actual presentation itself, we will also implement accesses to the business methods of the `EmployeeServices` session bean. For example, we will add information to configure the Web application in the corresponding deployment descriptor. Lastly, we will combine all parts of the project in a Web archive—the WAR.

3.7.1 Creating a Web Module Project

Container for Web Resources

To create a Web module project, we will again start the **New Project Wizard** via the menu option **File · New Project**. In the displayed wizard window, we choose the **J2EE** category in the left section and **Web Module Project** in the right section. To open the next wizard window, we click on **Next**, and there we enter "EmployeeWeb" as the project name. For the other values, we adopt the default settings and close the procedure by clicking on **Finish**.

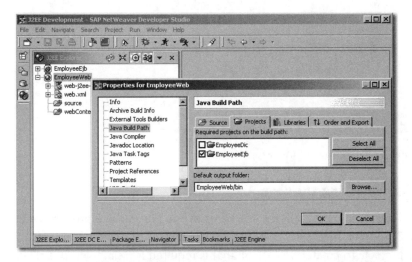

Figure 3.22 Java Build Path for Project EmployeeWeb

To look at the project frame, it is best to do so in the J2EE Explorer. In the JSP, we also want to access the resources from the EJB module project. Therefore we need to take this project dependency into consideration. To do so, we select the project name **EmployeeWeb** and choose the menu

---

19 Normally, a JSP-based Web application consists of a combination of JSPs and servlets, and possible other Java beans as auxiliary classes. While JSPs are used for presentation display and therefore preferred as view components, servlets usually act as controllers and depict the application logic.

option **Properties** from the context menu. Then, we select the attribute **Java Build Path**, select the **Projects** tab, and assign the required project (see Figure 3.22).

3.7.2 Implementing the User Interface with JSP

To create a JSP for the new project, we select the project node in the J2EE and choose the menu option **New · JSP...** In the wizard, we enter the name **NewEmployee**. Other specifications are not required, so we end the procedure by clicking on **Finish**. A standard template for the JSP is issued immediately in the JSP editor preview.[20]

In the **Source** tab, we have write access to the JSP editor, where we perform the JSP implementation.

In the JSP source code, you have two sections: An HTML basic frame that defines, for the most part, a static input form for the Web application, and a dynamic, Java-based part that you can use to access the business logic.

HTML Basic Frame

The form for registering new employees could hardly be simpler. It contains the two input fields for first and last names, a drop-down list with the corresponding departments, and a pushbutton with which the user can generate a registration process. All the aforementioned interface elements are aligned within an HTML table (see Figure 3.23). The basic frame from Listing 3.9 already has certain page directives whose import attributes contain the required packages.

```
<%@ page language="java" %>
<html>
<body style= "font-family:Arial;"  bgcolor="D2D8E1">
<%@ page import="javax.naming.*" %>
<%@ page import="javax.ejb.*" %>
<%@ page import="com.sap.demo.*" %>
<%@ page import="java.util.*" %>
<h2>
Register New Employee
</h2>
```

---

20 The preview always shows only the static HTML parts of the JSP. The dynamic parts of the implementation that cover the server-side functions are therefore not shown in the preview.

```
<form action="NewEmployee.jsp" method="POST"
  name="NewEmployee">
<table border=0 align=center>
<tr>
<td width="220" >First name: <td>
<input type="text" name="firstname" value = "" size="20">
<tr>
<td width="220" >Last name: <td>
<input type="text" name="lastname" value = "" size="20">
<tr>
<td width="220" >Department: <td>
   <select name="department" >
    <option value="DEVELOPMENT">Development</option>
    <option value="TRAINING">Training</option>
    <option value="MANAGEMENT">Management</option>
    <option value="ARCHITECTURE">Architecture</option>
  </select>
<tr>
<td><td><br><input type="submit" value="Create"
  name="create">
</table>
<br>
</form>
<!-- Access the business logic -->
</body>
</html>
```

Listing 3.9 HTML Basic Frame for JSP

Accesses to Business Logic

To get the reference to the session bean, a JNDI lookup is performed on the context variable jndiContext. You should remember that with ...ejb/EmployeeService in Listing 3.10 we are using a symbolic name for the session bean. This name has yet to be created as a reference name in the deployment descriptor of the Web application. The result of the lookup is assigned to the home object empHome after successful casting. The session bean is actually accessed using the home interface method create(). Afterwards, the session bean object empSession calls the business method registerEmployee(). The local variables lName, fName, and eDepartment are passed as parameters. These variables were defined in the first line of the source code extract and they

Figure 3.23 JSP of the Employee Application in the Preview Page

adopt the values entered by the user only now. Whenever the business method is successfully executed in the EJB container, it always returns a valid ID. Otherwise, an exception is triggered and appropriate text is output on the user interface.

```
<%
String lName = request.getParameter(" lastname" );
String fName = request.getParameter("firstname");
String eDepartment = request.getParameter( "department");
if(lName == null || fName == null
  || lName.length() == 0 || fName.length() == 0) return;
try {
Context jndiContext = new InitialContext();
Object ref = jndiContext.lookup(
  "java:comp/env/ejb/EmployeeService");
javax.rmi.PortableRemoteObject.narrow(ref,
  EmployeeServicesHome.class);
EmployeeServicesHome empHome =
  (EmployeeServicesHome) ref;
EmployeeServices empSession  = empHome.create();
long empId = empSession.registerEmployee(fName, lName,
  eDepartment);
if(empId == 0)
out.println("<H3> Failed!  </H3>");
else
out.println("<H3> Success! </H3>");
}
```

```
catch(Exception e){
    out.println("<H3>"+e.toString()+"</H3>");
    e.printStackTrace(System.out);
    return;
}
%>
```

Listing 3.10 Dynamic Part of JSP

3.7.3 Descriptions in the Deployment Descriptor web.xml

In the deployment descriptor *web.xml*, we include the information on the configuration of the Web application. The entries contained there are evaluated at the time of deployment. On the one hand, the Web container contains information regarding how the individual resources of the project match each other. On the other hand, security role assignments are contained in the *web.xml*. These can be used to control the access authorization for the Web application as a whole at runtime.

However, we will limit ourselves to storing only some mapping information in the descriptor. In the following step, we'll define—as an example—a reference to the required session bean using a symbolic name. In addition, we will need to specify a virtual path for JSP access.

Symbolic Name for the Session Bean

Reference to Session Bean

To access the session bean, we have not used a real bean name in the JSP source code (see Listing 3.10), but a symbolic name. In order that the container can correctly assign such a name at runtime, we need to store a corresponding mapping rule in the deployment descriptor.

To define a symbolic name for a reference to the session bean, we open the multi-page editor for the deployment descriptor *web.xml*. There we select the **EJBs** tab, choose the entry **EJB references**, and then click on the pushbutton **Add**, which is now activated. Finally, we select the session bean to be referenced.

As you can see in Figure 3.24, we change the proposed name to "ejb/EmployeeService", so that it matches the entry in the JNDI lookup in the JSP source code from Listing 3.10.

The new entries for the XML source are automatically entered at a suitable position. You can view this by selecting the **Source** tab and then navigating to the element <ejb-ref> in the displayed XML source (see Listing 3.11).

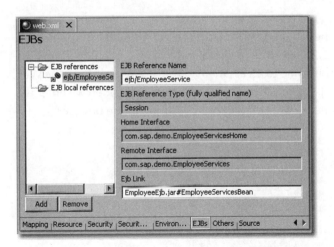

Figure 3.24 Creating a Symbolic Name for the EJB Reference to the Session Bean

With this entry, we have now defined a mapping between an arbitrary reference name (symbolic name) and the real bean name, as it is passed in the form of an *EJB Link*. In this way, the reference name assigned once in the source code of the JSP can be used for the session bean and remains unchanged there, even if the bean name should change.

```
<ejb-ref>
   <ejb-ref-name>ejb/EmployeeService </ejb-ref-name>
   <ejb-ref-type>Session</ejb-ref-type>
   <home>com.sap.demo.EmployeeServicesHome</home>
   <remote>com.sap.demo.EmployeeServices</remote>
   <ejb-link>EmployeeEjb.jar#EmployeeServicesBean
   </ejb-link>
</ejb-ref>
```

Listing 3.11 Generated XML Source for the Reference to the Session Bean

URL Mapping

For JSPs as well as for servlets, the Web container on the J2EE Engine provides support for so-called *URL patterns*. URL patterns are virtual paths that are used within an application instead of the real path names. This kind of mapping is not prescribed as mandatory by the servlet specification, but it should always be considered when thinking about the portability of the application. This is always a prudent approach to take, particularly if the real URL changes over time.

Virtual Path for the JSP

To add a URL pattern to our JSP, we now switch to the **Mapping** tab page. There we select the required JSP[21] under the entry **Servlet Mappings**. As shown in Figure 3.25, we enter a virtual path named */view* to access the JSP. You can use this name to access the JSP from a servlet or from the Web browser, for example. We will only use this virtual path when we enter the URL for the start page of the employee application in the browser.

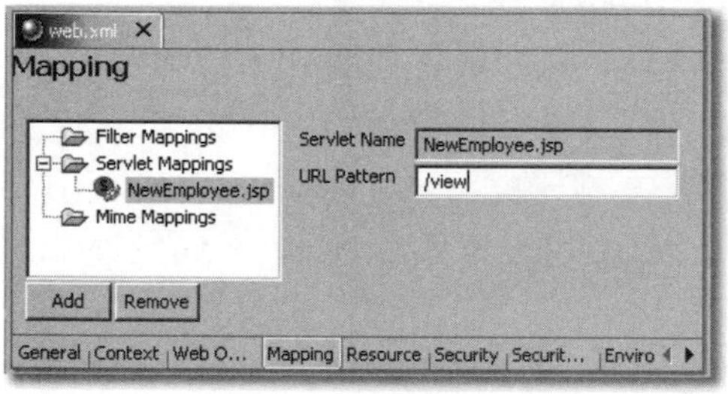

Figure 3.25 Entry for a URL Pattern for the JSP

3.7.4 Creating the Web Archive

Web Resources in Best Packaging

Finally, we will now unite the components of the Web module in a Web archive (WAR). To create this archive, we simply select the project node **EmployeeWeb** and choose the menu path **Build Web Archive** from the context menu. The created archive file is given the name *Employee-Web.war*. The same-name node is also added to the project structure.

We can now view this archive as the result of our Web module project and will close our activities within this project. Remember, however, that this archive (just like the JAR) does not represent a deployable unit in the Developer Studio. Only when we assign it to an enterprise archive (EAR) can it be deployed on the J2EE server from the Developer Studio.

3.8 Defining and Deploying the Entire J2EE Application

While we provided the business functions with the JAR archive, the matching Web components were added with the Web archive. Now we must combine all the components to create a type of complete J2EE application. For this purpose, the Developer Studio provides a special project type—an enterprise application project.

---

21 It should be noted here that a JSP is converted at deployment time, and very definitely at runtime, into a servlet. It is then executed in the Web container. Therefore, servlets as well as JSPs can be associated with the description *Servlet Mapping*.

To create the complete employee application, we will first create an enterprise application project called "EmployeeEar". Here we must also enter some descriptions in the standard deployment descriptor *application.xml* before we generate the corresponding EAR file as an archive and subsequently deploy it on the J2EE server.

3.8.1 Creating an Enterprise Application Project

To create the project, we again start the New Project Wizard via the menu option **File · New Project**. In the displayed wizard window, we choose the **J2EE** category in the left section and the **Enterprise Module Project** in the right section. To open the next wizard window, we click on **Next**. There we enter "EmployeeEar" as the name for the new project. Again we click on **Next** and then select the two projects **EmployeeEjb** and **EmployeeEar**. For the other values, we simply adopt the default settings and close this procedure by clicking on **Finish**.

3.8.2 Creating Descriptions for application.xml

We enter a context root as the sole entry for the deployment descriptor. In this way, we define the URL with which our employee application will be published on the J2EE server.

As before, we call the multi-page editor for *application.xml* by double-clicking the same-name node in the project structure. There we switch to the **Modules** tab and select the Web archive *EmployeeWeb.war*. As shown in Figure 3.26, we enter the name "employee" as the **Context Root**. This entry will allow us to address all the components of our employee application via the URL *http://<my_server>:<port>/employee*.

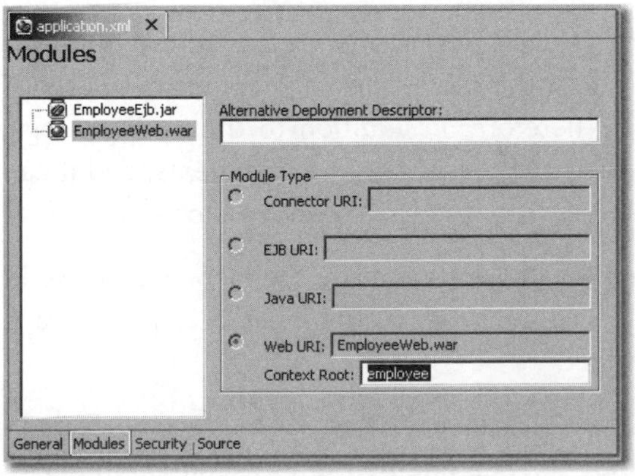

Figure 3.26 Entry for Context Root in the Deployment Descriptor application.xml

3.8.3   Creating a Data Source alias

As you remember, we entered a name for the Data Source alias in the deployment descriptor *persistent.xml*. However, we haven't yet created this kind of Data Source alias. We will now do this in the enterprise application project.

The procedure for creating a Data Source alias is really simple. All we need to do is select the project node **EmployeeEar** in the J2EE Explorer, open the corresponding context menu, and choose the menu option **New · META-INF/data-source-aliases.xml**. In the displayed dialog box, we enter "TMP_EMPLOYEES_DATA" as the alias name and click on **Finish**. With this step, we create the XML file named *data-source-aliases.xml*, which is now also visible in the project structure. The alias name is assigned to the system data source during deployment. To see this, we can view the generated XML source. It is exactly like the lines in Listing 3.12.

```
<data-source-aliases>
  <aliases>
    <data-source-name> ${com.sap.Data Source.default}
    </data-source-name>
  <alias>TMP_EMPLOYEES_DATA</alias>
  </aliases>
</data-source-aliases>
```

Listing 3.12 com.sap.Data Source.default Represents the System Data Source on the Server

3.8.4   Creating and Deploying the Enterprise Application Archive (EAR)

The Enterprise Application Archive (EAR) combines the archives JAR and WAR with the information from the corresponding deployment descriptors to create one archive. Therefore, in addition to the business logic components, the EAR contains the presentation components, and it can be deployed on the J2EE server from the Developer Studio.

To create the EAR, we select the project node and the menu option **Build Enterprise Archive** from the context menu. The created archive data is added as a node to the project.

To deploy the archive on the J2EE server, we select the archive node in the J2EE Explorer and **Deploy to J2EE engine** from the context menu.

Executing the Employee Application

Provided the J2EE server has the name **my_server** and can be reached under the "port_number," we can start our employee application using the URL *http://my_server:port_number/employee/view* (see Figure 3.27).

Figure 3.27 Starting the Employee Application in the Browser

3.9 Providing Business Logic as a Web Service

To provide the functions of our employee application to external clients, we now want to provide a Web service from within the session bean EmployeeServices. In this chapter, however, we will not develop the topic of Web services any further. You will find a detailed view of Web services in the context of the SAP Web AS in Chapter 5.

In the following step, we'll learn a simple procedure for creating the Web service. A session bean implementation is used as the Web service end point. With only a few mouse clicks, we will create the virtual interface as well as the appropriate Web service definition and configuration. Then, we can deploy the new Web service. We'll also display how a deployed Web service can be tested in the Developer Studio.

3.9.1 Creating a Web Service

As shown in Figure 3.28, we proceed to the J2EE Explorer to the node for the session bean (**ejb-jar.xml · EmployeeServicesBean**) and choose the menu option **New · Web Service ...** from the context menu.

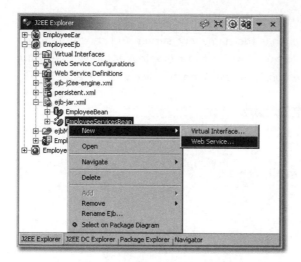

Figure 3.28 Calling the Web Service Creation Wizards in the EJB Module Project

Web Service Creation Wizard

Now a wizard is displayed in which we can specify some attributes of the Web service more precisely. The new Web service will be called "EmployeeRegister." We adopt the default settings from the first wizard window, in particular the entry "Simple SOAP" for the **Default Configuration Type**. Then we continue the creation process by clicking on **Next** (see Figure 3.29).

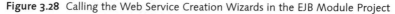

Figure 3.29 Creating a New Web Service with a Preset Configuration

In the following dialog box, we can determine which business methods of the session bean will be displayed with the Web service. We adopt the preset values for the two business methods `getAllEmployees` and `registerEmployee` and click on **Next** to go to the next dialog box. Here, already, names for the virtual interface and the Web service definition are proposed. All we need do now is enter "EmployeeEar" as **EAR Project** for the deployment and we trigger the generation by clicking on **Finish**.

The wizard automatically creates a virtual interface with the name **EmployeeRegisterVi**, the appropriate Web service definition **Employee-RegisterWsd**, as well as a configuration named **Config1**. It also adds the corresponding nodes to the structure of the EJB module project (see Figure 3.30).

Figure 3.30 Nodes Added to EJB Module Project

3.9.2 Deploying the Web Service

In the Developer Studio, we can deploy the new Web service with the EAR file. To do this, we update the JAR in the EJB module project and then the EAR archive before we deploy it again on the server using **Deploy to J2EE Engine**.

3.9.3 Calling the Web Service in the Test Environment

The Developer Studio provides an integrated test environment for Web services. We want to use it to call the two business methods.

To start the test environment, we open the Web service perspective via the menu path **Window · Open Perspective**. In the standard version, the **Web Service Navigator** is also displayed with this perspective. Here, all the Web services that were deployed on a server are listed. We select our Web service **EmployeeRegister** from the Navigator, and start an overview list for the Web service via the menu option **Open**. By clicking on **Test** we get to the test environment (see Figure 3.31). Now we can execute both methods consecutively.

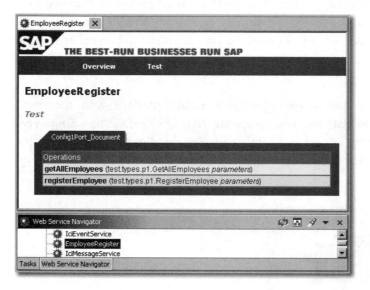

Figure 3.31 Integrated Test Environment for Web Services in the Developer Studio

4 Java Persistence in the SAP Web Application Server

JDBC, entity beans, and JDO are three standards that are available to Java developers for making objects persistent. This chapter examines how they are implemented in SAP Web AS. First, you will learn about the underlying infrastructure.

4.1 Open JDBC for Java

In Java, Java Database Connectivity (JDBC) is the standard for dynamic database queries on which object-relational persistence frameworks such as Enterprise JavaBeans (EJB) and Java Data Objects (JDO) are based. At runtime, strings are created dynamically and passed to the database using statements, where they are interpreted, executed and returned in the form of ResultSets.

Database-Independent Programming with Open JDBC

JDBC defines only the programming interface, not the content and syntax of the SQL string. Of course, this can be used to exploit the special properties of the underlying database system, although it has the disadvantage that an application cannot be ported to other databases without much effort. Using vendor specifics makes complete sense for projects where you know which database will be used, although application programmers are often unaware of which databases their applications will later run on. Furthermore, the partly different SQL syntax from database manufacturers requires additional work for programming and testing applications.

Open JDBC for Java as part of the SAP NetWeaver infrastructure enables developers to write database-independent code using Open SQL grammar. This is based on the ISO standard SQL-92 (ISO/IEC 9075, third edition) and contains extensions that enable inner and outer joins to be used and dynamic parameters to be specified. Statements that are created with Open SQL can be executed by all supported databases once they have been converted to the database by the Open SQL runtime.

The reduction to SQL, which is understood by all databases, initially appears to be a restriction. In exceptional cases, you can use the auxiliary class `com.sap.sql.NativeSQLAccess` to continue using any SQL. There is still one small problem: Open SQL for Java (Open SQLJ) is not fully compatible with JDBC. The Java Application Programming Interface (API) is restricted to the classes and methods that are supported by all databases.

4.1.1 Features of Open JDBC for Java

In addition to the portability between different database systems, Open JDBC has the additional functions:

▶ Open SQLJ for static database queries

▶ Table buffering

▶ SQL trace

▶ Statement pooling

▶ Syntax check of SQL queries

▶ Semantic check of SQL queries at runtime for tables that were defined using the Java Dictionary (see Chapter 2)

We will examine the first four functions listed above in greater detail later on.

4.2 Persistence Infrastructure of the SAP Web AS at Runtime

Open JDBC's persistence infrastructure consists of three hierarchical layers, representing a higher abstraction of the underlying database with each step (see Figure 4.1). The previous section contains a general overview of the top level, Open JDBC. We will now look at the underlying *Vendor JDBC* and *Native JDBC* layers in more detail.

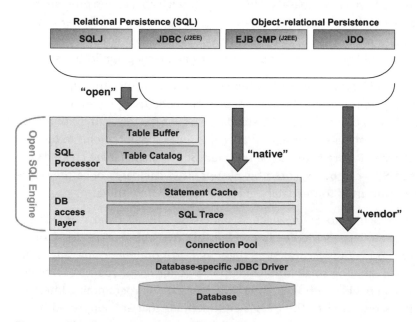

Figure 4.1 The Three Layers of Open JDBC for Java

4.2.1 Vendor JDBC

The lowest level is *Vendor JDBC*, which contains the manufacturer's JDBC implementation. Only the database connections are encapsulated using the JDBC pool. This encapsulation is standard for all J2EE servers and essentially takes place for two reasons: Databases can keep only a limited number of connections open, and time is required to set up a database connection. The JDBC drivers are tested thoroughly for the databases that are supported by SAP NetWeaver, although, in principle, any databases can be integrated using their JDBC drivers. This may be necessary for applications that have to access existing data, for example. These databases should be accessed by using only the JDBC API, however, not the object-relational mechanisms.

4.2.2 Native JDBC

As with Vendor JDBC, SQL queries are passed unchanged to the database. The syntax is therefore not checked, and database-dependent queries are possible. From a technical point of view, Native JDBC is only an encapsulation of the JDBC driver for the database that passes everything on, but can save the statements in trace files on demand and can keep frequently used queries in the cache. With regard to the connection of databases that are not supported and the use of object-relational persistence, the same restrictions for the underlying layer apply here.

4.2.3 Statement Pooling

Prepared statements enable performance to be increased with static database queries. In the Java source code, their usage looks like what you see in Listing 4.1.

```
public void findEmployeeByName(Connection con,
  String name) throws SQLException
{
  String sql ="Select * from EMPLOYEE where NAME = ?";
  PreparedStatement ps = con.prepareStatement(sql);
  ps.setString(1, name);
  ResultSet rs = ps.executeQuery();
  ...
  ps.close();
}
```

Listing 4.1 Prepared Statements

Increased Performance

The SQL query is passed to the database when the `preparedStatement(String sql)` method is called, where it is analyzed and an optimum procedure is determined. Generally, this is a time-consuming operation. As long as the Prepared statement is not closed, the `executeQuery()` method can be called as often as you like without the database having to analyze the statement and prepare the execution plan. With Native JDBC, the statement is not closed but is placed in a pool. One such pool exists for each database connection. As the connections are not released, the query can be reused later, thereby reducing load on the database. Since prepared statements are used intensively in SQLJ, JDO, and EJB implementations, performance clearly increases as a result.

4.2.4 SQL Trace

Browser-Based Analysis of Database Queries

You can activate the SQL trace for the Native SQL layer if necessary. It is managed and assessed using the browser and URL *http://<hostname>:<port>/SQLTrace* can only be carried out by a user with administrator rights. The application enables the trace to be switched on and off, and existing files to be deleted and evaluated. For the evaluation, you can set a filter for the database accesses that are to be displayed. This filter includes the session, the application, the user, and the duration of the access. This makes it possible to filter out all of user *Guest*'s SQL queries in the *JDO PersistenceManager* application that lasted longer than 1,000 milliseconds, for example Each query can be examined in detail (see Figure 4.2).

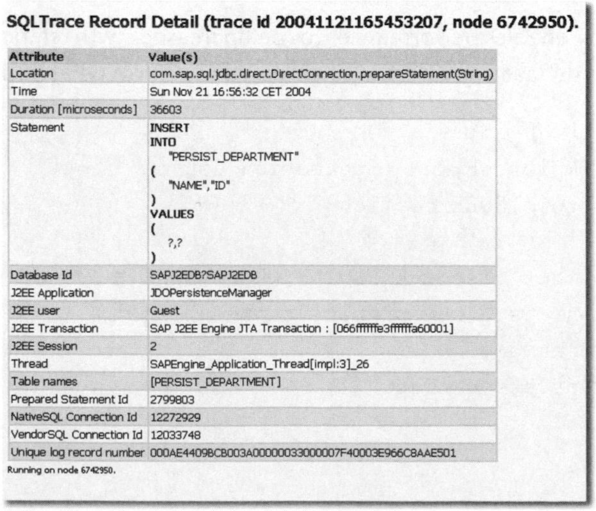

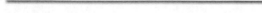

SQLTrace Record Detail (trace id 20041121165453207, node 6742950).

Attribute	Value(s)
Location	com.sap.sql.jdbc.direct.DirectConnection.prepareStatement(String)
Time	Sun Nov 21 16:56:32 CET 2004
Duration [microseconds]	36603
Statement	**INSERT** **INTO** "PERSIST_DEPARTMENT" ("NAME","ID") **VALUES** (?,?)
Database Id	SAPJ2EDB?SAPJ2EDB
J2EE Application	JDOPersistenceManager
J2EE user	Guest
J2EE Transaction	SAP J2EE Engine JTA Transaction : [066ffffffe3ffffffa60001]
J2EE Session	2
Thread	SAPEngine_Application_Thread[impl:3]_26
Table names	[PERSIST_DEPARTMENT]
Prepared Statement Id	2799803
NativeSQL Connection Id	12272929
VendorSQL Connection Id	12033748
Unique log record number	000AE4409BCB003A00000033000007F40003E966C8AAE501

Running on node 6742950.

Figure 4.2 Detailed View of a Database in SQL trace

The trace files can reach a maximum of 10 MB, and up to 10 files are created for each trace. This means that a trace can reach up to 100 MB in size. Once the tenth file reaches its maximum size, the first file is overwritten. You can change these settings in the *Log Configurator* for the server using the *Visual Administrator*.

4.2.5 Table Buffering

The table buffer is a local cache that is created on every server node in the SAP NetWeaver Web Application Server (Web AS). The data that this cache contains is defined at design time using the Java Dictionary. This data can be complete tables, or only parts of tables that are defined using areas of key fields. Buffering is transparent for an application programmer; his or her SQL query is analyzed in the Open SQL layer. If the table to which the query refers is in the buffer, then no database communication is necessary. However, this applies only to queries that refer to one table. Select queries over several tables are always analyzed in the database.

As buffering is active on all server nodes in a cluster, an invalidation mechanism ensures that the data remains consistent. If buffered data is changed, the data in the corresponding key areas on the other nodes is invalidated and reloaded from the database as necessary. This is why this function should only be used for tables with very infrequent write access.

4.2.6 Managing Database Connections

You use the Visual Administrator to manage database connections. Navigate in the left tree structure to the JDBC Connector Service of any server node (see Figure 4.3).

To integrate a new database, the corresponding JDBC driver must first be included in the list of all drivers. To create a new pool, you need a name with which it is stored in the JNDI, the driver class, the connection parameters, and a database user and password. Choose JDBC Version 2.0 if the pool supports distributed transactions. In this case, the driver class expects parameters in the form of name-value pairs, which can be entered on the **Additional** tab.

Furthermore, multiple aliases can be created for a pool, which can be used to call it in the JNDI. This compensates for a weakness in the J2EE specification: the lookup path is specified in the Web or EJB archive's deployment descriptor, and has to be adapted before deployment.

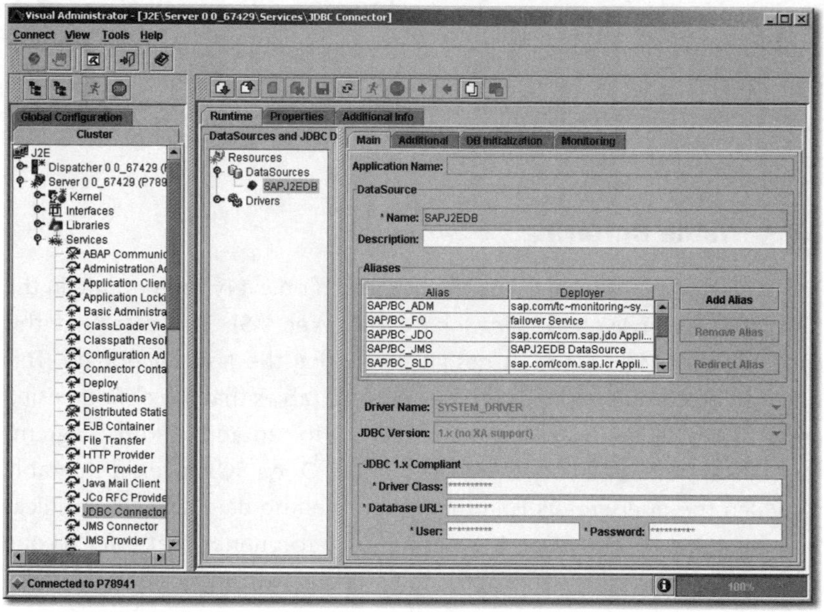

Figure 4.3 Administration of Database Connections in the Visual Administrator

Defining an alias means that the application can be deployed unchanged in the descriptor.

SAP Web AS is installed with a separate configuration database. A default datasource is created for this database with connection parameters that cannot be changed.

On the **Additional** tab, you can also set the maximum number of pool connections and decide which access layer should be used: Vendor JDBC, Native JDBC, or Open JDBC. Open JDBC is only an option for the default database, however. Given this restriction, the Java Dictionary in NetWeaver '04 can only be used for the system database, since Open JDBC requires its metadata. The whole definition of a database pool can be imported and exported as an XML file.

4.3 Java Dictionary

The metadata of the data types and tables that are used by the Web Dynpro and the persistence layer at runtime are defined in the Java Dictionary, which was described in Chapter 2. At this point, we will focus on the metadata that is relevant for persistence—table structures.

The first question you have to ask yourself is "What are the benefits?" The next question you have to ask is "Why should you take the effort to maintain metadata?" The answers to these questions are software logistics, portability, and type safety at runtime and at design time:

Benefits

▶ **Software Logistics**
An application doesn't just run on one database. In a development process, an application runs on developer databases, test databases, and lastly, on the live database. Changes to the database structure must be transported through this landscape together with the software, which is why you must be able to assign versions to the metadata.

▶ **Portability**
By describing database structures and data types in XML, you no longer have to maintain SQL scripts for every database type. The software delivery manager uses the metadata to create, change, or delete database objects (such as database tables, indexes, and so on).

▶ **Type Safety at Design Time**
The SQLJ preprocessor compares the table names, column names, and data types of the queries with the metadata when Open SQLJ is converted to Open JDBC. With JDO or CMP entity beans, consistency is ensured by the corresponding XML files (*.map or persistent.xml). For JDBC, a test at design time is not possible because the queries cannot generally be localized in the source text and don't have to be static.

▶ **Type Safety at Runtime**
Open JDBC for Java can use the table descriptions to map the JDBC data types to the corresponding types of the underlying database.

4.3.1 Defining Database Tables in the SAP NetWeaver Developer Studio

Only predefined or simple data types can be used to define database tables; the Developer Studio does not support the mapping of structured types. Of the information that you can enter for simple data types, only the database default value and the information on whether null is permitted as a value are considered in the persistence layer. The added value of self-defined data types becomes apparent when you develop Web Dynpro applications; they're not really required for persistence.

The Developer Studio has its own *Dictionary* perspective and corresponding project type for defining database objects. The central view is the **Dic-**

Defining Database Objects

tionary Explorer, which displays the logical structure of the project (see Figure 4.4). You can use the context menu of the project node to pack the metadata in the form of XML files into an archive and deploy it. The tables are created by the Software Delivery Manager (SDM) in the server's configuration database, or existing tables are adapted. At the same time, the metadata is stored in special database tables and is therefore available to the Open JDBC layer at runtime. Developers can also deploy individual tables using the context menu for the corresponding table node. You can also create new tables or delete existing ones.

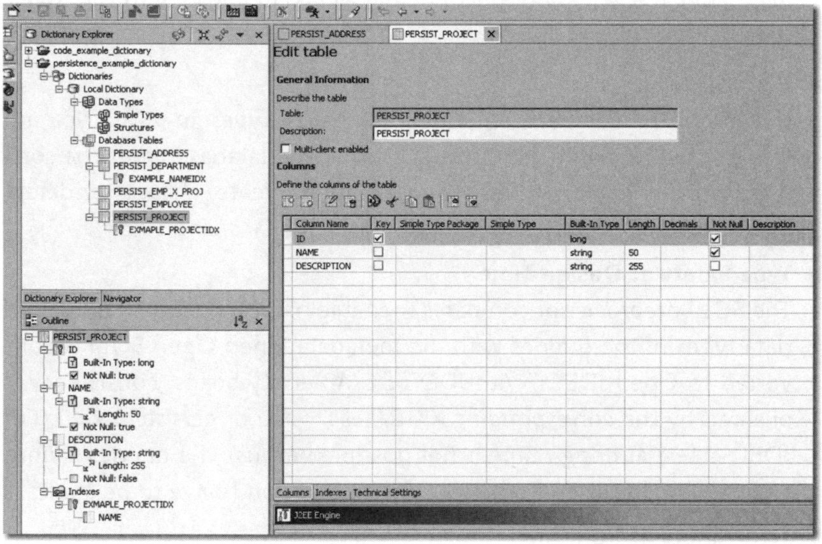

Figure 4.4 Dictionary Perspective with the Dictionary Explorer and Table Editor

Metadata in a Table Column

The metadata of tables is maintained in the Table Editor, which has three tabs for defining columns, indexes, and the buffer granularity. The description of a column consists of the following information:

▶ The name of the column

▶ Information whether the column belongs to the primary key

▶ The data type—this may be a self-defined simple data type or one of the predefined types: *binary, date, decimal, double, float, integer, long, short, string, time,* or *timestamp*

▶ Depending on the data type, the length or the number of decimal places

▶ Information whether `null` is permitted as a value

- ▶ A short description
- ▶ A default value for the database

If you activate table buffering for a table, you can also set the granularity for the buffer. You have the option of caching a whole table, table areas, or individual rows. The latter in this case means that a row is only placed in the buffer if it is read from the database. Table areas can be selected if the primary key consists of more than one column. The granularity is specified by a number that is at least one (1) and less than the number of the key's columns. If you select the first n columns and read a record, the first select statement loads all records that are identical in the buffers in the first n primary key columns into the buffer. Therefore, full and individual buffering are only the extreme cases where $n = 0$ or $n = number of key fields$.

4.4 Developing an Example Application

Now that you're familiar, at least theoretically, with the persistence infrastructure of SAP Web AS, we'll show you how to develop applications using the SAP NetWeaver Developer Studio (SAP NWDS) with the help of an example application. We'll describe the implementation with each of the following technologies: Open SQLJ, Java Data Objects, and entity beans.

4.4.1 Example Project Management Scenario

Our application should map a simple project management scenario. We are considering employees who have an address, belong to a department, and who can work on one or more projects. In other words, we're implementing the four persistent classes Employee, Department, Address, and Project, and their interactions. The classes, their attributes, and their relations with each other are shown in Figure 4.5.

We implement the application logic as methods of a stateless session bean. This has the advantage that we can expose the functions as a Web service and test it in the IDE with only a few mouse clicks. Because both the parameters and the return values must be serializable for a Web service, we're using Data Access Objects (DAOs), which we need anyway for the SQLJ implementation. To keep the example simple, we are not adhering strictly to the pattern definition from the J2EE pattern catalog on the Sun Web site *http://java.sun.com/blueprints/patterns/DAO.html*; instead, we're skipping the interfaces and using the DAOs in the session bean's interface.

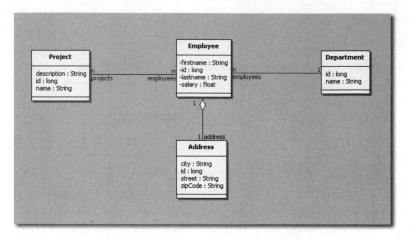

Figure 4.5 The Persistent Classes of the Example Application

The session bean's methods should show the basic operations with persistent objects. The `ProjectManagementLocal` interface has the following methods:

```
public long createEmployee(String firstname,
    String lastname, float salary, String departmentName);


public long createDepartment(String name);


public long createProject(String name, String description);


public long assignAddressToEmployee(long employeeId,
  String city, String street, String zipCode);


public void assingProjectToEmployee(long employeeId,
    String projectName);


public EmployeeDAO[] findAllEmployeesInProject(
    String projectName);


public EmployeeDAO[] findEmployee(String lastname);


public float getOverAllSalaryOfDepartment(
    String departmentName);


public void removeEmployeeFromProject(long employeeId,
  long projectId);
```

Once we have defined the structure and functions of the application, we divide the implementation into four steps, each of which corresponds to a project in the Developer Studio:

1. Definition and deployment of the necessary tables
2. Implementation of auxiliary classes; here, these classes include the DAOs and a class for creating keys
3. Implementation of the session bean and the persistent objects
4. Definition of the Web service and deployment of the application

We will show steps 3 and 4 for each of the SQLJ, CMP, EJB, and JDO persistence mechanisms.

4.4.2 Definition and Deployment of the Tables

Now that we've explained how you create a Dictionary project and tables, and how you deploy the project, we can focus on how our tables look. For each persistent class we need a table, so we create the PERSIST_ EMPLOYEE, PERSIST_ADDRESS, PERSIST_DEPARTMENT, and PERSIST_ PROJECT tables. It's also easy to map the attributes in the data model; the table for employees, for example, has columns ID, FIRSTNAME, LAST-NAME, and SALARY, where the first column is the primary key. We represent an employee's membership to one department using only the DEPARTMENT_ID column in the employee table, which should contain the department's foreign key. At the same time, we define the ADDRESS_ ID for the address assignment. The m:n relationship between employees and projects requires a PERSIST_EMP_X_PROJ assignment table with two columns, in which the employees and projects are connected by their key. In this table, both columns form the primary key so that an automatic lock can be activated on this table. This does not refer to locks at database level, but those locks that are kept in the enqueue server's lock table.

The name should be unique for projects and departments. If you've looked closely at the methods of the session bean, you will have noticed that some of the methods don't make sense otherwise, such as findAll-EmployeesInProject(String projectName). To ensure that they are unique, you should define a unique index for the table columns on the **Indexes** tab.

Of course, we could also have chosen the name as the key. Renaming a project from **Paris** to **New York** would have affected not only the record in the project table, but also the foreign key in the assignment table.

4.4.3 Implementation of the Auxiliary Classes

We create a separate Java project for the four Data Access Objects. The implementation of the ProjectDAO class looks as follows (see Listing 4.2):

```java
package com.sap.examples.persistence.dao;

import java.io.Serializable;

public class ProjectDAO implements Serializable
{
    //private attributes
    private long id;
    private String name;
    private String description;

    //constructors
    public ProjectDAO(long id, String name,
                        String description)
    {
        this.id = id;
        this.name = name;
        this.description = description;
    }

    public ProjectDAO()
    {
    }


    //getter and setter for private attributes
    public long getId()
    {
        return id;
    }
        //more getter and setter ...
}
```

Listing 4.2 Implementing the ProjectDAO Class

Although the class doesn't have any attributes for relationships to employees, there is no harm in including the list of employees in the object. However, you need to think about this carefully before you do it. In the DAOs, if you can navigate from the projects to the employees and from the employees back to the projects, then, in the worst-case scenario, all employees and projects may be connected indirectly to a project. Possible solutions to this problem (although this list is certainly incomplete) are as follows:

▶ A project can contain a list of employee keys.

▶ You can implement different DAOs, such as *ProjectDAO* and *ProjectDAOWithEmployees*.

▶ The DAOs permit all navigation using references, although they are only really created to a certain depth. You must document this thoroughly; it is probably not suitable for published interfaces.

The project also has the `IdGenerator` auxiliary class, whose static `public static synchronized long getNewId()` method creates unique keys for the persistent objects. The implementation on the DVD is not cluster-enabled and is therefore not suitable for a real world project.

4.4.4 Implementation of the Session Bean and Deployment of the Application

In Chapter 3, you learned how to handle Enterprise JavaBeans in the SAP NetWeaver Developer Studio. At this point, we assume that you already know how to create a stateless session bean and its business methods.[1] We also refer to other chapters for defining a Web service and deploying the application. The implementation of the business methods depends on the persistence mechanism that was selected and is described in the following sections.

4.5 Open SQL/SQLJ

This section describes the SAP implementation of the SQLJ standard. SQLJ offers type safety at design time and makes it very easy to use ResultSets.

---

1 For this example, you also have to create references to the project using the auxiliary classes and the Dictionary project. To do this, choose **Properties** from the project's context menu. You add the references in the *Java Build Path* on the **Projects** tab.

If you have already developed applications in Java that were connected to a relational backend via JDBC, you will know that JDBC merely defines an interface, which allows you to send dynamic queries in different SQL dialects for communicating with any relational database. This is why type checks are not possible at runtime or at design time.

This lack of type safety is a constant source of errors that involves many code iterations, and can therefore even jeopardize project deadlines. The ability to generate SQL queries dynamically at runtime is not usually used; static SQL is adequate in most cases. Just reading a ResultSet element using the index and one of the getter methods corresponding to the expected Java type by specifying the column name is time-consuming and prone to errors.

Even after the end of the development phase, the problems aren't over: If the database manufacturer changes, coding in a special SQL dialect results in the entire persistence layer being reworked.

4.5.1 Open SQL/SQLJ: Basic Principles

Although Open SQL addresses the issue of portability and provides type safety at runtime, only Open SQL/SQLJ can provide an elegant way of dealing with ResultSets and supporting typing at design time. But using Open SQL/SQLJ comes at a price, namely that dynamic statements cannot be used. However, this should rarely be a problem, because Open SQL and Open SQL/SQLJ can be used together in the same source code, and operations can be performed on the same database connection.

Open SQL/SQLJ statements have their own syntax that is different from SQL and that is embedded directly in the Java code. But, unlike Open SQL or pure JDBC, Open SQL/SQLJ statements are not embedded in the source code as character strings; rather, they are marked with special keywords.

Together with the restriction to static statements, this enables the *SQLJ Translator* to perform syntax and type checks at design time. The checks in the database schemas used are based on the logical schema definitions of the Java Dictionary, which has already been described, and the *OpenSQL Catalog*, which is part of the SAP NetWeaver Java Development Infrastructure (JDI) and is also used at runtime.

Since source code containing Open SQL/SQLJ statements cannot be translated, the SQLJ Translator preprocesses them into Java-compliant source code that can be compiled, and translates the Open SQL/SQLJ statements into Open SQL/SQLJ runtime calls.

All of this is completely transparent: The Open SQL/SQLJ Translator is fully integrated in the NetWeaver Developer Studio and developers edit Open SQL/SQLJ source code in the same way as if it were pure Java source code (see Figure 4.6).

Figure 4.6 Open SQL/SQLJ Translator

Now we'll explain how to implement the project management scenario using Open SQL/SQLJ and describe the features of Open SQL/SQLJ.

4.5.2 Implementing the Project Management Scenario with Open SQL/SQLJ

We assume that all table definitions that were described earlier were created using the Java Dictionary and have been deployed, and that the session bean for the example scenario has already been created.

To separate the database logic from the business logic to be implemented in the `ProjectManagementBean` session bean, we want to encapsulate the database accesses in a separate `DataAccess` class, which will contain the Open SQL/SQLJ statements. The `ProjectManagementBean` session bean calls the methods of this class to communicate with the database.

Encapsulating the Database Logic

Creating the Database Connection

The first step in communicating with the database consists of creating a database connection. The Open SQL/SQLJ project management example will use the default database using the `PERSISTENCE_EXAMPLE` alias. Database connections are not requested directly from the DataSource, however; instead a database connection is represented by a *Connection-Context*.

The ConnectionContext is a separate class that we have to declare using SQLJ syntax in which the required DataSource is specified. For the sake of simplicity, we will call it *Ctx* and associate it with the `PERSISTENCE_ EXAMPLE` DataSource.

Connection-Context Class

A special wizard for creating Open SQL/SQLJ classes is available in the NetWeaver Developer Studio. We will use this wizard to create the Data Access class.

Creating the ConnectionContext Class Ctx

To create the `Ctx` class in the SAP NetWeaver Developer Studio, proceed as follows:

1. Open the **persistence_example_sqlj** project in the Explorer view and activate the context menu for this project by clicking the right mouse button.

2. Choose **New · Other ...**

3. Select **Persistence** in the left column and then **SQLJ Source** in the right column. Then, click on **Next**.

4. In the **Package** input field, enter the following classpath: `com.sap.examples.persistence.sqlj`

5. In the **Name** input field, enter the name of the SQLJ class (`Ctx`) and then click on **Finish**. The class that you have just created is automatically displayed in the SQLJ Editor.

The class that was created can easily be recognized as an Open SQL/SQLJ source code file by its suffix `.sqlj`.

`Ctx.sqlj` contains the following content:[2]

```
package com.sap.examples.persistence.sqlj;

#sql public context Ctx with (dataSource =
  "java:comp/env/PERSISTENCE_EXAMPLE");
```

Once you have saved `Ctx.sqlj`, the SQLJ Translator creates a Java file that contains the calls of the Open SQL/SQLJ runtime.

At the time of translation, the SQLJ Translator also performs semantic and syntax checks. As the ConnectionContext class specifies the DataSource, the SQLJ Translator can determine the corresponding logical database schema of the Java Dictionary against which the checks are executed. The checks therefore take place offline and not against the physical database schema.

---

2 **Caution:** When you create a ConnectionContext class, the class body has to be removed. In this example, replace `public class Ctx {}` with a `#sqlj` expression.

Unfortunately, for our session bean project, it is necessary to manually introduce the generated Java sources to the project:[3]

Inserting the Generated Java Source Code in the Project

To create the Ctx class in the SAP NetWeaver Developer Studio, proceed as follows:

1. Open the **persistence_example_sqlj** project in the Explorer view and activate the context menu for this project by clicking the right mouse button.

2. Choose **Properties**.

3. In the left column, select **Java Build Path** and then in the right column, choose **Add Folder ...** on the **Source** tab.

4. Choose the **gen_sqlj** folder and click on **OK**.

5. Then click on **OK** on the **Properties** panel.

Once we have declared the database connection using ConnectionContext, we can work with the ConnectionContext.

Data Manipulations: Insert, Update, Delete

Within our Data Access class, we will now create ConnectionContext instances and send SQLJ queries. First, however, you must create the Data Access class. You do in the same way that you created the Ctx class; the fully qualified name is com.sap.examples.persistence.sqlj. DataAccess.[4]

We can now start to bring our project management example to life and write our first SQLJ queries. All manipulating database queries (Insert, Update, and Delete) are exemplified using the Insert statement for creating a project. We therefore implement DataAccess.createProject()(see Listing 4.3):

```
public long createProject(String name,
  String description) throws SQLException
{
  Ctx ctx = new Ctx();
  try
```

---

3 Another way of dealing with this problem is to create all SQLJ classes in a separate Java project and to reference this project from the *persistence_example_sqlj* session bean project.

4 The class body must be replaced for the ConnectionContext class only!

```
{
  long id = IdGenerator.getNewId();
  #sql [ctx] { insert into PERSIST_PROJECT (ID,
                  NAME, DESCRIPTION)
              values (:id, :name, :description)};
  return id;
}
finally
{
  if (ctx != null)
  {
    ctx.close();
  }
}
}
```

Listing 4.3 Implementing the DataAccess.createProject() Method

The creation of an instance of the `Ctx` class creates a connection to the database:

```
Ctx ctx = new Ctx();
```

In this context, the SQLJ queries are now executed; this is why the context instance `ctx` in the special SQLJ notation is placed in front of the SQLJ Insert statement: `[ctx]`.

SQLJ statements are embedded between the SQLJ keyword and a closing semicolon (;).

The braces now contain the actual Insert statement. The Java host variables `id`, `name`, and `description` are used to exchange data between the Java host language and the embedded SQLJ. They are identified by a prefixed colon (:).[5]

Releasing Resources Database connections are valuable resources in a J2EE server and they must be returned to the server's connection pool as quickly as possible. Regardless of whether an error occurs or the database query was submitted successfully, you must always close the ConnectionContext in the finally block to ensure that the resources of the underlying database connection are released properly:

---

5 You can also use *Java host expressions* that contain more complex calculations.

```
finally
{
  if (ctx != null)
  {
    ctx.close();
  }
}
```

The first records have been written. The next section explains how they are read.

Database Queries: Single Row Queries

First, we want to implement a database query that returns a maximum of one record as the return value, which is called a *single row query*. Because the name of a project is defined in the Java Dictionary as *unique*, we can use the name to search for a certain project (see Listing 4.4).

```
public long findProject(String projectName) throws
  SQLException
{
  Ctx ctx = new Ctx();
  try
  {
    long id;
    #sql [ctx] { select ID
                   into :id
                   from PERSIST_PROJECT
                   where NAME = :projectName };
    return id;
  }
  finally
  {
    if (ctx != null)
    {
      ctx.close();
    }
  }
}
```

Listing 4.4 Single Row Query Project Search

Of course, single row queries are also perfect for querying the relevant record using the key attributes. However, because single row queries are generally suitable for all queries that provide a single record as a return value,[6] we can also use them for aggregate functions. To calculate the total salaries of all employees in a department, we use the following single row query in the getOverallSalaryOfDepartment(String departmentName) method of the Data Access class:

```
float salary = 0;
#sql [ctx] { select sum(SALARY)
             into :salary
             from PERSIST_EMPLOYEE e, PERSIST_
DEPARTMENT d
             where e.DEPARTMENT_ID = d.ID and d.NAME =
                :departmentName };
```

Now we'll look at database queries that return several data records.

Database Queries: Multiple Row Queries

A single row query is not suitable if you wanted to list all employees with a certain last name, such as Smith. We need a construction that can handle a number of returned data records. Open SQL/SQLJ provides several constructs for this, the most elegant of which are surely *named iterators*.[7] It is at this point that the power of Open SQL/SQLJ becomes most apparent. It has never been easier to retrieve ResultSets without having to worry constantly about parameter indexes, column names, or JDBC types.

A named iterator is specified in a user-defined class and wraps the database cursor. In other words, a named iterator is used as a handle for the ResultSet on the database side. The named iterator is instantiated and iterated to process a Select statement's ResultSet.

We create a SQLJ class com.sap.examples.persistence.sqlj. NamedIteratorEmployees in the same way as we did with the Ctx SQLJ class.

Because we're interested in all of the employee's attributes, this SQLJ class has the following content:

---

6 Note that a single row query may not contain ORDER BY clauses or UNIONS.
7 There is also what is called a *positional iterator* and an *untyped iterator*.

```
package com.sap.examples.persistence.sqlj;

#sql public iterator NamedIteratorEmployees (long id,
    String firstName, String lastName, float salary);
```

This determines which columns are mapped to which Java types, although uppercase and lowercase letters are not distinguished, and the sequence of the columns is equally unimportant. Of course, the JDBC types must correspond to the Java types. This is also checked by the SQLJ Translator when the SQLJ code is translated.

In the implementation of our findEmployees(String lastName) method, the named iterator is instantiated as follows:

```
NamedIteratorEmployees namedIter;
#sql [ctx] namedIter = { select ID, FIRSTNAME, LASTNAME,
                                SALARY
                         from PERSIST_EMPLOYEE
                         where LASTNAME = :lastName };
```

Now let's look at how the named iterator is iterated:

```
ArrayList employeesList = new ArrayList();

while (namedIter.next()) {
  EmployeeDAO empDAO = new EmployeeDAO(namedIter.id(),
    namedIter.firstName(), namedIter.lastName(),
    namedIter.salary());
  employeesList.add(empDAO);
}

namedIter.close();
```

The ResultSet is iterated for each namedIter.next() and an EmployeeDAO instance is created for each element in the set.

Its constructor is filled by method calls of the namedIter named iterator, where the names of the getter methods and return parameter types correspond to the column names that are declared in the NamedIterator-Employees class.

Once the named iterator has been processed—as we already explained when the ConnectionContext was introduced—it is important that the resources associated with it are released. This is why the named iterator is closed by close().

In addition to the named iterator, Open SQL/SQLJ has two other iterator types for processing ResultSets: the *positional iterator* and the *untyped iterator*.

Unlike the named iterator, column names are not declared when the positional iterator is declared; only a list of the column types is declared in Java. Here too, the iterator is instantiated by assigning the ResultSet.[8] A special SQLJ `fetch` statement is used to assign the column values to Java host variables. Because the column names are not declared, they now have to be assigned to the host variables in the sequence that is determined by the ResultSet; no getter methods are available.

If the column types are not known in a query (admittedly this is rare), the *untyped iterator* can be used.

In this case, the ResultSet is assigned directly to a variable of interface type `sqlj.runtime.ResultSetIterator`, which offers the possibility to return the JDBC ResultSet. Using the ResultSet's metadata or using reflection, the JDBC ResultSet can be read dynamically without being devoid of the SQLJ Translator's syntax and type checks at design time.

Now that we have addressed reading ResultSets, in the next section, we return to the subject of manipulating data records. This time, however, we'll focus on processing large sets of data.

Mass Data Processing: Batch Updates

When large sets of data records are processed and the same operation is executed on each record, we don't recommend that you save every single change with a separate query. Instead, we suggest that you send a request including parameters to the database, compile the query there, execute it, and then return the result to the database clients. The throughput can be significantly increased by using *mass data updates*, also known as *batch updates*.

The query is prepared only once, the parameters of the individual records are collected (called the batch), and the query is not executed until all records have been processed. Finally, the whole batch is sent to the database, where it is executed. Creating a large number of new projects is a good example here.

Mass updates are performed in Open SQL/SQLJ using a special *Execution Context*. In our previous examples, we didn't need to specify an execution context because a standard execution context was assumed implicitly.

---

8 That is, by specifying the Select query in a SQLJ expression.

Now we're going to work with a *BatchExecutionContext*. Like the ConnectionContext, it is instantiated and placed after the SQLJ keyword as a second argument of the bracket that precedes the SQLJ query:

```
BatchExecutionContext bCtx =
new com.sap.sql.BatchExecutionContext();
try
{
  for (int i = 1; i <= 100; i++)
  {
    long id = IdGenerator.getNewId();
    String name = "Project " + i;
    String description = "Project having id " + i;
    #sql [ctx, bCtx] { insert into PERSIST_PROJECT (ID,
                            NAME, DESCRIPTION)
                        values (:id, :name, :description)
};
  }
  bCtx.executeBatch();
}
finally
{
  if (ctx != null)
  {
    ctx.close();
  }
}
```

Once all projects to be created have been added to the batch, executeBatch() is used to trigger the execution of the database query and the ConnectionContext is closed in the finally block.

In all previous examples, we used the J2EE standard JTA transactions that we already declared in the session bean. The following section discusses how you can use another option in Open SQL/SQLJ.

Transaction Management: Controlling Local Transactions

Instead of leaving transaction management to the J2EE server's transaction monitor by using global JTA transactions implicitly (in the *ejb-jar.xml Deployment Descriptor*) or explicitly (via JNDI lookup), transaction management can also occur locally when you use Open SQL/SQLJ, just like in Open SQL or pure JDBC.

We want to demonstrate this using the `removeEmployeeFromPro-ject()` method as an example. First, the implicit transaction control must be deactivated for this method in the *ejb-jar.xml* of our session bean project by selecting the **Never** transaction attribute. Figure 4.7 shows the settings that must be made in the *ejb-jar.xml*.

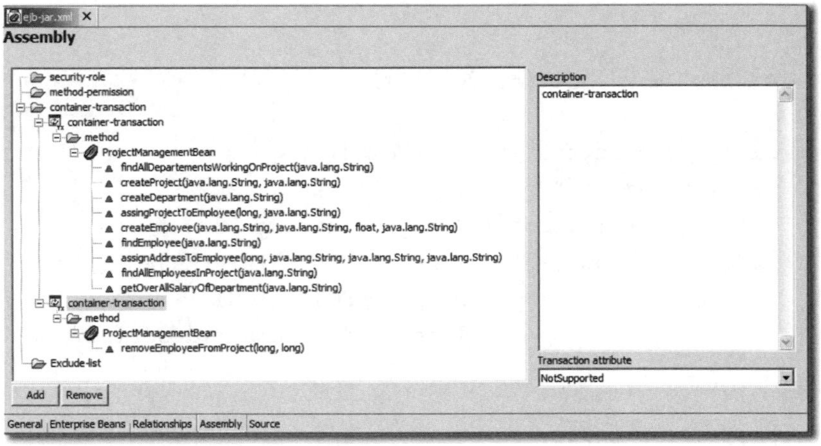

Figure 4.7 Deactivating the Implicit Transaction management

Local Transaction Management

Transaction management still has to be declared explicitly. How is a local transaction committed to a ConnectionContext or rolled back? Once the database query is triggered, this takes place in an additional embedded SQLJ declaration:

```
#sql [ctx] { commit work };
```

This is the complete method implementation:

```
public void removeEmployeeFromProject(long employeeId,
            long projectId) throws SQLException
{
  Ctx ctx = new Ctx();
  try
  {
    #sql [ctx] { delete from PERSIST_EMP_X_PROJ
                where EMPLOYEE_ID = :employeeId
                and PROJECT_ID = :projectId };

    #sql [ctx] { commit work };
  }
  finally
```

```
  {
    if (ctx != null)
    {
      ctx.close();
    }
  }
}
```

Now that we've seen how the project management scenario is implemented using Open SQL/SQLJ, we'll look at the two component-based and object-oriented approaches respectively that can be used in SAP Web AS in the next two sections.

4.6 Enterprise JavaBeans—Container-Managed Persistence

If you still aren't excited about getting into the relational paradigm of the persistence media of business applications in the Java object-oriented world—even after reading about the assets of Open SQL and the comfort of Open SQL/SQLJ—then, SAP Web AS offers two solutions: Enterprise JavaBeans with container-managed persistence entity beans (EJB CMP) and Java Data Objects (JDO).

Both solutions are based on the principle of transparent persistence, that is, as developers we don't have to worry about synchronizing our main memory objects with the database. A mechanism automatically populates our main memory objects with database values when object attributes are accessed and the object graph is navigated through. Changes to attribute values are logged and written to the database at the time of the commit. So that this conversion can be performed automatically, in both cases you must declare the mapping of classes with their attributes to tables and columns as well as the mapping of object relationships using logical foreign key relationships.

Transparent Persistence

This section shows how we can implement our persistence scenario using EJB CMP without having to program a single line of SQL. In general, Enterprise JavaBeans (EJBs) are not merely a way of making data persistent. Rather they are a conglomerate of concepts for implementing business applications that makes life easier for developers in many respects. In addition to transaction management, they also afford security and remote capabilities. Persistence is only one of many EJB's features.

This section assumes that you're already familiar with the basic concepts of Enterprise JavaBeans and how they're used in the SAP NetWeaver Development Studio, which was addressed in Chapter 2.

4.6.1 Implementing the Project Management Scenario Using EJB CMP

As in the previous example, we also want to implement the business logic in the Project Management session bean, from which, in turn, we want to access our data management logic implemented in EJB CMP. We want to create an entity bean for each of the UML classes. These are the names of the beans that should be created: Address, Employee, Department, and Project.[9] As our entity beans should only be addressed locally from the Project Management bean, it will suffice if we have only local interfaces generated. You have already learned how to create simple entity beans whose attributes are not related. In each entity bean, declare the *id* field as a simple key attribute of type `java.lang.Long`.

Relationships Between Entity Beans

Declaring Relationships in ejb-jar.xml

This section looks more closely at creating relationships between entity beans, using the unidirectional 1:n relationship between the department and employee class as a template. If you understand how this relationship is mapped, you will easily be able to create the remaining relationships yourself.[10] To do this, a relationship called *employeesOfDepartment* must be created in *ejb-jar.xml* for the Department bean on the **Relations** tab (see Figure 4.8).[11]

The cardinality of the Department is one (1), the name of the CMR field is **employees**. Its type is `java.util.Set`. We still have to select the `com.sap.examples.persistence.ejb.EmployeeBean` class as the target class of this **CMR** field and declare the cardinality n (*many*).

Here are the other relationships that are still missing: The Employee bean is given the relationships *address* and *projects*; the Project bean has the *employeesOfProjects* relationship.

---

9   The wizard enhances the names of each of the beans with the additional "Bean" appendix: **Address** • **AddressBean**.

10 All relationships are coded in the fully implemented *persistence_example_ejb* project on the accompanying DVD.

11 Because relationships are declared outside of the declaration of the respective beans in a separate section in *ejb-jar.xml*, we have to differentiate this *employee's* relationship from the Project bean, which is why we give it a more comprehensive name.

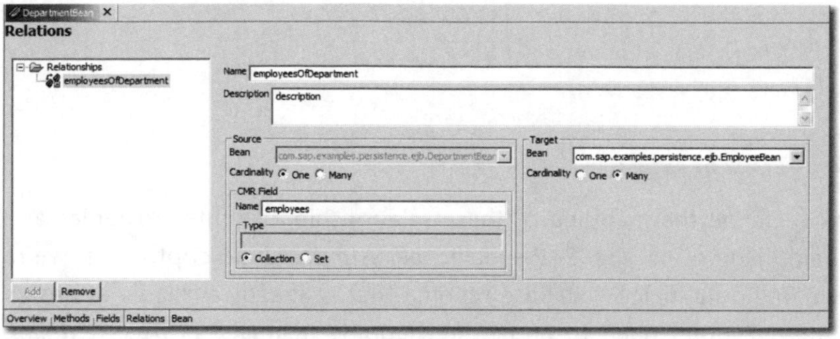

Figure 4.8 Creating the employeesOfDepartment Relationship in ejb-jar.xml

For the *employeesOfDepartment* relationship, the *ejb-jar.xml* contains the following entries:

```
<relationships>
  <ejb-relation>
    <description>description</description>
    <ejb-relation-name>
      employeesOfDepartment
    </ejb-relation-name>
    <ejb-relationship-role>
      <ejb-relationship-role-name>
        com.sap.examples.persistence.ejb.DepartmentBean
      </ejb-relationship-role-name>
      <multiplicity>One</multiplicity>
      <relationship-role-source>
        <ejb-name>DepartmentBean</ejb-name>
      </relationship-role-source>
      <cmr-field>
        <cmr-field-name>
          employees
        </cmr-field-name>
      </cmr-field>
    </ejb-relationship-role>
    <ejb-relationship-role
      <ejb-relationship-role-name>
        com.sap.examples.persistence.ejb.EmployeeBean
      </ejb-relationship-role-name>
      <multiplicity>Many</multiplicity>
      <relationship-role-source>
        <ejb-name>EmployeeBean</ejb-name>
```

```
        </relationship-role-source>
      </ejb-relationship-role>
    </ejb-relation>

...

</relationships>
```

Database Mapping in persistent.xml Now define the mapping of these relationship attributes to tables and their columns in the SAP-specific *persistent.xml* descriptor. As we're working on a logical database schema that is already available at design time, we don't need to enter the mapping manually in *persistent.xml*; instead, we can easily select tables and their columns to specify the foreign key and primary key of our relationship. This is why the first step consists of specifying our DataSource or its already known DataSource alias PERSISTENCE_EXAMPLE in *persistent.xml* (field **Datasource Name** on the **General** tab in *persistent.xml*).[12]

On the **Relationships** tab, we can find our *employeesOfDepartment* relationship that is declared in *ejb-jar.xml* and its associated Department bean and Employee bean entity beans.

For the Department bean, the primary key is mapped to the foreign key of the table of the other (that is, the Employee) bean.

For the Employee bean, the primary key is not used to describe the relationship; this side of the relationship contains the foreign key column. We select DEPARTMENT_ID as the foreign key column relating to the primary key of the Department bean. The Entity Bean Wizard generates the following entry from this primary key for the *employeesOfDepartment* relationship in *persistent.xml*:

```
<relationships>
  <table-relation>
    <table-relationship-role key-type="PrimaryKey">
      <ejb-name>DepartmentBean</ejb-name>
      <cmr-field>employees</cmr-field>
    </table-relationship-role>
    <table-relationship-role key-type="NoKey">
      <ejb-name>EmployeeBean</ejb-name>
      <fk-column>
        <column-name>DEPARTMENT_ID</column-name>
```

---

12 If you adhered to declaring the simple attributes of our entity beans, you will already have specified the DataSource alias and assigned a table to each entity bean.

```
      <pk-field-name>id</pk-field-name>
    </fk-column>
  </table-relationship-role>
 </table-relation>
...
</relationships>
```

Creating, Manipulating, and Deleting Entity Beans

The EJB wizard has served us well up to now, but we have to stand on our own two feet again to code the business methods. As we have decided on CMP, we don't need to code the abstract getter and setter methods of the persistent attributes. We still have to specify the creation of our entity bean's initial state in the ejbCreate method.

For all entity beans, the *id* key field must be assigned a unique value, which we create using the IdGenerator class.[13] All ejbCreate methods of our abstract entity bean classes have the following form:

```
public Long ejbCreate() throws CreateException
{
  Long id = new Long(IdGenerator.getNewId());
  setId(id);
  return id;
}
```

Consequently, our entity beans are fully described in the sense of persistent objects. The following shows how you work with them within the Project Management session bean.

In order to use entity beans within the session bean, some preparatory work is still necessary. We show this using the Department bean as an example, which represents all entity beans that are used.

Thus far, we could refer to just the entity bean. The EJB wizard has largely prevented us from having to differentiate between the (local) Home interface, (local) Component interface, and the abstract bean class. To understand how entity beans are addressed within a session bean, we must now consider these differences. For the sake of simplicity, we'll omit the *Local* addition, especially since the entity beans don't have to support remote-capability with the session façade pattern.

---

13   This helper class is located in the *data_access_objects* project. To use this class in the *persistence_example_ejb* project, add the *data_access_objects* project to the required projects in the Java build path of the properties of the *persistence_example_ejb* project.

Declaring Local EJB References

The DepartmentLocalHome Home interface serves as a factory for Department entity bean instances and declares creation and deletion methods.[14] As Home interfaces are looked up in the JNDI context, we must enter all our entity beans there. Because local EJB references should only be visible in the local context of the Project Management session bean, we declare these references there (see Figure 4.9).

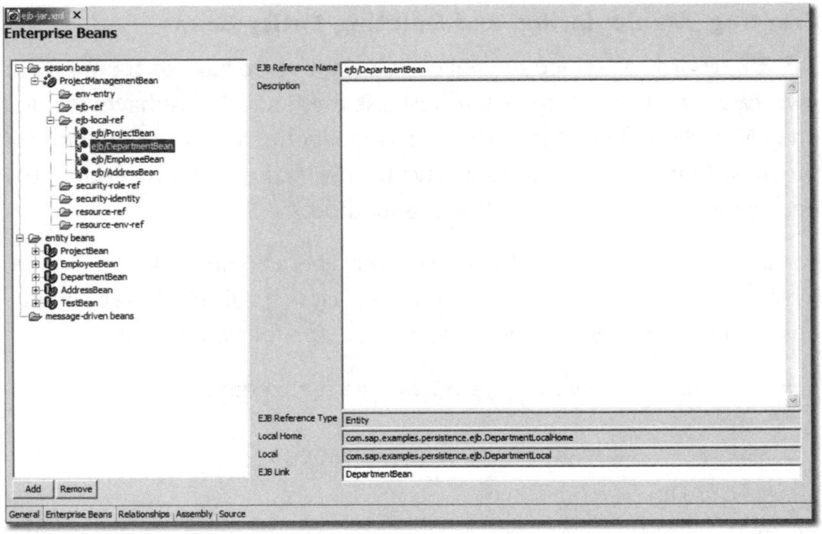

Figure 4.9 Local EJB References in the Project Management Session Bean

We can now perform the Java Naming and Directory Interface (JNDI) lookup, taking into account the EJB reference name declared above.

JNDI Lookup

Because a JNDI lookup is a relatively expensive operation, all entity bean lookups are summarized in the initial life-cycle method setSessionContext () of the Project Management bean.[15] The Home interfaces are kept in private attributes (see Listing 4.5):

```
public class ProjectManagementBean
  implements SessionBean
{
  private DepartmentLocalHome departmentHome;
  ...
  public void setSessionContext(
```

14 In the following sections, we'll see that a Home interface can also declare additional methods.

15 Of course, this is irrelevant for our stateless session bean, but it is considered to be generally good programming practice.

```
                javax.ejb.SessionContext context)
  {
    javax.naming.Context myContext;
    try
    {
      myContext = new InitialContext();

      departmentHome =
        (DepartmentLocalHome) myContext.lookup(
          "java:comp/env/ejb/DepartmentBean");
      ...
    }
    catch (NamingException e)
    {
      throw new EJBException(
        "Error in lookup of lookup bean home: "
          + e.getMessage());
    }
  }
}
```

Listing 4.5 JNDI Lookup of Home Interfaces

Since we don't want to deal with the details of transaction management, we declare the *Required* transaction attribute for all methods of all beans on the **Assembly** tab of the *ejb-jar.xml* (see Figure 4.10).

The following createDepartment() business method of the Project Management session bean shows how you use this Home interface to create a persistent Department instance[16] and call the setter method for the department name:

```
public Long createDepartment(String name)
{
  DepartmentLocal department;
  Long id = null;
  try
  {
    department = departmentHome.create();
    department.setName(name);
    id = department.getId();
```

---

16 Entity bean instances are always persistent, unlike JDO, which allows for transient states of persistence-capable objects.

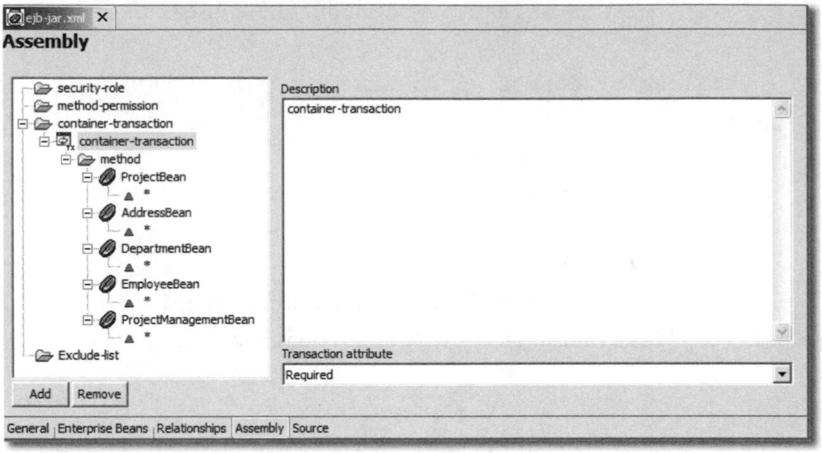

Figure 4.10 Global JTA Transactions for All Methods of All Beans: Required

```
    }
    catch (CreateException e)
    {
      e.printStackTrace();
    }
    return id;
}
```

When the Home interface's `create()` method is called, the EJB Container creates a new bean instance or uses a pooled bean instance, and calls the `ejbCreate()` method that we have implemented. This fills the key fields and the EJB Container creates an identity object that receives the values of the key fields. This identity object is uniquely assigned to the EJB object that is addressed from the Project Management session bean using the Component interface.

Similar to the `create()` method, each Home interface or EJB object has a `remove()` method with which a persistent entity bean instance is deleted.

To implement the project management example scenario, more functionality is required than merely creating, changing, and deleting objects.

Database Queries: Finder and Select Methods

If we know the employee's key and the name of the project, let's look at what we need in order to assign a project to that employee. Of course, you must be able to find an employee by specifying his or her unique key, search for the project with the specified name, and then use the setter methods of both entity beans to assign them to each other.

If you've been following the generation process of the entity beans carefully, you'll note that the EJB Container has generated a `findByPrimary-Key` method for every bean in the Home interface. These types of methods are known as finder methods. They have the primary key[17] that we defined as an argument and return the corresponding bean as the return value. Consequently, it's easy to search for an employee if you know his or her key. Unfortunately, we only know the project name; we need another finder method that has the project name as an argument and returns the corresponding project.

Finder methods are always declared in the Home interface of the bean whose Component interface is the return value. This is why our new `findProjectByName(String name)` finder method is declared via the EJB wizard in the Project bean's Home interface; the same mechanism that we have already seen for the `create()` method applies to the method name, the parameter, and the return value (see Figure 4.11).

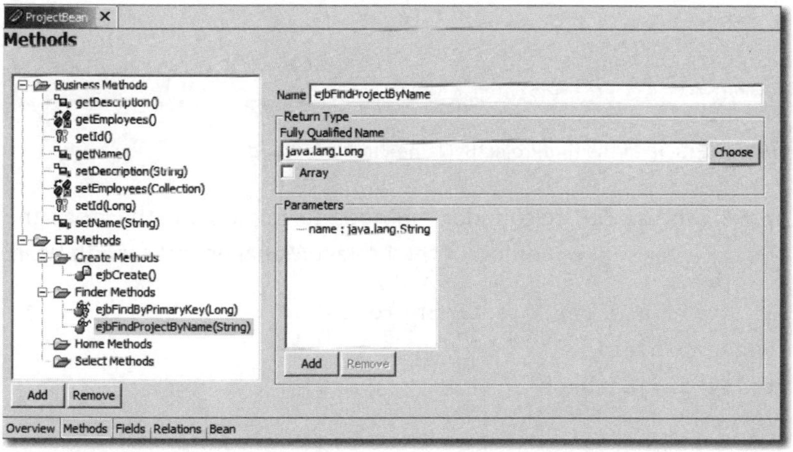

Declaring Finder Methods

Figure 4.11 Creating the New Finder Method for the Project Bean

Unfortunately, because the EJB Container cannot guess which semantic we intended to use with the new finder method, we have to specify it ourselves. This is done declaratively in the *ejb-jar.xml* deployment descriptor using a special query language for the object model: EJB Query Language—EJBQL. At the time of deployment, the EJB Container gener-

Specifying Finder Methods in ejb-jar.xml

---

17 Which is of type `java.lang.Long` for all of our entity bean instances.

ates the necessary database queries from this declaration and the signature of the finder method. Once you have declared the new finder method as described above, select *ejb-jar.xml* and open the **query** folder for the Project entity bean, and specify the corresponding database query in EJBQL for our `findProjectByName` finder method:

```
select object(p) from ProjectBean p where p.name
  = ?1
```

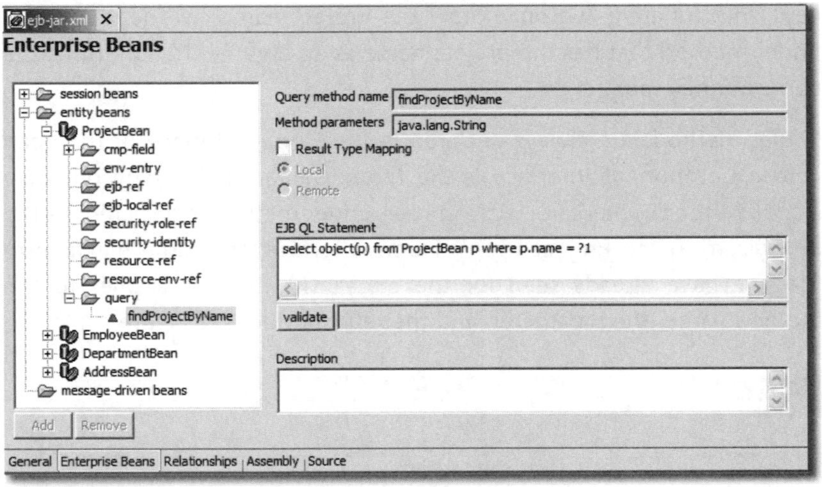

Figure 4.12 EJBQL of the findProjectByName Finder Method

Now we can use our two finder methods to implement the `assignProjectToEmployee` method of the Project Management session bean:

```
public void assignProjectToEmployee(
  long employeeId,
  String projectName)
{
  try
  {
    ProjectLocal project =
      projectHome.findProjectByName(projectName);
    EmployeeLocal employee =
      employeeHome.findByPrimaryKey(
      new Long(employeeId));


    Collection projects = employee.getProjects();
```

```
    projects.add(project);
  }
  catch (FinderException e)
  {
    e.printStackTrace();
  }
}
```

Note that we are dealing with a bidirectional m:n relationship here, and that we would also have to add the employee to the project's employees set to keep our model consistent. EJB does this work for us:

Managed Relationships in EJB CMP

The `project.getEmployees()` call returns a result set that also includes the employee to whom this project has just been assigned.

Of course, finder methods can also be used for result sets, as we have just shown, not just for results that consist of a single element.

Next, we turn our attention to implementing the method that calculates the total salary of all employees in a certain department.

To do this, use the summation aggregate function that is available with the EJBQL 2.1 extensions. Unfortunately, they cannot be used in combination with finder methods, because finder methods' return values are restricted to individual entity beans or sets of entity beans as described above.

Another group of database queries form so-called *selector methods*. They permit even individual CMP fields and their aggregates as return values. Selector methods can only be used within an actual bean instance, therefore, we cannot declare them in the Home interface. Instead, we have to take a short detour and expose the `selector` method's functionality with a business method that encapsulates the selector method. This means that we must use an actual bean instance, which is why we declare this business method on the Component interface of the Department bean as follows:

Declaring Selector Methods in the Component Interface

```
public float computeOverallSalary()
  throws FinderException;
```

The implementation in the abstract bean class occurs as soon as the `selector` method is implemented.

Implementing Select Methods in ejb-jar.xml

In *ejb-jar.xml*, use the EJB wizard to create a selector method called `ejbSelectAllSalary` for the Department bean and assign it a *name* parameter of type `java.lang.String`.[18]

For declaring the `float` return value type, we have to trick the EJB wizard, whose behavior is slightly too restricted when you select the permitted types. Choose any one of the types that are offered and save your changes. Then, open the abstract Department bean class in the Java editor and change the return value types manually as follows:

```
public abstract float ejbSelectAllSalary(String name)
  throws FinderException;
```

When you save it, your EJB wizard for the Department bean should look like the wizard displayed in Figure 4.13.

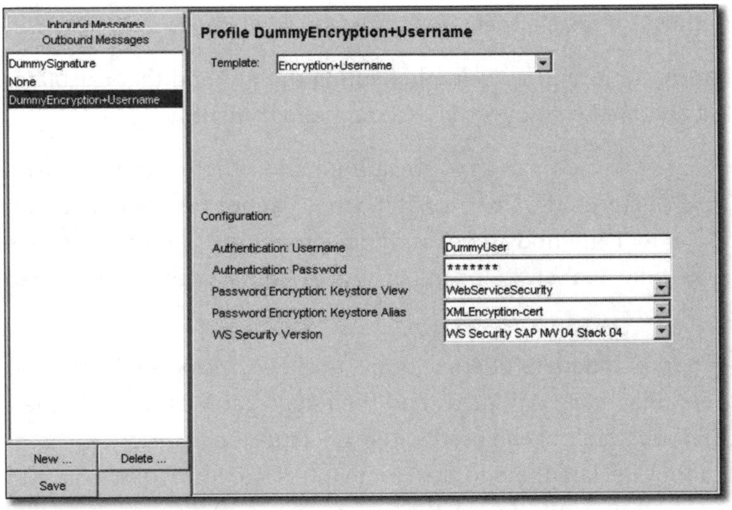

Figure 4.13 Bypassing the EJB Wizard to Specify the Return Value Type

Activating EJBQL 2.1 Extensions

Next, we have to specify the use of EJBQL 2.1 extensions (the sum aggregate function) by setting the corresponding flag for the Department bean's selector method in the *persistent.xml*.

In *ejb-jar.xml*, we express our query in EJBQL as follows (see also Figure 4.14):

```
select sum(e.salary) from DepartmentBean d, in
                    (d.employees) e where d.name = ?1
```

18 Of course, you can also work directly with the department's *id* attribute instead of its name, in which case you also need to change the EJBQL query accordingly.

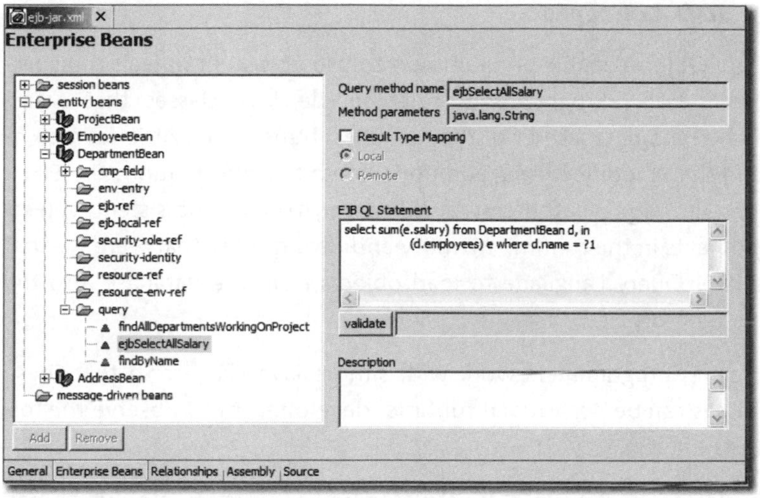

Figure 4.14 Formulating the EJBQL for the Selector Method

We declared the `computeOverallSalary()` business method in the Component interface of the Department bean. This is how it is implemented in the abstract bean class.

```
public float computeOverallSalary()
  throws FinderException
{
  float overallSalary = ejbSelectAllSalary(getName());
  return overallSalary;
}
```

4.7 Programming with Java Data Objects

We will now program our example application using Java Data Objects (JDO). To give you an understanding of JDO, we'll start with a short introduction explaining the basic principles of this programming model. The example application will enable you to program and deploy simple applications using JDO in the Developer Studio, and also to assess JDO's advantages and disadvantages. If you want to use JDO for larger applications, you will require more detailed documentation. Good sources of information on the Internet are the JDO specification *http://jcp.org/aboutJava/communityprocess/final/jsr012/index2.html* and the JDO community page *http://jdocentral.com*.

4.7.1   JDO Concepts

Java Data Objects enable programmers to use persistent objects transparently and easily. Programmers write simple Java classes that aren't mapped to the database until they've been translated by the Java compiler and then modified using additional metadata information. The `PersistenceManager` is the central interface. It makes persistent objects out of objects in the runtime memory and uses queries that were created in the JDO Query Language to load objects from the database into the runtime memory.

In principle, programmers work with simple Java classes. So that these Java classes can be persisted at runtime, developers must observe the following rules:

▶ The classes must have a constructor without arguments, which can also be declared as *private*. Additional constructors can be implemented optionally.

▶ There must be a unique key class for each class. Rules also apply to this key class; we will discuss these rules during our example implementation.

These classes are translated using the standard Java compiler. The Java bytecode files that are created are modified by the *enhancer*. To do this, the enhancer needs information about the attributes to be made persistent and it needs the key class. This information is specified in an XML file, whose format and content is defined in the JDO specification. The name of the XML file is determined by the naming convention. For a `com.package.Name.java` class, the name of the XML file is *com.package.Name.jdo*. Alternatively, you can also specify the metadata for the whole Java package in the *com.package.jdo* file.

If you want to know exactly which modifications are performed by the enhancer, you can decompile the modified classes. For programmers, only one fact is relevant: Their classes are derived from the `javax.jdo.spi.PersistenceCapable` interface that the *persistence manager* expects for its methods.

The mapping of persistent attributes and relations to database objects is defined in another XML file that is read at runtime. The format of this file is not determined in the specification and is therefore SAP-specific.

4.7.2 Preparing the JDO Project

Because we want to access the JDO classes using a session bean, we create an EJB module project. We must include the necessary archives with the JDO interfaces and classes manually in the build path. This is done in the project's *Java Build PathProperties*. On the **Libraries** tab, choose **Add Variable ...** and on the window that appears, select **SAP_SYSTEM_ADD_LIBS** (see Figure 4.15). A file browser opens when you click on **Extend ...**

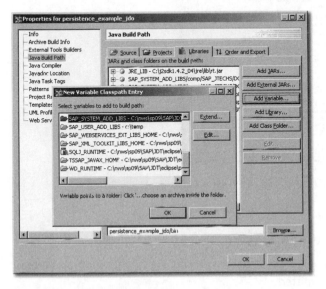

Figure 4.15 Selecting SAP_SYSTEM_ADD_LIBS

The two JDO archives *jdo.jar* and *sapjdoapi.jar* are located in:

/comp/SAP_JTECHS/DCs/sap.com/com.sap.jdo/comp/gen/default/ public/default/lib/java (see Figure 4.16).

Archives that are included as an extension of **SAP_SYSTEM_ADD_LIBS** in the project's build path are not packed in the Enterprise Archive (EAR). The steps that are required so that the application can access the JDO classes at runtime are described in Section 4.5.7.

4.7.3 Programming the Example Classes

Now we want to see how a JDO class is programmed. First we need a key class for each persistent class. As in our example, all keys are of type `long`, so we program a `LongKey` class, which is the base class for all our key classes. The rules for the key classes addressed in the previous section are:

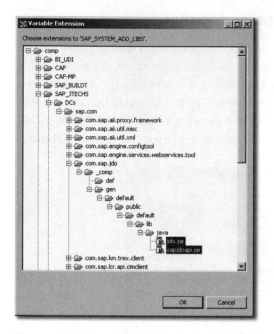

Figure 4.16 Adding JDO Archives as a Variable Extension to the Build Path

► It must be *public*.

► It must implement the `java.io.Serializable` interface.

► It must have a *public* constructor without arguments. Additional constructors are permitted.

► All attributes that are not static have to be serializable. The specification requires that all primitive data types and `String`, `Date`, `Byte`, `Short`, `Integer`, `Long`, `Float`, `Double`, `BigDecimal`, and `BigInteger` must be supported.

► All attributes that are not static must be declared *public*.

► The names and types of these attributes must correspond to the primary key attributes of the corresponding classes.

► The `equals()` and `hashCode()` methods have to consider all values of the corresponding primary key attributes.

► If the key class is an inner class, it must be static.

► It must have a constructor with a `String` parameter.

► It has to overwrite the `toString()` method. If the return value is used as a parameter of the constructor, the key class has to create an object that returns the value **true** when the original object is compared using the `equals()` method.

In view of these rules, our LongKey class looks as it appears in Listing 4.6:

```java
package com.sap.examples.persistence.jdo;

public class LongKey implements java.io.Serializable
{
    public long id;

    public LongKey() {}

    public LongKey(long id)
    {
        this.id = id;
    }

    public boolean equals(Object o)
    {
        if (!(o instanceof LongKey))
            return false;
        return (this.id == ((LongKey) o).id);
    }

    public int hashCode()
    {
     // taken from the hashCode calculation
      // of java.lang.Long
        return (int) (id ^ id >>> 32);
    }

    public String toString()
    {
        return Long.toString(id);
    }
}
```

Listing 4.6 Implementation of the General Key Class

As the primary key for all example classes is assigned to the *id* attribute and is of type long, we can derive the key classes from LongKey. We have included the key class as an inner class in the Employee class in Listing 4.7:

Employee Class

```
package com.sap.examples.persistence.jdo;

import java.util.Set;
import com.sap.jdo.SAPJDOHelper;

public class Employee
{

  // provide static inner class for primary key handling
  static public class Key extends LongKey
    implements java.io.Serializable
  {
    static {SAPJDOHelper.registerPCClass(Employee.class);
}

    public Key() {}

    public Key(String str)
    {
       this.id = Long.parseLong(str);
    }

    public Key(long id)
    {
      this.id = id;
    }
  }

  //persistent attributes
  protected long id;
  protected String firstname;
  protected String lastname;
  protected float salary;
  protected Set projects;
  protected Address address;

  //getter and setter
  public Address getAddress()
  {
    return address;
  }
```

```
//.....
}
```

Listing 4.7 Implementation of the Employee Class

The `Employee` class contains only the persistent attributes and their getter and setter methods. The inner, statically declared key class contains only the constructors and static call `SAPJDOHelper.registerPC-Class(Employee.class)`. This informs the JDO runtime about the assignment between the key and persistent classes.

The term POJO (plain old Java object) has become popular in the Java community in the last few years. It harks back to the days when Java programming was easy, and developers did not have to battle with complicated specifications to write their applications. As you can see from the implementation of the `Employee` class, JDO is an approach that enables persistence with POJOs.

4.7.4 Modifying Bytecode with the Enhancer

Unfortunately, the SAP NetWeaver Developer Studio does not provide any support for JDO in terms of wizards. This is why we have to create the *jdo* files manually and write an ANT script that modifies the bytecode. Fortunately, much of this work can be done using copy and paste as soon as you have created the first *jdo* file. Even the ANT script can be reused for new JDO projects.

The *Employee.jdo* file in our example is structured as follows:

```
<?xml version="1.0" encoding="UTF-8"?>
<!DOCTYPE jdo SYSTEM "jdo.dtd">
<jdo>
   <package name="com.sap.examples.persistence.jdo">
     <class name="Employee"......>
        <field name="id"....../>
        <field name="firstname"....../>
          .
          .
     </class>
   </package>
  ..
</jdo>
```

The metadata file begins with information about the XML format and the jdo element that frames the whole metadata. Within the JDO data, additional brackets are set by the *package* and *class* elements. The *class* element has the *name*, *identity-type*, and *objectid-class* attributes. In our case, the name is Employee and the object ID class is the inner Employee$Key key class. The identity type that is supported by the NetWeaver runtime is *application*. The alternative *datastore* is not supported. For simple attributes, the field element usually contains only the name; the persistence indicator *persistent, transient*, or *none*; and information on whether it is a primary key field is as follows:

```
<field name="id" persistence-modifier="persistent"
       primary-key="true"/>
<field name="firstname" persistence-modifier=
  "persistent"/>
```

For attributes of type *collection*, the additional information pertaining to which Java classes its elements are from is required; in our example, this is the Project class. You can use the *default-fetch-group* to determine whether the projects—along with the employees—are read from the database:

```
<field name="projects" persistence-modifier="persistent"
       embedded ="false" default-fetch-group="false">
       <collection element-type="Project "/>
</field>
```

The embedded element specifies whether the attribute is saved as part of the containing instance. The element types and attributes are standardized in the JDO specification.

We'll now turn to the ANT script that should call the bytecode modification. To do this, we create the *build.xml* file in the project's root directory. The file can easily be adapted to new JDO projects. The project **jdo_example** with default target *build holds our script together.*

```
<project name="jdo_example" default="build"
         basedir=".">
```

In the following four project-specific rows, we specify the directories of our source code files, the translated Java classes, and the Eclipse plug-ins for the Developer Studio and the Java Dictionary project.

```
<property name="src.dir"value="${basedir}/ejbModule"/>
<property name="bin.dir" value="${basedir}/bin"/>
```

```
<property name="plug.dir"
          value="C:/nws/sp09/SAP/JDT/eclipse/plugins"/>
<property name="ddict.dir"
value="../persistence_example_dictionary"/>
```

The Java class com.sap.jdo.enhancer.Main is responsible for modifying the bytecode. We use the com.sap.jdo.sql.util.JDO class later to check our metadata and persistent classes:

```
<property name="enhancer.class"
          value="com.sap.jdo.enhancer.Main"/>
<property name="checker_class"
          value="com.sap.jdo.sql.util.JDO"/>
```

Next we have to define the classpath for these two classes. The paths to the archives are relative to the directories specified above and are therefore project-independent. Conversely, the directories are project-dependent:

Project-Dependent Directories

```
<property name="jdo" value
  ="${plug.dir}/com.sap.ide.eclipse.ext.libs.jdo/lib/
  jdo.jar"/>
<property name="xml" value="${plug.dir}/
  com.tssap.sap.libs.xmltoolkit/lib/sapxmltoolkit.jar"/>
<property name="jdoutil" value
  ="${plug.dir}/com.sap.jdo.utils/lib/sapjdoutil.jar"/>
<property name="dictionary" value
  ="${plug.dir}/com.sap.dictionary.database/lib/
  jddi.jar"/>
<property name="logging" value
  ="${plugin.dir}/com.tssap.sap.libs.logging/lib/
  logging.jar"/>
<property name="catalogreader" value
  ="${plugin.dir}/com.sap.opensql/lib/opensqlapi.jar"/>
<property name="classpath.enhance" value
  ="${jdo};${jdoutil};${xml};${logging}"/>
<property name="classpath.check" value
  ="${classpath.enhance};${dictionary};${logging};
  ${catalogreader};${bin.dir}"/>
```

The entire build procedure consists of two substeps. First, all files apart from the source code are copied to the directory of the compiled classes. These are the JDO files and the MAP files in which the object-relational mapping of the persistent classes to the database tables is defined. In the second step, the modification is applied:

```
<target name="build">
  <echo message="Sourcepath: ${src.dir}"/>
  <antcall target="examples.copy"/>
  <antcall target="examples.enhance"/>
</target>

<target name="examples.copy">
  <copy todir="${bin.dir}/com/sap/examples/
    persistence/jdo">
    <fileset dir="${src.dir}/com/sap/examples/
      persistence/jdo">
      <exclude name="**/*.java"/>
    </fileset>
  </copy>
</target>
```

The enhancer class is responsible for modifying the Java bytecode files. The -f (force overwrite) option overwrites the binary files and -v (verbose) gives detailed information about the individual modification steps. With -d <outputdir> you can redirect the modified classes to a different directory:

```
<target name="examples.enhance">
  <java
    fork="yes"
    failonerror="yes"
    classname="${enhancer_class}"
    classpath="${classpath.enhance}">
    <arg line= "-f -v -d" />
    <arg value= "${bin.dir}" />
    <arg value= "${src.dir}/com/../Project.jdo" />
    <arg value= "${bin.dir}/com/../Project.class" />
    <arg value= "${src.dir}/com/../Employee.jdo" />
    <arg value= "${bin.dir}/com/../Employee.class" />
    <arg value= "${src.dir}/com/../Address.jdo" />
    <arg value= "${bin.dir}/com/../Address.class" />
    <arg value= "${src.dir}/com/../Department.jdo" />
    <arg value= "${bin.dir}/com/../Department.class" />
  </java>
</target>
```

The parameters are always pairs of JDO files and the corresponding translated Java classes. For the sake of clarity, we have not written the complete name of the Java *Package*. You can use the -h option to display a detailed description of the options and parameters.

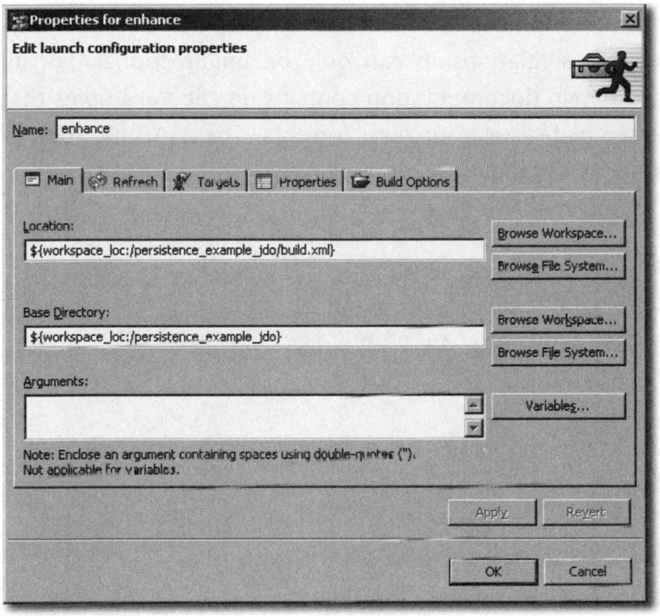

Figure 4.17 Including External Tools in the Build Process Using a Wizard

Now we can use a feature of Eclipse so that our ANT script is called automatically after every compile operation. To do this, we open the project's properties and choose **External Tools Builder** in the left-hand window. In the right-hand window, we use the **New** button to add a new build to our ANT script. There follows a wizard (see Figure 4.17), which you use to specify the parameters of the ANT call. We choose **enhance** as the name, our *build.xml* is the location, and our project's directory is the Base Directory. The **Targets** tab displays all the targets that we defined in *build.xml*. Here the option is the *build* target; that is, copy and subsequently modify the bytecode.

4.7.5 Object-Relational Mapping of Persistent Classes to the Database

Mapping the persistent attributes of a Java class to database tables and columns is defined in the MAP file. The format of this file is not determined in the JDO standard, for example, because the specification doesn't want to exclude object-oriented databases. The format for the SAP-specific JDO implementation is described in detail in the help documentation for the Developer Studio. The cases of simple attributes and all relationships (1:1, 1:n, n:m, unidirectional, and bidirectional) are also described in detail there. Furthermore, the mapping of relationships to generic types such as interfaces and collections is handled with unspecified object types. This relationship can only be unidirectional. For all mapping types, the help documentation contains detailed examples that you can use as templates for your own projects. The MAP file for our Employee class looks as follows (see Listing 4.8):

```xml
<?xml version="1.0" encoding="UTF-8"?>
<!DOCTYPE map SYSTEM "map.dtd">
<map version="1.0">
  <package name="com.sap.examples.persistence.jdo">
    <class name="Employee">
      <field name="id">
        <column name="ID" table="PERSIST_EMPLOYEE"/>
      </field>
      <field name="firstname">
        <column name="FIRSTNAME"
                table="PERSIST_EMPLOYEE"/>
      </field>
      <field name="lastname">
        <column name="LASTNAME"
                table="PERSIST_EMPLOYEE"/>
      </field>
      <field name="salary">
        <column name="SALARY"
                table="PERSIST_EMPLOYEE"/>
      </field>
      <relationship-field
        name="address" multiplicity="one">
        <foreign-key name="EMPLOYEE_TO_ADDRESS"
          foreign-key-table="PERSIST_EMPLOYEE"
          primary-key-table="PERSIST_ADDRESS">
          <column-pair
            foreign-key-column="ADDRESS_ID"
            primary-key-column="ID"/>
        </foreign-key>
      </relationship-field>
```

```
<relationship-field name="projects"
  multiplicity="many" join-table="true">
  <foreign-key name="EMPLOYEE_TO_PROJECTS"
    foreign-key-table="PERSIST_EMP_X_PROJ"
    primary-key-table="PERSIST_EMPLOYEE">
   <column-pair
      foreign-key-column="EMPLOYEE_ID"
      primary-key-column="ID"/>
  </foreign-key>
  <foreign-key name="PROJECTS_TO_EMPLOYEE"
    foreign-key-table="PERSIST_EMP_X_PROJ"
    primary-key-table="PERSIST_PROJECT">
   <column-pair
      foreign-key-column="PROJECT_ID"
      primary-key-column="ID"/>
  </foreign-key>
</relationship-field>
  </class>
 </package>
</map>
```

Listing 4.8 MAP File for the Employee Class

For the simple attributes *id*, *lastname*, *firstname*, and *salary*, it will suffice to specify a table column to which they are mapped. For the 1:1 relationship of the employee to the address, we specify that the primary key ID of the address in the PERSIST_ADDRESS table is assigned to the employee using the ADDRESS_ID foreign key in the PERSIST_EMPLOYEE table. The n:m relationship of projects to employees is mapped using the PERSIST_EMP_X_PROJ assignment table. In the MAP file, we specify that the employee's primary key ID is represented by the EMPLOYEE_ID foreign key and the project's primary key by the PROJECT_ID foreign key.

We can check the correctness of the mapping at design time. To do this, we add an additional target to the *build.xml* file:

```
<target name="check.examples" depends="examples.copy">
  <java
    fork="yes"
    failonerror="yes"
    classname="${checker_class}"
    classpath="${classpath.check}">
```

```
        <arg line= "-v -p" />
        <arg value= "${basedir}/checker.properties" />
        <arg value= "-c" />
        <arg value= "${ddict.dir}/gen_ddic/dbtables/" />
        <arg value= "check" />
        <arg value= "com/../Employee.class" />
        <arg value= "com/../Address.class" />
        <arg value= "com/sap/../Project.class" />
        <arg value= "com/../Department.class" />
    </java>
</target>
```

This ANT target calls the `com.sap.jdo.sql.util.JDO` class for our persistent classes. During the check, the `-v` option informs you which classes were checked, and the `-c <table directory>` compares the tables specified in the MAP file and their columns with the table definitions in the Java Dictionary project. In the *checker.properties* file, you can determine what should be checked:

```
com.sap.jdo.sql.mapping.checkConsistency=true
com.sap.jdo.sql.mapping.checkConsistencyDeep=true
```

The *checkConsistency* property determines whether a check should take place. In this case, all simple attributes are checked. The *checkConsistencyDeep* property also includes the relationships and the classes that can be reached by navigation through the relations in the check.

You can call the check by selecting **Run Ant ...** in *build.xml*'s context menu. A window appears with all targets that you defined in the file. Select the *check.examples* targets and click on **Run**. The result of the check is displayed in the Developer Studio's console window.

4.7.6 Programming the Application Logic

As we already mentioned in our brief introduction to the JDO concept, the persistence manager is the central class for creating, finding, and deleting persistent objects. According to the JDO specification, every manufacturer must provide a class that implements the `Persistence-ManagerFactory` class. An instance of this class gives application programmers access to the persistence manager with the `getPersistenceManager()` method.

In the NetWeaver application server, you get an instance of the factory using a JNDI lookup. The default factory, which uses the system database as the datasource, is bound in the global JNDI under the path *jdo/defaultPMF*. To access the default factory in our session bean, we have to create a resource reference with the identical name **jdo/defaultPMF** of type `javax.resource.cci.ConnectionFactory` in the *ejb-jar.xml* deployment descriptor. We can now reach the persistence manager in our session bean as follows:

```
private PersistenceManager getPersistenceManager()
{
  Context ctx = new InitialContext();
  PersistenceManagerFactory pmf =
    (PersistenceManagerFactory) ctx.lookup(
        "java:comp/env/jdo/defaultPMF");
  PersistenceManager pm =
    pmf.getPersistenceManager();
  return pm;
}
```

Accessing the Persistence Manager

To avoid complicating this information, we are not including error handling in the coding above. We have also limited ourselves to handling at *try-catch-printStackTrace* level in the source texts on the accompanying DVD. Similarly, we will not concern ourselves with transaction management. In *ejb-jar.xml*, we specify *required* as the container transaction attribute for all methods of the bean and rely on the server to *begin*, *commit*, and *rollback* the transactions.

We can now use the persistence manager to write the first object to the database.

Creating a Department

```
public long createDepartment(String name)
{
  PersistenceManager pm = null;
  long result = 0;
  try
  {
    pm = getPersistenceManager();
    Department department = new Department();
    department.setId(IdGenerator.getNewId());
    department.setName(name);
    pm.makePersistent(department);
    result = department.getId();
  }
  finally
```

```
{
   if (pm != null)
     pm.close();
   }
   return result;
}
```

To create a new *Department*, we must call the default constructor and set
the attributes. The pm.makePersistent(department) call writes the
(up to now) *transient* object to the database with the next commit. The
close method of the persistence manager closes the database connection again. We have only described this here to show you how to program the call correctly according to the specification. Because the transactions are adopted by the server's transaction manager, the call does not
have any effect and is automatically initiated during the next commit. The
transaction manager—to which the persistence manager is bound—is
responsible for the entire transaction handling.

Finding a
Department Next we want to find the department using its name. Our table definition
ensures a unique name for departments. We use the JDO Query Language for the first time:

```
private Department findDepartmentByName(
   PersistenceManager pm, String name)
{
   Extent departmentExtent =
     pm.getExtent(Department.class, true);
   String filter = "name == departmentName";
   Query query = pm.newQuery(departmentExtent, filter);
   query.declareParameters("String departmentName");
   Collection col = (Collection) query.execute(name);
   pm.retrieveAll(col);
   Iterator iter = col.iterator();
   Department department =
     (Department) (iter.hasNext() ? iter.next() :null);
   return department;
}
```

First we create an *extent* of the Department class. An extent is a JDO
construction that contains runtime information about the persistent class
and its subclasses. We then create a filter that contains our search criterion and define our search using the extend and the filter. We still have to
notify the search that the departmentName parameter is of type

String. The name parameter is recognized by the JDO runtime as an attribute of the Department class. Once we've assigned a value to the departmentName placeholder, we start the search using the query.execute() call. The search returns a collection; we already know that it contains either one department or no departments.

We can now create an employee and assign that employee to a department. The only unexpected fact in the program code below may be that we don't make an explicit call for the transient object, which is representing our new employee, to make it persistent. However, by assigning a potentially persistent object to an object that has already been made persistent, the persistence manager recognizes that it also has to store the transient object.

```
public long createEmployee(
    String firstname, String lastname,
    float salary, String departmentName)
{
    long result = 0;
    PersistenceManager pm = getPersistenceManager();
    Employee emp = new Employee();
    emp.setId(IdGenerator.getNewId());
    emp.setLastname(lastname);
    emp.setFirstname(firstname);
    emp.setSalary(salary);
    Department department =
    findDepartmentByName(pm, departmentName);
    if (department != null)
    {
        department.getEmployees().add(emp);
        result = emp.getId();
    }
    else
    {
        //do some exception handling
    }
    return result;
}
```

Creating an Employee

We used a query to search for a department using its name. Finding an object using its key is considerably easier. The following program code shows you how to find an employee using his or her *ID*:

```
private Employee findEmployeeById(
    PersistenceManager pm, long employeeId)
{
    Employee.Key key = new Employee.Key();
    key.id = employeeId;
    Employee employee =
        (Employee) pm.getObjectById(key, true);
    return employee;
}
```

The second parameter of the getObjectById(Object key, boolean validate) method specifies whether the persistence manager should determine if the object really exists in the database. If you set the value to **false**, an empty object is created apart from its key, and the attributes are not loaded until they are required. In this case, this could lead to a negative outcome.

For our application, we need additional methods such as finding employees using their last name, creating projects, and discovering projects using their name or key. These methods are programmed similarly to those previously described.

The assignment of an address to an employee shows us something else: The JDO runtime can't fully handle managing relations automatically. If you create a new address and assign it to the employee, the old address remains but it is no longer assigned to an employee. This is why we always first verify whether the employee already has an address. If he or she does have an address, we change its attribute to the new values; otherwise, we create a new address and assign it to the employee.

```
public long assignAddressToEmployee( long employeeId,
    String city, String street, String zipCode)
{
    PersistenceManager pm = getPersistenceManager();
    Employee employee =findEmployeeById(pm, employeeId);
    Address address = null;
    if (employee.getAddress() != null)
    {
        address = employee.getAddress();
    }
    else
    {
        address = new Address();
```

```
    address.setId(IdGenerator.getNewId());
    employee.setAddress(address);
  }
  address.setCity(city);
  address.setStreet(street);
  address.setZipCode(zipCode);
  return address.getId();
}
```

We have defined an n:m relationship between employees and projects.
An employee is assigned to a project by adding him or her to the set
(*java.util.Set*) of all of the employee's projects. Because our work is
object-oriented and the relationship is bidirectional, we must also specify
the inversion programmatically, that is, we must add the project to the set
of projects of the employee so that our object model remains consistent.
Otherwise, JDO does not ensure that the object model in the runtime
memory is consistent with its representation in the database. This appears
in the source code as follows:

```
public void assingProjectToEmployee(                          Assigning an
  long employeeId,                                            Employee to
  String projectName)                                         a Project
{

  PersistenceManager pm = getPersistenceManager();
  Project project =findProjectByName(pm, projectName);
  Object obj = new Employee.Key(employeeId);
  Employee employee =
    (Employee) pm.getObjectById(obj, true);
  project.getEmployees().add(employee);
  employee.getProjects().add(project);
}
```

To remove the relationship between a project and an employee, you must
replace the last two program lines with:

```
project.getEmployees().remove(employee);
employee.getProjects().remove(project);
```

We now want to perform a query in the JDO Query Language that
involves not only one object type, but several object types.

Certainly, you can also search for all employees in a project by finding the
project *p* and displaying all employees using p.getEmployees(). Using
a query, the solution would look as follows:

```
public EmployeeDAO[] findAllEmployeesInProject(String
  projectName)
{
  PersistenceManager pm = getPersistenceManager();
  Extent employeeExtent =
    pm.getExtent(Employee.class, true);
  String vars = "Project proj";
  String filter = "projects.contains (proj) &
    proj.name == projectName";
  Query query = pm.newQuery(employeeExtent, filter);
  query.declareParameters("String projectName");
  query.declareVariables(vars);
  Collection col =
    (Collection) query.execute(projectName);
  pm.retrieveAll(col);
  ...
  // loop over Collection with iterator and extract
  // data into the Data Access Objects
}
```

First, we construct another extent for the Employee class. As the search extends projects, we define a *proj* variable for the Project class. The first search condition is that the employee's projects contain a project that is described in the second condition by its name. We now give the query the variable and the parameter for the project name. We use query.execute(projectName) to start the search and the result is a collection whose elements are the required employees.

To conclude our discussion of Java Data Objects, we want to show the limits of JDO. The JDO Query Language does not support any set functions such as *average*, *sum*, *max*, and *min*. The sum of the salaries in a department cannot be determined by a query. Instead, you have to find the department, load all of its employees in the runtime memory, and total the salaries manually. In reality, you could circumvent this problem by using a JDBC query.

JDBC and JDO can easily be interchanged. If the *PersistenceManagerFactory* is configured on the same connection pool that you are using in the program code for JDBC, the same database connection is used in the same JDO and JDBC transaction. In the following program code, we have assumed that the transactions are managed by the container:

```
Context ctx = new InitialContext();

PersistenceManagerFactory pmf =
  (PersistenceManagerFactory) ctx.lookup(
    "java:comp/env/jdo/defaultPMF");

DataSource ds = (DataSource)
  ctx.lookup("java:comp/env/SAP/BC_JDO");

PersistenceManager pm = pmf.getPersistenceManager();
// work with JDO
  ...
Connection conn = ds.getConnection();
// work with JDBC
...
```

4.7.7 Deploying the Application

Deploying a JDO application is almost the same as deploying a typical EJB application. First, determine whether you've configured transaction management and the *PersistenceManagerFactory* correctly in the *exj-jar.xml*. You must also ensure that your application can access the server's JDO runtime. To do this, in the SAP-specific *application-j2ee-engine.xml* deployment descriptor, insert a reference to the JDO implementation that runs as an application in the JCA adapter. Your XML file should look as follows:

```
<application-j2ee-engine>
  <reference
    reference-type="hard">
    <reference-target
      provider-name="sap.com"
      target-type="application">com.sap.jdo
    </reference-target>
  </reference>
      <provider-name>sap.com</provider-name>
      <fail-over-enable
            mode="disable"/>
</application-j2ee-engine>
```

Finally, we also want to respond to the question "How can I reconfigure the JDO runtime so that it runs on any database, and not just the server's default database?" Our answer is simple: "You never configure the JDO runtime to run on a different database!"

With the NetWeaver Application Server, SAP is also providing a series of applications that run on the server. The JDO runtime must use the system database so that these applications continue to function. However, there is an alternative—cloning the PersistenceManagerFactory. To do this, navigate in the Visual Administrator to the connector container service of any server node. Select the **sap.com/com.sap.jdo/SAPJDO** connector and click on **Clone** in the menu bar above the **Runtime** tab. You can choose any name for the new connector. Select the new connector and choose the **Managed Connection Factory · Properties** tab. Here you can change the datasource to a different one than the default database. For your application, this changes only the path where the *PersistenceManagerFactory* is located in the JNDI (see Figure 4.18).

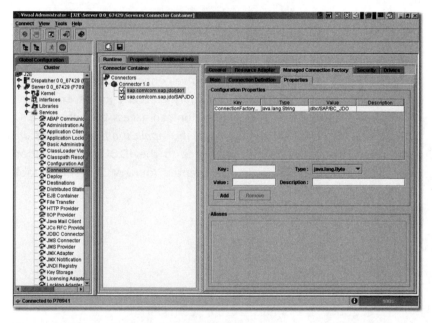

Figure 4.18 Cloning the PersistenceManagerFactory

4.8   Persistence for Experts

You've just seen how an actual persistence scenario was implemented using one relational and two object-relational technologies in the SAP NetWeaver Developer Studio for SAP Web AS. Therefore, you should now be able to use, develop, and tailor this knowledge to your own projects.

We're fully aware that we haven't addressed all aspects of Java persistence. We've only touched on transaction management, since much of this topic is defined in the J2EE standard. We also haven't discussed locking and cascading delete. Discussing optimization strategies and the infrastructure's behavior in detail, such as when certain statements are written to the database, is beyond the scope of this book. However, the SAP NetWeaver Developer Studio documentation and the SAP NetWeaver online help at *help.sap.com* are excellent references for such additional questions.

5   Web Services in the SAP Web Application Server

Web services form the technological basis of Enterprise Services Architecture (ESA). When implemented, IT infrastructures can be converted—step by step—into service-oriented architectures (SOAs). With the use of an example in this chapter, you will learn how to create a Web service, how to publish it in a UDDI registry, and how to bind this Web service in an application. We will focus primarily on the security of Web services.

The enhancement of business processes in heterogeneous system landscapes poses a great challenge for companies. Solutions for tasks of this type have been available for years. However, none of the solutions provided—such as CORBA, Java RMI, or DCOM—have been successful. Conversely, with Web services this target can be reached. As a result of intensive efforts to establish accepted standards for Web services and due to the commitment of most software providers—including Microsoft, IBM, Sun Microsystems, SAP, and many others—to apply these standards, systems with the most diverse types and technology can communicate with one another through Web services.

The extension of business processes is often a complicated, time-consuming undertaking, as shown by the following example. An airline carrier would like to enable rental car bookings in its Internet portal. So that the customer does not need to book the desired car himself through the appropriate Internet pages, the airline company portal will assist in processing the required booking. It is assumed that the developer of the portal application cannot only access the data of the rental car company, but is also familiar with the technical environment, that is, the programming language of the car rental application or the various middleware approaches.

If, on the other hand, the car rental company provides the Web service *Check Availability of a Rental Car*, this service could be used as a black box by any number of applications, without the need to start complicated development projects. To implement this kind of solution, a Web service must fulfill certain requirements.

Definition of Web Services	A Web service is a modularized, executable unit. It can be called in heterogeneous system landscapes and across system boundaries. Output is determined on the basis of the assigned input parameters. This output is then passed back to the caller.
Enterprise Services Architecture	While Web services represent a technical concept, the Enterprise Services Architecture (ESA) provides a complete solution for a business application.[1] Web services, components of mySAP Business Suite, and external software can be linked together in business processes. With Web services, existing company solutions can be optimized and supplemented, and existing functions do not have to be replaced. The ESA provides customers with a powerful tool to adapt, for example, Supply Chain Management (SCM) and Customer Relationship Management (CRM) to customer requirements through the combination of services. In this case, the SAP Enterprise Portal (SAP EP) ensures that instead of users having to know anything about the combined services and components, they can simply use a role-specific user interface that is tailored to a certain task.

SAP NetWeaver has been developed as a platform for the expansion, provision, and management of services. When implemented, IT infrastructures can be converted—step by step—into service-oriented architectures.

5.1 The Web Service Framework

The SAP Web Application Server (SAP Web AS) can function both as a *server* for Web services and as a Web service *client*. SAP Web AS implements the following basic Web services standards: eXtensible Markup Language (XML), Simple Object Access Protocol (SOAP), Web Service Definition Language (WSDL), and Universal Description, Discovery, and Integration (UDDI). SOAP, WSDL, and UDDI are core components of the Web service approach. SOAP provides a general, application-independent format for XML messages, which can then be exchanged between the individual communication partners through different transport protocols. WSDL adds on the application-related component. The Web services interface is described with this language. The description consists of names of operations—such as methods—and inbound and outbound messages. These messages are packed into SOAP messages at runtime and then transmitted. UDDI adds the option of being able to publish and

---

1 For a detailed description of the Enterprise Services Architecture, see Section 1.4, *Prospects: SAP NetWeaver as a Platform for Enterprise Services Architecture*.

look for Web services. Figure 5.1 shows the basic structure of the Web Service Framework.

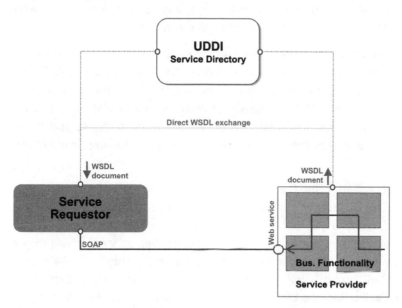

Figure 5.1 Architecture of the Web Service Framework

If the Web AS Java functions as a service provider, a Web service interface **Service Provider** is created for the implemented function. This can be an Enterprise Java Bean (EJB) or a Java class. The interface displays the Web service to the user. It is an abstraction layer that is independent of the implementation. Based on this interface, the so-called *virtual interface*, you configure the Web service that can be called at runtime.

You can store released Web services in a UDDI registry. Web services can **Service Directory** be searched for and published in all registries that adhere to the standard. SAP also offers a public UDDI Business Registry under *http://uddi. sap.com*.

If the Web AS Java functions as a service requestor, a Web service client **Service Requestor** can be created in a few steps using a WSDL file.

5.2   Standardizing Web Services

The Web service technology must be based on generally accepted standards. If application modules developed in different programming languages—on different hardware and in different systems—are to be linked up to the business process with the help of Web services, the critical question of interoperability and adherence to prescribed standards arises.

SOAP, WSDL, and UDDI	Established standards from the Internet world are used for communication. WSDL provides you with specifications for the Web service interface. SOAP enables you to transfer long-distance procedure calls. And UDDI allows you to publish and find Web services.
W3C	There are established organizations that ensure that these general standards are adhered to. The World Wide Web Consortium (W3C), for example, is responsible for core technologies within the Web Service Framework. The W3C comprises several provider-independent work groups whose goal is to create standards for specific technological areas. SAP is a member of the Web Services Architecture Working Group of the W3C.
OASIS	The Organization for the Advancement of Structured Information Systems (OASIS) deals, in particular, with processes; that is, with the interaction of Web services and their integration in business applications. The directory services and security for the use of Web services play a major role here. As part of business-oriented initiatives in the area of Web services, SAP supports not just OASIS but the United Nations Centre for Trade Facilitation and Electronic Business (UN/CEFACT). Both boards are concerned with the development of standards for Web services in the business environment, for example, Universal Business Language (UBL) or Web Services Security (WS-Security).
WS-I	The Web Services Interoperability Organization (WS-I) is an open industry chartered to promote Web services interoperability across platforms, operating systems, applications, and programming languages. WS-I delivers practical guidance, recommended procedures, and tools to support the development of interoperable Web services. The interoperability of Web services should be ensured through the definition of WS-I profiles, which include a number of specifications. If a Web service is to conform to a particular WS-I profile, it must meet all the specifications contained therein. With the Basic Security Profile (BSP), WS-I also handles WS-Security.
J2EE	SAP also contributes its business acumen to the Java 2 Enterprise Edition (J2EE) specifications, which are closely linked to Web services. In addition, SAP is involved in the Java Community Process (JCP), which is responsible for advancing the development of Java technology and is designed to ensure that Java standards bring forth a compatible, stable, and reliable platform.

Moreover, not only is SAP represented in other technology panels, but also primarily involved in groups concerned with the adoption of business standards in the various application areas.

Even if standards such as SOAP, WSDL, and UDDI have established themselves to a large extent, there is still much work ahead for standardization groups. New standards are being created while existing standards are being further developed. These extended standards—such as security standards or additional protocols—can easily be integrated in the Web Service Framework via SAP.

Table 5.1 summarizes the standards supported in the Web Service Framework.

Area	Standard
WS-I	WS-I BP 1.0
Java-API	JAXP 1.2, JAXM 1.1, SAAJ 1.1, JAX-RPC 1.0
XML	SOAP 1.1 w/ Attachments, WSDL 1.1, UDDI v2, Web Services Inspection Language
Security	WS-Security (1.0), SSL/TLS

Table 5.1 Standards Supported by the Web Service Framework

Standards such as SOAP 1.2, WSDL 2.0, and UDDI 3.0 have immediate effects on the development of the SAP Web Service Framework.

5.3   Providing a Web Service—The Server Side

Standard business functions that exist in independent and modular form can be provided as Web services. These could include, for example, a credit card check, conversion of a currency, or an Employee Self-Service (ESS).

In Figure 5.2, the SAP Web Application Server is represented in its function as a Web service provider. The usual standard interfaces, such as EJBs and classes, can be transformed into Web services without additional programming effort in the Web Services perspective of the SAP NetWeaver Developer Studio.

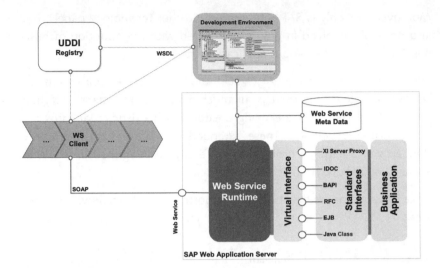

Figure 5.2 Web Service Provider

There are two procedures available for creating a Web service: using the *Web Service Creation Wizard* or using a *step-by-step procedure*. The Web Service Creation Wizard contains predefined profiles. With just a few mouse clicks, security settings or settings of a used transport protocol are assigned to the Web service. Alternatively, using the step-by-step procedure, you can configure a Web service from scratch. Compared to the Web Service Creation Wizard, this procedure involves more effort, but it also enables you to implement individual requirements directly. Note that these two options for creating a Web service are not mutually exclusive. When using the Web Service Creation Wizard, you can quickly create a Web service and then process it further with the editors in the step-by-step procedure.

In Chapter 3, Section 3.9, you learned how to use the Web Service Creation Wizard to provide business logic as a Web service with only a few mouse clicks, how to deploy the Web service on the J2EE Engine, and how to test a Web service by using the Web service home page.

The Web Service Creation Wizard uses typical settings that are employed in Web service scenarios. These settings are grouped together to form predefined configuration profiles. The **Simple SOAP** profile is set for stateless Web service calls for which no additional security measures are necessary. This profile contains no authentication or authorization functions, and it specifies the use of SOAP through HTTP for data transport. If calling a Web service on the client side requires the authentication of the caller—with the help of a user ID and a password—you should choose the profile **Basic Auth SOAP**. In this case, calling Web service operations is protected through security roles. The **Secure SOAP** profile also handles authentication with the help of X.509 client certificates. Data that is sent to the server from Web service clients using SOAP requests is encrypted using the Secure Sockets Layer (SSL) protocol.

In the following sections, we will demonstrate—using an example for checking the creditworthiness of a customer—how you create a Web service step by step, how you publish it in a UDDI registry, and which options exist for subsequently binding the Web service into an application. A high level of security is required to display sensitive business processes in heterogeneous system landscapes. In Section 5.3.3, you will learn how to perform security settings for a Web service.

Step-by-Step Procedure

5.3.1 Creating a Web Service

On the DVD supplied, you will find a ZIP file called *CreditLimit.zip* in the **Examples** directory. Unpack this file into a directory on your computer and import the project **CreditLimitCheck** using **File · Import · Existing Project into Workspace**.

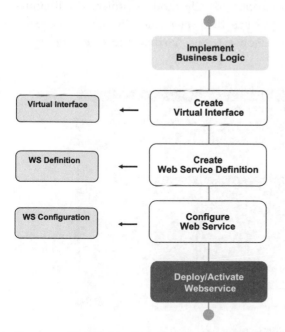

Figure 5.3 Step-by-Step Procedure for Creating a Web Service

The steps shown in Figure 5.3 must be executed when you create a Web service.

Implementing the Application

The application that is to be transformed into a Web service is an EJB or Java class. You must observe certain restrictions when you implement the application. Not all types from the Java packages or remote objects are allowed in the end point.[2]

Creating a Virtual Interface

A virtual interface is the visual representation of a Web service to the outside world. It is the interface that provides the Web service to clients. By using virtual interfaces, you can define several views of the interface of a Web service end point and publish each view separately. In a virtual interface, you can:

▶ Hide operations and parameters

▶ Replace names for operations and parameters with meaningful names

▶ Set fixed values for hidden parameters

▶ Convert parameter data types

▶ Define parameter representation in the SOAP message

To create a virtual interface, open the EJB module project **CreditLimit-Check** in the Web Services perspective, select the EJB under *ejb.jar.xml*, and, in the context menu, choose **New · Virtual Interface** (see Figure 5.4).

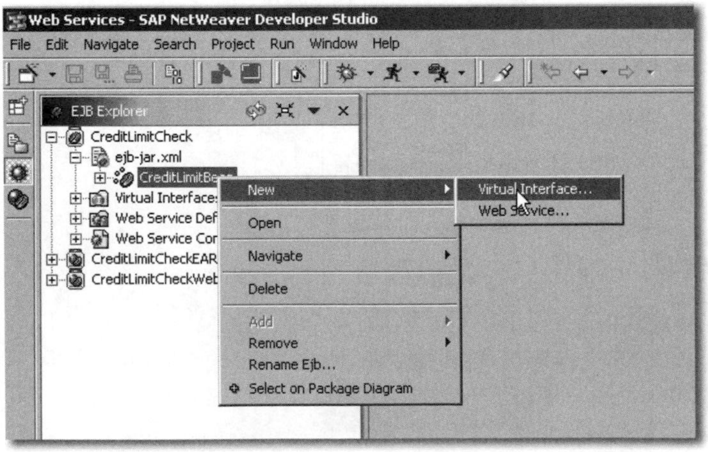

Figure 5.4 Creating a Virtual Interface

---

2 You will find more information in Section 5.3.4, *Restrictions for Web Service End Points*

Enter the name of the package and the name of the virtual interface (**CreditLimitCheckVI**) in the following dialog box.[3] Choose **Next** and select the methods that are to be provided in the virtual interface. Complete your entry by clicking on **Finish**. In the **Mapping** tab in the editor, make the settings for the methods and parameters contained in the EJB, as shown in Figure 5.5.

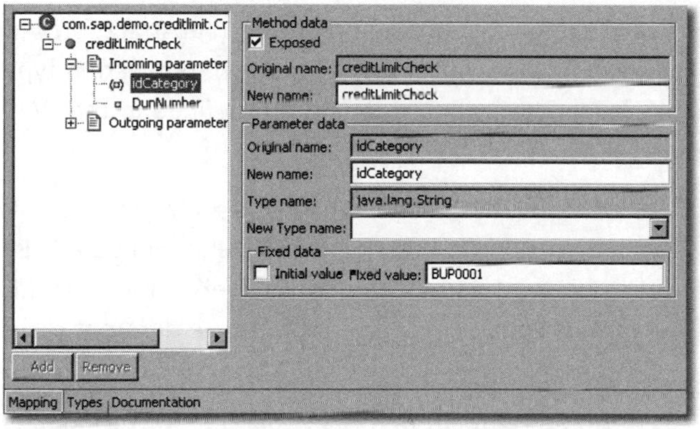

Figure 5.5 Settings for Methods and Parameters Contained in EJB

Remove the checkmark in the checkbox **Exposed** if the method is not offered in the Web service. If necessary, change the name of the method in the **New name** field. The name of the method appears in the WSDL document.

For the parameters, you can make changes in the following fields:

▶ **New name**
Enter a new name for the parameter.

▶ **New Type name**
Choose a new data type. Java-compliant standard conversions for simple and built-in types are possible.

▶ **Fixed value**
Here, enter a standard value. In Figure 5.5, the default value BUP0001 was assigned for the "idCategory" parameter. The parameter will no longer be offered in the Web service interface. When the service is called, the default value will be used and the method will be called with all its parameters.

---

3 For demonstration purposes, the EJB module product already contains the objects required for a Web service. You can delete these objects in order to be able to replicate the steps described in the following sections.

▶ **Exposed**

Remove the field selection if you want to hide the parameter. You can do this only if you have entered a standard value and you have a simple data type (int, string, and so on).

Save your entries using **Save Editor Contents** or **Ctrl+S**.

Step 3 **Creating a Web Service Definition**

With the Web Service Definition, you assign features in abstract form to the Web service. This can include, for example, the communication type or the authentication level. The technical details are defined in the Web service configuration.

Session handling is an example of this. This behavior is switched on or off in the Web Dervice Definition, but it is not technically configured. By assigning these abstract features, you ensure that a Web Service Definition can be used for various application servers that have different technical features.

In larger companies, it can be assumed that the developer of the application that is to be provided as a Web service is the one who determines whether the application—as a Web service—requires stateful communication. However, he or she may not be the person responsible for defining whether this is to be implemented, for example, through HTTP cookies or by using URL extensions. If necessary, this task can be performed by an administrator who knows the system landscape and the technical requirements of the application server on which the Web service is to be called.

You can publish the Web Service Definition as a tModel (that is, technical model) in the UDDI. tModels describe the interface of a Web service in a UDDI registry and serve as reusable units for the publication of business services.

To create the Web Service Definition (WSD), select the virtual interface. Then, in the context menu, choose **New · Webservice Definition**. In the following dialog box, enter the name of the WSD (**CreditLimitCheck-Wsd**), complete your entry by clicking on **Finish**, and choose the **Features** tab (see Figure 5.6).

The selection options in the lower section of the screen refer to the features selected in the upper section. The following options are available:

▶ Select **Session** to specify whether the communication is to be **stateful**.

▶ Select **Authentication** if you want to choose from among the following values: **Basic (User/Password)** and **Strong (incl. Certificates)**. In the first instance, the execution of a Web service requires, on the client side, the authentication of the caller using a user ID and a password. In the second instance, the authentication takes place with the additional help of X.509 client certificates.

▶ Select **Transport Guarantee** if you want to define—using **Integrity + Confidentiality**—that data sent from Web service clients to the server by SOAP requests is to be encrypted with the help of the SSL protocol.

▶ Select **Message ID** if you want to send an additional SOAP header containing a unique ID (GUID) that identifies the Web service message. The application can recall and retrieve this information at a later time.

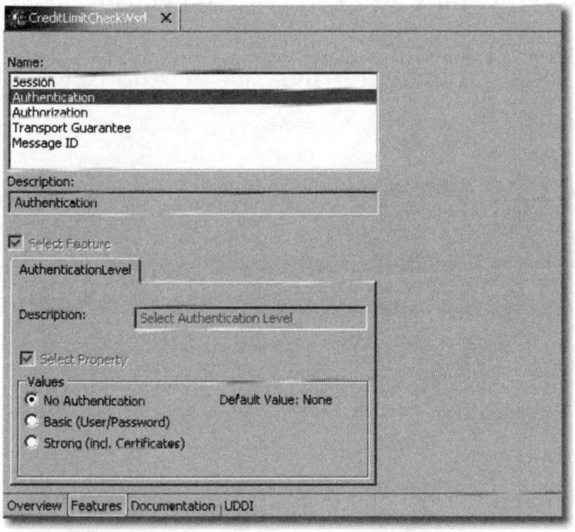

Figure 5.6 Selection of Features in the Web Service Definition

The documentation that you record in the **Documentation** tab is displayed as documentation of the Web service on the Web service home page.[4] In the **UDDI** register, the Web service definition can be published as a tModel.[5] Save the Web service definition by selecting **Ctrl+S**.

---

4 See also Section 5.3.2, *Testing a Web Service with the Web Service Home Page*.
5 This step is executed at a later time (see also Section 5.4).

Step 4   **Creating the Web Service and the Web Service Configuration**

Different application servers can have different technical options. In this step, the general functions that were configured in the Web service definition are assigned to the actual technical features of the server.

A Web service configuration defines the features of the Web service at runtime. One or several Web service configurations are assigned to a Web service.

Select the EJB module project. In the context menu, choose **New · Web Service Deployment Descriptor**. A deployment descriptor is an XML file in which the options you use to deploy an application are described. In the following dialog box, confirm this by clicking on **Finish**. On the right, you see the Web Service (WS) Deployment Descriptor Editor. Select the node for the WS Deployment Descriptor Editor and click on **Add**. Choose the EJB reference and the Web Service Definition (WSD). Assign the name for the Web service (**CreditLimitCheck**) and click on **Finish**. Create a Web Service configuration. Select the node created for the Web service (below the **Web Service Configuration** entry) and click on **Add** (see Figure 5.7).

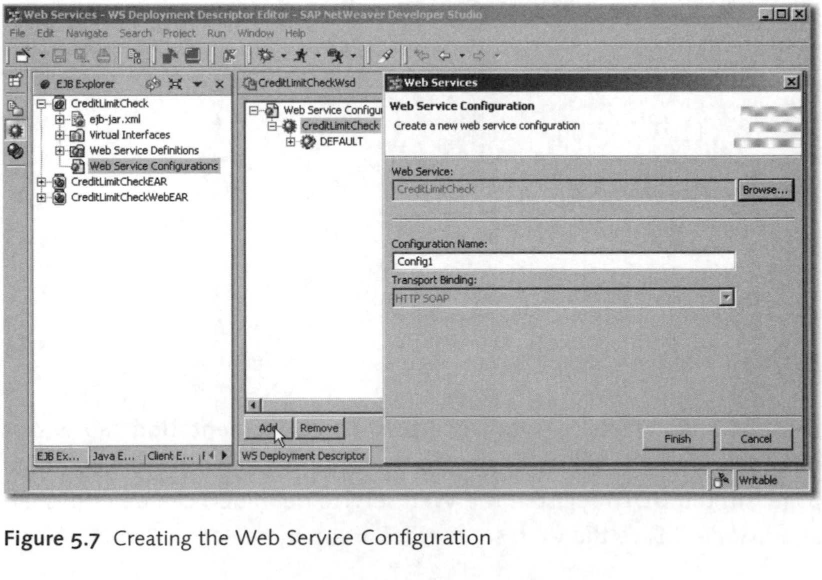

Figure 5.7 Creating the Web Service Configuration

Enter the required data in the following dialog box. Choose the appropriate transport binding (HTTP SOAP). The following transport bindings are available: HTTP SOAP, HTTP GET, HTTP POST, and SOAP with attachments.

SOAP messages must be transmitted between the individual SOAP nodes. This is done using a transport system that can be based on different protocols. The cooperation between SOAP and any arbitrary transport protocol is referred to as *Binding*. HTTP SOAP is a standardized binding method that is suitable for typical Web service calls. The GET variant should be used if the Web service call has no side effects; that is, if no resources are changed on the server side. POST should be used if the message ensures that the state of a resource changes at the server. SOAP with attachments is an extension for SOAP in order to be able to send attachments (images and so on).

The transport binding is the same for all configurations of a Web service. You can only choose a SOAP or HTTP binding only when you create the first configuration.

Define the Web Service (WS) Configuration. Click on the subnode of the WS configuration and enter the appropriate settings (see Figure 5.8).

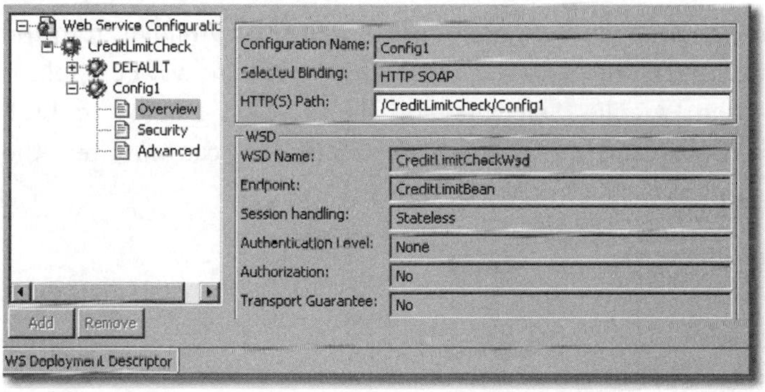

Figure 5.8 Settings in the Web Service Deployment Descriptor

Under **Overview**, you will see information on the Web service definition and on the EJB that is the basis of the Web service configuration. The URL postfix in the **Path** field is set automatically. You can change the relative path specification, if required.

Under **Security**, you determine the required **authentication type** for the Web service. The only options allowed are those that do not conflict with the authentication already defined in the WSD. If the **Authorization** option was selected at design time, roles are assigned for the operations of the Web service. You can change the assignment by choosing **Use Authorization**.

Under **Advanced**, you can enter the WSDL port name, the WSDL binding name, and the address of the target server. Save the Web service definition through **Ctrl+S**.

Create a JAR file. A JAR file (stands for Java Archive) is a platform-independent file format in which different files can be grouped together. Choose **Build EJB Archive** in the context menu of the module project node.

Step 5   **Deploying a Web Service**

The Web Service Deployment function corresponds to the standard procedure in the SAP NetWeaver Developer Studio. All the necessary objects and descriptors are managed in the Enterprise Application Archive and deployed with the application.

Create an enterprise application project. Choose **File · New · Project · J2EE · Enterprise Application Project**. Assign the JAR file that is to be included in the EAR project.

Select this EAR project and choose **Build Application Archive** from the context menu. An EAR file is a JAR archive that contains a J2EE application. Deploy the EAR file. Select it, and then choose **Deploy to J2EE Engine** from the context menu (see Figure 5.9). You can now test the Web service and publish it in a UDDI registry.

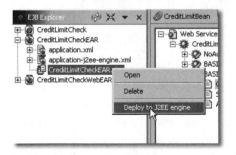

Figure 5.9 Deploying a Web Service on the J2EE Engine

For reasons of flexibility and reusability, you can set up different virtual interfaces for an end point, several Web Service Definitions for a virtual interface, and various Web services or Web Service Configurations for each Web Service Definition (see Figure 5.10).

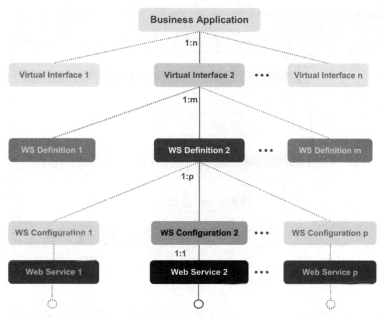

Figure 5.10 Reusability of Web Service Objects

5.3.2 Testing a Web Service with the Web Service Home Page

The Web service home page is a tool you can use to simplify the cycle from development, testing, and error corrections. The Web service home page combines all the documentation, displays the appropriate WSDL files, enables the generation of client proxies, and provides you with testing options. In this way, you can check each Web service without the requirement for additional coding to implement a test client. The home page is complemented with a complete status overview that displayes certain features, such as the UDDI publishing status.

Simply call the Web service home page from the Web Service Navigator in the Web Services perspective. You start the Web Service Navigator via **Window · Show View · Others · Webservices · Webservice Navigator**. Select the required Web service and choose **Open** in the context menu.

Using the test page, you can test the Web service operations. Choose the operation you that you want to test, enter the appropriate values, and click on **Send** (see Figure 5.11). The return values appear subsequently on the right hand of the screen. To see how the return values are represented with the SOAP response, simply display them by scrolling down and choosing **Wrap/Unwrap**.

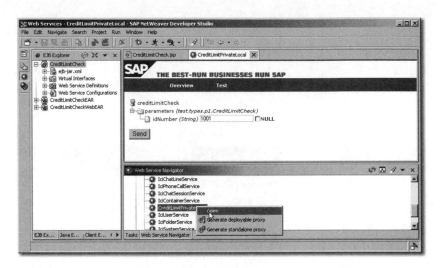

Figure 5.11 Test Function for Web Service Home Page—Calling the Home Page Through the Web Service Navigator

If you call the home page using the Web service URL or the Visual Administrator, you will see additional Web Service Definition Language (WSDL) documents displayed in different styles (see Figure 5.12).

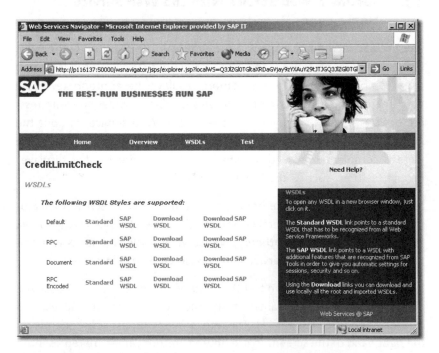

Figure 5.12 WSDL Styles of a Web Service

Both standard and SAP WSDL documents are offered in the various styles (Default, RPC, Document, RPC Encoded). Standard WSDLs can be useful if you want to create Web service clients with non-SAP tools. For SAP users there is a SAP WSDL—an extended variant of WSDL— that is available with additional features.

5.3.3   Securing the Web Service

Since Web services are provided to enable you to use functions across security domains as well as system and company borders, the question arises as to how these Web services can be protected against external attacks. In times where new security problems in operating systems or Internet browsers are regularly publicized, the question of data security is critical, particularly when it comes to Web Service technology.

SSL[6] is, in many cases, a good and secure method used to protect the data to be transported from unauthorized viewing. A secure point-to-point connection is set up between two hosts, and all the transmitted messages are encrypted so that they can be read by only the party to whom they are being sent. In addition, SSL enables you to ensure that the communication partner is exactly the person he or she purports to be. Therefore, you can ensure that not only is your connection safe, but that you are connected to a trustworthy partner.

Restrictions with SSL

Both of these aforementioned features of SSL can be viewed in a positive light. However, they can also become disadvantages when you have many messages, which require much effort for encryption and decryption and also demand an unnecessary amount of computing time with increasing numbers of connections. Often, it would suffice to encrypt only a small amount of sensitive data.

Moreover, SSL connections are pure point-to-point connections. As such, it is not possible, for example, to set up a message in such a way that it can be passed from the recipient to a third party without having to completely decrypt it beforehand.

If we look at the goal and the potential of Web Services technology on the basis of these facts, it soon becomes apparent why relying solely on SSL is sufficient only in rare cases. To be able to efficiently organize various security requirements in complex scenarios, it is necessary to shift the implementation of these security mechanisms from the transport level to the level of the message itself.

---

6   Secure Sockets Layer is a generally accepted standard developed by Netscape for the secure transmission of data.

If data is signed and encrypted at message level, its secure transmission no longer depends on the transport protocol used. This enables you to encrypt only parts of a message and to create secure end-to-end connections, for example. To benefit from these advantages, an increased amount of implementation effort is required at the outset. However, this investment should prove invaluable within only a short period of time because of improvements in flexibility and security.

The Web Services Security standard of OASIS supports the signing and encryption of data at message level and has been integrated into the Web Service Framework for this reason. It is tailored to meet the requirements of complex Web Service infrastructures, and it integrates the recommendations for XML Encryption and XML Signature of the World Wide Web Consortium (W3C).

XML Encryption Let us look at a simple example. Imagine a direct service for ordering books from an online bookseller. To ensure that the ordering procedure can be executed successfully, certain personal details—such as name, address, shipping address, telephone number, email address, credit card number, and bank details—as well as the actual list of books to be ordered—have to be sent over the Internet. While most of the data for further processing remains in the bookseller's system, the information required for payment processing is sent to the bank, which can then perform the appropriate financial transactions.

If such sensitive data is transferred within this scenario through SSL, the entire message is encrypted before data transmission can occur, and must then be decrypted accordingly by the recipient before it can be processed further. The bookseller can then subsequently trigger the delivery and transfer the account data of the customer to his or her bank. Since this data is now available as a visible text, it must again be encrypted by the system before transmission to the bank can occur. This kind of message would then look as follows:

```
<BookOrder>
  <Order>
    <Item>
      <ISBN>0345391802</ISBN>
    </Item>
    <Quantity>10</Quantity>
  </Order>
  <ShippingAddress>
    <Name>Arthur Dent</Name>
```

```
  <Country>GB</Country>
  <City>SomeCity</City>
  <Street>SomeStreet<Street>
</ShippingAddress>
<Payment>
  <CreditCard>
    <CardName>ProcterGoldCard</CardName>
    <Number>230539333248</Number>
  </CreditCard>
</Payment>
</BookOrder>
```

How would this kind of scenario look if XML Encryption were implemented? While most of the personal data is information that requires very special protection, the order list itself is non-critical. In this case, you could forego using encryption, which would most likely reduce the computation time.

Furthermore, you should note that not all sensitive data is relevant for the bookseller. Using XML Encryption, you can secure various sections of a message with different keys or even different encryption procedures. Nesting is also possible here. Therefore, only the shipping address and the order list is relevant for the shipment of the articles. The credit card number or the bank data could be transmitted by the online bookseller directly to his or her bank, without having to be processed in the interim. In this way, you prevent the bookseller from ever gaining the customer's credit card number because this information could be secured with a different key. The message would look roughly like this:

```
<BookOrder>
  <Order>...</Order>
  <EncryptedData xmlns="http://www.w3.org/2001/04/xmlenc#">
    <EncryptionMethod Algorithm="..."/>
    <KeyInfo> ... </KeyInfo>
    <CipherData>
      <CipherValue>XNASZiuzpiwe6d8qg...</CipherValue>
    </CipherData>
  </EncryptedData>
</BookOrder>
```

After decryption, the online bookseller would receive the following code, and he or she could then send the yet encrypted part, for example, by Web Service to his or her bank:

```
<BookOrder>
  <Order>...</Order>
  <ShippingAddress>...</ShippingAddress>
  <EncryptedData xmlns="...">
    <EncryptionMethod Algorithm="..."/>
    <KeyInfo> ... </KeyInfo>
    <CipherData>
      <CipherValue>OiUZ4VWXBiuz768...</CipherValue>
    </CipherData>
  </EncryptedData>
</BookOrder>
```

XML Signature With the help of XML Encryption, the secure transmission of data is ensured. However, there still exists the problem of authenticity with regard to this information, that is, validating the identity of the originator. This problem is solved with XML Signature. Here, you should note that XML Encryption and XML Signature are two entirely separate standards, independent of one another. It is therefore not absolutely necessary to sign encrypted content—and signed messages do not always have to be encrypted—even though, ideally, the two technologies complement one another. Similar to the situation with XML Encryption, individual parts of a message can be signed. In this way, various sections of a message can be signed by different individuals, and content that is already signed can be signed again.

In the case of our online bookseller, for example, it might be appropriate to have the messages signed by the customer in order to prevent unauthorized orders from being placed. For the same reason, the bookseller, for his part, could sign the message that he or she sends to his bank.

The implementation of XML Signature, however, is considerably more complex than that of XML Encryption. This is primarily due to the fact that a signature, unlike encryption, is closely linked to the content of the message to be signed and is valid for only precisely the same content. This refers exactly to the actual character representation, and not to the semantics of the message. It could happen, for example, that in the course of message processing, the semantics are reformatted slightly. From the first message in the following listing, you could get the second message, for example:

```
<CreditCard>
  <CardName>ProcterGoldCard</CardName>
  <Number>230539333248</Number>
```

```
</CreditCard>
<CreditCard>
  <Number>230539333248</Number>
  <CardName>ProcterGoldCard</CardName>
</CreditCard>
```

With this change in the message, its actual information has not changed in any way. However, the corresponding signature loses its validity. In effect, every insertion or removal of a blank space or a line break would mean that the signature and the content no longer match.

To avoid this problem, "canonization" is used. This specifies how a document is to be formatted, that is, where blanks and lines are to be set, and in which sequence properties and arguments are to appear in the document. Thus, before data is signed or a signature is checked for its validity, the corresponding data is normalized.

Canonization

Another important question arises regarding the common use of XML Signature and XML Encryption. To verify the signature, it is necessary to know whether the signing took place before or after the encryption. Since an explanation of the exact technical details would be too extensive, we will use a code fragment to illustrate the functioning of the XML Signature and its interaction with XML Encryption:

Verifying the Signature

```
<ds:Signature xmlns:ds="http://www.w3.org/2000/09/xmldsig#">
  <ds:SignedInfo>
    <ds:CanonicalizationMethod Algorithm="..."/>
    <ds:SignatureMethod Algorithm="..."/>
    <ds:Reference URI="#ShippingAddress">
      <ds:Transforms>
        <ds:Transform Algorithm="..."/>
      </ds:Transforms>
      <ds:DigestMethod Algorithm="..."/>
      <ds:DigestValue>DDvkjh8...</ds:DigestValue>
    </ds:Reference>
    <ds:Reference URI="CreditCard">
      <ds:Transforms>
        <ds:Transform Algorithm="..."/>
      </ds:Transforms>
      <ds:DigestMethod Algorithm="..."/>
      <ds:DigestValue>o7ycNN...</ds:DigestValue>
    </ds:Reference>
  </ds:SignedInfo>
```

```
<ds:SignatureValue>aZoIQ8cfHpF9OKQxDe...<ds:SignatureValue>
</ds:Signature>
```

Listing 5.1 Joint Use of XML Signature and XML Encryption

Web Services Security integrates, among other things, XML Encryption and XML Signature. It is intended to close the gaps between hitherto existing security technologies, SOAP, and the demands placed on a complex Web Service infrastructure. WS-Security does not define any new, fixed security mechanisms, but rather combines and integrates standards that already exist, thus enabling the flexible implementation of special security needs.

Security Tokens WS-Security specifies the appearance of a security header for SOAP messages. In this header, you will find the security information relevant for the recipient of the message. One way of inserting this information is to use security tokens. This kind of security token can contain, for example, a user name and a password, or even an X.509 certificate. In general, WS-Security does not prescribe any special content of these tokens. Therefore, you can define your own security tokens. Other information in the header could include specifications on signed or encrypted parts of a message.

The Web Service provider and the Web Service consumer can therefore agree on a combination of different tokens that meet the security demands of both sides. If the security header of a SOAP message doesn't match the agreed profile, it is rejected by the recipient.

The following example shows the header of a SOAP envelope whose security header contains a timestamp and the security token Username-Token. Both elements, in this case, are not encrypted and not signed, which is why we can use this example for demonstration purposes only, even if it is theoretically accurate:

```
<SOAP-ENV:Header>
  <wsse:Security
    xmlns:wsse="http://docs.oasis-open.org/wss/2004/01/
      oasis-200401-wss-wssecurity-secext-1.0.xsd"
    xmlns:soap="http://schemas.xmlsoap.org/soap/envelope/">
    <wsu:Timestamp
      xmlns:wsu="http://docs.oasis-open.org/wss/2004/01/
        oasis-200401-wss-wssecurity-utility-1.0.xsd"
```

188   Web Services in the SAP Web Application Server

```
  wsu:Id="timestamp">
  <wsu:Created ValueType="xsd:dateTime">
    2004-11-09T13:44:29Z
  </wsu:Created>
 </wsu:Timestamp>
 <wsse:UsernameToken>
  <wsse:Username>DummyUser</wsse:Username>
  <wsse:Password Type="http://docs.oasis-open.org/wss/
    2004/01/oasis-200401-wss-username-token-
    profile-1.0#PasswordText">
   DummyUsersPassword
  </wsse:Password>
  <wsu:Created
    xmlns:wsu="http://docs.oasis-open.org/wss/2004/01/
    oasis-200401-wss-wssecurity-utility-1.0.xsd"
    ValueType="xsd:dateTime">
    2004-11-09T13:44:29Z
  </wsu:Created>
 </wsse:UsernameToken>
 </wsse:Security>
</SOAP-ENV:Header>
```

Listing 5.2 Security Header with Timestamp and Security Token UsernameToken

Using the Web Service **CreditLimitCheck**, which we already employed in the previous chapters, we will now describe how you can design a Web service—with the help of SAP development tools—to leverage WS-Security.

Example: Web Service Security

For this new security configuration, you first need to create another Web Service configuration. In the NetWeaver Developer Studio, open the WS Deployment Descriptor Editor for the **CreditLimitCheck** project. Then, add a new configuration with the name **WSBASIC** to the Web Service **CreditLimitCheck.** Afterward, display these security settings. Both authentication through HTTP as well as Document Authentication are available as authentication mechanisms. The former has to do with standard mechanisms, such as sending an HTTP user ID and a password, or an X.509 certificate. You set the use of the SAP Logon Ticket there as well. In this case, however, we don't want to depend entirely on the transport layer to ensure security, but rather to have all security-relevant information inserted directly into the message. For this reason, we choose **Document Authentication**.

SAP Web AS provides you with different templates for WS-Security configuration. These profiles are characterized by the use of different security tokens in the security header. Common to all templates is the use of a timestamp. The timestamp is used to prevent inauthentic messages from being sent to a third party and, based on the validity of the security tokens, to prevent it from being accepted by the Web service provider.

Since we want to configure the Web Service for authentication by user name and password, select the radio button **Basic (username/password)** in the section **Authentication.** In the lower right of the screen, select the **Document Security** tab (see Figure 5.13)

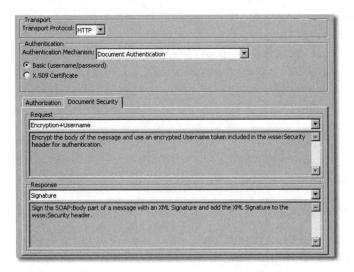

Figure 5.13 Selection of Template for Document Security

Under **Request**, you can now choose the template that you expect from the incoming SOAP message. If you select the **Username** template, its security header will be searched for a Username token. In addition to a user name and a password, this template must have another timestamp in order to be verified. The same holds true for the **Encryption+Username** template. Here, the Username token must also be encrypted if this option is chosen. In our example, the Web Service is to be transmitted using HTTP. We do not want to send the user name and passwords as clear text over the Internet. Therefore, we choose the template **Encryption+Username**.

Under **Response**, you can also choose a profile template that will be applied to the outgoing message of the Web Service **CreditLimitCheck**. The **Signature** template is available. In this case, the SOAP body and the timestamp are signed. An appropriate statement is then included in the security header. For our example, choose the **Signature** template.

Save your changes. After you have regenerated the EJB archive and the application archive, you can deploy your changed Web Service on the SAP J2EE Engine.

Appropriate profiles must be assigned—during runtime of the Web services—to the templates chosen during design time. For example, you must specify which certificate will be used for signing the message. This occurs within the Visual Administrator.

Start the Visual Administrator. Under the services of the server, select the **Web Services Security** entry. On the right, you will see a tree structure with all the Web services and Web Service clients that exist on the J2EE Engine. You will find the service **CreditLimitCheck** under **Security Configuration · Webservices · sap.com · CreditLimitCheck EAR**. Then, select the entry **CreditLimitCheck*WSBASIC**. On the right, you see the WS-Security settings of the WSBASIC Web Service configuration. There, you will also see that the security templates set in the SAP NetWeaver Developer Studio are listed as policies for the operation **CreditLimitCheck**. The profile **default_Encryption+Username** is already selected for the inbound message (see Figure 5.14). The **XMLEncryption** key from the **WebServiceSecurity Keystore** View is automatically used for encryption of the Username token.

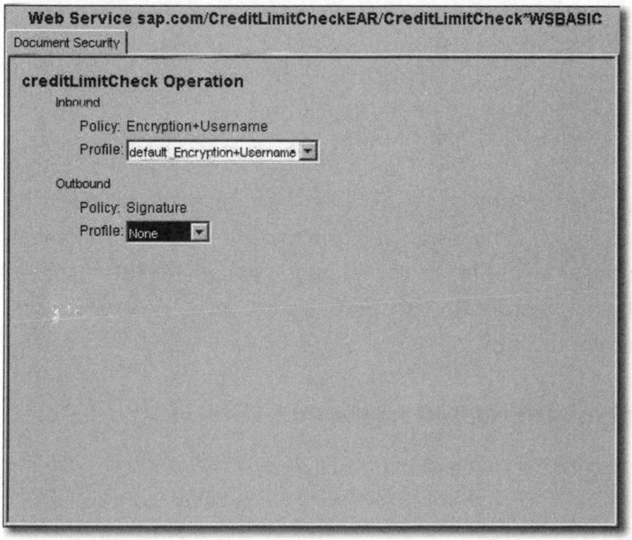

Figure 5.14 Selection of Security Profiles for Inbound and Outbound Messages

To configure the outgoing message, that is, the answer from the Web Service, you first need to create a suitable profile (Figure 5.15). After you have activated the tabs **Profile Administration** (lower part of the window) and **Outbound Messages** (upper part), you will receive a list of all the existing profiles for outbound messages.

With the help of the **New ...** pushbutton underneath this list, you can create a new profile with any name you choose. Since we have entered this accordingly during Web Service design, choose the **Signature** entry as a template. In the **Configuration** section, you can now select a corresponding Keystore View or Keystore Alias that will be used for signing the SOAP body and the timestamp in the security header.

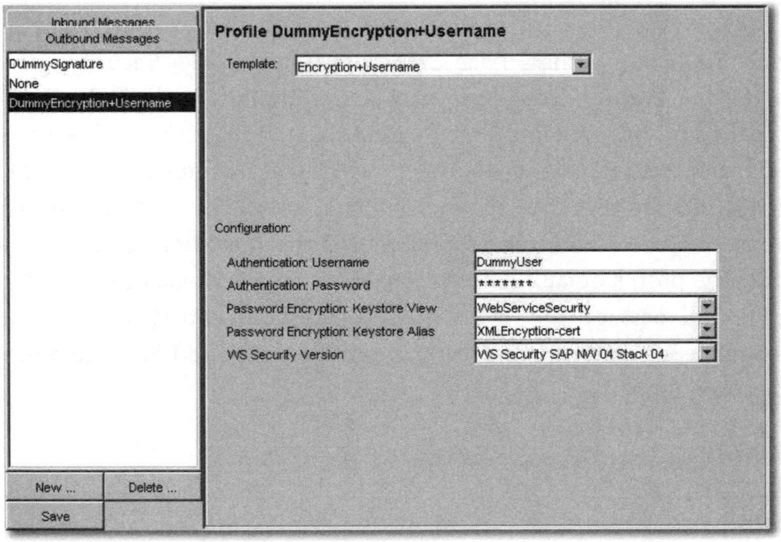

Figure 5.15 Creating Profile for Outgoing Message

After you have saved the profile, you can now return to the **Security Administration** screen by activating the corresponding tab. In the selection list for the outbound profile, the profile you have just created should now be included as an entry and can be selected. Now save your data again and the configuration of the Web Service is complete.[7]

5.3.4 Restrictions for Web Service End Points

The following restrictions apply to Java Web service end points:

---

7 In the section entitled *Using Web Services Security for Java Web Service Clients* at the end of this chapter, you will learn which settings should be made on the client side.

If the Web service is based on a session bean, the session bean must contain a remote interface. The methods of this interface can be offered as operations of the Web service. The following types must not exist in the WS end point:

▶ Remote objects (EJBs)

▶ Classes that implement more than one interface

▶ Classes that inherit from other types and implement an interface

▶ Hash table types

▶ Classes/objects that cannot be serialized

Interfaces and abstract classes are allowed in an end point only if at least one runtime class (implementation of an abstract class or an interface) has been created.

You cannot include constructor methods with parameters in the virtual interface of a Web service. For session EJBs, you should use a constructor method without parameters and depict everything else through business methods. In particular, this restriction applies whenever entity beans are wrapped by session beans.

5.3.5 Supported Types in Web Service End Points

The following types from java*.packages are supported in Web service end points:

Type Groups	Types
Simple Type Wrappers	java.lang.Void java.lang.Boolean
Simple Type Wrappers (cont.)	java.lang.Byte java.lang.Short java.lang.Integer java.lang.Long java.lang.Float java.lang.Double java.lang.String
Marker Interfaces	java.io.Serializable java.lang.Cloneable java.lang.Comparable

Table 5.2 Support of java*.packages in Web Service End Points

Type Groups	Types
Array classes	java.util.ArrayList java.util.HashSet java.util.LinkedList java.util.List java.util.Stack java.util.Vector
Date/Time	java.util.Calendar java.util.Date java.util.GregorianCalendar java.sql.Date java.sql.Time
Long numbers	java.math.BigInteger java.math.BigDecimal
Exception	java.lang.Throwable java.lang.Exception java.rmi.RemoteException
Object	java.lang.Object

Table 5.2 Support of java*.packages in Web Service End Points (cont.)

5.4 Providing Web Services in Public Directories

When using Web services, we distinguish between the service provider and the service requestor. In the simplest case, we can assume that the service provider—the person who provides the services—knows the service requestor and informs the latter where services can be found. However, this contradicts the idea of Web services as a global service platform. What makes the use of Web services so attractive is the idea that applications can be built from Web services that are available globally. This service can be provided with Universal Description, Discovery, and Integration (UDDI).

UDDI is an essential module of the general Web Service architecture. Therefore, it is clear that UDDI is directly supported by SAP NetWeaver. SAP customers can create a connection to any arbitrary UDDI directory to publish Web services developed using the SAP Web AS or to integrate external Web services. Many companies provide public UDDI servers; for example, SAP (*http://uddi.sap.com*), Microsoft (*http://uddi.microsoft.com*), and IBM (*http://uddi.ibm.com*). Web services should not be provided in a public registry in every case. Sometimes, providing Web services for a *private group* of business partners will suffice. In this section, we will describe how you configure your own UDDI server with a UDDI registry, and how you publish a Web service in this registry.

With the help of a UDDI server, you can set up public as well as private registries. Companies can provide private directories, for example, to which business partners also have access. However, within the intranet, you can set up Web service registries. With the currently used UDDI Version 2.0, it can be assumed that private directories will be used more frequently than public catalogs, for reasons of safety. Currently, companies tend to implement Web services first in networks that are protected from the outside through firewalls.

UDDI defines four data structures on which the UDDI registry is based. These data structures are stored in XML format. Figure 5.16 shows the framework of these four structures.

UDDI Data Structures

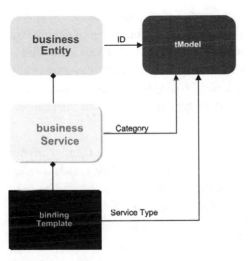

Figure 5.16 UDDI Data Structures

The businessEntity structure contains the name and the description of a company. This includes addresses, contact information, and so on. The company information can be stored in several languages. The actual description of the provided Web services is specified in the business-Service and bindingTemplate elements that are contained in the business-Entity.

businessEntity

The businessService structures represent a logical group of Web services. They do not contain any technical information on services, but allow these services to be collected in a particular category. Each businessSer-vice is contained in a businessEntity that, in turn, holds information that describes the Web services contained in the businessService. A businessService element, in addition, allows you to allocate Web services to business categories.

businessService

bindingTemplate The bindingTemplate structure is contained in a businessService. This template contains the technical information on the service, which is necessary for the user to be able to access and interact with the server. Several bindingTemplates can be defined for a Web service if this can be used through several transport protocols. The bindingTemplate elements can be equipped with metadata to allow you to find templates based on certain criteria.

tModel The reusability of interface and structure definitions is a design target of the UDDI data structure. These commonly used definitions are represented by tModels, which are managed outside of the businessEntity, businessService, and bindingTemplate structure.

tModels are created and stored for each unique specification. If a Web service that fulfills certain specifications is described in the UDDI registry, references to the tModels that represent these specifications are included in the bindingTemplate elements. Existing tModels can be reused in different bindingTemplates on this basis. bindingTemplates have the same *technical fingerprint* and are of the same type if they point to the same set of tModels.

Documents and technical specifications that describe the tModel are not stored in the UDDI registry. In addition to the actual key, which is referenced through a tModel, a tModel contains addresses, which can be used to find the appropriate documents. For example, a tModel could contain a URL with the address of a WSDL document that belongs to the Web service.

A tModel is not solely bound to a WSDL document. A technical model can be an arbitrary specification, a namespace, a protocol, or a completely different structure that is described by the referenced documents.

UDDI Server Using the UDDI server, customers can create their own registries. A UDDI business registry is a central database in which companies can have their services registered free of charge. The registry is similar to an address book where providers and services are listed. A UDDI business registry provides three types of information: white pages, yellow pages, and green pages.

White Pages The white pages are a register that is sorted by the name of the provider. The white pages get their information from the businessEntity element. The name, address, and industry sector of the Web service provider are stored here. As already mentioned, the businessEntity element functions as a type of container in which all Web service information is held. Therefore, one main prerequisite for the publication of a Web service in a UDDI registry is the availability of a businessEntity.

The yellow pages are a registry sorted by categories. The service informa- **Yellow Pages** tion in the yellow pages is stored in the businessService element. They serve the purpose of sorting services into groups, for example, on the basis of the business processes for which they were conceived. A group of services can include e-business services for purchasing goods, for example.

The green pages have technical details on services provided. They contain **Green Pages** binding templates, that is, technical data, which enable a user to access a Web service and communicate with it. This category includes the Web address under which a service can be reached, for example. The tModel element provides even more detailed data. It describes the specification of the interfaces that a Web service uses.

UDDI servers have the architecture according to Figure 5.17 as their basis. **Architecture of a UDDI Server**

Web User Interface

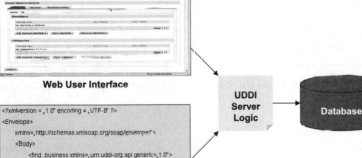

SOAP API

Figure 5.17 Architecture of a UDDI Server

The user interface for a UDDI server is the UDDI client. It enables you to perform a browser-based search for data and a means to publish data on the UDDI server. You call the UDDI client as follows *http://<host>: <port>/uddiclient*. The *<host>* field is the required computer name. In the *<port>* field, enter *50000*. The prerequisite for this is that a J2EE Engine is started and that the UDDI server was configured on this computer. UDDI servers can be operated either manually via the browser or with client programs using Web service application program interfaces (APIs).

To access the data of a UDDI registry, the client software uses SOAP through HTTP. UDDI provides, as a Web service, an inquiry API and a publishing API in accordance with the specifications. The calls for applications that search through the business registry form the inquiry API.

These include calls such as `find_business` and `find_service`. On the other hand, applications must be able to create and change this information. For this purpose, calls such as `save_business` and `save_service` are available. You can use these calls to create or update information for a businessEntity or a businessService.

The following SOAP APIs can be used with the UDDI server:

▶ Inquiry API: *http://host:port/uddi/api/inquiry*

▶ Publishing API: *http(s)://host:port/uddi/api/publish*

In the Visual Administrator, you can decide whether to use the publishing API HTTP or HTTPS. At SAP, we recommend that you install the Cryptographic Library and ensure the use of HTTPS.

The data of a UDDI registry is usually stored in a relational database.

The UDDI logic implements the search and publication functions defined in the standard version. The data searched for using a SOAP API or a Web user interface is read from the database using UDDI logic. Similarly, data is published and written to the database with the help of the appropriate utilities.

Configuring the UDDI Server
You configure the UDDI server with the help of the Visual Administrator in the J2EE Engine. Before using the UDDI server, you must reset the database. In the same step, you import standard tModels and taxonomies.

Caution: UDDI data that already exists will be deleted. In the Visual Administrator, choose **Webservices Container Service · Runtime · UDDI-Server**. In the **General** register, select the checkbox **Preload base tModels and taxonomies (UNSPSC, ISO-3166, NAICS, etc ...)** and then click on **Reset DB** (see Figure 5.18).

Now create a UDDI registry. In the Visual Administrator, choose **Web Services Container Service · Runtime · UDDI Client**. Choose **New Registry** and enter the name of the registry, the inquiry URL, and the publish URL (see Figure 5.19).

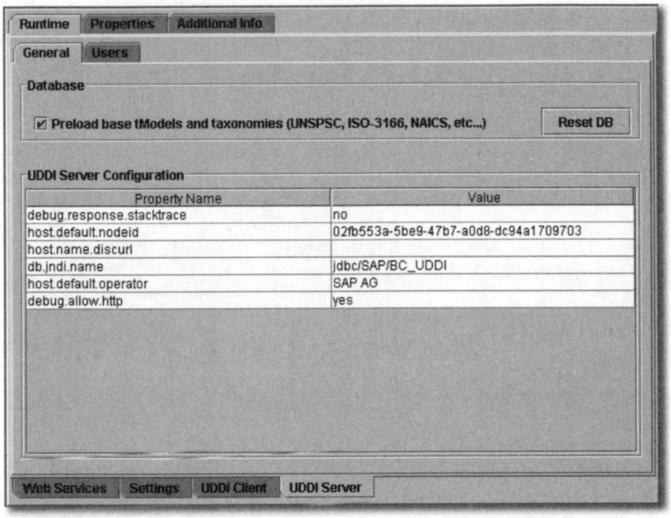

Figure 5.18 Configuration of the UDDI Server

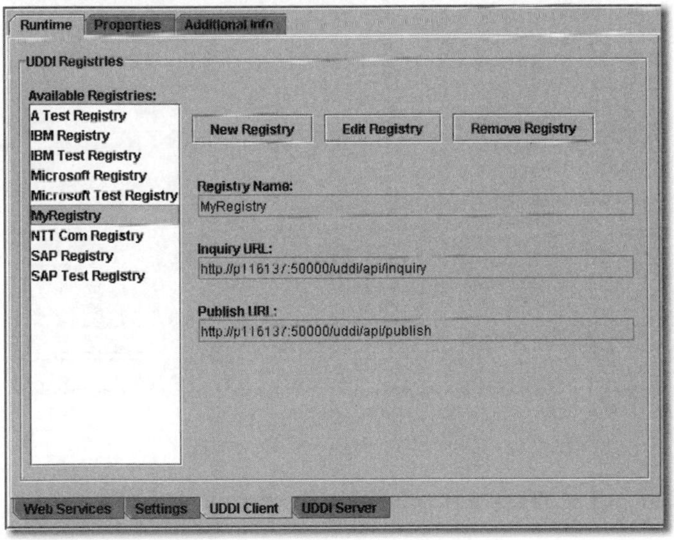

Figure 5.19 Creating a UDDI Server

Users and roles play an important part in the publication of services in UDDI registries. If you have a non-public registry, only a selected circle of users should be allowed to make entries in the UDDI database.

Table 5.3 shows which authorization levels can be selected (see also Figure 5.20).

UDDI User Groups	Authorization
Level Tier 1	The user can create the following: businessEntity Four businessServices Two bindingTemplates per Business Service 100 tModels
Level Tier N	The user can create any number of UDDI objects.
Level Admin	The user can create any number of UDDI objects and delete UDDI data of other users.

Table 5.3 Possible Authorization Levels

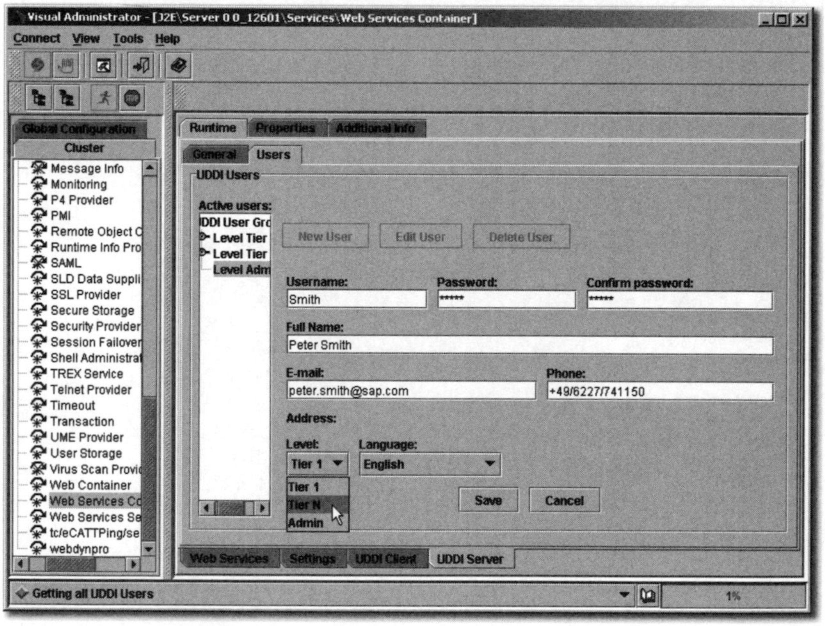

Figure 5.20 UDDI User Groups

5.4.1 Publishing a Web Service in a Registry

To publish a Web service in a registry, you need to perform the following steps:

Step 1 **Creating a Business Entity**

Call the UDDI client on (*http://<host>:<port>/uddiclient*). Choose **Publish Business Entity**, and then select the registry you have created. Enter the user name and password of a user you have created for the registry in the Visual Administrator.

In the following screen, choose **Publish Business Entity**. Enter a name for the business entity. You can add descriptions in various languages, names of contact persons, and sector-specific information.

Creating a tModel

Step 2

Call the SAP NetWeaver Developer Studio and choose the Web Service Definition of the service that you want to publish in the UDDI registry. On the right-hand side, choose the **UDDI** tab and then **Publish**. Identify yourself using the administrator password for the J2EE Engine.

Remember that, in the Developer Studio, the host of the UDDI server must be entered under **Windows · Preferences · SAP J2EE Engine**. The browser will be started immediately. Choose the registry you have created and identify yourself. Enter a short text for the tModel and choose **Publish**. Deploy the Web service so that the tModel key for the Web service can be found in the J2EE Engine.

5.4.2 Creating a Business Service

Step 3

Start the Visual Administrator and choose **Webservice Container · Runtime · Webservices**. Choose the Web service to be published and then **Publish**. The UDDI client is started. In different tabs, you can enter the names and descriptions in various languages. You can classify the service using categories and also store information on the bindingTemplate. It is important that you make the address of the service known.

In summary, one can say the following: UDDI servers should enable companies to register Web services and provide these services to internal and external users. A UDDI server can be set up for each J2EE Engine. In addition to the public UDDI servers, the use of otherUDDI servers is set up so that certain services can be provided to a group of appropriately authorized users. You configure a UDDI server by setting up registries and users for the UDDI server. You can publish Web services in a UDDI registry by publishing the tModel in the SAP NetWeaver Developer Studio and then making the Web service available with the Visual Administrator. It is imperative that you have a business entity that contains the general information on the name, address, and business sector of the Web service provider.

5.5 Consuming a Web Service—The Client Side

Binding a Web service into an application can be done in three steps:

1. Call the WSDL description of the Web service.

2. Generate a Web service proxy.

3. Implement the client application.

A Web service can be called from a Web Dynpro application,[8] from a bean, a servlet, or a Java Server Page (JSP). In Figure 5.21, the SAP Web Application Server is represented as a Web service requestor.

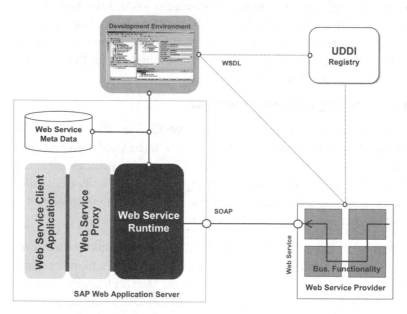

Figure 5.21 Web Service Requestor

In the following example, calling a deployable proxy from a JSP is displayed.

5.5.1 Calling the WSDL Description of the Web Service

A Web service description that conforms to standards is the starting point for the implementation of a client application. Whether the description is called with the integrated UDDI browser or in another manner is not important.

---

8 See also Section 7.1, *Web Dynpro Calls a Web Service – Five Steps to an Application*. In this case, a Web service is used to store business data via a Web Dynpro user interface and then display it.

The proxy is created with the WSDL document. The WSDL document can be called either via URL, in the local file system, or in a UDDI registry. You start the UDDI client by choosing the selection button **UDDI or URL when creating a proxy.** You can choose a registry and search for a Web service. If you do not know the exact name of the Web service, use the percentage symbol (%). For example, if you are searching for a Web service that begins with *My* and you do not know the remainder of the name, enter "My%" in the **Name** field and choose **Search**. If you enter "%" only, all the Web services that have been created in the selected registry will be displayed. In the detailed display for a Web service, you can find the URL for a Web service under the tab **Service Definition Details** (see Figure 5.22).

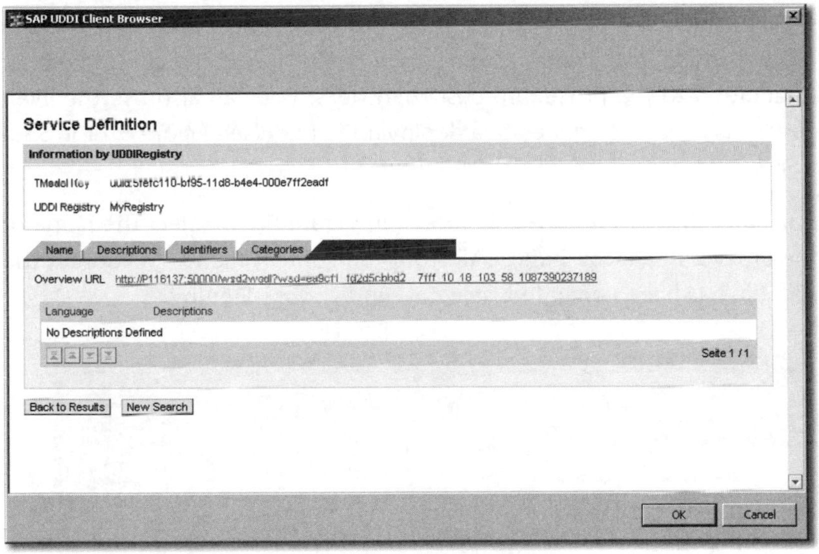

Figure 5.22 Address of the Web Service in a UDDI Registry

If the UDDI client is not to be called, configure the HTTP proxy settings in the Web Service Container Service of the Visual Administrator.

You can also copy the URL of a Web service from the home page or use a WSDL document from the local file system.

5.5.2 Generating a Web Service Proxy

To bind a Web service, you can create a deployable or a standalone proxy for the Web service in the SAP NetWeaver Developer Studio, using a WSDL document as a basis. This can be done with just a few mouse clicks. To have a deployable proxy, the application of the Web service client must be deployed on the J2EE Engine. A stand-alone proxy can be executed without the J2EE Engine.

You generate a Web service client proxy with a valid WSDL file as input. The proxy enables the application developer to concentrate on the business functions, while technical aspects—such as the creation of a valid SOAP message—are automatically dealt with through the proxy implementation. The creation of the proxy is supported by a wizard. In this way, creating a client proxy is a task that takes only a few minutes. During creation, all the necessary objects are created in the target project.

To bind a Web service, you first create a Web service client proxy definition, which is then called by an application. Choose **File · New · Project · Webservices · Deployable Proxy Project**. Select the name of the project and choose **New · Client Proxy Definition** in the context menu. In addition to the procedure described here, you can also use the Web Service Navigator to generate a deployable proxy (see Figure 5.11 in Section 5.3.2).

Build and deploy the proxy, as shown in Figure 5.23. Select the name of the proxy and choose **Build EAR** from the context menu. As soon as the EAR file has been generated, select it, and choose **Deploy**.

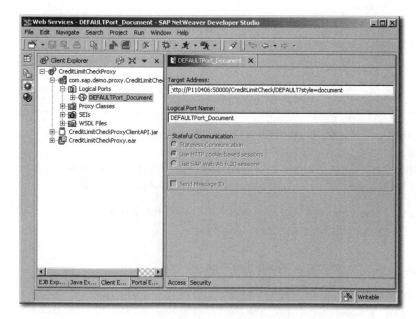

Figure 5.23 Client Proxy of a Web Service

During proxy generation, all the objects required to call a Web service are **Logical Ports** created. These include, in particular, the so-called *Logical Ports*. This is an SAP-specific concept for the configuration of runtime features for Web service client proxies. Runtime features are features that must be configured in the runtime environment (runtime) when the Web service client is activated. Logical ports contain, for example, the URL address of the Web service. In standard Web service infrastructures, this URL has already been generated directly into the proxy object.

This procedure, however, has disadvantages. Say, for example, that you are having recurring problems whenever the proxy is moved into a system landscape from the test system to the productive system. In this case, the proxy would still attempt to call the Web service on the test server, although it should call the productive system. To avoid this problem, the proxy would have to be regenerated or the coding would need to be adapted manually. Since such individual adjustments are very prone to errors, the configuration data is separated from the implementation in the SAP Web Service Framework. After transport or re-deployment of the proxy, you can adapt the URL and other important parameters by using a simple editor.

Service Endpoint Interfaces (SEIs) are created by the proxy generator in accordance with the *<port Type>* information in the WSDL document. SEIs are used by client applications for Web service calls. The actual structure of an SEI depends on whether an Remote Procedure Call (RPC)-style or document-style proxy was generated.

5.5.3 Implementing the Client Application

To find out how you bind a Web service into a Web Dynpro application, see Section 7.1. In this section, we will explain how a Web service can be called from a JSP.

Create a Web module project through the menu path **File · New · Project · J2EE**. Select the name of the Web project and choose **New · JSP** to create a new JSP.[9] Enter the required data and click on **Finish**. To add a Web service client API library, select the Web project, and choose **Add Webservice Client API Library** in the context menu. In this way, you can use the client API of the deployable proxy.

---

9 You will find a template (*CreditLimitCheck.jsp*) in the Web module project **Credit-LimitCheckWeb** under *web.xml*.

Implement the application. Open the Web project. Underneath **web-Content**, double-click the name of the JSP. On the right-hand side, select the **Source** tab. Program the JSP and the Web service call:

```
<%@ page import="javax.naming.InitialContext" %>
<%@ page import="javax.rmi.PortableRemoteObject" %>
<%@ page import="com.sap.demo.proxy.
                 CreditLimitCheckViDocument" %>
<%@ page import="com.sap.demo.proxy.CreditLimitCheck" %>
<%@ page import="com.sap.demo.proxy.types.CreditLimit
                 CheckResponse" %>

<% InitialContext ctx = new InitialContext();
   CreditLimitCheck obj = (CreditLimitCheck)

   ctx.lookup("java:comp/env/CreditLimitCheckProxy");
   CreditLimitCheckViDocument port =
     (CreditLimitCheckViDocument)

   obj.getLogicalPort("DEFAULTPort_Document",
     CreditLimitCheckViDocument.class);
   CreditLimitCheckResponse result =
     new CreditLimitCheckResponse();
   result = port.creditLimitCheck(request.
     getParameter("idNumber"));
   if (result.getScore() == null) {
     result.setScore("  ");
   }
   if (result.getCreditLimit() == null) {
     result.setCreditLimit("  ");
   }
   if (result.getLimitCurrency() == null) {
     result.setLimitCurrency("  ");
   if (result.getValidTo() == null) {
     result.setValidTo("  ");
...
```

Listing 5.3 Calling a Web Service from a JSP

Instantiate `InitialContext()` to be able to access the proxy in the J2EE *Naming and Directory System* (JNDI). Use the constructor `Initial-Context` without parameters.

Execute a lookup on the proxy using the JNDI context name. The context name contains the prefix *java:comp/env*.

With the help of a logical port, you can access a service end point. You will find the service end point in the proxy project under the subtree **SEIs**. Since several logical ports can be generated within the framework of a proxy project, you can set up one logical port as the default. To access this, program as follows:

```
CreditLimitCheckViDocument port =
   (CreditLimitCheckViDocument)
obj.getLogicalPort(CreditLimitCheckViDocument.class);
```

You can also pass on the name of a logical port with the help of a parameter:

```
CreditLimitCheckViDocument port =
   (CreditLimitCheckViDocument)
obj.getLogicalPort("DEFAULTPort_Document",
CreditLimitCheckViDocument.class);
```

Call the method for checking the credit limit.

```
CreditLimitCheckResponse result =
   new CreditLimitCheckResponse();
result = port.creditLimitCheck(request.getParameter
   ("idNumber"));
```

So that your application can access the functions of the server or interface components of the J2EE Engine, create a reference from the JSP to these components.

Open the file *web-j2ee-engine.xml* and choose **References**. Select the folder **jndi mapping** and click on **Add**. Now enter the required data (see Figure 5.24):

▶ **Application local JNDI name**: This is the name you use in the JSP to determine the server components (in our example, this is **CreditLimitCheckProxy**).

▶ **Server component type**: Use the input help to select an appropriate type.

▶ **Server component JNDI name**: Enter the name under which this component is assigned to the JNDI. The following convention is used for the name of the JNDI context: */wsclients/proxies/<provider name>/ <ApplicationName>/<ProxyName>*.

► **<ApplicationName>** is the name of the proxy application that is generated when the enterprise archive is generated for the deployable proxy project. The application automatically receives the same name as the proxy project. If the application name contains the character "/", this character must be replaced by "~".

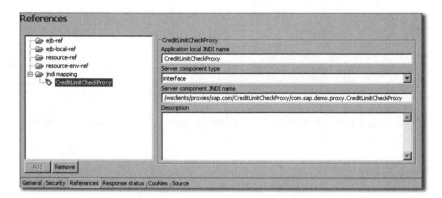

Figure 5.24 Creating JNDI Mappings

Assign a URL pattern to the JSP. Open *web.xml*, choose **Mapping · Servlet Mappings**, and then click on **Add**. Select your JSP and click on **OK**. Enter "/" in the field **URL Pattern**.

Now create a Web archive file for the Web project. In the context menu of the Web project, choose **Build Web Archive**. So that the JSP can be generated and deployed in the form of an EAR file, choose **File · New · Project · J2EE · Enterprise Application Project**. Enter the required data and click on **Next**. In the following dialog box, choose the **Web Project** so that a reference to this project can be set up. Complete your entry by clicking on **Finish**.

So that your client application can access proxy classes, you must also set up a reference to the deployable proxy application. Open the *application-j2ee-engine.xml* editor of the **EAR** project. Choose **General · References · Add · Create New**.

Enter the project name of the proxy in the field **Reference Target**. In the field **Reference Type**, enter **hard**. This means that your application will not be started if the proxy application is not already running. **Weak** means that it will be started, irrespective of whether a deployment for the proxy application was executed; otherwise, it can be used only when the proxy application was started. Choose the **Application** option as **Reference Target Type**. Enter "sap.com" as **Provider Name**.

Edit the value for the context directory of the **WAR** project in order to get the correct place to call the JSP. Choose **application.xml · Modules · Context Root** and enter the required value, for example, "/CreditLimit Check/JSP".

Build and deploy the EAR application. You can then test the application under *http://<host>:<port>/CreditLimitCheck/JSP.*

You will find an example of this kind of application on the DVD supplied with this book. There, the check for creditworthiness of a customer has been built into the mobile phone order function. If you click on the **Order** pushbutton, the system will check the creditworthiness before the order is registered (see Figure 5.25).

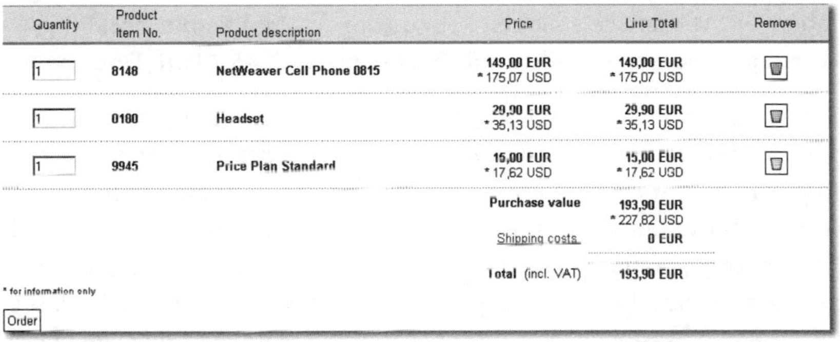

Quantity	Product Item No.	Product description	Price	Line Total	Remove
1	8148	NetWeaver Cell Phone 0815	149,00 EUR * 175,07 USD	149,00 EUR * 175,07 USD	🗑
1	0180	Headset	29,90 EUR * 35,13 USD	29,90 EUR * 35,13 USD	🗑
1	9945	Price Plan Standard	15,00 EUR * 17,62 USD	15,00 EUR * 17,62 USD	🗑
			Purchase value	193,90 EUR * 227,82 USD	
			Shipping costs.	0 EUR	
			Total (incl. VAT)	193,90 EUR	

* for information only

Order

Figure 5.25 JSP for Ordering a Mobile Telephone with Check for Creditworthiness of a Customer

Using Web Services Security for Java Web Service Clients

To use a Web Service configuration that was set up for Web Services Security, you must adjust the setting for the Web Service client. This primarily concerns the logical port. A logical port with the name **WSBASICPort_Document** should have been generated automatically when the proxy was created. Open this port in your SAP NetWeaver Developer Studio. You will see some general settings for the logical port, but we do not want to change these settings. Choose the **Security** tab in order to display the security settings. Since this port points to a Web service configuration that expects the use of WS-Security, choose **Document Authentication** as the authentication method and click on the pushbutton **Basic (username/password)**. Similar to the creation of the Web Service configuration, you can also assign a security profile template to the message of the Web Service call here as well as to the Web Service reply. Under **Request**, choose the entry **Encryption+Username** in order to insert an encrypted Username token into the security header of the query to the Web Service.

Because we've configured the Web Service **CreditLimitCheck** in such a way that it signs parts of its reply and we want to verify this signature, choose the **Signature** template under **Response**. Save your changes. After you have re-generated the EAR archive of the project **CreditLimit-CheckProxy**, you can deploy the changed proxy on the SAP J2EE Engine.

As you did when you created the Web Service itself, it is now necessary to assign valid profiles to the selected templates. Once again, this task is performed in the Visual Administrator under the Web Services Security settings. You will find these settings under the services on the server. Under the tree structure, you will see our Web Service client at **Security Configuration · Webservice Clients · sap.com · CreditLimitCheckProxy · com.sap.demo.proxy.CreditLimitCheckProxy*WSBASICPort_Document**.

First, you see general Web Service properties and settings for transport security. We do not want to change these properties and settings. Therefore, switch to the configuration for WS-Security by activating the **Document Security** tab. Here, too, you will find a picture similar to the Web Service configuration. The default Signature profile has already been selected for the inbound message, that is, for the reply from the Web service. Here the system checks whether the certificate used for signing was also signed by a Certification Authority (CA) who is listed in the **Trusted-CAs Keystore** View.

We want to create a new profile for the outbound message. Switch to the profile administration and create a new profile under **Outbound Messages**. Now choose the template **Encryption+Username** this time as the Web Service requires. Under **Configuration**, you can now make the required specifications for user name, password, and the key to be used. Note that the Web Service always uses the XMLEncryption key from the WebServiceSecurity Keystore View for encryption. After you have stored the profile, you can again activate the tab **Security Administration** and specify this as the profile to be used for outbound messages. As soon as you have saved your settings, the configuration of the Web Service client is complete.

So that the correctly configured logical port **WSBASICPort_Document** can be used, you must now adapt the client application accordingly.

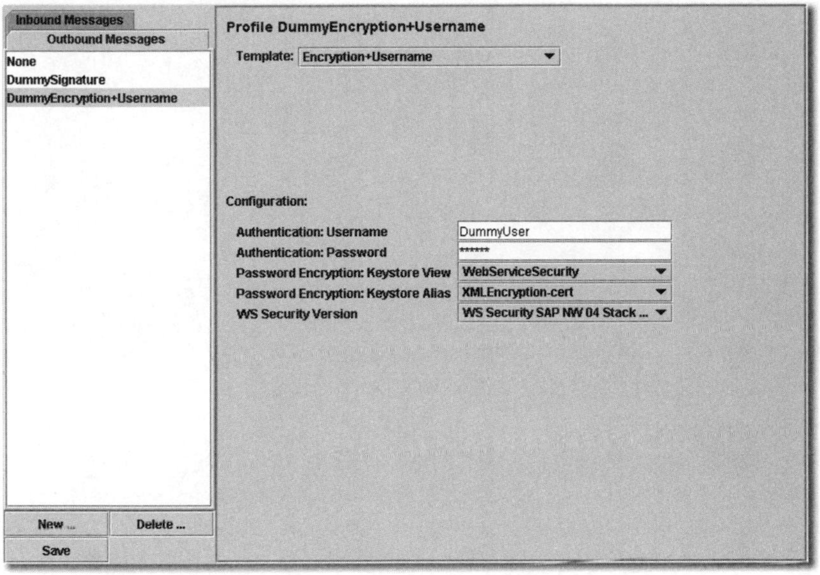

Figure 5.26 Security Settings for Outbound Messages

6   Web Dynpro: Developing User Interfaces

If you had the impression that there are no alternatives to Java Server Pages (JSPs) or servlets for server-based applications in Java, we will now attempt to change your mind. With Web Dynpro, SAP NetWeaver provides a technology for building user interfaces where the emphasis is on structuring and modeling. The bad news is that this means your knowledge of HTML won't help you here.

6.1   Working with the View Designer

Web Dynpro is a technology that you can use to create user interfaces for your applications. So let us begin our tour of the world of Web Dynpro at the point where we decide what will be displayed on the screen: in the View Designer in the Web Dynpro perspective of the SAP NetWeaver Developer Studio.

6.1.1   Views and Layouts

Since we are all by now familiar with the terminology of the Internet browser, you will naturally assume that a page will fill the entire screen. In Web Dynpro however, the screen contents are generally made up of smaller units, which are known as *views*. Views are processed in the screen painter of Web Dynpro, which is why it is called the *View Designer*. As we will soon learn, views can be combined and nested within one another in many different ways and thus several of them can be displayed on the screen simultaneously.

Views and the View Designer

The different tabs in the View Designer (**Properties**, **Layout**, **Context**, **Plugs**, **Actions**, **Methods**, and **Implementation**) indicate that a view is made up of many parts.

The screen content of the view is designed in the **Layout** tab. Here you can arrange user interface (UI) elements, which are provided in trays, via Drag & Drop (in Figure 6.1, you see the UI elements offered in the tray **Simple Standard**).

Layout

The fact that the individual UI elements—buttons, elements, and so on—are not positioned exactly where they are placed using Drag & Drop will take some getting used to for many new Web Dynpro users.

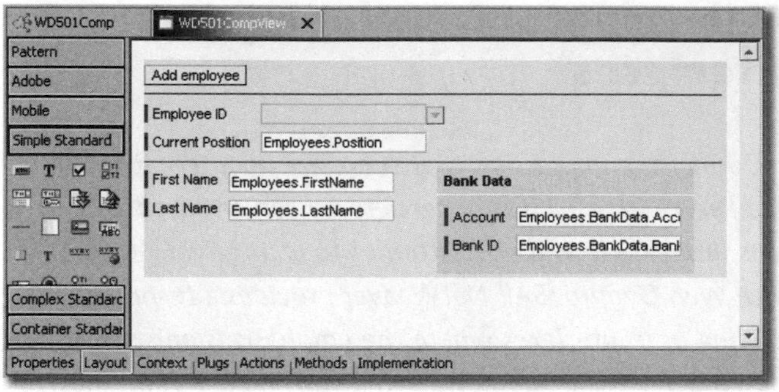

Figure 6.1 Layout Tab in the View Designer

If the positioning was pixel accurate, however, the layout would have to refer to a specific screen resolution, and you wouldn't be able to use the same layout for different clients (laptops, PDAs, and so on). Therefore, this kind of UI element placement supports an important objective of Web Dynpro: The same abstract toolkit should be able to provide user interfaces for various different devices and absolute positioning would make this practically impossible.

Relative Positioning of UI Elements Using the Layout Manager

In Web Dynpro, invisible containers control the arrangement of the UI elements and a *Layout Manager* in each container defines the strategy:

► A **FlowLayout** attempts to arrange its contents side by side and automatically inserts line breaks whenever there is insufficient space.

► The **RowLayout** is equivalent to the **FlowLayout**, but also enables the forcing of fixed line breaks at specified points.

► The **MatrixLayout** is similar to the **FlowLayout**, but also ensures that contents that are at the same position in adjacent lines are aligned in columns one below the other.

► Like the **MatrixLayout**, the **GridLayout** arranges its contents in columns. However, the line breaks are inserted according to predefined, fixed column numbers and you cannot include additional line breaks.

Because containers can be nested in other containers using the UI element **TransparentContainer**, you can combine the different layout strategies into any arrangement of UI elements that you desire. However, SAP recommends that you use a simple structure, in which a **RowLayout** defines the basic structure. The resulting horizontal strips contain only simple UI elements and containers in the **MatrixLayout**, which are themselves not nested to any greater depth. Not only can the Internet browser display this layout very quickly, but it also enables the automatic mechanisms of Web Dynpro to create an ergonomic screen structure—with regard to the padding and spacing between UI elements, for example—particularly well.

Whenever the **Layout** tab is active, the **Outline** window displays the hierarchy of the containers in the layout. If you select one of the containers in the outline, it is displayed in the layout and you can edit its properties in the **Properties** window. For example, you can edit the **Layout** property, which selects the Layout Manager for the container. Depending on how you set this property, the container obtains different additional properties and, depending on the type of Layout Manager, the UI elements nested in the containers also gain additional special properties. For example, the UI elements in a **RowLayout** can determine via their **LayoutData** property whether they are **RowHeadData**—always at the start of a new line—or just normal **RowData**—adhering to automatic line wrapping.

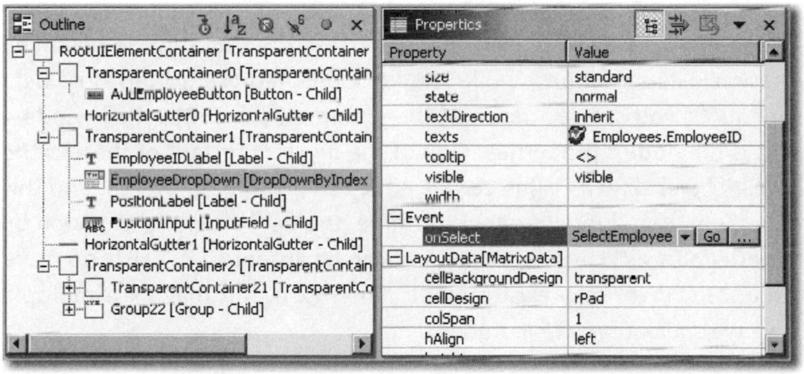

Hierarchical Display of the Layouts

Figure 6.2 Layout Display in the Outline Window. The Properties Window Provides Details on the Selected Element.

Exercise: Start the Developer Studio and switch to the *Web Dynpro perspective*. Now load the project WD501 from the book DVD. It contains a single view with a somewhat more complex layout. Analyze the structure of the containers and move the input field **Position**, including its label, under the input field **LastName**. Note the display of the nesting hierarchy in the **Outline** window (see Figure 6.2); it is often easier to work with Drag & Drop here than in the WYSIWYG view.

In the **Web Dypro Explorer** window, search for the application WD501App (it is the only one in the project). Right-click the application and choose **Deploy new archive and run** to see your changes in action.

6.1.2 Local Data: The Context of a View

Context and Controller

The next part of a view for us to deal with is its *context*. In accordance with the Model View Controller (MVC) principle, which is almost universally used for the structuring of user interfaces today, the active sections in the user interface are called *controllers* in the Web Dynpro environment. A controller handles and triggers events; it provides methods, which other controllers can call, calls methods of other controllers itself, and so on. A controller generally has at its disposal a set of data that it can access locally, without reference to other controllers. This data is known as the *context of the controller*.

View Controller

The reason why every view is linked with a context is that each view has its own controller, which essentially handles the events originating from UI elements in the view layout. This controller is therefore called the *view controller*; its context is displayed on the **Context** tab in the View Designer when a view is being edited.

The context is always modeled as a hierarchy. The *nodes* in the hierarchy represent data structures, while the attributes represent individual data elements. If you select a node in the hierarchy, the **Properties** window displays the node's properties. One of the most important of these is the *cardinality property*: Its value can be either 0..1, 1..1, 0..n, or 1..n, and this defines whether, during program runtime, the data structure modeled by the node must exist at least once (1..), can be absent (0..), exists no more than once (..1), or may exist multiple times (..n). If it may exist multiple times, we speak of *multiple* nodes.

Tabular Data Structures

With multiple nodes, Web Dynpro models tabular data structures: A fixed layout of data fields is repeated any number of times. By nesting nodes, you can create more complex data structures. For example: If you insert an additional multiple node with four attributes below a multiple node with three attributes, this results in a table with three columns, of which every single line is connected to an additional table with four columns. This pattern can be continued to any nesting depth that you require.

> **Exercise:** Look at the context of the WD501CompView in the project WD501. Insert an additional value node called *AddressData* below the **Employees** node and some suitable value attributes below the former node, for example, **City**, **Street**, and so on. To insert this text, right-click on the relevant parent node. Ensure that you give the new node the cardinality 1..1 (in the **Properties** window) and set the value of the **singleton** property to **false**.

> You can execute a test run of the application to ensure that everything is functioning correctly. However, you will have to wait until the next exercise to the see the results of your changes.

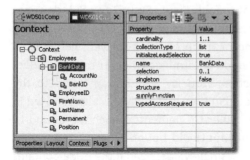

Figure 6.3 Context Tab in the View Designer; the Properties Window Provides Details on the Selected Element

The importance of using the cardinality 1..1 warrants its own explanation: For a node of this cardinality, Web Dynpro automatically creates a corresponding data structure at runtime and assigns it to the node; that is, the node can immediately store values. This is not possible for any other cardinality, as the runtime system does not know how many instances of the data structure are needed. Therefore, you (the programmer) must create these instances and bind them to the context. We will explain the exact procedure in Section 6.4.3.

Just one final remark regarding the **singleton** property: If you leave its value as **true**, only one instance of the **BankData** node would ever exist at runtime. However, for our example, we require a separate instance of **BankData** for each instance of the **Employees** node.

6.1.3 Binding Data

If you select individual UI elements in the layout of a view, their properties are displayed in the **Properties** window. You can then change the properties, for example, by creating a fixed character string for the **Text** property of a **TextView** element, which the **TextView** is to display. However, you can also bind properties of UI elements to data elements in the view context instead. For most properties, such as the **Text** property, a special button (marked "...") leads to the context display, where you can select a suitable data field and bind it to the property. The effect of the binding is that the Web Dynpro runtime transports any data changes, and does so in both directions. If the property of the UI element changes—for

Binding Transports Data Between Layout and Context

example, if the user makes an entry in an input field—the value of the bound data element in the context also changes. If, on the other hand, the value of a data element changes, this, in turn, affects all properties bound to the element.

Binding also Transfers the Selection Status

Furthermore, some UI elements (**TableView**, **DropDownByIndex**) are suitable for displaying the contents of multiple nodes. In these UI elements, you can then select one or more of the displayed elements. A property of the bound context node determines whether multiple selections are permitted. This selection property is also transferred to the bound data: The elements selected in the UI element are also selected in the context, and this can affect other UI elements, which are bound to the same data. For example, an **InputField** bound to an attribute in a multiple context can display only a single value, even if the node contains multiple instances of the data structure and thus also multiple values for the attribute. Therefore, a multiple node always has one special element, the *lead selection*, and the **InputField** displays this element's values. Since other UI elements—such as the **TableView**—can influence which element will be the lead selection, you can use a **TableView** to control which table row will be displayed and edited in other bound UI elements, such as in **InputFields**. This is schematically illustrated in Figure 6.4. The table and form are bound to the same multiple node; the node element selected in the table is displayed in the form. Note that you can create such a scenario in Web Dynpro without having to add a single line of source code.

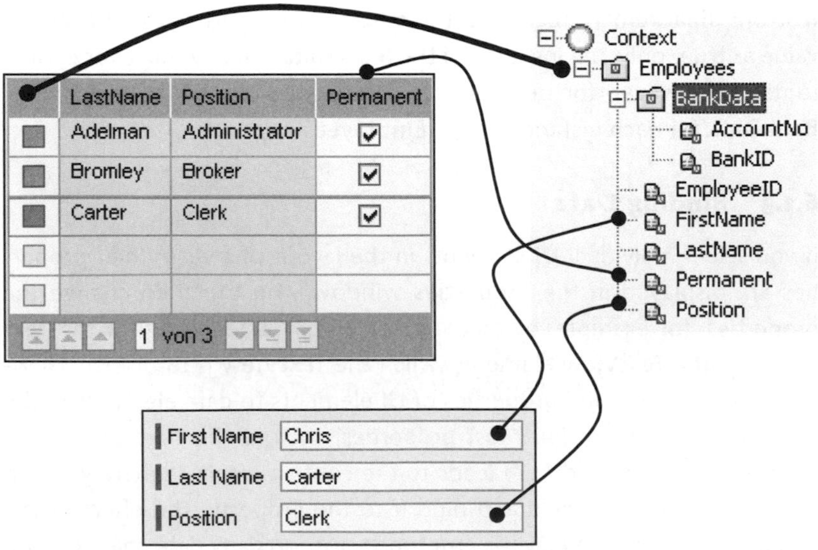

Figure 6.4 Binding UI Elements

Exercise: The project WD501 contains a similar scenario to that displayed in the graphic. You will now add UI elements to the form section and bind them to the attributes in the context that you just inserted in the last exercise.

You create the UI elements by dragging them from the palette on the left side of the **Layout** tab and dropping them in the WYSIWYG display of the layout or in the **Outline** window. For now, you will only require the UI elements **Label** and **InputField** from the palette **Simple Standard**. Bind each **value** property of an **InputField** to an attribute of the type `string`, which you want to display in the element.

In addition, create a **Checkbox** and bind its **checked** property as well as the **enabled** property of at least one **InputField** to the *Permanent* attribute, which is of type `boolean`.

Now start the application and enter some values. Toggle between the data records to verify that the application is storing the entered data. Furthermore, the **Checkbox** should now control the input-ready status of the **InputField**.

We should emphasize the last point illustrated by the exercise: The binding of data is useful for more than the obvious properties of UI elements such as **text** or **value**. Multiple binding of the same attribute and the binding of properties such as **enabled** or **visible** in particular, often enables you to create scenarios in which the value of one UI element influences the visibility or input-ready status of one (or more) other UI elements, without any need for programming.

Binding Different Properties

Exercise: As your last modification of the project WD501, delete the **DropDownByIndex** and replace it with an element of the type **TableView** for selecting the element to be edited. This UI element is in the **Complex Standard** palette.

A table wizard supports you when binding the **TableView** to the **Employees** node (right-click on the **TableView** element in the **Outline** window and choose **Create binding**). On the first screen of the wizard, you can select specific value attributes for the table columns. On the second screen, you can arrange the chosen table columns and select a UI element as the editor for each column. If, for example, you also want to be able to edit the table, you should select the editor **InputField** for some columns.

6.2 Interactive Forms with Adobe Technology

While we cannot cover all the interesting UI elements of Web Dynpro in this book, we would at least like to mention the interactive forms you can build using Web Dynpro.

Interactive Forms
as a Special UI
Element
In Section 6.1.1, we stressed that the pixel-accurate positioning of UI elements is not possible in Web Dynpro. Instead, the layout results from the interaction of containers nested within one another. With the UI element **InteractiveForm**, we can circumvent this restriction: The positioning of the **InteractiveForm** on the Web Dynpro view is relative, but it contains a complete form created in the Adobe Forms Designer.® You can then place anything provided by Adobe Technology on this form, and the positioning will be pixel accurate.

If you use this UI element in a Web Dynpro application, this creates a new restriction with regard to client selection: The Adobe Reader® must be running where the application is to be displayed. However, due to the widespread use of Adobe Reader, this limitation is not really a problem.

6.2.1 The Adobe Forms Designer in the Developer Studio

As already stated, the embedding of an interactive form begins with the insertion of the UI element **InteractiveForm** into a view. In the first instance, **InteractiveForm** is a UI element like any other: It can share a view with other UI elements, according to the layout regulations, and it has a range of properties—such as the **DataSource** property—with which you can bind it to a context node.

However, for the further processing of the UI element **InteractiveForm**, the Developer Studio allows you to branch to the Adobe Forms Designer, where you can edit the form to be displayed in the UI element (see Figure 6.5).

In the **Data View** tab of the Designer, you can see the contents of the context node used as the **DataSource**. A suitable UI element is listed for each data element—such as a checkbox for a Boolean value or an input field for a string. The developer can move these UI elements onto the form using Drag & Drop and then combine them with other UI elements from the **Library** tab—such as static graphics, and so on.

Binding Data
to Forms
As you can see, what we learned in Section 6.1.3 about binding UI elements to data in the context also applies here: The UI elements in the form are also bound to the values in the context. Therefore, the applica-

tion can exchange data with the form by operating on the context. For instance, it can predefine values for specific fields and it can obtain entered data from the context and check it for correctness online. Among many other things, it can also support the user when entering values by compiling a list of possible values.

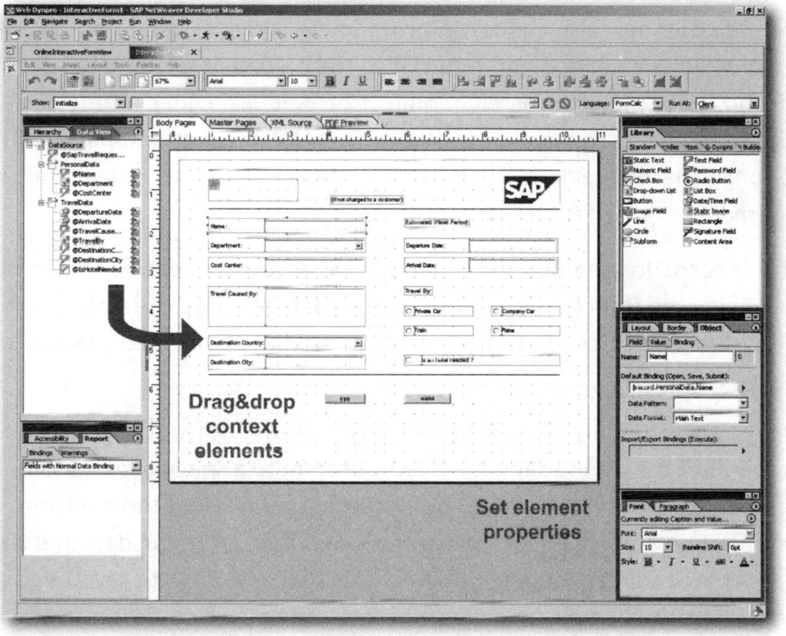

Figure 6.5 The Adobe Forms Designer® in the Development Environment of Web Dynpro

In anticipation of the topic *eventing*, we'll just mention here that every interactive form holds two predefined events (onCheck and onSubmit), which can be bound to actions. Eventing is discussed in more detail in Section 6.4.

6.2.2 Further Scenarios with Interactive Forms

Although this is outside the scope of this chapter, it is worth discussing the fact that the use of Adobe form technology is not limited to the Web Dynpro development environment or Web Dynpro runtime system. In fact, there is a wide range of possible uses for this technology.

The basis for such scenarios is the fact that the *Adobe Document Services* (ADS) are integrated in the SAP Web Application Server (SAP Web AS) as of SAP NetWeaver '04. A Java application can address these services

Adobe Document Services

directly, for example, to write data into the fields of a form or extract user entries from a form. This is precisely what the Web Dynpro runtime system does automatically—without the Web Dynpro programmer having to worry about it—in the online scenarios described above.

Offline Scenarios In the variants described so far, it is assumed that the user fills out the form while still connected to the Web Dynpro application online. However, the user may also choose to save the file on his or her computer, fill it out when convenient, and return it to the system at a later date. To fill out the form, the user merely requires the Adobe Reader on his or her PC; a permanent connection to the running Web Dynpro application is no longer necessary. In contrast to the interactive online variant, this is referred to as an *offline scenario*.

Offline scenarios can be further subdivided according to how the forms are transferred from the application to the user, or from the user back into the system. The most important methods are file upload and download, HTML, and email.

Using Email and File Transfer An application could, for example, provide forms for download online and request the user to send the filled-out form to a specific mail address. Another application could filter out incoming forms from the mail inbox, use ADS to extract the data they contain, and then store the data in database tables or directly trigger further processing. Needless to say, the user interfaces of such applications can be created with Web Dynpro, which provides a separate UI element for file uploads and downloads. Anyone who would rather avoid programming such scenarios altogether will be interested to know that, with the *Guided Procedures* technology, SAP NetWeaver provides such scenarios in the form of executable application templates, which the customer can adapt to the specific workflow situation.

Alternative to Paper Forms The major advantage of Adobe technology is that the electronic form can be an exact copy of an original form, which the user will already be familiar with from paper-based processes such as tax returns, damage reports, orders, and so on. Therefore, the user will immediately feel more at home with the electronic variant of the process and won't require any special instructions or support.

Of course, the offline variant has some restrictions when compared to its online counterpart: Context-sensitive help and complex checks are only possible if a running Web Dynpro application displays the form online. For example, if a customer is selected, the **Contacts** field lists only the contact persons for this customer. However, Adobe forms can also provide input helps and input checks in the offline case. Adobe technology even incorporates a macro language that enables you to conduct calculations directly in the form. This feature is only available in newer versions of the Adobe Reader,® but can significantly improve the processing of offline forms.

6.3 Applications with Multiple Views

In Section 6.1, we used an example in which a table layout and a detail layout of the same data worked together on a single view. In this section, we will deliberately separate the table layout and the data layout and place them on two different views. Initially, we see that this causes nothing but problems. How can we get the data from one view to the other now?

6.3.1 Data Transfer Between Multiple Views Using Mapping

Fortunately, when examining the application more closely, we discover that the data was not originally created in the controller connected with the view. This controller merely obtains the data from another controller via *mapping*.

The other controller also has a context and a mapping connection exists between the two contexts of the two controllers. This mapping connects certain nodes of one context with similar nodes of the other context. Consequently, any changes made to the contents of one node are immediately carried over to the other. If you change a field value in one of the two nodes, it automatically changes in the other node. If you're dealing with multiple nodes, the number and contents of the attributes for both nodes will always be the same. If you select a different attribute in one of the nodes, the corresponding attribute is also selected in the other node.

Data Exchange Between Contexts

Mapping is a one-way relationship: It points from one context to the other. The direction is important; for example, if you want to change the mapping, as in this case you must find the context from which the mapping originates. Furthermore, the controller from which the mapping originates must have a *use relationship* with the other controller (see Section 6.7.1). However, the direction is not relevant for the exchange of information: Any changes made on one side are immediately reproduced on the other, regardless of the mapping direction.

You can also use mapping to create chains of connected controllers and map several contexts onto the same context. Figure 6.6 illustrates why this solves our problem of transferring data between views: If both controllers create a mapping context for a common third controller, the data flows automatically from one view to the other via this intermediary.

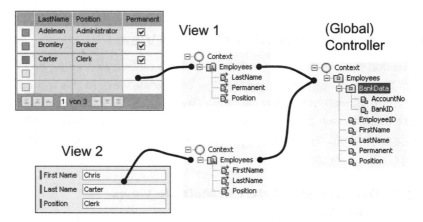

Figure 6.6 Mappings Between Multiple Contexts

The obvious question as to why we introduce a third context here, instead of initiating the mapping directly between the two views, will be answered later.

Exercise: Load the project WD502 and start the contained application. You'll see that the view **WD502DetailView** displayed on the Detail tab is still completely empty. Create a new node **Employees** in the context of this view and then select **Edit Context Mapping ...** in the context menu for this node. In the wizard that appears, you see the context of the global controller **WD502Comp.** Select the **Employees** node and click on **Next.** On the next screen, select some of the attributes of the node and click on **Finish.**

You have now created a context in the view that automatically receives data from the global controller **WD502Comp** via mapping. Now insert some UI elements into the view layout and connect them with attributes in the context.

When you start the application, the **Detail** tab lists all existing data in a table. If you then select any table row and switch to the second tab, you will see the view **WD502DetailView** filled with the data of the selected row.

Just a quick word about where the other controller obtains the data from: It is contained in an XML file in the directory *...\workspace\WD502\src\ mimes\Components\com.sap.somepackage.WD502Comp\Employees.xml* in the file system. You can add a few data records to this file if you want to make the example more interesting.

You may have noticed an important fact when testing the result of the last exercise: Values entered in an input field on the **Detail** tab don't immediately appear on the table tab when you switch back to it; they only appear after you have selected a different row in the table. Just make a note of this fact for now; it will be explained in more detail in Section 6.3.3.

6.3.2 Arranging Views in the Navigation Modeler

So what have we achieved? We've broken down our user interface into smaller units, which we can now combine in any way we wish. The tool we use to do this is the *Navigation Modeler*, in which we process *windows*. A window occupies a rectangular area of the screen and specifies where and in what order views appear in this area.

Navigation Modeler and Window

The Navigation Modeler starts when you select a window for editing. To do so, right-click on a window in the Web Dynpro Explorer and choose **Edit**. To help you locate a window in the hierarchy of the Web Dynpro project, it's useful to know that a window is always subordinate to a component. We'll explain this relationship in more detail in Section 6.6.

You can fill the entire area managed by the window with a single view by embedding it in the Navigation Modeler as the only view. The whole thing becomes more interesting if we first split the area into several smaller areas into which we embed a *view set*. It divides the available area into several *view areas*. There are different types of view sets for different arrangements of view areas. You can also insert views into each of the view areas; the former are then displayed next to each other on the screen. Instead of views, you can also insert view sets into the view areas and thus divide up the view areas even further.

View Sets and View Areas

> **Exercise:** Open the Navigation Modeler in the project WD502 and choose the **ViewSet** tab to display its properties in the **Properties** window. Set **tabCount** to the value 3 and enter a descriptive header for the newly created property **tabCaption[3]**.

You have now created another view area in the view set; you can see this view area on a third tab when the application is running. Then, you can add views or additional view sets to this new view area. For example, the project contains a third view, which displays the same data in a different way; you can insert this view by choosing **Embed View** from the context menu for the new view area.

You can also display all three views adjacently in a view set. In the toolbar on the left of the Navigation Modeler, select the **Create a View Set** icon. Enter a name for the view and choose one of the layouts for the view set type. You then receive three new view areas which you can distribute the three views to. So that your new view set is displayed instead of the **TabViewSet** when you start the application, you must set the former's **Default** property to **true.**

ViewContainer and Nesting Views in Views

It's worth mentioning that, in addition to the predefined types of view sets, developers can easily create additional view arrangements. Using the UI element **ViewContainer** in the layout of a view creates a space for displaying more, nested views. In the Navigation Modeler, this space is displayed as a separate view area and it can be filled with views, just like the view areas of the view sets. The **ViewContainer** is useful in cases where, for example, the layout of a view is to flow around other, embedded contents. Views that feature several **ViewContainer** elements in their layout can also be used as full-fledged replacements for unavailable variants of view sets.

6.3.3 Round Trips and Actions

If you look at the architecture of the Web Dynpro runtime environment illustrated in Figure 6.7, you see that the majority of an application runs on the server. On the client—the end user's PC—there is only one universal frontend, the *Web Dynpro Client*. The client can display specified screen contents and report user actions to the server. The Web Dynpro Client is currently based on HTML and resides solely in the Internet browser used on the PC.

Round Trip

All the client knows is the screen to be displayed. All deeper, underlying dependencies in the user interface are hidden from it and reserved solely for the server. In particular, the client knows nothing of contexts. Therefore, a change of screen content can only be converted to a change of context content on the server. In turn, only the server can convert a change of context content into screen content. For this synchronization to occur, the client must send a message to the server. The server then processes the messages and all changed screen content. It sends back a new screen, which the client then displays. This process is known as a *round trip*.

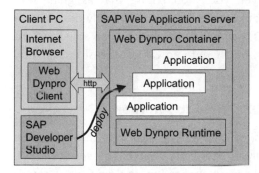

Figure 6.7 Architecture of the Web Dynpro Runtime Environment

Programmers can define which user operations trigger a round trip by binding specific user operations to *actions*. Which user operations are involved depends on the UI elements used. Most UI elements trigger events as a result of specific user operations. If you bind such an event to an action, the user operation triggers the action and thus a round trip.

Actions = Handlers for User-Triggered Events

> **Exercise:** Open the project WD502 again and add a UI element of the type Button to the view with the detail view. Bind the button to an action by setting the **onClick** property of the UI element: Choose the button marked "..." to create a new action. In the wizard that is displayed, you must enter a **Name** and **Text** for the new action and then click on **Finish**. Although the new action doesn't trigger any processing itself, this modification still causes a noticeable change, as you can see when testing the application. If, after changing values, you now press the new button and then switch to the table view, you'll see that your change has taken effect immediately without having to select a new table row.

We can now explain the role played by the button that we created in the last exercise. Only when the button is pressed is the round trip triggered; the changed values are transferred to the context and therefore, also to the table.

Incidentally, strictly speaking you don't require a button to send events. If you want, you could try binding one of the input fields in the example ap-

Sending Events by Data Input

plication to an action. The only event you could use in this case is **on-ValueChange**, as no other event exists for UI elements of the type **InputField.** You'll notice that any subsequent changes made to the value of the chosen field will also result in the transfer of the changed data from all fields to the context. However, you should note that assigning `on-ValueChange` to an action could prove to be a very costly design decision. For performance reasons, you will most likely not be able to afford a separate round trip for every newly entered value, at least not for very large forms.

6.3.4   Navigation from One View to Another

Based on our previous examples, it is not yet clear how the Navigation Modeler got its name. Typically, the term "navigation" describes the different paths that a user can take in an application. In Web Dynpro terminology, the subject of navigation therefore pertains to the transition from one view to another. In fact, you can outline such transitions in the Navigation Modeler. The basis for this is formed by the so-called *plugs*:

▶ *Inbound plugs* mark the possible entry points into a view.

▶ *Outbound plugs* indicate the possible ways of navigating out of a view.

Navigation links connect one outbound plug with one inbound plug. Usually, but not necessarily, the two connected plugs are in different views.

Navigating =
Firing Outbound
Plugs

The outbound plugs of a view allow it to initiate navigation: When an outbound plug is fired (for example, as a result of an action), all links originating from the plug are followed and the views at which they end are displayed after the round trip. Note that the view does not have access to the information regarding where the navigation leads. The view merely selects the outbound plug; it is the navigation graph for the window that defines the effect of the resulting navigation. This principle ensures that you can change the navigation paths of an application without having to worry about the inner workings of the individual views.

Navigation with
View Sets and
View Areas

Attaching several links to the same outbound plug can be very useful, provided they lead to views in different view areas. It is in fact possible to assign more than one view to a single view area, something that we have so far not addressed. When the application is running, the view area can display only one view at a time, but through navigation you can have the view area display alternating views. Another option that we haven't yet mentioned is that, in addition to simple views, you can also embed view sets in a view area. You can imagine that there is always a superordinate, virtual view area that comprises the entire navigation scenario contained in a window. If a view becomes visible due to a navigation step, this also results in the view area that contains the view being displayed and, in turn, the view set containing the view area. It is therefore necessary to flag one of the nested views or view sets in the view area that becomes active when the latter is to spontaneously appear. To do so, you must select the view or view set in the Navigation Modeler and set its **Default** property to **true** in the **Properties** window.

As you will have noticed, the level of complexity of the navigation scenarios you can create in the Navigation Modeler is unlimited. The example in Figure 6.8 illustrates just some of these scenarios.

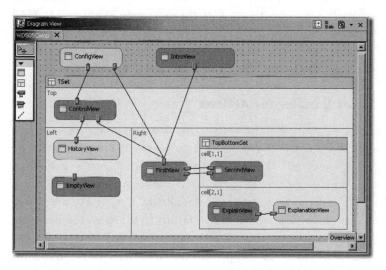

Figure 6.8 Modeling View Sequences in the Navigation Modeler

You can see, for example, that you can make the **HistoryView** visible from the **ControlView**. Can you think of a way to make the **HistoryView** disappear again? If not, the following exercise will show you how to do just that.

Exercise: The project WD505 contains the navigation scenario from the figure above. First, let the application run and observe the different navigation paths. Now add an outbound plug to the **HistoryView** (to do so, choose the **Out** icon in the toolbar and then click on the view). Connect the new plug with the inbound plug of the **empty view** in the same view area (choose the **Link** icon in the toolbar and use the mouse to drag a link from one plug to the other).

In order to fire the plug and make the **HistoryView** invisible, create a button in the layout of the **HistoryView** and bind it to a new action. You can proceed as you did in the last exercise, but with one difference: For the button to actually fire the plug, you must check the **Fire Plug** checkbox and select the relevant plug when creating the action in the corresponding wizard.

6.4 Generated and Custom Source Code: Working with Event Handlers

In Section 6.3.3, we saw that actions trigger a round trip to the server, and that input and output data is aligned with the context during a round trip. However, this is by no means all that can happen in a round trip. All our previous example applications were created using the graphical tools of the Web Dynpro perspective; we'll now add some of our own Java code to our application, which will then run during a round trip.

6.4.1 Event Handler for Actions

Let's turn to the **Implementation** tab in the View Designer. The Java code visible here is the part of the program that implements the view when the application is executed. This source code is predominantly generated from what you created on the other View Designer tabs. Therefore, it would not make sense to edit the code manually. It will be generated in exactly the same way the next time we return to the tab. It is therefore quite safe for you to try it out: Make some changes to the generated source code, then switch to another tab and then back to **Implementation**. You'll see that your changes are no longer there.

Custom Code
You are only allowed to add your own code to a few specially marked areas in the source code. These sections are enclosed with @@begin .. @@end. Anything you insert in such an area is not lost, but is retained in exactly the same place every time a generation takes place. This type of source code is also referred to as *custom code*, if you want to distinguish it from the other, generated source code (see Figure 6.9).

Event Handlers
For every action we create, the generated source code contains a method with a corresponding name (for example, the method onActionUser-Panic for the action UserPanic). The method is initially of little use, but it contains one of the aforementioned sections for adding your own source code. When an action then triggers a round trip, the relevant source code is also executed. This method is known as the *event handler* of the action.

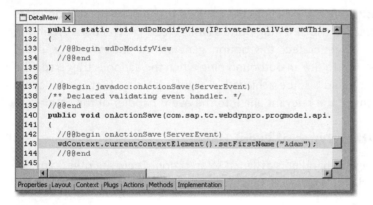

```
  DetailView  X
131    public static void wdDoModifyView(IPrivateDetailView wdThis,
132    {
133      //@@begin wdDoModifyView
134      //@@end
135    }
136
137    //@@begin javadoc:onActionSave(ServerEvent)
138    /** Declared validating event handler. */
139    //@@end
140    public void onActionSave(com.sap.tc.webdynpro.progmodel.api.
141    {
142      //@@begin onActionSave(ServerEvent)
143      wdContext.currentContextElement().setFirstName("Adam");
144      //@@end
145    }
```

Properties | Layout | Context | Plugs | Actions | Methods | Implementation

Figure 6.9 Custom Code Editor in the Implementation Tab of the View Designer

It is important to note that the event handler runs after the edited screen data was transferred to the context, but before the edited context data is transferred to the screen. This allows the event handler to manipulate the context for its own purpose.

Exercise: In an earlier exercise, you created a button with an empty action in project WD502. Find the event handler for this action in the **Implementation** tab and add the following line of source code:

```
wdContext.currentEmployeesElement().
  setFirstName("Adam");
```

Pressing the button should now set the **FirstName** element in the context, and thus all bound UI element properties, to the value "Adam."

Chapter 7 will cover the editing of context contents in much more detail. Just one recommendation at this point: In principle, the API does not only allow the Web Dynpro runtime environment to edit the values of context content via programs, but also the properties of UI elements in the layout. For example, you could use a program to set the **enabled** property of a UI element to **false** if the UI element shall not be ready for input. However, a better method was described in Section 6.1.3: Bind the property to a context element of the type `boolean` instead and assign the value **false** to this context element in the custom code. Not only is this technique less performance-intensive when implemented by the Web Dynpro runtime environment, but it also generally results in more clearly designed programs, because a single context element can now control the input-ready status of several fields simultaneously.

Finally, just a quick word about the exercise in the previous section: Here we had checked the **Fire Plug** option while creating an action. When the application is generated, this option generates a line of source code, whose task it is to fire an outbound plug when the action is triggered. The same effect could also be achieved in a different way, that is, you could manually insert the relevant line into the event handler of the action.

6.4.2 Other Types of Event Handlers

Not every event handler is assigned to an action. There are other types of event handlers, which are triggered in completely different ways, for example:

▶ Every inbound plug in a view has its own event handler. The event handler runs for each navigation into the view via this inbound plug.

▶ The so-called *supply functions*, which are discussed in Section 7.3.4, can be regarded as a special type of event handler. The event they handle is the first access to specific data in the context. They are used to make data available in the context on demand, that is, only when it is actually needed by the application.

Custom Events
▶ Controllers can declare any number of their own events (custom events) and trigger them in their custom code. Other controllers can register themselves for such events and provide event handlers for this purpose, which run when the first controller triggers the event.

We'll discuss sending events between controllers in Section 6.7.2 using an example. The following exercise shows the benefits of using event handlers in an inbound plug.

Exercise: In project WD505, the view **FirstView** has two inbound plugs: **ConfigView** and **ControlView** navigate to the view via the plug **StartTransaction**, while **SecondView** uses the plug **NextTransaction**.

We can take advantage of this difference by inserting the following code into the event handler for the plug **StartTransaction**.

```
wdContext.currentContextElement().setCurrentValue(
    wdContext.currentContextElement().getDefaultValue()
);
```

If you now navigate to the view from **ConfigView** or **ControlView,** the field **Your input** contains the default value set by the **ConfigView**. However, if you navigate from the **SecondView**, the default value remains ineffective.

6.4.3 API of the Web Dynpro Runtime Environment

In addition to general Java statements such as calculations, string manipulations, decisions, and so on, the custom code of a Web Dynpro application will generally contain many operations that affect the specific runtime environment of Web Dynpro. Which operations are possible is defined by the Web Dynpro API. The exact description of the API is available as a Javadoc both in the online help of the Developer Studio and in the SAP Developer Network (*http://sdn.sap.com*) under the URL *https://www.sdn.sap.com/sdn/javadocs.sdn*.

The API is quite substantial, so the following are just a few of the most important areas an application can become involved in by calling it:

▶ Manipulating the structure and content of the context

▶ Creating UI elements in the layout

▶ Sending messages and error messages

▶ Managing connections to external services, Web services in particular

▶ Reading the user master record and checking authorizations

▶ Triggering navigation steps by firing outbound plugs

▶ Dynamically filling selection lists and drop-down lists

▶ Triggering custom events

▶ Accessing other controllers and calling their methods

Figure 6.7 illustrated how the SAP Web AS executes Web Dynpro applications, albeit in an extremely simplfied form. The layer in the J2EE server described as the *Web Dynpro container* is based on servlet technology. In this container, the same standardized servlet runs for every Web Dynpro application, but the servlet calls the application-specific source code in each case. This application-specific source code is mainly generated from the metadata created by the programmer in the graphical tools of the Developer Studio. However, the generated code branches into the custom code, which the programmer stored in the event handlers, at precisely defined points. Both the generated source code and the custom code have access to the services in the Web Dynpro runtime environment, whose interface is defined in the Web Dynpro API.

6.4.4 Simple Code Examples for the Web Dynpro API

In the following, we've provided a few simple but common code fragments as examples for the use of API calls. Section 6.5 covers a somewhat more complex subject, the Web Dynpro API, which concerns the dynamic creation of Web Dynpro objects at program runtime.

The objects and methods of the Web Dynpro API are usually accessed via the object `wdThis`, which represents the controller to which the event handler belongs. For example, `wdThis.getContext()`—for which the short form `wdContext` is also offered—returns an object that represents the context of the controller. `wdThis.getAPI()` is also very important; it leads to the generic interface of the controller of the type `IWDController` or `IWDViewController`.

Furthermore, note that you will often use types from the libraries under `com.sap.tc.webdynpro.*`, which implement the API, to address the API. If the compiler does not recognize some of these types, choose **Source · Organize Imports** after right-**clicking in the code editor.** The development environment then automatically generates the required import statements in your Java project.

Code Example: Initializing a Context Node

In the exercise in Section 6.1.2, we had to restrict ourselves to nodes of the cardinality 1..1, because we didn't know how to initialize a multiple context node. Now, we'll compensate for this in our first example, which describes how to add elements to a multiple node. The context of the view **AddEmployeeView** contains a multiple node **Employees** with some attributes such as *First Name*, *Surname, and so on*, as well as a multiple subnode **Skills** with attributes such as *Description*, and so on. With Listing 6.1, you will add a new employee.

```
// get a reference to the Employees node
IPrivateAddEmployeeView.IEmployeesNode
    myEmployeeNode = wdContext.nodeEmployees();
// create a new element that can be added to the node
IPrivateAddEmployeeView.IEmployeesElement
    myNewEmployee =
        myEmployeeNode.createEmployeesElement();
// set a few attributes
myNewEmployee.setFirstName("Joe");
myNewEmployee.setLastName("Black");
// add the new element to the node as the last element
myEmployeeNode.addElement(myNewEmployee);
// make the new element the lead selection, because we
// now want to add the skills for this element
```

```
myEmployeeNode.
    setLeadSelection(myEmployeeNode.size()-1);
// get node and create element for skills
IPrivateAddEmployeeView.ISkillsNode
    mySkillNode = wdContext.nodeSkills();
IPrivateAddEmployeeView.ISkillsElement
    myNewSkill = mySkillsNode.createSkillsElement();
// attributes can also be set more dynamically
myNewSkill.setAttributeValue("SkillName", "Coding");
// add the Skill for the new Employee
mySkillNode.addElement(myNewSkill);
```

Listing 6.1 Adding an Employee

Code Example: Dialog Boxes

As a second example of working with API calls, we will look at the source code for two event handlers, which together implement a modal dialog box. The first event handler starts the dialog box and the second event handler closes it again. The example is quite simple but requires some preparation:

First, you must, in addition to the main window that becomes active with the application, create a second window called **PopupWindow** under the same component (to do so, right-click the component in the Web Dynpro Explorer) and then fill this second window with views in the Navigation Modeler. In such cases, you can compose both navigation graphs from the same pool of views in the Navigation Modeler. However, the view containing the event handler for opening the dialog box should be in the main window, while the view with the event handler for closing the dialog box should be in the **PopupWindow**.

The code for the first event handler starts the additional window as a dialog box on the main window. The second event handler must close this window, but to do so it requires a reference to the instance of the window created by the first event handler. So how does this reference get from one event handler to the other if both handlers are in different views? The answer: In the same way that views always exchange data. There must be a context element in a global context onto which both views map one of their local context elements. The only noteworthy difference from the relevant example in Section 6.1.3 is that this context element cannot have a simple type like `string`, `int`, or similar, but instead must have a type from the Web Dynpro API, namely `com.sap.tc.`

webdynpro.services.session.api.IWDWindow. With this in mind,
we can now proceed to the source code (see Listing 6.2).

```
public void onActionPopupOpen( ... wdEvent ){
//@@begin onActionPopupOpen(ServerEvent)
// get window information for the popup window
IWDWindowInfo myWindowInfo = wdComponentAPI
    .getComponentInfo().findInWindows("DetailsPopup");
// create the window from the given window information
IWDWindow myWindow = wdComponentAPI.getWindowManager()
    .createWindow(myWindowInfo, true);
// save the window handle in a (mapped) context element
wdContext.currentContextElement()
    .setPopupWindowHandle(myWindow);
// set some parameters for the window and open it
myWindow.setWindowSize(400, 150);
myWindow.setWindowPosition(WDWindowPos.CENTER);
myWindow.open();
//@@end
}
public void onActionPopupClose( ... wdEvent ){
//@@begin onActionPopupClose(ServerEvent)
// get the window handle from the context element
wdContext.currentContextElement()
    .getPopupWindowHandle().close();
//@@end
}
```

Listing 6.2 Dialog Boxes

Code Example: Messages and Error Dialogs

Our last code fragment shows how an application program can display
messages on the screen. Once more, the source code is not very complex,
but there are some special aspects of Web Dynpro that you need to consider:

Message Pool ▶ Web Dynpro supports multilingual applications. It is therefore not sen-
sible to write the texts of user messages, and so on, directly into the
source code. Instead, such texts are kept in a *message pool*. The source
code refers to these texts using keys, and the Web Dynpro runtime
environment then ensures that the text is displayed in the correct language.

- Sending error messages affects the navigation in the application. Depending on the severity of the error, the Web Dynpro runtime environment automatically changes the navigation accordingly.

- You can link error messages with specific context contents. The Web Dynpro application then automatically carries out an adapted error dialog with the user, in which it specifically refers the user to the screen fields that display the context contents. For example, if the user clicks on the displayed error message, he or she can be automatically taken to a UI element bound to the relevant context element.

The code example that starts on the next page (Listing 6.3) assumes that there are two texts in the message pool: *ChecksOk* of the type text and *MustNotBeZero* of the type error. If you want to create your own texts in the message pool, it can be found in the Web Dynpro Explorer, where, just like the window objects, it is located under the component to which it is assigned. Also, note the different notation of the same key in the message pool (*ThisIsAKey*) and the source code (THIS_IS_A_KEY).

```
// check the attribute MyNumber in context node MyNode
if (wdContext.currentMyNodeElement().getMyNumber()>0) {
    // get access to the texts in the message pool
    IWDTextAccessor myTexts =
        wdComponentAPI.getTextAccessor();
    // send success message with text ChecksOK
    wdComponentAPI.getMessageManager()
        .reportSuccess(myTexts.getText("CHECKS_OK"));
} else {
    // report an error for a certain context attribute
    wdComponentAPI.getMessageManager()
        .raiseInvalidContextAttributeMessage (
            // the node that contains the attribute
            wdContext.currentMyNodeElement(),
            // the attribute itself
            wdContext.getNodeInfo()
                .getAttribute("MyNumber"),
            // the text for the message (coming from
            // component MyComp's message pool !)
            IMessageMyComp.MUST_NOT_BE_ZERO,
            // no dynamic message parameters
            null,
            // cancel all pending navigation
```

```
          true
      );
}
// if the check fails, this navigation (and every other
// pending navigation) will not happen
wdThis.wdFirePlugStandardOut();
```

Listing 6.3 Messages and Error Dialogs

6.5 Changing the User Interface Dynamically

With what we have learned about binding in Section 6.1.3, we can already change the properties of UI elements dynamically. You simply bind the property to an element in the context and then change the value of this element at runtime.

Dynamically Controlling Visibility in the Layout

In this way, you could, for example, bind the *visible* property of one or more UI elements to an element in the context and then simply display or hide UI elements at runtime. However, this requires some advanced knowledge, as the *visible* property needs a context element with a very specific data type for binding, namely the Java Dictionary type `com.sap.ide.webdynpro.uielementdefinitions.Visibility`.

Furthermore, we would have to assign the values of this context element in an event handler, since the possible values of this type (`WDVisibility.VISIBLE`, `WDVisibility.BLANK`...) cannot be generated in the user interface. Therefore, while this solution is not exactly trivial, it does follow a very simple basic principle, which we have already discussed.

However, when using this method, you need to know the maximum number of UI elements (and context elements), their types, and their positions in advance. But what if you don't know all this? We will now answer this question.

6.5.1 Creating Context Elements Dynamically

For every context element defined in the static metadata, the generated source code derived from the metadata must, among other things, create a Java object instance that represents the element at runtime. For this purpose, the source code uses specific calls in the API of the Web Dynpro runtime environment. However, the same calls are also available in the custom code. At runtime, the application program can thus add additional nodes and attributes to the contexts defined in the development environment.

The following example illustrates the most important calls from this area of the API: It creates an additional node **MySubNode** below the node **MyNode** and assigns it an attribute of the type `string`. We select the simplest case for each of the parameters for creating the node; many of the parameters refer to concepts explained in Chapter 7.

```
// get access to MyNode's meta-data
IWDNodeInfo myNodeInfo =
    wdContext.nodeMyNode().getNodeInfo();
// add the sub-node as a value node with ..
myNodeInfo.addChild("MySubNode", null, true,
    // .. cardinality 1..1 (mandatory and non-multiple)
    true, false,
    // .. with matching selection handling
    true, false, false,
    // .. without a fixed structure from the dictionary
    null,
    // .. and no automatic initialization / disposal
    null, null);
// define variables for access to the node ..
IWDNode mySubNode = wdContext.nodeMyNode()
    .getChildNode("MySubNode", 0);
// .. and for access to the node's meta-data
IWDNodeInfo mySubNodeInfo = mySubNode.getNodeInfo();
// add an attribute of type string to the sub-node
mySubNodeInfo.addAttribute("MyAttribute",
    "ddic:com.sap.dictionary.string");
// give the new attribute an initial value
mySubNode.getCurrentElement()
    .setAttributeValue("MyAttribute", "my value");
```

Listing 6.4 Creating Context Elements at Runtime

6.5.2 Creating UI Elements Dynamically

As we have seen, when changing the context dynamically, we're dealing with a hierarchical structure that can be traversed and extended. The dynamic changing of the layout in a view is very similar: Starting from a root node, you move through the hierarchy, adding more containers and UI elements. In doing so, you either set the properties of the new UI elements to fixed values or you bind them to context elements (which may also have been created dynamically).

However, dynamically changing the layout is only possible in one event handler called wdDoModifyView, which exists in every view controller. It is called before each display of the view and is the last event handler to be called. We recommend that you restrict yourself to the dynamic modification of the layout in the custom code for wdDoModifyView. In this event handler, changing the context is generally not advisable.

The following constructions are typical for this area of the API. Note that the root node of the container hierarchy is passed along with wdDo-ModifyView as the parameter view. Because you usually want to generate the dynamic elements only once per program run, an additional parameter firstTime specifies whether a particular call is the first call of the routine.

**Creating Layout
Elements at
Runtime**

The source code in Listing 6.5 assumes that the layout already includes a container element called MyContainer. Into this container, the example generates two elements: an InputField with a corresponding Label. At the same time, the InputField is bound to the context attribute created dynamically in the previous example.

```
if (firstTime) {
// create two new elements (inputfield + label)
IWDInputField myField = (IWDInputField)
    view.createElement(IWDInputField.class, "MyField");
IWDLabel myLabel = (IWDLabel)
    view.createElement(IWDLabel.class, "MyLabel");
// set Text property of the label from the context
myLabel.setText(wdContext.currentContextElement()
    .getMyLabelText());
// set LabelFor property of the label to a constant
myLabel.setLabelFor("MyField");
// bind Value property of the field to the context
myField.bindValue(wdContext.nodeMyNode()
    .getChildNode("MySubNode", 0).getNodeInfo()
    .getAttribute("MyAttribute"));
// find the right container for the two new elements
IWDUIElementContainer myContainer =
  (IWDUIElementContainer)view.getElement("MyContainer");
// add the two new elements at the end of the container
myContainer.addChild(myLabel);
myContainer.addChild(myField);
}
```

Listing 6.5 Creating Layout Elements at Runtime

6.5.3 Binding UI Elements to Actions

UI elements generated by the custom code at runtime can, like other UI elements, be bound to actions. As you would expect, this must also be done in the custom code. However, you cannot create new actions with corresponding event handlers at runtime. The events of the new UI elements can thus only be bound to the actions already statically created. Consequently, it will often be necessary to bind several UI elements to the same action. However, to make the system react differently to different UI elements, you will normally create actions with parameters in this case and, when binding the UI elements to the actions, ensure that each UI element sets the parameter differently.

Listing 6.6 demonstrates this technique. It creates several elements of the type Button. All the buttons trigger the same action (ButtonPressed), but each button passes a different value for the buttonId parameter of the action. As in the previous example, the parameter belongs in the event handler wdDoModifyView and refers to an existing container, which should already exist in the variable myContainer.

Dynamic Binding to Actions with Parameters

```
// get access to the action we have prepared statically
IWDAction myAction =
    wdThis.wdGetAPI().getAction("ButtonPressed");
for (int i = 0; i < 3; i++) {
    // create an individual ID for the button ..
    String myId = "Button".concat(String.valueOf(i));
    // .. and use it the button ID and text ..
    IWDButton myButton = (IWDButton)
        view.createElement(IWDButton.class, myId);
    myButton.setText(myId);
    // .. as well as for the action parameter buttonId
    myButton.setOnAction(myAction);
    myButton.mappingOfOnAction()
        .addParameter("buttonId", myId);
    // finally, add the button to an existing container
    myContainer.addChild(myButton);
}
```

Listing 6.6 Dynamic Binding to Actions with Parameters

The multiple use of the same action also has a beneficial side effect. User interface elements and actions both have a method setEnabled. Deactivating an action with this method also blocks user interaction for all UI

Activating and Deactivating Actions

elements bound to this action. In our example, a single statement can set all dynamically created buttons to **disabled**:

```
myAction.setEnabled(false);
```

6.5.4 Statically and Dynamically Created Elements

Further examples of the use of the two APIs can be found in every Web Dynpro project. For every view **MyView**, this version of the development environment creates, amongst other things, a file *InternalMyView.java*. It contains all calls that create the static parts of the context and layout at runtime. To find this file in the file system, follow the path *...\gen_wdp\ packages\... my package ...\wdp* from the workspace directory.

> **Tip:** You can often explore unknown API calls for dynamic modifications by creating the desired end product statically in the View Editor, and then examining the generated file to find a call sequence that can create such a result.

Note that it can often be useful to mix both techniques: The programmer can statically prepare basic parts of the user interface in the View Designer, while situation-specific parts can then be added dynamically in custom code.

Resetting to Initial Status However, you should bear in mind the following: The dynamically added elements normally remain intact until the end of the application and there are no API calls for deleting individual, dynamically added elements. There are only `reset` methods available, with which you can reset the context or layout to the static portion, that is, restore the status from the start of the application.

6.6 Web Dynpro Components

For some of the Web Dynpro elements that we have encountered so far—views and controllers in particular—we have already stressed their significance for the structuring of a Web Dynpro application. However, we have yet to cover the most important unit for the modularization of projects with Web Dynpro, namely the *component*.

Web Dynpro Components, SCs, and DCs To avoid any obvious confusion from the outset, we would like to point out that the term *component* also plays a major role in the context of the SAP NetWeaver Development Infrastructure (NWDI). To be more precise, the latter features so-called *software components* (SCs) and *develop-*

ment components (DCs). However, the only relationship that exists between these components and our Web Dynpro components is that one SC can contain several DCs and each DC can, in turn, contain several Web Dynpro components. Because this chapter and Chapter 7 pertain only to the world of Web Dynpro, we will for the sake of brevity simply refer to *components* where we should more precisely say *Web Dynpro components*.

6.6.1 Components and Applications

The first thing you must learn about components is that you cannot do without them. Every *application* starts exactly one component and, in doing so, defines exactly one of its windows as the main window. The wizard for creating the application thus requires the specification of a component as well as a window of this component. The reason we haven't noticed this before is that we normally have the component and window generated automatically when creating the application. If you're wondering what a component would do with more than one window, then think back to the code example for starting a dialog box in Section 6.4.3. In that example, we required two windows in the same component. We'll revisit this scenario when we discuss *interface views* in Section 6.6.3.

Component + Start Window = Application

Like views, components also have inbound and outbound plugs:

▶ As with views, inbound plugs define the entry points into the component and can carry their own event handlers with custom code.

▶ Firing an outbound plug ends the application.

A new feature is that inbound plugs of components can carry parameters. The user can pass values for these parameters when starting the application, for example, in the URL. Depending on the passed values, inbound plugs can, for example, decide which view the application should navigate to first, or they can simply write the values into the context of a controller.

Parameters of Components

In addition to the controllers for the individual views, each component contains at least two other controllers: One of them is the *component controller*, which has the same name as the component itself. The other, the *interface controller*, is discussed in more detail in Section 6.6.2.

Component Controller and Interface Controller

Exercise: The application in the project WD505 uses the inbound plug **Default** to start the component **WD505Comp**. This inbound plug has a parameter called **UserDefault**. When you start the application, you can add a value for this parameter to the URL, as follows:

```
... &app.UserDefault=17
```

The corresponding event handler `onPlugDefault` already contains source code for converting the entered value to an integer (the event handler can be found under **WD505Comp · Component Interface · Interface Views · WD505CompInterfaceView**). Add the following code to store the integer value as the default for the input field **Your input** in the context of the component controller:

```
wdThis.wdGetWD505CompController().wdGetContext()
    .currentContextElement()
    .setDefaultValue(myDefault);
```

6.6.2 Components as Reusable Units

Apart from serving as the basis of applications, the most important task of components is to encapsulate reusable units. As the term suggests, a component should provide a precisely defined set of services and, in doing so, conceal as far as possible how the individual services are implemented.

Interface Controller Defines the API of a Component

The interface controller is used for this *information hiding*. It is the only controller of a component that is visible externally. Therefore, a component that creates another component can, for example, map the context of the other component's interface controller or call the interface controller's methods; however, it cannot establish direct contact with the component controller or the various view controllers of the other component.

Data Modeler

To display and edit all these aspects of a component, Web Dynpro features a special graphical tool, the *Data Modeler* (which is started by choosing **Edit** from the context menu for a component). Figure 6.10 shows how a component is displayed in the Data Modeler. The different parts of the component are shown on the right, distributed over the three layers—view, controller, and model. The view level contains the controllers of the individual views. The middle, controller level shows the obligatory component controller, which is connected to the only view of the component. To the right, you can see the interface controller, which makes available some of the component's functions. The left side contains the interface controllers of the components that are used by the displayed component.

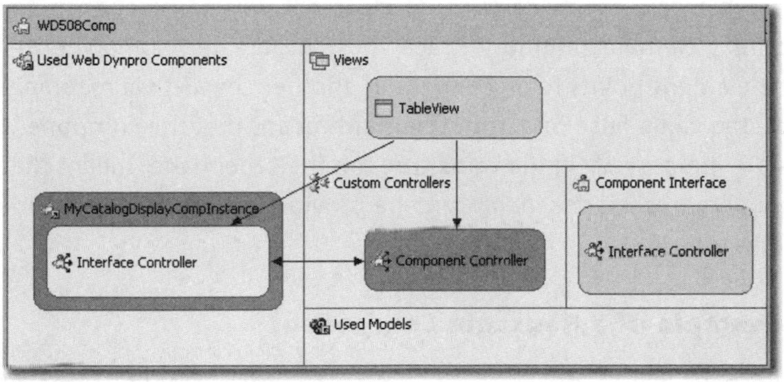

Figure 6.10 The Data Modeler

The term *reuse* usually implies that an assembly is exported from the project as a separate unit so that it can then be used in various projects like a library. (In Section 6.6.3, we'll take an in-depth look at such an example.) However, in Web Dynpro, components are also useful for a related but significantly different scenario that could be referred to as multiple usage—they are the only constructs from which you can dynamically create any number of instances at runtime.

Assemblies and Multiple Usage

According to the two different ways in which components can be used, the user can decide whether to create the instances of the used component explicitly—that is, with custom code in an event handler—or have instances automatically generated by the Web Dynpro runtime. If a user uses only one instance, he or she will generally want the lifetime of the used components controlled automatically (though there can be exceptions). If a user wants to instantiate a dynamic number of components, he or she will have to take care of this in the custom coding.

Lifetime of Components

Mappings that extend beyond and across component boundaries can go in both directions: They can be directed from a controller in the external component to the interface controller of the used component or vice versa. However, these *external mappings* have a special feature. The elements in the context of the interface controller have a property that dictates the direction of any mappings for a particular element:

External Mappings Between Components

▶ If, for an attribute, the **isInputElement** property has the value **false**, any user of the component can map its context onto this element.

▶ However, if the **isInputElement** property has the value **true**, the user of this component must (!) map this element onto the context of one of its own controllers.

This somewhat confusing rule is made clearer if you consider that, for every context element, memory space must be created somewhere—unless the element points to an element in another context via mapping. Therefore, the value **false** for **isInputElement** means that the component provides the memory itself; the value **true**, on the other hand, means that the component expects the memory to be provided by the external component that uses it.

6.6.3   Example of a Reusable Component

We would now like to demonstrate—in a practical example—some of what was theoretically discussed in the preceding sections. For this, let's look at the component **CatalogDisplayComp**.

Component Catalog-DisplayComp

CatalogDisplayComp is a perfect example of a reusable assembly. The component receives a table and displays its contents in the form of a goods catalog, as often encountered on commercial sites on the Internet (see Figure 6.11). There is no specific, predefined structure for the display of an entry in the catalog. The user of the component can specify which UI elements in this standard structure are to be filled with which data from the table; unfilled UI elements remain invisible. The user also specifies how many entries should be placed on a page. The component then automatically provides the user with the means for scrolling from page to page.

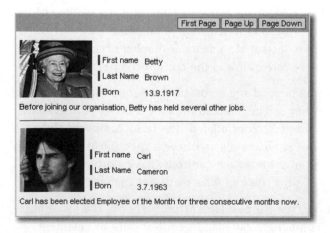

Figure 6.11 The Component CatalogDisplayComp in Action

Many of the techniques discussed in the last few pages are used in this component:

▶ The interface controller of the component features *input elements*—for example, the node **DisplayData** for the table that the user wants to display—as well as elements created in the component itself and onto which the user can map his or her contexts. An example of the latter is the attribute **PageSize**, which specifies the number of entries per page.

▶ In addition, the interface controller provides the user with a method (showCatalog), which he or she can use to trigger the display of the data that was passed and refresh it later if any changes have been made to the data.

▶ With the **PageSize** attribute, the user can externally specify the number of catalog entries to be displayed per page. Therefore, the view that displays the catalog must dynamically create all the screen elements for displaying the entries.

▶ The context elements, to which the catalog display is bound, are also created dynamically; they are not created in the interface controller of course, but in the local context of the controller for the view **Catalog-View**, so that they don't become visible in the interface.

▶ The data structure, which assigns the table data to the UI elements in the standard catalog entry, belongs to the interface controller so that it's always accessible. Both views in the component use the data structure via mapping and the user of the component also utilizes it (see Figure 6.12).

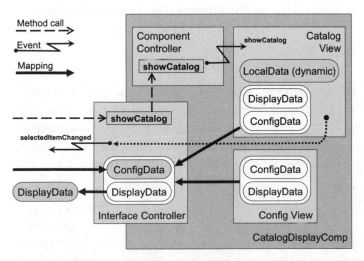

Figure 6.12 Relationships Between Controllers in the Component CatalogDisplayComp

We now need to explain how the visual portion of a component is transferred to the screen. For any component that is embedded, there is another component that embeds it, and we will refer to the latter as the *using* component for the embedded component. There is a rule in Web Dynpro that each window of an embedded component appears as an additional view in the using component. Such views are known as *interface views*, as they basically represent the visual interface with the processes in the view, like the program interface in the interface controller. However, for the using component, there is no difference between the interface views and the other, atomic views, which are simply created directly in the using component. The Navigation Modeler can combine both types of views in view sets and connect them with one another using navigation links. When the using component dedicates screen space to an interface view, a complex navigation scenario made up of views of the embedded component may run in this space.

Since most components work with a single window, they usually have only a single interface view. Our component **CatalogDisplayComp** is also particularly interesting in this respect, as it has two windows. In addition to the main window for displaying the catalog, the component also features a second window for configuration purposes. Incidentally, both windows contain only one view, but this is just by coincidence and need not necessarily be the case. In the configuration window, the user can specify which of the columns in the table that was passed to the component are to be part of the catalog. The user can also specify how these columns are to be displayed. The using component can then decide whether it wants to incorporate the second interface view in one of its view areas and thereby enable the user to customize the catalog entries while the application is running.

> **Exercise:** Project WD508 already contains **CatalogDisplayComp**. However, the using component **WD508Comp** initially uses only one of the two interface views of the embedded component **CatalogDisplayComp**. Your task is to integrate the second interface view (**ConfigWindowInterfaceView**) into the window of **WD505Comp**.
>
> First, you need to create space for this second view by increasing the value of the sole view set's **row** property from 2 to 3. Then, you have to embed the second interface view in the newly created view area (choose **Embed interface view of a component instance**). This enables the user of the application to change the catalog display at runtime.

6.7 Communication Between Controllers

We have encountered many different types of controllers—view controllers, component controllers, interface controllers—and it should now be apparent that, in complex Web Dynpro applications, the relationships between the different controllers make up the framework for the structuring of a project. Therefore, we would like to compare and contrast the possible relationships between controllers.

6.7.1 Usage Relationships

For a controller to be able to use parts of another controller, a *usage relationship* must be defined in the metadata of the first controller. A usage relationship is created automatically if you link two controllers together in the Data Modeler. However, when editing a controller, this relationship is also listed under **Required Controllers** on the **Properties** tab of the editor (not to be confused with the **Properties** window). If controller C1 has a usage relationship with controller C2, it can:

Usage Relationships

▶ Create mappings from its context to the context of C2

▶ Call methods of C2

▶ Register for custom events of C2

The Navigation Modeler depicts the usage relationship between the controllers as links, but does not indicate whether and in what way C1 actually uses the controller C2.

For calling the local methods of C2, the controller C1 can use the getControllerC2() method to obtain a reference to this controller. This call returns the same object instance that would be available to an event handler in C2 as wdThis.

References to Other Controllers

Registering for events simply involves C1 defining a local event handler for the foreign event. This is done on the **Methods** tab in the editor for controllers in the development environment. Here you can define event handlers and the local methods, which the controller makes available to other controllers, provided a usage relationship exists between them.

Registering for Foreign Events

There is a separate **Events** tab for the creation of custom events. For every custom event created, the development environment generates a separate method (for example, the method wdFireEventMyAlert for the event MyAlert), which the controller can then call in its custom code to trigger the event.

Creating Events and Methods

**Lifetime of
Controllers** We should use this opportunity to point out that the lifetime of controllers can play a very important role when determining which controller uses another. For example, the global controllers in a component—that is, component controllers and interface controllers—exist as long as the component exists. By comparison, the lifetime of view controllers is shorter; in extreme cases, they exist only as long as the view is displayed on the screen.

**Global Controllers
and View
Controllers** As a result, a usage relationship can only be directed from, for example, a view controller to a global controller, but not the other way around. It is therefore not possible for a mapping to be directed from, for instance, a component controller to a node in the context of a view controller. Similarly, a global controller cannot call a method of a view controller. In a situation where a global controller is to trigger a view controller to become active, this would generally be implemented with eventing. The global controller throws a custom event and the view controller catches it.

6.7.2 Communication Using Events

Now we'll illustrate the advantages of using custom events in an example, namely "How can the component `CatalogDisplayComp` from Section 6.6.3 inform the outside world that the user has scrolled to another page?". After all, other controllers, which display the same or related data, would perhaps like to synchronize their lead selection with the processes in the component.

In the component, the data passed for display gets copied elsewhere, so this problem cannot be solved via mapping. In fact, one main reason for copying this data is that the using component will usually not want the component to change the data that was passed to it, nor even change the lead selection in that data.

Solving the problem with a method call is also not possible, as the component does not know its user and thus cannot call a method in one of the user's controllers. It would theoretically be possible for the user to pass an object to the component, whose methods the component could use as a callback interface, but this would needlessly complicate the matter.

**Component Sends
Events to Its
Users** Therefore, the simplest solution is for the component to trigger a custom event to inform the user—or any other controllers that are interested— when the scroll function is used. In fact, the component **CatalogDisplay-**

Comp, which we looked at in Section 6.6, already offers this service. In the following exercise, you will add the event to the user's controller and evaluate it.

> **Exercise:** In project WD508, register the controller of the component **WD508Comp** for the event `selectedItemChanged`, which is triggered by the instance of the component **CatalogDisplayComp** embedded in it. To do this, create a new event handler for the component controller of the embedding component on the **Methods** tab and specify the embedded component and the event as the source. Then insert the following line of code in the event handler created by the registration:
>
> ```
> wdContext.nodeEmployees().setLeadSelection(
>     wdContext.currentConfigDataElement().getFirstIndex()
> );
> ```
>
> Check that this synchronizes the lead selection of the table in the view **TableView** with the relevant element selected in `CatalogDisplay-Comp`.

6.8 Summary

Our tour of the basic Web Dynpro concepts is now over. Before we proceed to the advanced topics covered in Chapter 7—the binding of Web Dynpro user interfaces to back-end systems in particular—we would like to briefly summarize and organize what we have learned so far.

The topics we have discussed in this chapter can be broadly split into three areas, according to the relevant tool for each subject:

▶ **Views and Layout (Tool: View Designer)**

  ▶ Web Dynpro provides an extensive range of UI elements.

  ▶ Web Dynpro works primarily with relative positioning. If pixel-accurate layouts are required, you can use interactive forms based on Adobe® technology.

  ▶ Developers normally design the layout statically in the View Designer, but it is also possible to add elements dynamically at application runtime.

▶ **Navigation (Tool: Navigation Modeler)**

  ▶ Transitions between views are prepared statically and then called dynamically at application runtime.

  ▶ Several views can be displayed simultaneously. The user can divide up the screen area in any way he or she wants.

▶ **Relationships Between Controllers Form the Application Framework (Tool: Data Modeler)**

  ▶ In the context of a controller, you model the data that the controller works with.

  ▶ Mappings between the contexts of two controllers result in an automatic exchange of information.

  ▶ You can add custom code to the event handlers of controllers. Controllers can declare their own methods and events.

  ▶ Components are used to encapsulate reusable program sections. They can only be addressed from outside via a specifically defined interface.

In general, we have seen that Web Dynpro attempts to place the emphasis on modeling rather than programming: Virtually all our examples required only a few lines of custom code. In each case, the bulk of the source code of an application was generated by the development environment.

6.8.1 The Metamodel of Web Dynpro

Now that you have had firsthand experiences with Web Dynpro, it's time to make an evaluation: How does Web Dynpro differ from the alternatives, JSPs and servlets in particular?

Metamodel Enables High Level of Abstraction The most obvious difference is that Web Dynpro works on a higher level of abstraction. The runtime environment of Web Dynpro uses a lot of servlet technology in the background, but the programmer remains unaware of this technology. He works with a predefined *metamodel*, which provides specific types of objects, such as views, components, controllers, and so on. The programmer can create instances of these objects—either statically in the View Designer, for example, or dynamically at runtime—and then combine them with one another according to predetermined rules—for example, by binding UI elements to a context or having controllers exchange events. Since the object world is predefined, the development environment can provide support in the form of easy-to-use tools. Furthermore, the developer doesn't need to deal with client technology.

The focus of Web Dynpro is currently on user interfaces running fully in Internet browsers. However, SAP has already frequently hinted at the existence of prototypes for Smart Clients, that is, specialized Web Dynpro display machines, based on .NET front-end technology, for instance.

It is inevitable that some users may feel restricted by the transition to such a higher level of abstraction: The developer cannot break out of the metamodel—he cannot structure his user interface according to completely different principles—and the level to which he can influence how his program is displayed on the screen is limited by predefined boundaries. The maintainability and longevity of the created programs are two major advantages of this approach, but these properties of Web Dynpro may still appear to be too restrictive in particular projects.

Another disadvantage that is usually stated about Web Dynpro is that the its metamodel cannot (currently) be enhanced by the user, for example, by adding new UI elements. If you are disappointed by this, bear in mind that components enable you to do many things that initially appear to be impossible. In Section 6.6.3, we saw how you can implement a complex UI element as a component. In fact, it is often useful to create components without any views in their interface (faceless components) to hide complex processes from the outside world. This is especially advisable if these components often reoccur in a similar shape. The Web Dynpro metamodel allows for the definition of components in the form of interfaces—a fact that we won't discuss further in this book—thus opening up a whole new range of possibilities for ambitious Web Dynpro developers to make far-reaching enhancements to the concepts of Web Dynpro.

Enhancing with Components

No matter how you appraise the fact that Web Dynpro is based on a fixed metamodel, it does have some definite advantages that cannot be denied:

Advantages of an Abstract Metamodel

▶ Web Dynpro is independent of the underlying platform, that is, the runtime system. For example, SAP will also make the Web Dynpo concept available for its own programming language ABAP and, as far as possible, with an identical metamodel.

▶ Web Dynpro is also independent of any specific client technology. As shown above, the focus on HTML featured in the clients currently offered is due to the current market situation and not in any way caused by specifications of Web Dynpro.

▶ Web Dynpro offers an excellent basis for providing optimal support to application developers in integrated tool environments in the form of graphical and other tools.

6.8.2 Outlook

As you will probably have noticed, we have so far avoided the question of where the data that appears in the UI elements actually comes from. We have not even explained how to append an additional line to a multiple node, nor has it been discussed how data changes entered in the user interface remain intact—even after the application has finished. All this will change in Chapter 7, which focuses on the data: Where does it come from? How is it modeled? How can you permanently change it?

Another important subject that we have yet to address is the multitude of services that Web Dynpro automatically provides to the user, thus avoiding a lot of programming, which would normally have to be carried out by the developer. Examples of this are input helps, checks, error handling, and so on. In all cases, the runtime environment actively participates, thus considerably reducing the amount of work required from the programmer. The basis for such automatic services is usually information about the types of data with which the user interface works. Therefore, these services are also discussed in Chapter 7.

Finally, it is important to note that our brief introduction to the screen contents that you can develop with Web Dynpro is by no means complete. There are many more UI elements, from simple captions to complex business graphics, which aren't covered in this book. We hereby encourage readers to explore these unchartered waters during their travels in the world of Web Dynpro.

7   Web Dynpro: Developing Business Applications

Having just covered the development of user interfaces with Web Dynpro in Chapter 6, we now turn to the missing third dimension of the Web Dynpro programming model: Working with business data via the incorporation of models. In doing so, we will encounter some important concepts of the Web Dynpro programming model: controllers and their APIs, contexts and their APIs, and the use of Dictionary types.

In the previous chapter, we introduced fundamental concepts and principles of Web Dynpro, which significantly simplify the development of Web-based applications: From the visual design of user interfaces in the Web Dynpro View Designer, via the data containers of controllers known as *contexts*, to the powerful mechanism of *data binding* between the user interface and the context, as well as the general strengths of the underlying metamodel. All these capabilities clearly demonstrate the advantages of Web Dynpro over alternative approaches.

However, one central aspect is still missing. With regard to the *Model View Controller* (MVC) *principle* used by Web Dynpro, the following questions arise: How does the new programming model link up with the underlying business logic? How does the connection to the *model* layer take place? What can be defined using the Web Dynpro tools and what must be programmed in the controller view? Contexts are still used as data containers for the display of business data, but how does the business data get from the backend to the context? What services does Web Dynpro provide to enable you to implement—with minimum programming effort—the data transport between the user interface and the backend?

Models

The first part of this chapter (Section 7.1) consists of the description of a simple Web Dynpro application, which uses the *employee* Web service from Chapter 3 as a model. Based on this example application, we will already be familiarized with the most important principles by which models can be used in Web Dynpro applications.

In Section 7.2, we'll discuss the Web Dynpro controller concept and the interfaces involved in more detail, before moving on to the central topic of the data flow between the backend and the frontend in Section 7.3. Controller contexts play a major role in this flow of data, because they act

Controllers, Contexts, and Models

as a link between the user interface (data binding) and the persistence layer (model binding). To understand the foundations of context programming, we will learn about the different context interfaces as well as the difference between value elements and model elements. Furthermore, this chapter will also cover the subjects of calculated context attributes and the use of supply functions for filling context nodes.

Using Data Type Information Finally, in Section 7.4, we'll turn to the definition of Dictionary types and learn about generic UI services for input helps based on the use of Dictionary information.

7.1 Web Dynpro Calls a Web Service—Five Steps to an Application

In the first example application, we'll learn simply and quickly how an existing Web service can be used to store and display business data via a Web Dynpro user interface. For this, we'll use the employee Web service developed in Chapter 3, *which is implemented using* an Enterprise Java Bean (EJB). In addition to the registration of an employee via the three properties—*firstname*, *lastname*, and *department*—the employee Web service also enables you to read all employees already registered from the database. The example application is developed in the following five steps:

Step 1 **Importing the Web Service Model**

The Web Dynpro tools provide a special wizard for importing a Web service model. It automatically creates all classes and files required for communicating with the employee Web service.

Step 2 **Model Binding**

If the imported model is used in an actual Web Dynpro component, you can define the binding of a custom context to the model. The term *model binding* describes the definition of a hierarchical context structure according to the classes contained in the model and their relation to one another at design time. The context structure consists of *model nodes and model attributes*. The Web Dynpro tools also provide a wizard for defining model binding. Model binding occurs at a declarative level at design time and doesn't involve any application code.

Step 3 **Context Mapping**

After the model binding of a custom context, you can also connect the contexts of view controllers with the same model via context mapping. The business data stored in the model can thus be used in multiple contexts without any need for programming.

View Layout and Data Binding

Step 4

Data binding is responsible for the automatic data transport between the user interface and the view context. The input form for registering a new employee and the table for displaying all registered employees in the view layout can be easily created using the relevant template wizards.

Controller Implementation

Step 5

The implementation comprises two view controllers and a custom controller. In the view controller, methods are implemented for checking user inputs, for the event handling of actions (registering an employee, displaying and hiding the employee table, emptying form field), and for a navigation (displaying the employee table).

In the example application, the communication with the employee Web service is encapsulated in a special custom controller. It exposes the two Web service calls for registering and displaying employees and the initialization of the registration data via an appropriate interface extension, so that the methods can also be called from view controllers.

The model binding is defined at design time on the level of model classes, model relations, and a corresponding hierarchical structure in the custom context. At runtime, the employee Web service model contains real object instances, which are referenced by the controller context. The code in the custom controller covers both the actual Web service calls and the binding of model objects to the context.

Project Template

To develop the example, you can use a predefined project template on the book DVD. It already contains the fundamental components of the application, the definition of which was discussed in detail in the previous chapter. Therefore, you don't have to create another Web Dynpro project. The two views **EmployeeView** and **EmployeesTableView**, along with the view composition,[1] are also already defined in the project template. Furthermore, you're provided with the required actions and the templates of the finished view layouts.

The functioning of the example application is quite simple, comprising the registration of an employee via an input form, the resetting of input

---

1 The term *view composition* describes the set of all view assemblies that can be reached via navigation. A view assembly is an arrangement of views displayed in a browser window at a particular point in time. View compositions are defined in the Navigation Modeler of the Web Dynpro tools. Further details are available in Chapter 6, Section 6.3.2.

fields, and the tabular display of all employees already registered (see also Figure 7.1). This table can be displayed or hidden via two corresponding buttons.

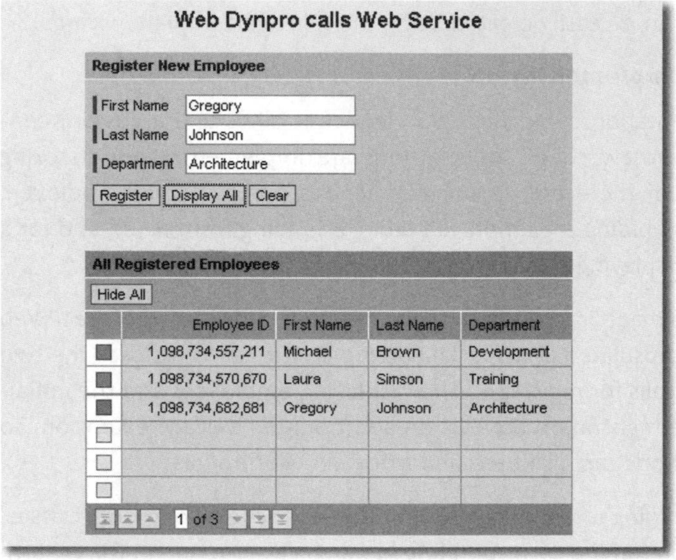

Figure 7.1 Web Dynpro Application for the Employee Web Service

Exercise: Importing the Project Template

To import the project template, perform the following steps in the SAP NetWeaver Developer Studio (SAP NWDS):

1. Unpack the entire contents of the zip file from the book DVD *WebDynpro_EmployeeWS_Init.zip* into the workspace directory or another directory of your choice.

2. Start the SAP NWDS.

3. Open the Web Dynpro perspective (**Window • Open Perspective … • Web Dynpro**).

4. Choose **File • Import** followed by Existing Project into Workspace. Then, click on Next.

5. In the input field Project Content, enter the name of the directory containing the unpacked Web Dynpro project (**WebDynpro_ EmployeeWS_Init**) and click on Finish. The project **WebDynpro_ EmployeeWS_Init** is then displayed in the Web Dynpro Explorer view.

7.1.1 Importing the Model for the Employee Web Service

We can now start developing our first model-based Web Dynpro application. Based on the predefined project template, we begin by importing the **employee** Web service model.

In this step and in subsequent steps, we'll be working with the *Data Modeler*, an easy-to-use tool for various definitions of the data flow. These include model import to the project, use of a model in a component, adding a custom controller along with the model-binding definition, interface extension of the custom controller for exporting Web service calls, context mapping—right up to the definition of actions and their event handling, and template-based extension of the view layout with integrated data binding. Therefore, all definitions required for developing the example application can be carried out in the Data Modeler, without having to branch out to the relevant entities in the Web Dynpro Explorer.

Data Modeler

First, we'll display the Web Dynpro component **EmployeeWSComp** in the Data Modeler[2] (see Figure 7.2).

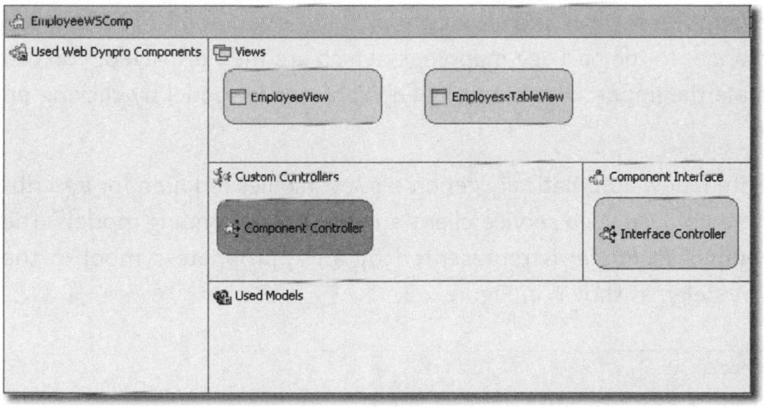

Figure 7.2 Component EmployeeWSComp of the Project Template in the Data Modeler

The models used by a Web Dynpro component are displayed in the lower part of the Data Modeler. Models are inserted at project level, independently of the actual Web Dynpro components. The use of an existing

Model Import

---

2 The Data Modeler can be opened for any Web Dynpro component by double-clicking on a component symbol in the Web Dynpro Explorer. Alternatively, you can also choose the relevant context menu entry. Furthermore, by double-clicking the frame entitled **Diagram View**, you can expand the Data Modeler to fill the entire working area in the Developer Studio; or, you can use the **Overview** function on the bottom right to select the visible area.

model in a component is then defined in a second step. In the Data Modeler, both these actions can be carried out in a single step. To do so, choose the **Create a Model** icon from the toolbar on the left and then move the cursor over the **Used Models** area in the Data Modeler. Clicking on this area opens the wizard to import a model. In the list of possible model types, choose the entry **Import Web Service Model** and then proceed to the second step—defining the Web service model. Before you can provide a definition for this model, you must first specify the name of the model and the namespace that will contain the generated model classes. Call the new model **EmployeeWSModel** and enter "com.sap. was.wd.employeews.model" **as the package name**. You can select the first part of the package name by clicking on the **Browse** button and then add the extension **.model**. Consequently, the model is stored in a separate namespace. You must also specify from which source the Web Service Definition Language (WSDL) description for the Web service can be read. Because we want to use the employee Web service already deployed on the local J2EE Server, choose the first entry, **Local Server**.[3]

In the next step, select **EmployeeRegister** from the list of all locally deployed Web services and click on **Next**. Since you don't need to make any changes to the package mappings, which are then displayed, you can complete the import of the employee Web service model by clicking on **Finish**.

The system now automatically generates several files required for describing the employee Web service client and the corresponding model.[4] The new employee model is represented by an appropriate symbol in the Data Modeler, as shown in Figure 7.3.

Figure 7.3 Data Modeler Display of the Employee Web Service Model Added to the Web Dynpro Component

---

3 Alternatively, you can address the WSDL description of the employee Web service via the URL *http://localhost:50000/EmployeeRegister/Config1?wsdl*.
4 The generated proxy files and various WSDL descriptions can be seen as the technical infrastructure required for communicating with the Web service. The data model on which the employee Web service is based (that is, the Web service model) is visible to the application development.

Initially, the Web service model is available only in the form of a description based on the Web Dynpro metamodel, which is perfectly adequate for the declarative development. The different model classes are created by the Web Dynpro tools in a separate *build* step before being packed into the project archive (EAR file) for deployment (see Figure 7.4).

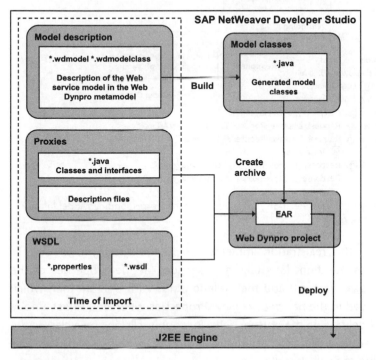

Figure 7.4 Model Import and the Components, Build Process, and Deployment Involved

Generated Model Classes and Their Relationships

After you have imported the model, the classes displayed in the model and their relationships with one another are displayed in the Web Dynpro Explorer. Our example model **EmployeeWSModel** contains a total of five model classes, some of which have individual relations (see Figure 7.5). Note the two different symbols for model classes. The circles positioned slightly to the right with lines on the left side represent *executable model classes*. We will later be able to trigger the actual Web service calls for objects of the type of an executable model class. In our example, these are the classes `Request_EmployeeRegisterVIDocument_get AllEmployees` for obtaining all registered employees as well as `Request_EmployeeRegisterVIDocument_registerEmployee` for registering a new employee.

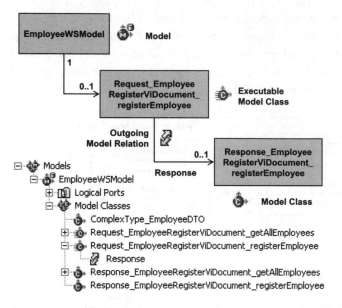

Figure 7.5 Model Class Relationships—Display of the Corresponding Model in the Web Dynpro Explorer

So how is this registration implemented in the employee model? To answer this question, let's take a closer look at the properties of the model classes involved and their relationships with one another, which are displayed in the perspective view **Properties** when you select a node in the model tree on the bottom right. By double-clicking on a class in the model tree, you can also see additional details for this model class. The executable model class `Request_EmployeeRegister-VIDocument_ registerEmployee` contains three *model properties* called *department*, *firstname*, and *lastname*, which are of the type `string`. At runtime, these properties will contain the entered form data. The executable model class is associated with the so-called *Response* from the Web service via the relationship. The exact technical name is actually somewhat longer, but that is no cause for concern here. Due to the property *targetCardinality=0..1*, the response consists of no more than one object from the class `Response_EmployeeRegisterVIDocument_registerEmployee`.

This model class has only one property *Result* of the type `long`. In this property, the Web service stores the ID of the entered data record when a new employee is registered.

The Web service for obtaining all registered employees can be called using the second executable model class `Request_EmployeeRegister VIDocument_getAllEmployees`. The related class `Response_`

`EmployeeRegisterVIDocument_getAllEmployees` also associates
the class `ComplexType_EmployeeDTO` as a representation of a registered employee (the model properties are *ID*, *department*, *firstname*, and
lastname). The corresponding relation *Result* is of the type 0..n, since several employees could already be registered.

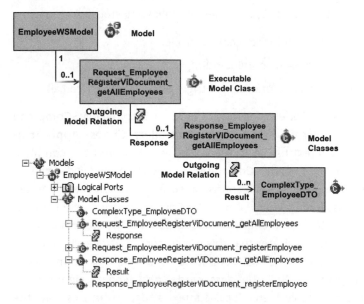

Figure 7.6 Model for Obtaining All Registered Employees

Now that we have examined the structure of the imported Web service
model more closely, we can define the binding of a suitable context structure to the model (*model binding*) in our next step.

7.1.2 Binding a Custom Controller to the Model

We recommend that you have a separate custom controller carry out the
communication with the employee Web service, even though this could
also be done by the component controller.[5] Via its service methods, this
custom controller can make its services (registering an employee,
requesting all registered employees) available externally. The connection
to the model view and the Web service calls are thus encapsulated in the
custom controller. The employee data in the context of the custom con-

---

5 View controllers can also communicate with the employee Web service directly,
   but as a result of this direct access to the business logic, there would no longer be
   any separation of different aspects (view control and user interaction, as well as the
   connection to the model layer) in the various controllers (view and custom controllers).

troller is later accessed via context mapping. For this purpose, you must now bind the custom context to the imported Web service model.

In the Web Dynpro tools, a custom controller with model binding and service methods for triggering Web service calls is also referred to as a *service controller*. The Data Modeler provides a special wizard for creating such service controllers. It incorporates the following steps:

▶ Adding a new custom (or service) controller

▶ Defining the context-to-model binding

▶ Adding a public service method for triggering a Web service call

Switch to the Data Modeler for the component **EmployeeWSComp** and place the cursor over the area **Custom Controllers**. Choose **Apply Template** from the context menu. In the wizard window, you can complete the first step with the **Service Controller** icon by choosing **Next**. The two executable model classes are then displayed in the EmployeeWSModel. Select the class ending with _registerEmployee and, in the upper input field, enter the name **EmployeeModelCust** for the custom controller. The ending **Cust** indicates that this is a custom controller. In our next step, we can define the actual context-to-model binding. Context-to-model binding means that the class model displayed in Figure 7.7 is mapped onto a suitable hierarchical context structure. In this way, the data model contained in the model is transferred to the context and is therefore available for further use in the Web Dynpro component (for example, context mapping followed by data binding). This step is predominantly automatic; we only need to specify which levels or elements should be included in the model binding. Check all checkboxes in the context hierarchy, as displayed in Figure 7.7, and then click on **Next**.

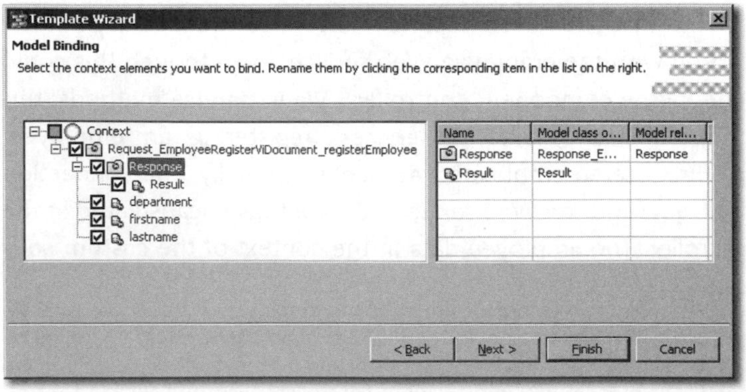

Figure 7.7 Selection of Context Elements for the Model Binding

Before we continue with the next step, we'll take a closer look at how the context structure created by the model binding began. Let's consider Figure 7.8. First, an identically-named, independent context model node is created for the executable model class `Request_EmployeeRegister VIDocument_registerEmployee`.[6] All properties defined in this class (*department, firstname*, and *lastname*) are added to this model node as model attributes. The cardinality of the node is 0..1, which means that at runtime, this node can contain no more than one node element pointing to an instance of the executable model class.

Context-to-Model Binding

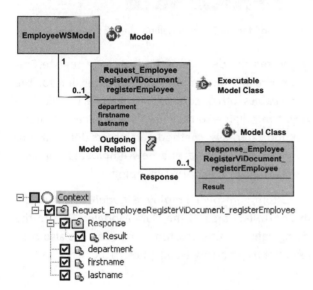

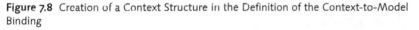

Figure 7.8 Creation of a Context Structure in the Definition of the Context-to-Model Binding

Now we turn our attention to the handling of model relationships for context-to-model binding. Exactly one 0..1 relation **Response** exists between the executable model class and the class `Response_ EmployeeRegisterViDocument_registerEmployee`. For this relationship, a new, dependent, and identically named child node is added to the context. The cardinality of this model node corresponds to the target cardinality of the underlying relationship in the model, that is, 0..1. In our case, the Web service returns a single model object with the property *Result* following a successful registration. Correspondingly, the dependent model node **Response** contains the model attribute *Result*.

---

6 Context nodes at the uppermost level—nodes that are directly below the root node—are described as independent. All lower-level nodes are dependent, since their contents usually depend on a node element in the parent node.

Service Method   In the last step of the service controller wizard, we add a public method to the controller, with which other controllers can trigger the calling of the registration Web service from the outside (see Figure 7.9).

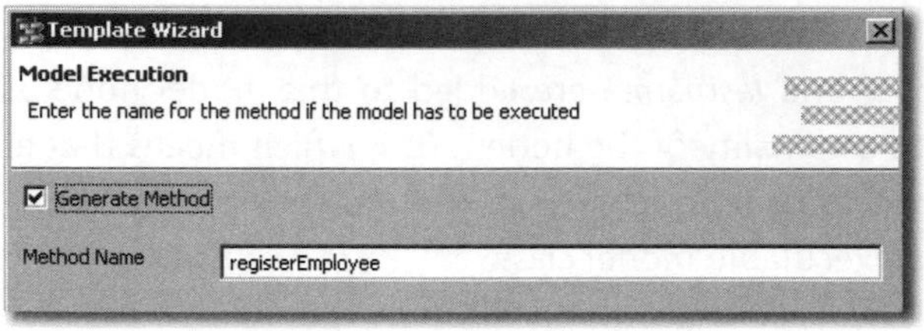

Figure 7.9 Adding a Public Method for the External Calling of a Web Service

For better readability, shorten the default method name to **registerEmployee** and then click on **Finish**. This simple interface extension for the new custom controller enables other controllers that use this custom controller—such as view controllers—to trigger a Web service call implemented by the new method externally. Method parameters don't have to be passed, since the data exchange (data of a new employee) between the controller contexts takes place via context mapping.

New Custom Controller   After adding the new custom controller **EmployeeModelCust**, it is displayed in the **Custom Controllers** area of the Data Modeler. Due to the context-to-model binding defined in this custom controller, it is also connected to the model symbol by an arrow (see Figure 7.10).

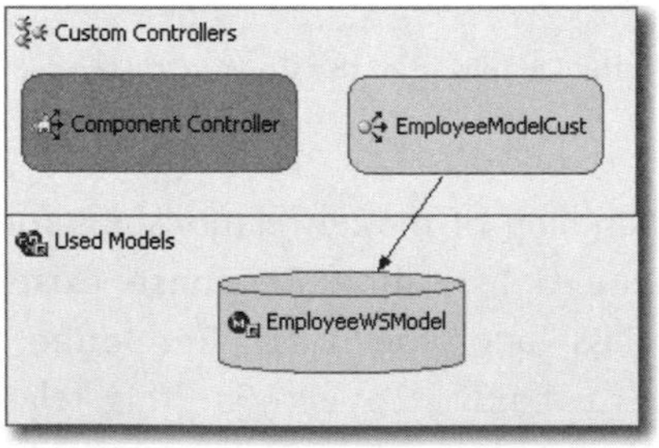

Figure 7.10 New Custom Controller in the Data Modeler

An entry is also inserted under the **Custom Controllers** node in the Web Dynpro Explorer (see Figure 7.11).

Note the structure of the context created after successful context-to-model binding. Its display in the context perspective (see Figure 7.12) corresponds to that in Figure 7.8. The used model is displayed on the right in the form of a hierarchy.

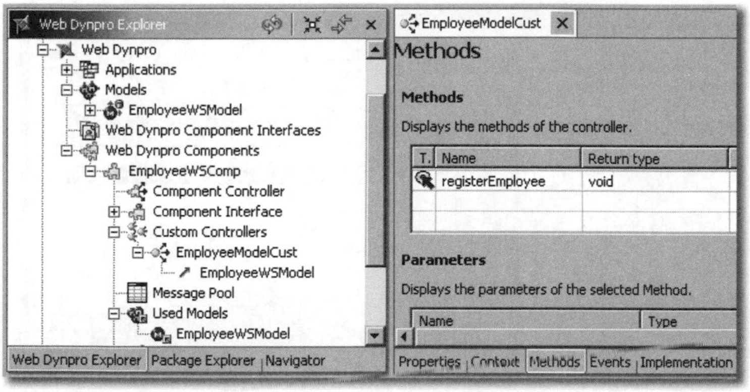

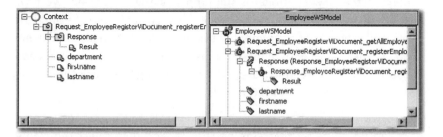

Figure 7.11 Added Custom Controller EmployeeModelCust in the Web Dynpro Explorer and the registerEmployee Method

Figure 7.12 Context Structure in the Context of the EmployeeModelCust Controller After Defining the Context-to-Model Binding

7.1.3 Defining the Context Mappings

In the next step, we'll use *context mapping* to enable access to the original context stored in the custom controller **EmployeeModelCust** from within the view controller. This means that the custom context bound to the employee model will be referenced from the view controller context, so that the context data can then be transported to the view layout (containing the form for employee registration) and back via data binding.

Context Mapping

The context mapping from the view context to the custom context in the Data Modeler can be easily implemented by defining a *data link*. To do so, open the Data Modeler for the component **EmployeeWSComp** and, in the toolbar on the left, choose the arrow icon for adding a data link. You then drag an arrow (data link) from the symbol for the view **Employee-View** to the custom controller **EmployeeModelCust**, after which you release the mouse button. Then, a window for defining the context mapping opens (see Figure 7.13).

Data Link

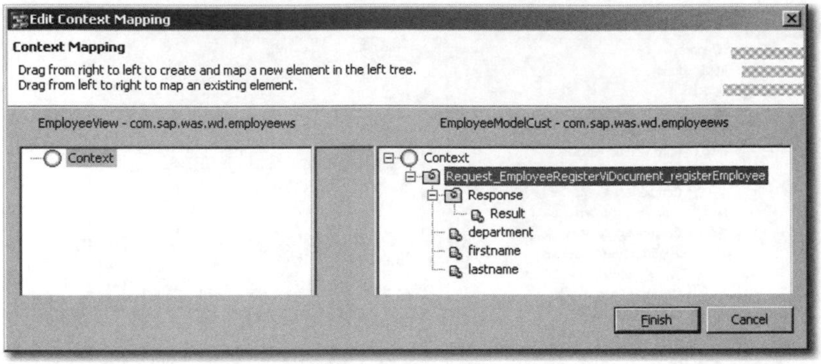

Figure 7.13 Definition of the Context Mapping

The original context in the custom controller is displayed on the right; the context in the view controller is still empty. Via Drag & Drop, we now move the symbol of the top model node in the custom context from right to left and drop it over the symbol of the root node (**Context**) in the view context. Then, a second window opens, similar to the one we already encountered for the context-to-model binding. Again, check the checkboxes of all context elements on the left.

Renaming a Mapped Node

Before we complete this step, we will rename the uppermost model node. To do so, select the node on the left and then select the **Name** entry in the first line on the right. You can now change the name of the model node to **RequestNewEmployee**. This step does not affect the name of the original node in the custom context. After you have clicked on **OK**, the wizard displays the context mapping, as shown in Figure 7.14.

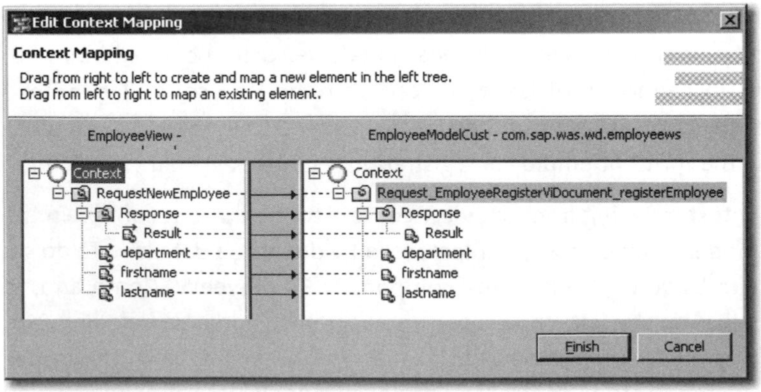

Figure 7.14 Context Mapping from the View Context to the Custom Context

Note the arrows displayed over the mapped context elements in the view context. The mapping direction is defined as the link from the view context to the original context in the custom controller. The mapping arrow also symbolizes that the mapped context elements reference the relevant elements in the original context. Figure 7.14 shows the different names of the two independent model nodes.

After **Finish** is clicked, the new data link (symbolizing the defined context mapping) between the view **EmployeeView** and the custom controller **EmployeeModelCust** is displayed as an arrow in the Data Modeler.

7.1.4 View Layout and Data Binding

Defining the context mapping enables us to make the employee data defined in the context of the view **EmployeeView** editable in the view layout via a corresponding form. In the context, the **RequestNewEmployee** node contains the three model attributes *department*, *firstname*, and *lastname*. The return value of the Web service is contained in the model attribute *Result* for the dependent node **Response**. It is displayed in a message text on the view interface using a **MessageArea** UI element.

Data Binding

You can simply add the input form for employee registration and define the data binding using the *form template of the* Web Dynpro tools. First, open the layout window of the view **EmployeeView** and select the UI element **RegistrationFormContainer[Transparent Container – Child]** in the **Outline** area. Then, choose the context menu entry **Apply Template** to add the new input form to the container UI element. In the wizard window, select the **Form icon**, choose **Next**, and check the context elements *RequestNewEmployee, lastname, firstname,* and *department*. Don't select the **Response** node or the *Result* attribute. In the next step, you can use the arrow buttons to change the order of the fields, or leave the fields as they are and exit the wizard by clicking on **Finish**. The added input form is now displayed in the view layout. The positioning of the fields, the adding of text to the labels, the binding of the *value* attributes to the individual context attributes—all these actions were automatically carried out by the form template. All we have to do is change the labels from the context attribute names to the correct texts, that is, *Last name, First name,* and *Department*.

Form Template

Now, let's take another look at the definition of the data transport between the view layout, view controller context, custom controller context, and model at design time (see Figure 7.15).

Data Transport

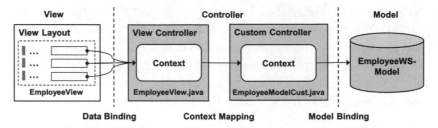

View	Controller	Model
Data Binding	Context Mapping	Model Binding

Figure 7.15 Definition of the Data Transport

After entering the employee data in the **EmployeeView** form, it's transported to the context of the corresponding view controller via data binding. Its context elements point to elements in the custom controller's context via context mapping. The context data is not transported, but saved only once in the original context (in this case, the custom context). The context mapping merely defines a reference to the custom context in the view context. The custom context is now connected to the Web service model via model binding. At runtime, the form data is transported from the context to the model and from here via the Web service client to the actual Web service, which then enables access to the persistence layer.

Binding an Action

We can now enter the registration data for a new employee in the view layout, but we cannot send it. For this, an action is required in the view controller, to which the onAction event of a button is bound (*action binding*). A wizard is also available for this declaration step. First, open the tab for the layout of the view **EmployeeView** and select the UI element **ButtonContainer[Transparent Container – Child]** in the outline area. Choose **Apply Template** from the context menu and then click on the **ActionButton icon**. You use the wizard to add a button that is bound to an action.[7] You can also define which method of a different controller should be called in the event handler of the action. In this example, it is the public method registerEmployee() of the custom controller **EmployeeModelCust** that should be called to trigger the Web service call. The wizard therefore enables us to carry out some of the required implementation in advance.

In the first step, select the action Register and the corresponding event handler onActionRegister from the list. Enter the text "Register" in the field **Button Label**. In the second step, we can specify the method of a controller to be called in the event handler of the action. Here, this is

---

7 In the project template, the action Register is already defined. You could also define it in the ActionButton wizard.

the method `registerEmployee` of the custom controller **Employee-ModelCust** after checking the **Call Method** checkbox. To exit the wizard, click on **Finish**. Finally, in the outline area, move the button UI element **Register[Button – Child]** into the container **ButtonContainer** via Drag& Drop.

7.1.5 Implementing Controllers

With these declarations in mind, we now ask ourselves which code lines we, as programmers, must still add to the custom code. The answer is none. However, that doesn't mean that no application code is required in the example application. In fact, this code was automatically inserted by the wizards at the relevant controller positions and it is these controllers that we will now discuss.

The model binding—the definition of a context structure according to the classes and relations contained in the model—occurs at design time, initially only at the metadata level. Examples of metadata are the context hierarchy itself (that is, the contained nodes and attributes according to the model classes and their relations to one another), the cardinalities of the context node, and the model classes belonging to the nodes,[8] as well as the so-called *supplying relation roles*.[9] At runtime, we should think of a model as a graph of model objects—a multitude of object instances for different business data—that can be interrelated. However, the model binding at design time does not yet include the direct connection of the context to the model at object level. We must at least ensure that the top context node—the model node **Request-NewEmployee in this case**—contains a node element pointing to an executable model object of the type `Request_EmployeeRegisterViDocument_register-Employee`. In other words, we must first instantiate such a model object and then *bind* it to the top model object. This is precisely the code that the wizard already inserted into the method `wdDoInit()` for the model binding (see Listing 7.1).

Binding an Executable Model Object to the Context

```
public void wdDoInit() {
    //@@begin wdDoInit()
    //$$begin Service Controller(-1718485108)
```

---

8 Depending on its cardinality, a node then contains object instances of this model class at runtime.

9 A *supplying relation role* specifies the relation between two model classes that is required for ascertaining object instances in the model object graph at runtime. The ascertaining of object instances is executed automatically by the Web Dynpro runtime environment and results in an update of the controller context.

```
wdContext.
        nodeRequest_EmployeeRegisterViDocument_
        registerEmployee().bind(
            new Request_EmployeeRegisterViDocument_
                registerEmployee());
    //$$end
    //@@end
}
```

Listing 7.1 Initialization of the Custom Controller EmployeeModelCust.java

At runtime, the top model node in the context of the custom controller **EmployeeModelCust** points to an executable model object for registering an employee. The form data entered on the view interface is then transferred directly to the executable model object instance at runtime via data binding and context mapping

If you look at the custom controller code, you'll notice that class compiling still fails due to missing import lines. Therefore, we automatically add these lines of code by choosing the context menu entry **Source · Organize Imports**.

How does the actual Web service call take place? When creating the custom controller, we added a public method `registerEmployee()` to its interface for this purpose; the interface was also automatically implemented by the model-binding wizard. We trigger the Web service call for the employee registration by calling the `execute()` method for the executable model object. We can access this object instance in the context via the node element that we just selected in the top model node. The currently selected node element is obtained using `wdContext.current<Name of Node>()` and the model object is accessed by adding `.modelObject()` (see Listing 7.2).

```
public void registerEmployee() {
    //@@begin registerEmployee()
    //$$begin Service Controller(2000151733)
```

```
    IWDMessageManager manager =
        wdComponentAPI.getMessageManager();
```

```
    try {
        wdContext.
```

```
            currentRequest_EmployeeRegisterViDocument_
                registerEmployeeElement()
```

```
        .modelObject().execute();
      wdContext.nodeResponse().invalidate();
    } catch (Exception ce) {
      manager.reportException(ce.getMessage(), false);
    }
    //$$end
    //@@end
}
```

Listing 7.2 Registration of an Employee by Executing the Web Service

So what is the significance of the code line after the execution of the model object wdContext.nodeResponse().invalidate(), that is, the invalidation of the response node? Before we can answer this, we need to know that the executable model object is not stored in the context, but in the model itself. After the Web service has been called, the object of the type Response_EmployeeRegisterViDocument_registerEmployee returned by the Web service is stored in the model. Initially, the context points to only the executable model object (see code in wdDoInit()) and is itself unaware of the new response object in the model. Therefore, we must *invalidate* the response node in the application code and declare its contents or any model objects to which it points as invalid. If such invalid context contents are then accessed on the user interface (via data binding), or in the application code (in our case, when the Web service response is displayed),[10] the Web Dynpro runtime environment validates the context. Here, *validation* refers to the binding of the object instances that are currently stored in the model to the context. The context contents are therefore updated, with regard to the current model status. The Web Dynpro runtime environment executes this data alignment automatically by processing the supplying relation roles contained in the context metadata.

Invalidating the Response Node

The Web service is called within a try-catch block. If an error occurs, the error message that is returned by the Web service is displayed on the interface by the Web Dynpro Message Manager.

The third location, where the wizards have already added application code, is the event handler onActionRegister for the Register action, with which the user sends the form data. At this point, we know that we must call the public method registerEmployee() of the custom controller **EmployeeModelCust** to execute the Web service call. So

Action Event Handling

---

10 Model attribute *Result* in the model node *Response*

how do we access the Application Programming Interface (API) of the custom controller in the view controller implementation?

Defining a Controller Use According to the principle of *information hiding*, all generally usable controllers are hidden from all other controllers by default. If, in a controller (in our case, in the controller of the view **EmployeeView**), you want to use the API of another controller or define a mapping to its context, you must define a corresponding controller usage. Due to the previously defined context mapping from the view context to the custom context, the use of the custom controller **EmployeeModelCust** was already added to the view controller **EmployeeView**.

Controller API: IPrivateEmployee View and wdThis How do we then access the API of the used custom controller in the action event handler? To answer this question, let's take a closer look at the controller class `EmployeeView.java`, which contains the *user coding areas* for our own application code. Here, we find the *hook methods* `wdDoInit()` and `wdDoExit()` used by the Web Dynpro runtime for initialization when creating the controller and for cleanup before destroying the controller. The hook method `wdDoModifyView()` is used for the dynamic modification of the view layout, the action event handlers, and the other defined methods. Lastly, we can add code, such as private instance variables or methods. All these areas contain our own application code. However, this class does not contain the entire controller implementation. The class `InternalEmployeeView.java` represents another, fully automatically generated part of the complete controller implementation. After all, where else could the controller context and the action objects be stored, for example, or where else could the interfaces of other used controllers be accessible? We don't need to trouble ourselves with the details of this controller class, since we will never insert any code into it. However, what we do need to understand is that the interface `IPrivateEmployeeView` enables us to access all the important parts of the complete controller implementation. The variable wdThis, which every Web Dynpro controller has, is precisely of this type `IPrivateEmployeeView`. This interface is automatically generated by the development environment and adapted to reflect the definitions made by the application developer. This means that the view controller API `IPrivateEmployeeView` is extended automatically when we define the view context or add actions, outbound plugs, methods, and particularly new controller usages. We'll discuss the API concept for Web Dynpro controllers in more detail in the next section.

The `IPrivate<Controller>` interface also enables us to access the interfaces of all used controllers, in our case, via the generated method

wdGetEmployeeModelCustController(). This method returns the
IPublic API of the used custom controller, which contains the regis-
terEmployee() method for registering an employee. This results in the
following code in the action event handler (see Listing 7.3).

**Calling a Public
Method Using the
IPublic API**

```
public void onActionRegister(
    com.sap.tc.webdynpro.progmodel.api.IWDCustomEvent
        wdEvent ){
    //@@begin onActionRegister(ServerEvent)
    //$$begin ActionButton(-277955917)
    wdThis.wdGetEmployeeModelCustController()
        .registerEmployee();
    //$$end
    //@@end
}
```

Listing 7.3 Event Handler of the Register Action in the Controller EmployeeView.java

Finally, we will now manually add some code to the custom controller. So
far, what's missing is the output of the result value returned by the Web
service. When an employee is successfully registered, the Web service
returns the ID of the entered employee data record to the caller. This
value of the type long is stored in the *Result* attribute of the context
node **Response** (see Listing 7.4).

**Displaying the
Web Service
Result**

```
public void registerEmployee() {
    //@@begin registerEmployee()
    ...
    try {
        ...
        wdContext.nodeResponse().invalidate();
        String id = String.valueOf(wdContext
            .currentResponseElement().getResult());
        String firstName = wdContext.currentRequest_
            EmployeeRegisterViDocument_
            registerEmployeeElement().getFirstname();
        String lastName = wdContext.currentRequest_
            EmployeeRegisterViDocument_
            registerEmployeeElement().getLastname();
        manager.reportMessage(
            IMessageEmployeeWSComp.SUCCESS,
            new Object[] { firstName, lastName, id },
```

**Displaying
Messages with
the Message
Manager**

**Accessing the
Web Service
Result in the
Context**

```
             false);
    } catch (Exception ce) {
        manager.reportException(ce.getMessage(), false);
    }
    ...
    //@@end
}
```

Listing 7.4 Output of Employee ID After Successful Web Service Call

A message text, for example: "The employee John Smith was successfully registered. The Web service returned the ID 1234567890," was defined in the message editor beforehand and can thus be passed to the Message Manager in the code using `IMessageEmployeeWSComp.SUCCESS`, along with the three placeholder values `firstName`, `lastName`, and `id`. This text is displayed automatically on the user interface, without the need to add a corresponding UI element.

We then insert the missing code line `import com.sap.was.wd.emp-lyeews.wdp.IMessageEmployeeWDComp` via the context menu entry **Source · Organize Imports**.

Building, Deploying, and Starting the Application

To start the Web service application, we open the path **WebDynpro_EmployeeWS_Init · Applications · EmployeeWSApp** in the Web Dynpro Explorer and then choose the context menu entry **Deploy new Archive and Run**. After creating the Web Dynpro EAR file (*Enterprise Archives*) and deploying it on the SAP J2EE Engine, the example application is opened in the Web browser. Once you have entered a first name, last name, and department and pressed the **Register button,** the employee registration is stored in the local database via a Web service call. In addition, a corresponding success message is displayed on the interface.

> **Exercise: Displaying the Employee Table**
>
> As an exercise, you can now extend the example application by adding the display of all registered employees in a table. For this purpose, the project template already contains the second view **EmployeesTable-View**, including an empty `Table` UI element. In the model, the employee data can be requested from the Web service using the executable model class:

```
RequestEmployee_EmployeeRegisterViDocument_
  getAllEmployees
```

1. Open the Data Modeler, select the custom controller Employee-ModelCust, and start the service controller wizard by choosing the context menu entry Apply Template. Define the model binding between the context and the second executable model class (with the ending _getAllEmployees). Change the name of the Response node to ResponseAll (see Section 7.1.3).[11] In addition, check the checkbox before the model node Result on the left.

2. Click on **Next** and add the new public method `getAllEmployees` in the controller interface. Then, click on **Finish**.

3. To define the context mapping, drag a data link from the view EmployeesTableView to the custom controller EmployeeModel-Cust. Then, in the wizard window, drag the second model node with the ending _getAllEmployees over the root node in the view context and select all context elements.

4. Switch to the layout of the view EmployeesTableView and select the UI element EmployeesTable [Table – Child]. Choose the context menu entry Create Binding and then select the context node Result. All attributes in the model node Result are inserted as columns into the table.

5. The Web service call for requesting all registered employees must be executed whenever the user navigates to the view EmployeesTable-View. To ensure this behavior, implement the following code line in the inbound plug event handler:

```
public void onPlugDisplayAllIn(
  com.sap.tc.webdynpro.progmodel.api.IWDCustomEvent
  wdEvent ) {
  //@@begin onPlugDisplayAllIn(ServerEvent)
  wdThis.wdGetEmployeeModelCustController()
    .getAllEmployees();
  //@@end
}
```

---

11 The renaming is necessary, because all nodes of a context must have different names. In the example application, the node name *Response* was already used for the first model binding.

6. Now build, deploy, and start the application EmployeeWSApp. Press the Display All button on the user interface to display all registered employees in the added table.

The solution to the exercise is available on the book DVD in the completed example project **WebDynpro_EmployeeWS_Final**.

In the example project **WebDynpro_EmployeeWS_Final+**, methods are implemented for resetting the input form with a non-validating action and for checking empty input fields before saving the employee data.

7.2 Web Dynpro Controllers and Their Interfaces

After the practical application examples in the previous section, we now turn to the basic principles of the Web Dynpro controller concept. We will start by looking at the general Model View Controller (MVC) model, which is consistently used by Web Dynpro. Then, we'll move on to the Web Dynpro controller architecture and, in so doing, familiarize ourselves with the underlying layer model, which consists of the different controller types as well as the corresponding generated and generic controller interfaces.

7.2.1 Model View Controller Model

MVC Model in Web Dynpro

Web Dynpro complies with the central *Model View Controller model* (subsequently referred to as the *MVC model*) for the architecture of Web applications. One important aspect of this MVC model is the *separation of concerns* in different parts of a Web Dynpro application. So, how is this separation implemented in Web Dynpro, according to the three aspects *Model* (business logic), *View* (user interface), and *Controller* (presentation and application logic)? If we look at the internal structure of a Web Dynpro project, we see that the separation takes place on several levels. At the top level, *applications* display the parts of a Web Dynpro project that are visible and can be addressed in the browser (*View* aspect). Imported models are also contained (*Model* aspect). An important Web Dynpro entity is the *Web Dynpro component*. Each component contains at least one controller and it can—but does not have to—combine the other two aspects of the MVC model within itself. Therefore, there are components that don't use a model and other components that don't contain any visual elements, such as windows, component interface views, or views.

Typical examples of these are non-displayable (*faceless*) model components, which encapsulate the connection to the business logic as Web Dynpro components and are used by other components, which are usually visible.

Another separation according to the MVC model takes place on the lower component level. The model connection is implemented via a usage relationship as well as the definition of a model binding between the custom or component context and model classes. The *controller* aspect is covered by different controller types. These include the component controller, which always exists, optional custom controllers, and the view controllers belonging to the views. We will discuss these controller types in more detail in the next section. The *View* aspect of the MVC model is covered by components. Within windows, the components combine several views into a user interface that can be displayed in a browser window. The windows of a component can be used by other components as component interface views for the modular design of user interfaces.

Finally, the MVC model is also implemented on the lowest level, that is, the level of Web Dynpro views. A view consists of a user interface implemented by the view layout as well as the *view controller*, which is responsible for the user interaction, data transfer, and navigation control. You connect to the model layer by defining the context mapping to a custom context bound to the model.

In Figure 7.16, the Web Dynpro entities mentioned above are assigned to the three aspects of the MVC model.

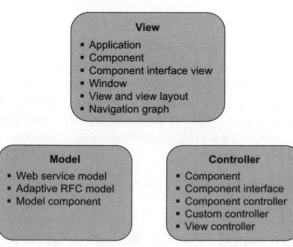

Figure 7.16 Web Dynpro Entities in the MVC Model

7.2.2 Controller Concept

Web Dynpro features its own controller concept, which enables a logically structured separation of the entire controller layer into several controllers. In the MVC model, controllers represent the intermediate layer between user interface (*View*) and the business logic (*Model*). All controllers reside in a Web Dynpro component and there are three different types—*custom*, *component*, and *view* controllers.

For the development of Web Dynpro applications, a precise knowledge of these three controller types and their relevant controller APIs is of central importance. They represent a pillar of the Web Dynpro programming model. In this section, we'll examine the classes of these controllers, the corresponding controller APIs, which grow along with the controllers, and the generic controller interfaces provided by Web Dynpro.

Controller Types · We'll begin by examining the differences between the three controller types, bearing in mind that that the first two types are closely related:

Non-View Controllers · ▶ **Component Controller**
By default, each Web Dynpro component has a component controller, which is automatically created and deleted by the Web Dynpro runtime system when required. The component controller acts as the central controller instance within the entire component. Data required across different views can be stored in its context. It can also form the intermediate layer between models and views, without having to take on the tasks necessary for data display.

A component controller can be accessed by all other controllers (view and custom controllers) within a component via its IPublic interface.

▶ **Custom Controller**
Custom controllers are optional controllers, which the application developer can add to a component as additional controller instances. They can be used to encapsulate different controller tasks—such as configuration, model connection, or functions that can be used across controllers—and thus promote the *separation of concerns* principle. The context of a custom controller is available to all other controllers of a component as additional data storage.

The other controllers of a component can access the custom controller via its IPublic interface.

View Controllers · ▶ **View Controller**
With their *view layout* (or *view,* for short), view controllers are the only controllers to have their own visual interface. As well as making the

user interface available, their task is to display data in the view, receive any user input made there, and respond to user actions.

Via data binding, the context of a view controller provides a view with all the required data. The business data displayed in the view is usually made available to the view context via context mapping onto a custom or controller context. This limits model layer access to the use of contexts and IPublic APIs of higher-level controllers.

The lifetime of view controllers can be defined with the two values framework_controlled and when_visible.[12] With the former, a view controller instance can exist for several navigation steps, without the corresponding view having to be visible in each step. In this case, the lifetime is longer than it is for the when_visible setting, for which a view controller is always deleted as soon as the corresponding view is no longer displayed on the user interface. The value when_visible should be used to reduce the memory requirements whenever a view is displayed on the user interface only once and not repeatedly. Typically, the lifetime of a view controller should be defined with the value framework_controlled.

Lifetime of View Controller

View controllers don't have a public interface and therefore aren't visible to any other controllers (view and non-view controllers, such as component controllers and custom controllers).

No IPublic API for View Controllers

IPrivate and IPublic APIs

When examining the controller code of our Web service example application (see Section 7.1.5), we already encountered the internal controller class containing the portion of the controller implementation that is generated fully automatically. The Web Dynpro runtime actually uses only this controller, which itself delegates to our controller containing the application code when necessary.

Internal Controller, IPrivate API, and wdThis

What is important for us to know is that the internal controller provides us with an API, with which we can use all the controller functions relevant to the application development, including those parts not implemented by ourselves. The interface generally referred to here as the IPrivate API[13] is accessed using the instance variable wdThis, which every instance variable contains. Figure 7.17 illustrates this concept.

---

12 In the **Properties** tab for a view, you can assign the **Lifespan** property to one of the two values when_visible or framework_controlled.
13 The exact name for this interface is made up of the prefix *IPrivate* and the name of the controller, for example, IPrivateEmployeeView.java for a view controller called EmployeeView.java.

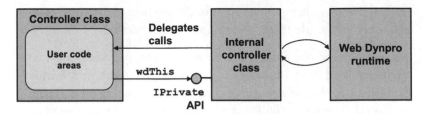

Figure 7.17 Controller Concept

While the `IPrivate` API represents the interface with a controller's functions within that controller, `IPublic` represents the interface for external users. This API is also generated automatically and contains the context API,[14] the public methods, and an access to the generic controller API, which we will address later. Other controllers can access the `IPublic` API of a controller only after its function has been defined.[15]

Because, in the Web Dynpro programming model, view controllers only act as consumers of higher-level controllers such as component or custom controllers, but don't provide them with any of their own functions, they don't have a corresponding `IPublic` API. Therefore, view controllers can't be used by other controllers and are therefore not visible to them.

The following table lists the characteristics of the controller interfaces `IPublic` and `IPrivate` for the different controller types. For non-view controllers, the `IPrivate` API extends the `IPublic` API, which causes the characteristics in the first column to apply to the second column as well.

Controller	IPublic API	IPrivate API
Component	Public methods, access to the context root node, context API, access to the IWDComponent API	Triggering of events, access to the API of used controllers

Table 7.1 Generated Controller APIs for Different Controller Types

---

14 The context interfaces of a controller that are generated for defining a context structure and contained in the `IPrivate` API are described as the *typed context API*. These interfaces specify the types of the nodes and node elements contained in the context. Furthermore, typed mutator methods (get and set methods) are generated for contained context attributes. More information is available in Section 7.3.2.

15 This is carried out in the **Required Controllers** area on the **Properties** tab.

Controller	IPublic API	IPrivate API
Custom	Public methods, access to the context root node, context API, access to the IWDController API	Triggering of events, access to the API of used controllers
View		Access to the API of used controllers, access to the context root node, context API, access to action objects, triggering of outbound plugs, event handlers for innbound plugs and actions, access to the IWDViewController API

Table 7.1 Generated Controller APIs for Different Controller Types (cont.)

Exercise: IPrivate and IPublic APIs in the Example Application

Look at the generated IPrivate API of the view controller **Employee-View.java** and the custom controller **EmployeeModelCust.java** in the example application. To do so, open the Navigator perspective next to the Web Dynpro Explorer and open the node **gen_wdp/packages/com/sap/was/wd/employeews/wdp**. It contains all the generated interfaces and the internal controller implementations.

▶ Open an IPrivate interface in the **Outline** view and examine its contents. Which methods do the interfaces contain? Compare it with the code completion after entering the shortcut variable wdThis in the controller implementation.

▶ Open the IPublic API of the custom controller **IPublicEmployeeModelCust.java**. It contains our defined public methods getAllEmployees() and registerEmployee().

▶ Which different controller interfaces does the wdGetAPI() method return in the interfaces IPrivateEmployeeView.java, IPublic EmployeeModelCust.java, and IPublicEmployeeWSComp.java?

▶ Display the type hierarchy for an IPublic API. To do so, select an IPublic API in the Navigator and then choose the context menu entry **Open Type Hierarchy** to see the layering of the IPublic API, IPrivate API, and the controller implementation.

Web Dynpro Controller Call—The Hook Methods

The Web Dynpro runtime automatically calls the *hook methods of a controller* class at specific times to process the application code they contain. To be more precise, the internal controller implementation delegates these methods to the controller that implements the application code. By default, each controller has two methods that are called at the beginning and at the end of a controller lifecycle:

Standard Hook Methods

▶ wdDoInit(): Called automatically by the Web Dynpro runtime after the creation of a controller. The call occurs only once.

▶ wdDoExit(): Called automatically by the Web Dynpro runtime shortly before the destruction of the controller instance. This hook method can be used, for example, to save data that would otherwise be lost when the controller lifecycle ends.

Component Hook Methods

Component controllers (but not custom controllers) also have two additional hook methods, which are called at specific times in a request response cycle:

▶ wdDoBeforeNavigation(): Called by the Web Dynpro runtime before each processing of the navigation destinations[16] collected so far. Only after this call does the Web Dynpro runtime assemble all the views visible on the user interface (the new *view assembly*), initialize the view controller instances not yet created, and then process the inbound plug event handlers specified by the navigation destinations. The method enables the application developer, for example, to conduct extensive checks of the context data beyond controller and component boundaries before the navigation takes place.

▶ wdDoPostProcessing(): Called automatically by the Web Dynpro runtime shortly before the rendering of the view layout, but after the handling of all events and navigation targets. At this time, the Web Dynpro runtime has also completed filling the controller contexts;[17] therefore, the contexts already contain the data displayed in the view and are *valid*. The method is primarily intended for handling errors that occur during the filling of controller contexts.

---

16 Navigation destinations are the inbound plugs of views to which the navigation links point. For every navigation transition, the Web Dynpro runtime calls or processes the relevant inbound plug event handlers.

17 The mechanisms for filling contexts via supply functions or calculated context attributes are discussed in more detail in the Section 7.3.3.

7.2.3   Generated and Generic Controller APIs

The controller interfaces automatically generated by the Web Dynpro development environment, IPrivate and IPublic, adapt to the declarations made by the developer. Therefore, they *evolve in parallel* and are specific to the individual controllers of an application. However, these *generated controller APIs* don't comprise all the controller functions that can be used at runtime, but only those relevant to the definitions made by application developers (controller uses, context structures, actions, events, inbound and outbound plugs, and public methods).

Furthermore, Web Dynpro controllers implement one or more *generic* interfaces (predefined by the Web Dynpro programming model), which we can use to access controller-relevant information, elements, and additional generic functions and services within our own application code. All Web Dynpro controllers implement the IWDController API, while component controllers also implement the IWDComponent interface, and view controllers implement IWDViewController.[18]

Generic Controller APIs

▶ **IWDController API**: Controller information, name information, context API, access to the corresponding component controller, access to action objects

▶ **IWComponent API**: IWDController API, component information, dynamic adding and removing of event handlers, corresponding application, Message Manager, validation service, Text Accessor, Window Manager

▶ **IWDViewController API**: IWDController API, firing of plugs, focus control in views, view information

The services provided by the generic controller APIs are especially significant. The IWDComponent API allows you to use the *Message Manager* for displaying messages and handling errors on the user interface, the *Window Manager for* displaying dialog boxes, or the *Text Accessor for* accessing the translated texts of a Web Dynpro project. You can also dynamically add or remove event handlers in a controller at runtime (see Figure 7.18).

Generic Services

---

18   The Javadoc information for these interfaces is available in the NetWeaver help under **SAP NetWeaver Developer Studio Documentation** • SAP Web AS for Java **Applications** • API WAS • Web DynproRuntime • com.sap.tc.webdynpro.prog-model.api.

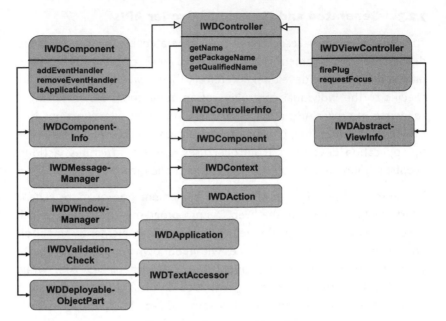

Figure 7.18 Generic Controller APIs and Contained Interfaces

IWD*Info APIs Depending on the controller type, we can obtain the metadata information for a controller instance via the three interfaces `IWDComponent-Info`, `IWDControllerInfo`, and `IWDAbstractViewInfo` in the package `com.sap.tc.webdynpro.progmodel.api`. This includes information about additional entities used by a controller such as event handlers, events, actions, other controllers, or plugs.

7.2.4 Shortcut Variables wdControllerAPI and wdComponentAPI

It's often necessary to use the generic controller APIs in your own controller implementations. The best example of this use of generic controller APIs is the utilization of the *Message Manager* for displaying message texts on the user interface. For instance, how do you access the `IWDMessageManager` API in a view controller? As we can see in Figure 7.18, the `IWDMessageManager` API can be accessed via the generic `IWDComponent` API. If we then look at Figure 7.19, we see that the following path exists from a view controller to the interface `IWDComponentAPI`: View controller – `IPrivate` – `IWDViewController` (implements `IWDController`) – `IWDComponent`. We can follow this path using the following program code:

```
wdThis.wdGetAPI().getComponent();
```

Calling the getMessageManager() method then returns the IWDMessageManager API:

```
IWDMessageManager msgMgr =
  wdThis.wdGetAPI().getComponent().getMessageManger();
```

Shortcut Variables

To enable quicker access to the generic controller APIs in a controller implementation, every controller contains the two *shortcut variables* wdComponentAPI and wdControllerAPI. These special instance variables represent short forms of frequently repeated Java code for accessing generic controller APIs:

```
wdComponentAPI = wdThis.wdGetAPI().getComponent();
wdControllerAPI = wdThis.wdGetAPI();
```

Using the shortcut variable wdComponentAPI simplifies our source code for accessing the Message Managers as follows:

```
IWDMessageManager msgMgr =
  wdComponentAPI.getMessageManger();
```

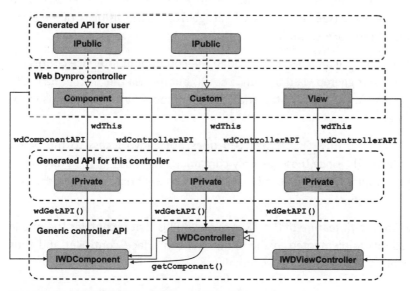

Figure 7.19 Controller APIs and Shortcut Variables

Component Interface (View) Controller

In our examination of the different controllers and their interfaces, we have so far omitted two important controllers, the *component interface controller* and the *component interface view controller*, both of which were already encountered in the previous chapter (see Section 6.6.1).

Component Interface Controller

Every Web Dynpro component has a *component interface controller*. It comes into play when an external user of the component requires an interface with the used component or when a component accesses context data in the user via external mapping. The user of a Web Dynpro component cannot see the internal structure of this component. The contained component and custom controller are completely unknown to the user. The only way of interacting with the component—for example, with method calls, context mapping, or reactions to events—is by using the component interface controller of the used component including its context. This interface controller implements the outer interface of a component.

IExternal API

So, which generated controller APIs exist for this special controller? As with the case of the other non-view controllers, an `IPrivate` API and an `IPublic` API are also generated for this controller. The component interface controller can access the `IPrivate` API via `wdThis`, and all other controllers within the same component can access the `IPublic` API after defining a corresponding use of the controller.[19] An embedding component **E**, on the other hand, can see only the `IExternal` API of a used component **U** (see Figure 7.6), which again limits the visibility of the component interface controller.[20]

For example, if an event is defined in the component interface controller, it can be triggered via the `IPublic` API, but not via the `IExternal` API. However, a controller in the embedding component can register itself for this event.

Furthermore, the `IExternal` API does not allow access to the typed context APIs, since these are only contained in `IPublic`. Therefore, context mapping should be used to access the context data of a used component-controller context.

An important feature of the `IExternal` API is that it contains the public methods implemented in the component interface controller and thus enables them to be called externally.

---

19 Figure 7.20 shows only the usage relationship between a component controller and a component interface controller. To be able to access the `IPublic` API of the component interface controller, it must also be defined for the custom controller and the view controller.

20 The following applies to the three generated controller APIs: `IPrivate` extends `IPublic` and `IPublic` extends `IExternal`.

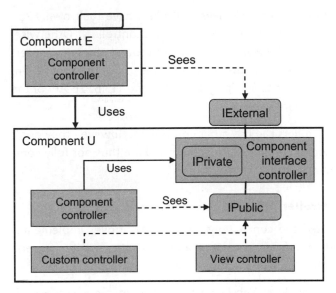

Figure 7.20 Visibility of the Component Interface Controllers

Component
Interface View
and Its Controller

A Web Dynpro component containing a window as a user interface makes this window available to external users via a visual interface, which is known as *the component interface view*. An external user embeds this view in his or her own user interface just like an ordinary view. The user cannot see the internal structure of this interface view (which exists as a window within the component), but he or she can use its inbound and outbound plugs to declare navigation links.

As we know, every view has its own view controller. In the same way, every interface view of a component has its own *component interface view controller*; however, the latter's functions are limited. The most important task of the interface view controller is to react to navigation events and the starting of the application;[21] it does so in its event handlers for *inbound* and *startup plugs*.

Importing URL
Parameters

Furthermore, the Web Dynpro runtime passes the parameters contained in the application URL to the event handler of the startup plug. But, before these parameters can be imported, identically named parameters of the type `String` must be defined for the startup plug.

---

21 A Web Dynpro application can be addressed in the browser window via its corresponding URL and displays an interface view of exactly one root component. When the application is started, the system navigates to the startup plug of the interface view, which was specified in its definition. After the creation and initialization of all relevant controllers, the Web Dynpro calls the event handler for the startup plug in the interface view controller of the root component.

Unlike view controllers, interface view controllers have their own IPublic API and can therefore be used by other controllers. Otherwise, other controllers wouldn't be able to fire the outbound plugs of an interface view for navigation transitions or its exit plugs to exit the application. It is precisely these methods for firing plugs that the IPublic API of the interface view controller contains.

Interface view controllers can use other controllers. However, they don't have their own context, methods, or actions and are thus not fully comparable with view controllers.

Summary—Controller APIs and Shortcut Variables

Figure 7.5 illustrated the connections between controller implementations, the generic interfaces IPrivate and IPublic, and the generic controller APIs, which include the following:

▶ All other controllers in a Web Dynpro component can access a non-view controller via the IPublic API.

▶ In a controller implementation, the corresponding IPrivate API is accessed using the variable wdThis.

▶ The IPrivate API allows you to access the lower-level, generic controller API using the wdGetAPI() method.

▶ The shortcut variables wdComponentAPI and wdControllerAPI enable direct access from the controller implementation to the generic controller API.

▶ In addition, the IExternal API is generated for component interface controllers; it is visible to external users of a Web Dynpro component.

▶ Interface view controllers have their own IPublic API, which enables other controllers to fire the outbound plugs and exit plugs defined in the interface view.

7.3 Contexts and Data Flow Between Backend and Frontend

In Web Dynpro, controller contexts represent an interface for the data flow between the backend and the frontend. The connection between the user interface and the context is established via data binding, as already discussed in detail in the last chapter. The connection between the context and the backend is based on *context-to-model binding*, in which a connection is defined between context elements and model classes, model attributes, and model relations at design time. To establish this connection, Web Dynpro uses the *Common Model Interface* as an abstract interface between model users and model providers (RFC in an SAP system, or Web services of a Web service provider). We'll begin with a general discussion of controller contexts and their interfaces before we move on to their binding to a Web Dynpro model.

7.3.1 Context Concept

In Chapter 6, you became familiar with the most important principles and terminology of the context concept in Web Dynpro. Particular attention was paid to the different aspects of the definition of controller contexts at design time. Therefore, the *nodes* and *attributes* defined in a context can be structured hierarchically. *Nodes* define data structures, which, at runtime, take the shape of data elements contained in the node, also known as *node elements*. The *cardinality* of a node specifies the maximum and minimum number of node elements stored at runtime. *Multiple nodes* are required for storing table data, which is automatically transported between the user interface and the context via *data binding*.

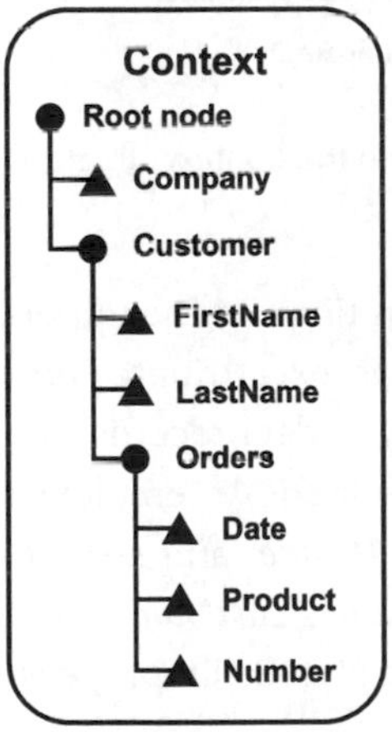

Description of Context Metadata at Design Time

Context	Property	Description

Context
● **Root node**
 ▲ **Company**
 ● **Customer**
  ▲ **FirstName**
  ▲ **LastName**
  ● **Orders**
   ▲ **Date**
   ▲ **Product**
   ▲ **Number**
	Attribute `name`	Name of context attribute

	`type`	Data type of attribute (such as *string*)
	`calculated`	Is the value of the attribute calculated via a method call?
	Node `name`	Name of context node
	`cardinality`	Minimum and maximum number of node elements the node contains at runtime (for example, *0..1*)?
	`selection`	Minimum and maximum number of node elements of a node that are selected at runtime
	`singleton`	Is the node created for each parent node (*true*) or for each parent node element (*false*)?

Context hierarchy   **Properties of context nodes and context attributes**

Figure 7.21 Description of Context Metadata at Design Time

The metadata of a controller context is described at design time in the Context Editor of the Web Dynpro tools. Figure 7.7 shows the hierarchical structure of a controller context and the individual properties of the contained context nodes and context attributes. These properties can be defined in the **Properties** view of the context editor.

The difference between the description of context metadata at design time and its structure at object level at runtime is critical to understanding the Web Dynpro context concept. The exact meaning of this difference is clarified in the following example (see Figure 7.8).

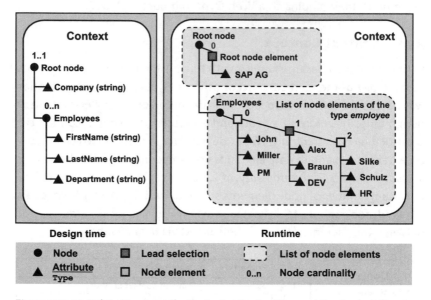

Figure 7.22 Metadata Structure of a Context at Design Time and the Context Structure at Object Level at Runtime

First, the hierarchy of the context is defined at design time. At the uppermost level, the company name is to be stored in the context attribute *Company of the type* `string`. To display several employee data records in a table, for example, a context node **Employees** is defined. An employee data record has the three properties *FirstName, LastName,* and *Department*. Accordingly, three context attributes *FirstName, LastName,* and *Department of* the type `string` are added to the context node **Employees**.

For the context node **Employees** to be able to receive a list of several employee data records (node elements) at runtime, a *cardinality* property of the type *x..n* should be selected. The list should be empty when the controller context is created by the Web Dynpro runtime, so the *cardinality* property of the **Employees** node is assigned the value *0..n*.

Now we'll examine the context at object level at runtime. Figure 7.8 shows that each context node contains a list of node elements at runtime. Nodes and node elements are represented by separate object instances. Since the root node always has the cardinality 1..1, it contains a list with exactly one node element object at runtime, which stores the company name in the variable (in the context attribute) *Company*. The value of this variable can be accessed or changed using corresponding methods. At runtime, the object instance of the **Employees** node can contain a list of node element objects (for storing employee data records) of any length. The values of the context attributes are thus always stored in variables of node element attributes at runtime. The type of these node elements—that is, which attributes and nodes they contain—is defined in the context hierarchy at design time.

7.3.2 Typed and Generic Context APIs

When examining the controller context at object level, the question arises, "Which interfaces are available to the application developer for context programming?" As we know, corresponding object instances are created for context nodes and node elements. So, the previous question can be rephrased as "Which interfaces are available for these objects or, to put it differently, how are these objects typed?"

To answer this question, we look at the API of the Web Dynpro programming model first. It contains the generic[22] context interfaces IWDContext, IWDNode, IWDNodeElement, IWDNodeInfo, and IWDAttributeInfo. IWDNode is implemented by all context nodes and IWDNodeElement is implemented by all node elements. The IWDContext API can be accessed via the generic IWDController API of a controller (shortcut variable type wdControllerAPI) and, among other things, allows you to access the root node of a context (IWDNode) and its metadata information (IWDNodeInfo). Lower-level context nodes can be accessed using the method IWDNodeInfo.getChildNode(). Information about a context attribute defined in the context node is provided via the IWDAttributeInfo API. Figure 7.23 shows how, starting with the shortcut variable wdControllerAPI, you can access the generic APIs of the node and node element objects stored in the context as well as the corresponding metadata APIs.

Generic Context APIs

The generic context interfaces are primarily required for dynamic context programming, for example, when new attributes are to be added to a context node at runtime and these attributes were not yet known at design time. In the broad sense, dynamic context programming involves

Dynamic Context Programming

---

22 The interfaces contained in the Web Dynpro runtime API are *generic*. According to Web Dynpro naming conventions, they begin with the prefix *IWD* for *Interface Web Dynpro*. To avoid naming conflicts, user-defined interfaces should not begin with this prefix.

the creation of context hierarchies and a description of context metadata at runtime via the processing of controller code. The metadata description of a controller context, which, typically, would have been defined at design time, is manipulated via a dynamic context programming at runtime.

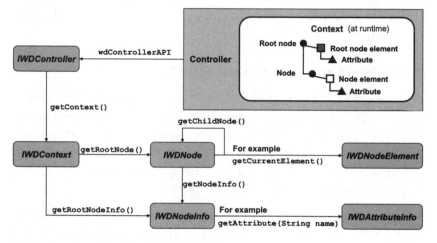

Figure 7.23 Accessing Generic Context APIs

Typed Context APIs

However, for statically defined context nodes and context attributes, Web Dynpro provides additional, automatically generated interfaces for programming purposes, which extend the IWDNode and IWDNodeElement APIs.[23] Furthermore, these interfaces are *typed*, that is, their method signatures use these typed interfaces and Dictionary types (for example, java.sql.Date) instead of IWDNode, IWDNodeElement, and java.lang.Object.

Figure 7.24 shows which additional, typed context interfaces are created. The IContextNode API for the root node and the IContextElement API for its node elements. For every other context node, the Web Dynpro tools generate a pair of correspondingly named interfaces, one for the node itself and one for the node elements, for example, for a node **Customers**, the two interfaces ICustomersNode and ICustomersElement are generated (see Figure 7.25).

---

23 Typed context APIs are generated only if the *typedAccessRequired* property is **true** at node level, which is the default case. Otherwise, the context programming for such nodes must be done using the generic context APIs.

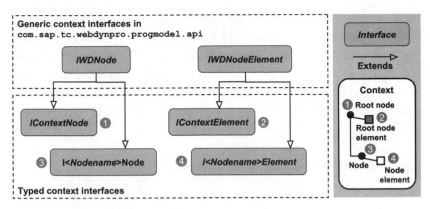

Figure 7.24 Generic and Typed Context Interfaces

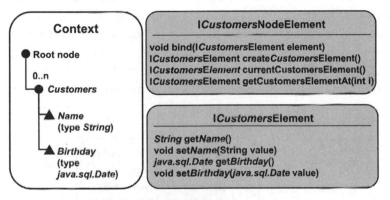

Figure 7.25 Example of Typed Context Interfaces

The main advantage of the typed context API over its generic counterpart is the typing itself; as you can see in Figure 7.11, the signatures of the different API methods contain the types `String`, `java.sql.Date`, and `ICustomersElement` instead of `java.lang.Object` and `IWDNode-Element`.

Data Binding Requires Dictionary Types

When defining types for context attributes, you can, in principle, use all Java classes that are visible via the class paths defined in the project. This enables you to store objects of any type in the controller context. Other contexts can then reference them via *context mapping*. However, if the values of context attributes are to be displayed on the user interface via data binding, you must use the data types provided in the package `com.sap.dictionary` in the Java Dictionary,[24] such as `com.sap.dictionary.string` or `com.sap.dictionary.time`.

---

24 With the exception of the type `binary`, since the display of *binary data* is possible with only additional knowledge of the MIME type.

If you use *Dictionary* types for the type definition of context attributes, note that there are two variations of these types at runtime. The first is the type in the controller context with which the typed context API also works. The second is the type required for displaying on the user interface. The type conversion from one variation to the other is carried out automatically by the Web Dynpro runtime environment. We'll discuss this topic in more detail in Section 7.4.

7.3.3 Context Programming Basics

The generic context APIs IWDContext, IWDNode, IWDNodeInfo, IWD-NodeElement, IWDAttribute, and IWDAttributeInfo comprise nearly 100 interface methods for context programming. Many of these methods are required for dynamic context manipulation, in which, for example, the definition of context structures or mapping relationships is implemented using controller code instead of being carried out statically at metadata level at design time. We will not discuss dynamic contexts in any more detail at this point; instead, we'll demonstrate the basics of context programming in a simple example.

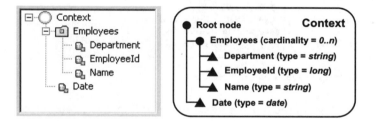

Figure 7.26 Definition of the Context Example (Left: Display in the Web Dynpro Tools, Right: Schematic Display)

Definition of the Context Example

As we continue with the Web service example that we introduced at the beginning of the chapter, let's examine a simple context structure containing an independent context value node[25] called **Employees**. Its *cardinality* property is defined as 0..n. It is therefore a multiple node, which can contain a list of any number of **Employees** node elements at runtime. The **Employees** node contains three context attributes: *Department* and *Name* of the type string and *EmployeeId* of the type long. The types

---

25 In the Web service example, the controller contexts contain *model* nodes and *model* attributes, since the data retrieval is implemented via the imported Web service model. No context-to-model binding exists for *value* nodes and *value* attributes. In this case, the data retrieval is carried out with user-defined controller code.

string and `long` are predefined types in the Java Dictionary. Further-more, a context attribute *Date* of the type `date` is defined directly below the root node in the example context.

We'll now address the question of how to implement the filling of the example context with runtime data. First, let's look at the context inter-faces automatically generated by the Web Dynpro tools: `IContextNode` and `IContextElement` in the case of the root node and its single node element; `IEmployeesNode` and `IEmployeesElement` for the **Emplo-yees** node and its node elements. While the root node already automat-ically contains a root node element at runtime (the cardinality property of the root node is 1..1), the node elements of the type **Employees** must first be created, then described with context attribute values, and finally added to the **Employees** node.

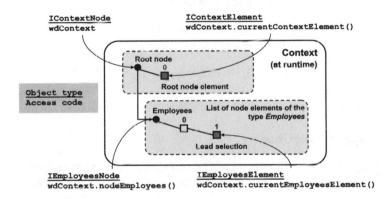

Figure 7.27 Accessing Context Nodes and Their Node Elements

For the creation of node elements and their adding to the **Employees** node, the `IEmployeesNode` API provides the methods `createEle-ment()` and `addElement()`. Listing 7.5 shows the resulting implemen-tation in the controller.

```
//@@begin imports
import com.sap.tc.webdynpro.contextapi.wdp
            .IPrivateMainView;
import com.sap.tc.webdynpro.contextapi.wdp
            .IPrivateMainView.IEmployeesElement;
//@@end
...
public void wdDoInit() {
    //@@begin wdDoInit()
```

Importing the IEmployees-Element Interface

```
IPrivateMainView.IEmployeesElement firstEmployeeEl=
    wdContext.createEmployeesElement();
IPrivateMainView.IEmployeesElement secondEmployeeEl=
    wdContext.createEmployeesElement();
```

Implementing
Value Assign-
ments for Context
Attributes for
Each Node
Element

```
firstEmployeeEl.setDepartment("Development");
firstEmployeeEl.setEmployeeId(1234);
firstEmployeeEl.setName("Peter Morgan");
secondEmployeeEl.setDepartment("Human Resources");
secondEmployeeEl.setEmployeeId(123456);
secondEmployeeEl.setName("Sarah Daniels");
```

Adding Node
Elements to the
List of the
Employees Node

```
wdContext.nodeEmployees()
    .addElement(firstEmployeeEl);
wdContext.nodeEmployees()
    .addElement(secondEmployeeEl);
```

```
wdContext.currentContextElement().setDate(
    new Date(System.currentTimeMillis()));
//@@end
}
```

Listing 7.5 Creation of Node Elements and Their Binding to Context Nodes

7.3.4 Supply Functions

The Web Dynpro programming model features a special type of controller methods, known as *supply functions*, for filling context nodes with node elements.

Supply functions can be defined for all value nodes (dependent or independent) by assigning a method name to the node property *supplyFunction* in a controller context at design time. The Web Dynpro tools then automatically add a supply function, including the user coding area it contains, to the corresponding controller class.

Supply functions are implemented by the application developer and are called[26] whenever the Web Dynpro runtime requires the list of node elements contained in a context node.

We will now demonstrate when this is the case and how supply functions are implemented.

---

26 Supply functions are always called implicitly by the Web Dynpro runtime environment and not explicitly with user-defined controller code.

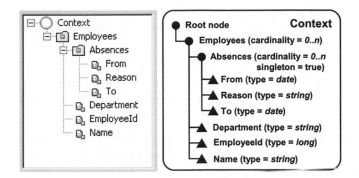

Figure 7.28 Adding the Dependent Context Node Absences

Figure 7.28 shows a context structure at design time; the **Employees** node contains a *dependent* context node **Absences** with the cardinality 0..n and of the type `singleton`. An employee's absences should also be stored in the context.

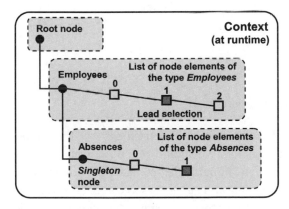

Figure 7.29 Dependent Singleton Node Absences

What does the property *singleton=true* mean in this case? The answer to this question is shown in Figure 7.29. For a singleton node, the Web Dynpro runtime creates a single node instance for each parent node. This means that only a single list of node elements of the type **Absences** can be stored in the context at any one time; the list that is stored is that of the node element marked as the lead selection in the parent node. If a different element is selected in the parent node (that is, if the lead selection changes), the list of node elements contained in the singleton node **Absences** must be regenerated. This task is carried out by the supply function defined for a context node. Its implementation is as follows (see Listing 7.6).

Definition of Singleton Nodes

**Transferring the
Singleton Node
and the Node
Element Currently
Selected in the
Parent Node**

```
public void supplyAbsences(IPrivateMainView.IAbsencesNode
    node, IPrivateMainView.IEmployeesElement parentElement
) {
    //@@begin supplyAbsences(IWDNode,IWDNodeElement)
    IPrivateMainView.IAbsencesElement absenceNodeElement;
    Collection absences = SomeBOL.getAbsencesForEmployee(
        parentElement.getEmployeeId());
    Collection absencesList = new ArrayList();
    for (Iterator iter = absences.iterator();
         iter.hasNext();)
        Absence absence = (Absence) iter.next();

        absenceNodeElement =
            wdContext.createAbsencesElement();
        absenceNodeElement.setFrom(absence.getFrom());
        absenceNodeElement.setReason(absence.getReason());
        absenceNodeElement.setTo(absence.getTo());
        absencesList.add(absenceNodeElement);
    }
    node.bind(absencesList);
    //@@end
}
```

**Creating a Node
Element and
Setting the
Attributes
Adding all Node
Elements to the
Node**

Listing 7.6 Implementation of a Supply Function

**Validating Invalid
Nodes Using
Supply Functions**

So when does the Web Dynpro runtime environment call the supply functions? To answer this question, we should remind ourselves of the actual task of controller contexts. In particular, contexts provide the user interface with data via data binding and generally serve as data storage for their own or foreign controllers (context mapping). However, to be able to carry out this task, contexts must meet a specific requirement at run-time: They must be in a *valid state*. If a context node is *invalid*, its list of node elements either doesn't exist or is invalid. Therefore, the Web Dynpro runtime conducts a validation by calling the context node's supply function[27] and thereby retrieving the required list of node elements.

In our example, the singleton node **Absences** becomes invalid whenever the lead selection of the parent node **Employees** changes. This happens, for example, when a different employee, (another node element in the **Employees node**) is selected in a table on the user interface, as a result of

---

27   If no supply function is defined, a single node element is added to the node element list for a node of the cardinality 1..n. When validated, nodes of the cardinality 0..n receive an empty list of node elements.

which the corresponding absence rows (node elements in the singleton node **Absences**), which are listed in a second table, become invalid and must be regenerated. To do so, Web Dynpro automatically calls the supply function defined for the **Absences** node. No further application code is required.

The main advantage of supply functions is that they are automatically called by the Web Dynpro runtime environment whenever node elements in invalid context nodes are accessed. In other words, Web Dynpro calls supply functions when necessary to validate invalid context nodes, which significantly simplifies the application code. In typical *master-detail scenarios*, the programming effort is thereby reduced to the implementation of a supply function. If the lead selection in the *master* parent node is changed (by selecting another *master* data record), Web Dynpro invalidates the lower-level *slave* node (of the type *Singleton*) and then calls its supply function.

Advantage of
Supply Functions

However, an invalid context node is also accessed if a table bound to a context node is to be filled with data records (node elements). After a context node has been initialized, it is at first invalid, since it does not yet contain a list of node elements. To validate it, Web Dynpro automatically calls the context node's supply function and retrieves the node elements to be displayed. Another example is the accessing of invalid context nodes via user-defined application code. If you use interface methods such as IWDNode.getCurrentElement() or IWDNode.getElementAt(index) to access a node element of an invalid context node, Web Dynpro first calls its supply function for validation purposes. Application developers can also use the methods IWDNode.validate() and IWDNode.invalidate() to manually validate or invalidate a context node. If a supply function was defined for the relevant node, using the method IWDNode.validate() automatically calls the supply function in the case of invalid nodes.

7.3.5 Calculated Context Attributes

Calculated context attributes are a special type of context attribute. They are created by assigning the value **true** to the *calculated* property when defining a context attribute. Unlike ordinary context attributes, they're not stored separately in node elements but calculated by the Web Dynpro runtime when necessary. This can occur when UI elements are to display the contents of a calculated attribute, or when a value is to be accessed in the controller code in a program. The calculation method is called automatically by the Web Dynpro runtime environment.

A calculated context attribute is determined in an automatically generated access method, which must be implemented by the application developer. For a calculated context attribute **FullName** of the type `string` in the **User** node of the context of the view **FormView**, the code for the access method would be as follows:

```
java.lang.String getUserFullNameCalc(
    IPrivateFormView.IUserDataElement element) {
    //@@begin getUserNameCalc(IPrivateFormView.
    //    IUserElement)
    return element.getFirstName()+ " "+ element.getLastName();
    //@@end
}
```

When the method is called, the system passes a reference to the node element `element`, to which the calculated context attribute refers (see Figure 7.30, right). If this were defined, for example, in a multiple node of the cardinality 0..n, the access method would be called for every node element contained in the node at runtime. In this way, you could display the full name of a customer, consisting of the first name and last name, in a third column of a table. The access method would then be called for every row (every node element) in the table.

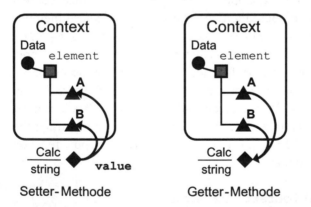

Figure 7.30 Methods for a Calculated Context Attribute with Property readOnly=false

It is assumed that the access method for determining a calculated context attribute is based on other attributes of the same node element.

Readable Calculated Context Attributes By default, calculated context attributes are only read, that is, the user cannot change their values. UI elements bound to readable, calculated context attributes are automatically displayed in only readable form.

If the *readOnly* property of a calculated context attribute has the value *false*, a set method with the following signature is generated in the controller class:

Calculated
Context
Attributes with
Property
readOnly=false

```
void set<NodeNameAttributeName>(<NodeName>element,
  <CalcAttrClass>value)
```

In the set method, the context attributes in the same node element are calculated based on the value of the calculated context attribute changed by the user. This means that the calculation method implemented in the get method is reversed in the set method, which is not always possible. Typically, most calculated context attributes are of the type *readOnly = true* (that is, read-only), but this is sufficient in most application cases.

The set method is called by the Web Dynpro runtime environment only when the value of a calculated context attribute with the property *readOnly=false* is changed on the user interface before an action is triggered. It is assumed that the context attributes of the same node element (parameter *element*) will be changed by the method (see Figure 7.30, left).

7.3.6 Web Dynpro Models and the Common Model Interface

The connecting of a model in Web Dynpro was covered in the Web service example application. Furthermore, the basic principles of the Web Dynpro context concept were discussed in the previous sections.

We will now take a more general look at Web Dynpro models and their relationship to controller contexts. The main question here is how a uniform connection of the different model types is achieved in the Web Dynpro programming model. The answer to this question is provided in the form of the *Common Model Interface* (CMI).

The CMI defines a common interface between the providers and users of models. This enables the separation of the application logic's accessing of the business logic from the underlying model implementation, for example, via Adaptive RFCs in an SAP system or using a Web service provider (see Figure 7.31). For Web Dynpro, this means that access to the business logic can be implemented via CMI.

In most cases, the application developer accesses the model via the context. Once a reference has been implemented between a model node element and a model object instance in the context, the corresponding business methods can be called in the controller (see Figure 7.32).

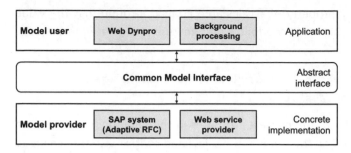

Figure 7.31 Common Model Interface

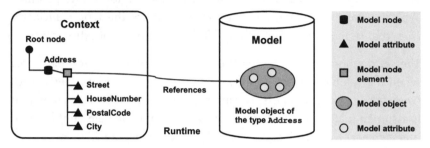

Figure 7.32 Reference Between Context Element and Model Object

For this reason, the current implementation of the CMI is based on the requirements resulting from context-to-model binding in Web Dynpro. In particular, these are the data transport (from and to the model layer), the metadata (required for developing generic functions), and the handling of events with which to react to changes. However, the CMI does not yet provide any additional services such as transaction handling, locking, or messaging.

Definitions of the Term Model

The totality of several model classes is known as a *model*. Every model class in a model implements the CMI to allow the model user access to the business data and the metadata (at least via reflection). The model itself also holds additional information regarding the transaction status, connection, or messages.

A model can contain either *typed or generic model classes* and, in rare instances, both classes. At runtime, the CMI is not responsible for the consistency of the contained model data.

What Are Model Classes?

A model class represents the most important form of data abstraction in the CMI. Similarly, context nodes constitute an abstraction for typed data records. A model class thus represents a single data type in the model. The properties of a model class correspond to the context attributes of a context node. Therefore, the properties of a model class are also referred to as its model attributes. Furthermore, relationships can exist between model classes. However, relations between model classes aren't limited to simple parent-child relations, like those that occur in the definition of hierarchical contexts.

7.3.7 Accessing the Business Logic with the Common Model Interface

In the CMI, there are two different types of access to the underlying business logic, *typed* and *generic*. This is not a revelation, since we already distinguished between typed and generic context APIs at context level.

Typed Access

For the typed model access, the model classes implementing the CMI have the get and set methods, as is also the case for Java Beans or typed context interfaces. To generate a typed model access via the CMI, at least part of the structure of the model and its model classes must be known at design time. This information must be accessible to model users, such as Web Dynpro, at design time via corresponding metadata. Furthermore, the CMI features some naming conventions with which the existing metadata is mapped onto the actual model implementation.

One big advantage of typed model classes is that their underlying metadata already exists at design time. In Web Dynpro, you can therefore declare context-to-model binding between context model nodes and model classes and access correspondingly typed context APIs—APIs that use the generated model classes—in the context programming.

Generic Access

For the generic, CMI-based model access, no information about the model structure is required at design time. Instead, a generic model class implements specific CMI interfaces, with which the model user can access the required metadata of a model at runtime. The accessing of the individual model attributes and of the relations between model classes is purely name-based, for example, using `setAttributeValue (name, value)`. Because no model metadata exists at design time, the binding of context nodes to the model can take place only dynamically at runtime.

The advantage of the typed model access over its generic counterpart is that it already enables code completion at design time and, moreover, includes the feature of type security (types known at design time, compiler checks). On the other hand, generic frameworks or generic applica-

Typed Model Access Compared to Generic Model Access

tion components favor the generic model access, because it doesn't depend on actual types, except for the CMI itself. Another alternative is to use both the typed and the generic access in a real model implementation.

Further details on the CMI are available in the NetWeaver help of the SAP NetWeaver Developer Studio under **SAP NetWeaver Developer Studio Documentation · SAP Web AS for Java Applications · API WAS · Common Model Interface**. The classes and interfaces of the CMI are contained in the packages under com.sap.tc.cmi.

7.3.8 Differences Between Model Nodes and Value Nodes in the Context

In Web Dynpro, we differentiate between *value* nodes and *model* nodes in the context. The main difference is that value nodes aren't bound to the model. The data stored in a value node is automatically lost when the corresponding Web Dynpro controller is destroyed. Value nodes therefore behave like the local instance variables of a controller. Typical services for model nodes, particularly the automatic data transport from and to the model, are not available for value nodes.

Model nodes, on the other hand, refer to the data managed in the underlying model layer. The lifecycle of the model layer is usually managed by transactional controllers. Model nodes must be bound to model classes (context-to-model-binding, see also Figure 7.33). For dependent model nodes, you can define a *supplying relation role*, which corresponds to the relationship between the relevant model classes. Based on this property, Web Dynpro can automatically adapt the references of the model node elements to the corresponding model objects at runtime. Alternatively, you can also define supply functions for dependent model nodes.

After the context-to-model binding, only a few lines of code are required.

1. **wdContext.nodeInput().bind(new Input());**
   In the first step, you must bind the executable model object instance in the model to the corresponding model node (**Input**) in the context. A new model node element then references this model object of the type Input.

2. **wdContext.currentInputElement().modelObject().execute();**
   In the second step, the model object is executed, for example, to obtain a list of model objects from the back-end system or store edited data there.

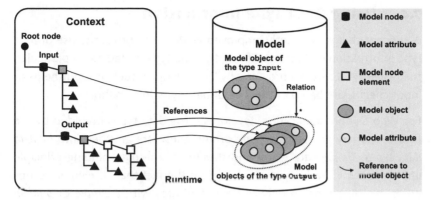

Figure 7.33 Context-to-Model Binding at Runtime

3. **wdContext.nodeOutput().invalidate();**

In the last step, you must invalidate the dependent model node **Output** below the **Input** node. This prompts the Web Dynpro runtime to follow the relevant relations in the model when accessing the **Output** node (for example, via data binding to fill a table on the user interface). The model node elements in the **Output** node then reference the corresponding model objects of the type `Output` in the model.

With regard to the third step, note that a model node in the context does not automatically point to the current relationships in the model (that is, the corresponding model objects) with the contained node elements. This means that the references between the context and the model can point to *old* model objects, even though the model contains *new* model objects after the `execute()` method is called again. Even if a *supplying relation role* was defined for a model node, the method `nodeOutput().invalidate()` must still be called to synchronize the context with the model.

With the class `WDCopyService`, the Web Dynpro API provides a service for copying node elements. You can also use the method `WDCopyService.copyCorresponding(Object source, Object target)` to copy node elements of different types (`IWDNodeElement` and `ICMIGenericModelClass`) from model nodes to value nodes and vice versa. Web Dynpro uses type information accessible in these node elements to find a type-compatible attribute in `target` for every attribute `source` and, if necessary, copy the attribute value to this location.

WDCopyService for Copying Node Elements

7.4 Using Data Type Information

A concept that is frequently employed in Web Dynpro is the use of data type information or, to put it differently, data type metadata. In particular, the (*generic*) UI services provided by Web Dynpro, such as input helps or input checks, are based on the use of data type information.

Java Dictionary   For Web Dynpro application developers, the data types provided by the Java Dictionary are especially important; these are grouped into *built-in data types*, *simple data types*, and *structures*. The data binding principle implemented in Web Dynpro is based on the fact that UI element properties can be bound to only context attributes with a *simple* or *built-in* Dictionary type.[28] *Built-in data types* are Dictionary types specially defined in the package `com.sap.dictionary`, for example, `string`, `time`, `long`, or `date`. *The dat*a type of context attributes can also be defined with any Java Native Type, such as `java.lang.Object`. However, this eliminates data binding for this attribute because only the Dictionary types provide the services required for the data exchange (data binding) between the user interface and the context. Such services include *formatting* (conversion of a context attribute of the type `java.sql.Time` into the *UI format* `java.lang.String`) or *parsing* (conversion in reversed direction).

Built-In Dictionary Types and the Typing of Context Attributes   Web Dynpro uses the built-in Dictionary types internally to display context attributes on the user interface. However, in the controller class itself, the attributes are stored using corresponding Java classes or primitive data types. Therefore, application developers program with context APIs typed with primitive data types (such as `long`, `double`, or `integer`) or Java classes (such as `java.lang.String` or `java.sql.Time`) instead of with built-in data types. The transfer of values between the user interface and context attributes is carried out automatically by the Web Dynpro runtime. Let's take a context attribute of the built-in type `date` as an example. The Web Dynpro tools generate the get method `public java.sql.Date getDate()` and the set method `public void setDate( java.sql.Date value)` in the API for the corresponding context element `I<Name of Node>Element`. Internally, Web Dynpro automatically converts the date value of the context attribute into the built-in Dictionary type `com.sap.dictionary.time` and displays it on the user interface via data binding.

---

28 With the exception of the built-in data type `binary`, since there is no general way of formatting or parsing binary data without specifying the MIME type.

Based on the built-in types, you can also define *simple data types* in the Dictionary. Simple data types are characterized by special metadata. This includes the built-in data type used, the type description, length restrictions, format specifications, the defined list of key/value pairs, or other metadata concerning the textual representation of the data type, such as field labels, column headers, or tooltips. A major advantage of simple data types is that Web Dynpro enables this metadata to be used for different services, including simple and extended input helps in particular.

Web Dynpro Uses Metadata of Simple Data Types

Another example is the binding mechanism for the UI element *Label* with reference to a simple data type in the Dictionary, as shown in Figure 7.34.

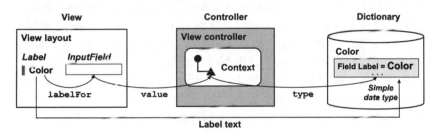

Figure 7.34 Binding Mechanism for Displaying Label Texts

For a UI element *Label*, the ID of an input field is assigned to the *labelFor* property. The *value* property for the corresponding input field is bound to a specific context attribute. The data type of this context attribute is a simple data type in the Java Dictionary. Finally, the metadata property *Field Label* is defined in this simple data type via the entry *Color*. The Web Dynpro runtime uses these binding connections and displays the label text of the type information on the user interface accordingly.

In addition to simple data types, you can also define structures in the Dictionary, and then use these structures to define context nodes. This is referred to as the *structure binding* of a context node. Such context nodes contain all fields defined in the Dictionary structure as identically named context attributes. Structure binding is particularly advantageous when using *Adaptive RFC models*, since it not only takes place at design time, but also at runtime. Therefore, at runtime, a context node defined using structure binding also contains any fields added to the structure at a later stage as attributes. The reason for this is that Web Dynpro doesn't import the metadata of Dictionary types until runtime, therefore adapting to any fields defined at a later stage.

Structures and Structure Binding of Context Nodes

7.4.1 Data Type Interfaces

Accessing Type
Information of
Context
Attributes At runtime, the type information of a context attribute can be accessed
via the interface IWDAttributeInfo in the package com.sap.tc.
webdynpro.progmodel.api. This interface is provided by the IWD-
NodeInfo interface of a context node:

```
IWDNodeInfo nodeInfo = wdContext.getNodeInfo();
IWDAttributeInfo attrInfo = nodeInfo.getAttribute("Color");
IDataType type = attrInfo.getDataType();
```

The interface IDataType knows only the data type name and the Java
class used for the representation of values. At runtime, the built-in data
types in the namespace com.sap.dictionary implement the interface
ISimpleType. For checking the data type of a context attribute,
IWDAttributeInfo provides the hasSimpleType() method. If a context attribute is of the type ISimpleType, you can access the corresponding simple data type using the method IWDAttributeInfo.
getSimpleType(). Otherwise, this method raises an exception.

The ISimpleType interface has the following features:

▶ It knows the labels for input fields, tooltips, and so on, provided such
metadata was defined (getTextServices()).

▶ It can return language-specific value sets, that is, key/text pairs (if
defined using getSVServices()).

▶ With the interface IWDAttributeInfo, a special instance of the simple data type can be created for a single context attribute, virtually all
properties of which can be modified at runtime.[29]

▶ You can convert from the language-specific string display (which is displayed on the user interface) to the object representation and vice
versa (format(Object) and parse(String)).

7.4.2 Local Dictionary

Every Web Dynpro project has its own *local* Dictionary. It initially contains the predefined, simple data types for currencies, Java wrapper
classes of primitive data types,[30] and for individual UI element properties

---

29 With the exception of the Java type.
30 For example, if a context attribute is typed with the simple Dictionary type
    com.sap.dictionary.predefined.objecttypes.integerObject, the Java wrap-
    per class java.lang.Integer is used instead of the data type int for typing this
    attribute in the generated context API.

like *Visibility*, *ButtonSize*, or *LabelDesign*. Simple data types are required for UI element properties if their values aren't defined statically but via data binding to context attributes. The context attributes for such properties must then be typed with the relevant Dictionary types.

Furthermore, the local Dictionary allows you to define your own simple data types, which you can use in all controller contexts of a Web Dynpro project for typing context attributes and for structure binding.

User-Defined Types in the Local Dictionary

7.4.3 Using Input Helps

Web Dynpro provides *generic UI services* for the simple integration of input helps on the user interface, which are based on the use of Dictionary types. Two different types of input help, *simple* and *extended*, allow the selection of a key value defined in a simple data type with a value set. The principle of these two input helps is based mainly on the fact that a suitable UI element is bound to a context attribute with a simple data type (containing a value set). The display of the input help on the user interface and the data transport from the user interface to the context take place fully automatically.

Simple Input Help

For a simple input help (also known as the *Simple Value Selector* or *SVS*) the *selectedKey* property of a `DropDownByKey` UI element must be bound to a context attribute that is typed with a simple Dictionary type. The display texts defined in the value set of this simple data type are then automatically displayed in the selection field (see Figure 7.35).

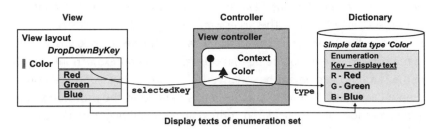

Display texts of enumeration set

Figure 7.35 Simple Input Help

If the user selects a display text from the selection list and an action is then triggered, the corresponding key for the display text is stored in the relevant context attribute. The display texts listed in the input help are obtained from the metadata of a simple data type in the Dictionary. Since the data transport also takes place automatically, this type of input help does not require any application code. This highlights the advantages of the declarative application development model supported by Web Dynpro particularly well.

Extended Input Help

The extended input help (also known as the *Extended Value Selector* or *EVS*) is based on a similar binding principle as the simple input help. The only difference is that, instead of a `DropDownByKey` UI element, an input field (`InputField`) is bound to a context attribute of the type *simple data type with value set*. The extended input help is intended for finding keys in large value sets. Its dialog interface allows you to sort and filter the entries contained in the value set (by entering the start of a key or display text). After you have selected a key/display text pair in the EVS user interface, the corresponding key value is stored in the context attribute. This key is then displayed in the input field.

Immediate Display of the Display Text with the Extended Input Help

Calculated Context Attributes and the EVS Input Help

After you've selected a key/display text pair in the extended input help, the Web Dynpro runtime environment stores the selected key value in the relevant context attribute. This occurs in a single server round trip, during which, by default, no application code is processed. So how, for instance, can the display text for the selected key be immediately displayed? The solution to the problem is to define an additional *calculated context attribute* called *DisplayTextCalc* in the same context node. In the view layout, you must then position an additional `TextView` UI element next to the relevant input field and bind it to the calculated context attribute *DisplayTextCalc*. The access method `getDisplayTextCalc()` is called in the same server round trip in which the selected key is stored in the context, the reason being that the value of a context attribute (key) in the same node element has changed. If an attribute *Color*, based on a simple Dictionary type with a value set, is defined in the root node, the access method for the calculated context attribute *DisplayTextCalc* has the following code (see Listing 7.7).

```
public java.lang.String getDisplayTextCalc(
    IPrivateMain.IContextElement element) {
  //@@begin
  String attributeName =
      IPrivateMain.IContextElement.COLOR;
  IWDAttributeInfo attributeInfo =
```

```
element.node().getNodeInfo()
    .getAttribute(attributeName);
ISimpleType simpleType =
    attributeInfo.getSimpleType();
ISimpleValueSet valueset =
    simpleType.getSVServices().getValues();
Object key =
    element.getAttributeValue(attributeName);
try {
    simpleType.checkValid(key);
    return valueset.getText(key);
} catch (DdCheckException e) {
    return "";
}
//@@end
}
```

Listing 7.7 Set Method for the Calculated Context Attribute DisplayTextCalc

Searching for Objects

The third type of Input help is the *Object Value Selector* (OVS). This UI service provides a generic user interface for finding objects generally provided by a model. While the input helps SVS and EVS use value sets (key/display text pairs) in simple data types, the OVS input help refers to *structures*.[31]

Object Value Selector (OVS)

Let's examine the OVS input help more closely via a flight data example. In an application, a flight number and the corresponding flight data is to be ascertained in an OVS and then used to fill an input form. For this purpose, a context node **Flight** of the cardinality 0..1 is defined in the view context, which is referred to here as the *application context*.

OVS Application Context

The data displayed in the generic OVS user interface is to be stored in a help context defined for this purpose (see Figure 7.36). This help context should be stored in a separate OVS custom controller. It contains an **Input** node of the cardinality 0..1 for storing the input data in the OVS search form and an **Output** node of the cardinality 0..n for storing the search hits (flight data records). In the simplest case, the context structure

OVS Help Context

---

31 These structures don't have to be defined in the Dictionary. With the context attributes it contains, a context node also represents a structure known as a *node element type* in context terminology. Context nodes can be bound to Dictionary structures.

created via binding to an *Adaptive RFC* flight data model will already contain the required input and output nodes.

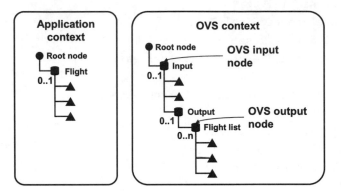

Figure 7.36 Contexts in the OVS Input Help

The Web Dynpro API provides the service class WDValueServices and the interface IWDOVSContextNotificationListener for implementing the OVS input help.

WDValueServices With the method addOVSExtension(...), the class WDValueServices provides a service with which the OVS search function can be added to the application context. The following references are passed in the addOVSExtension(...) method:

- IWDAttributeInfo[] startupAttributes: Array of the context attributes in the application context via which the OVS input help can be triggered. For input fields bound to these context attributes, user focusing displays a button to open the OVS user interface.

- IWDNode queryInputNode: OVS input node (cardinality 0..1) for storing the search data in the OVS input form.

- IWDNode queryOutputNode: OVS output node (cardinality 0..n) for storing the search hits to be displayed in the OVS table.

- IWDOVSContextNotificationListener queryListener: Listener object, which implements the interface IWDOVSContextNotificationListener for executing the search and for transferring context data between the application context and the OVS help context.

**IWDContext-
Notification-
Listener** The interface IWDOVSContextNotificationListener provides three special hook methods, which are called by the Web Dynpro runtime at three specific points during user interaction with the OVS interface. These methods can be regarded as event handlers for OVS actions, though the OVS actions are defined by the framework and not by the application

itself.[32] Furthermore, the relevant event handlers are not implemented in a view controller, but in the listener class.

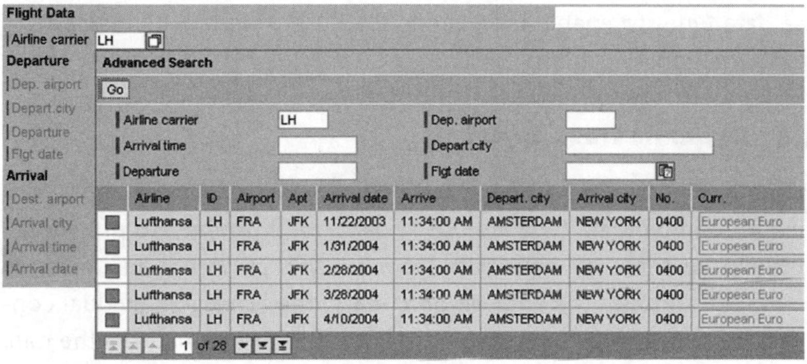

Figure 7.37 Generic OVS User Interface

The `IWDOVSContextNotificationListener` API defines the following three hook methods:

▶ `applyInputValues(IWDNodeElement ovsRequestingElement, IWDNodeElement queryInputNodeElement):`
Called by the Web Dynpro runtime when opening the OVS user interface to transfer values from the application context to the OVS help context. This enables the initialization of the fields in the OVS search form.

▶ `onQuery( IWDNodeElement queryInput, IWDNode queryOutput):`
Called after the user triggers the search on the OVS user interface. In this hook method, the hits are obtained based on the search criteria contained in the OVS input node. The search hits are stored in the OVS output node and then displayed in the OVS table via data binding.

▶ `applyResult(IWDNodeElement ovsRequestingElement, IWDNodeElement queryOutputElement):`
Called by the Web Dynpro runtime after an object (row) is selected in the OVS result table to transfer values from the OVS help context (OVS output node) to the application context. The search result of the OVS object search is thus transferred into the input form.

We recommend that you implement the `IWDOVSContextNotificationListener` API as an internal class in the OVS custom controller so that you can access the OVS help context there.

---

32 Therefore, these OVS actions are part of the class of Web Dynpro service events.

When defining the OVS help context, note that the context attributes contained in the input and output nodes must be typed with simple data types. Metadata such as field labels or table headers must be defined for these data types to enable the generic OVS user interface to display this text information.

7.4.4 Dynamic Data Types

In some application scenarios, the value sets (or other metadata) contained in a simple data type are not known until runtime. To provide an input help for these dynamic data types in Web Dynpro, you can make type modifications in the application code at the level of individual context attributes. Therefore, the type modifications aren't made to the data type centrally defined in the Java Dictionary, but only locally at context attribute level. For example, a context attribute *Color* can be typed with the built-in Dictionary type string at design time and then be dynamically changed to a simple data type with a value set at runtime (see Listing 7.8).

```
public void wdDoInit() {
    //@@begin wdDoInit()

    IWDAttributeInfo attributeInfo =
        wdContext.getNodeInfo().getAttribute(
            IPrivateMyView.IContextElement.COLOR);

    ISimpleTypeModifiable colorType =
        attributeInfo.getModifiableSimpleType();

    countryType.setFieldLabel("Color");
    IModifiableSimpleValueSet valueSet =
        colorType.getSVServices()
            .getModifiableSimpleValueSet();

    valueSet.put("R","Red");
    valueSet.put("G","Green");
    valueSet.put("B","Blue");

    wdContext.currentContextElement()
        .setColor("R");
    //@@end
}
```

Listing 7.8 Dynamic Type Modification for an Individual Context Attribute

In principle, the code example demonstrates how any dynamic type modification for an individual context attribute is implemented. The `IWDAttributeInfo` API of a context attribute is accessed using an automatically generated constant. After the definition of a context attribute *Color*, the Web Dynpro tools create the constant `IPrivate<Controller-Name>.I<Node-Name>Element.COLOR`. This avoids runtime errors caused by invalid attribute names—for example `nodeInfo.getAttribute("CALAR")` instead of `nodeInfo.getAttribute("COLOR")`. The dynamic type modification is then carried out via the interfaces `ISimpleTypeModifiable` and `IModifiableValueSet`.

7.4.5 Structures and Strengths of Adaptive RFC Models

The main advantage of the *Adaptive Remote Function Call* (Adaptive RFC) models supported by Web Dynpro is their use of Dictionary types. These models have a special feature in that they can adapt to specific changes in the RFC interfaces at runtime.

At design time, all structures and simple data types used in the Imported Adaptive RFC model are stored in the corresponding *logical Dictionary*. In this way, the Dictionary types contained in the ABAP Dictionary and used in the RFC interfaces (simple data types and structures) are replicated in a Java Dictionary. These Dictionary types can then be used for typing context elements (simple data types for context attributes and structures for context nodes). One advantage of context attributes typed in this way is that Dictionary information, like field lengths or value sets, is accessible and can be used by generic UI services (binding mechanisms for field labels, input helps, field lengths, tooltips, column headers).

Logical Dictionaries for Adaptive RFC Models

The flexibility of Adaptive RFC models is based on the logical Dictionary's ability to obtain information about any Dictionary types at runtime. For this, it uses a provider infrastructure to communicate with the SAP system in which Dictionary types are defined. The import of the logical Dictionary into a Web Dynpro project represents only a snapshot of the Dictionary at design time, after which declarations based on the Dictionary types can be made in the Web Dynpro tools.

When using Adaptive RFC models, you must configure two Java Connector (JCo) destinations in the *Web Dynpro Content Administrator*. The first destination refers to the model object instances, while the second destination refers to the runtime information about the RFC metadata (such as type information). The corresponding connection information is read by

Maintaining JCo Destinations in the Web Dynpro Content Administrator the *System Landscape Directory* (SLD). For this, the *SLD Data Supplier Service* must be configured in the SAP J2EE Engine.

In addition to simple data types, *Dictionary structures* are also supported in Adaptive RFC models. Context nodes can therefore be bound to the structures defined in the logical Dictionary (*context-to-structure binding*). The fields contained in the structures at design time are initially transferred to the generated and typed context APIs. Structure enhancements based on append structures that are defined in the ABAP Dictionary at a later stage can be accessed at runtime via the interfaces IWDNodeInfo and IWDAttributeInfo. For those context attributes that don't exist until runtime, the context programming is based on the generic context APIs (IWDNode.get/setAttributeValue(...)). When context node elements are copied using the service methods IWDCopyService.copyCorresponding(Object source, Object target), all fields contained in the structure at runtime are considered.

The fields and type information contained in an append structure (accessible via the interfaces IWDNodeInfo and IStructure) can be used in the hook method wdDoModifyView() to dynamically modify the user interface (see Listing 7.9).

```
public static void wdDoModifyView(
    IPrivateDynamicView wdThis,
    IPrivateSDynamicView.IContextNode wdContext,
    com.sap.tc.webdynpro.progmodel.api.IWDView view,
    boolean firstTime) {
//@@begin wdDoModifyView
IWDNodeInfo nodeInfo = wdContext
    .nodeCurrentAddressData().getNodeInfo();
```

```
IStructure structure = nodeInfo.getStructureType();
if (structure != null && firstTime) {
    boolean appendFound = false;
```

```
    for (Iterator iterator = structure.fieldIterator();
            iterator.hasNext();) {
        IField field = (IField) iterator.next();
        if (!appendFound)
            appendFound = field.belongsToAppend();
```

```
        else if (appendFound) {
            createCustomUI(view, wdContext, nodeInfo,
                        field.getName());
```

```
            }
        }
    }
    //@@end
}
```

Listing 7.9 Dynamic Adding of UI Elements Based on Fields of an Append Structure

8 SAP NetWeaver Java Development Infrastructure: Component Model and Services

Big application projects with long lifecycles require efficient and powerful processes for development and maintenance. With the Java Development Infrastructure, SAP has created an environment for Java-based development that supports all processes for the entire software lifecycle. These developments include the synchronized central storage of source data and archives, and a new model for structuring software.

8.1 Special Characteristics of Large Software Projects

SAP develops business applications on a large scale. The size and number of the development groups can prove challenging. In many projects, these groups are spread evenly over different development locations. Another challenge is the software lifecycle. The SAP solutions are maintained over a long period of time, during which they are repeatedly modified in customer systems, where big development teams may be working, too. Our customers now expect this kind of flexibility—for which ABAP-based applications have long since been famous—for the Java environment. Therefore, we must ensure both an outstanding stability in the software lifecycle and provide modification management in the setting of support package and release cycles.

The size of the projects and the long maintenance cycles multiply the problems that usually arise in small development groups. These problems include using libraries of different versions, composing source files and archives consistently, and simultaneously changing and using the same object. All these problems are addressed in the SAP NetWeaver Java Development Infrastructure (JDI), either by development concepts concerning the structure of the software itself, or by predetermined development processes that are implemented in the development tools.

With regard to the development process, this means that the environment must have the following characteristics:

Demands on a Development Infrastructure for Large-Scale Software Projects

▶ The goal of the development must be defined clearly. This starts with the definition of the product to be developed and the definition of its components.

- The starting point for the development must be the same for all developers. This applies to source files and all used libraries and archives alike.

- Software should be developed in components that encapsulate functions and can use one another via interfaces. This reduces the coupling between the software components and keeps them maintainable, because changes don't affect other components—or affect them only in a precisely defined way—unless the interface is involved. This considerably facilitates the reusability of all components. In addition, this form of structuring makes it possible to create an entirely new kind of development system that avoids the problems that usually plague large-scale software projects.

- The work of the developers must be synchronized during the development. This must be done automatically and systematically—while the developers perform the steps of their work—and not as an additional task. In this context, both source files and archives must be considered again; it is this last requirement, in particular, that is not adequately addressed in existing development processes.

- The steps after the development—central test, consolidation, and assembly—must be executed in a predefined manner. Also, the use of the new source files and archives in the next release and in other products must be ensured.

Although not every feature that is important for large-scale software projects is necessary for smaller teams, nevertheless, smaller software projects will profit from the features of the SAP NetWeaver JDI. The following example demonstrates these benefits.

8.1.1 Example of a Typical Development Process Without Central Infrastructure

Let's use an example in which two developers are working on software that is organized in projects. The second developer uses the build results of the first developer, which means that Project 2 depends on Project 1. To synchronize the developers' work, a central source file storage location is used; the build is executed in a central build process of the entire software. We'll call this process *Nightly Build*, because it usually runs at night to make the runtime objects available the next morning.

First, Archive 1 has been built in Project 1—with the runtime objects RTA1, and then RTA2 in Project 2—thereby using the current state of Project 1.

1. Developer 1 now changes the source files (sync) for Project 1.[1] After the local build, the developer performs the check-in, but the new version of RTA2 is not centrally available, because the nightly build has not yet run.

2. Developer 2, who uses Project 1, now changes Project 2, also using sync and check-out. This developer gets RTA1 (in the old version), which is used in Project 2, and introduces a new method.

   Developer 2 successfully builds Project 2 locally with the dependency to RTA1 (but still with the old version).[2] After a local test, Developer 2 checks in.

3. In the next central build, Project 1 is rebuilt with RTA1. If Project 2 is built, the old signature causes an error. Project 2 cannot be built centrally, even though no developer has done anything wrong. Before a successful build can be executed, manual changes are necessary. The results of the entire process are not available when the work begins.

This situation can occur independently of the group size of the developer team, but it's more likely to occur as the size of the group increases. The reason is the missing synchronization on the archive level. How you can improve this situation by using a central infrastructure is discussed in the following sections, especially in Section 8.3.2, *Component Build Service* (CBS).

The example illustrates what happens when the synchronization aspect of development objects on the archive level is not solved. For source files, usually a central storage with versioning functionality exists, but a problem arises as soon as the development team is working at different locations. When transporting source files, the synchronization becomes difficult at the moment when one version of a file is changed simultaneously in two locations.

We get a variation of this problem when customers want to modify delivered software. The delivery of the source files is simple, but the question arises as to how to deliver and load updates and support packages with-

---

1 If these changes are incompatible with the present state, the developer should inform all users so that they can make the required adaptations. To do this, the developer must know the identities of all users and be able to communicate with them directly as needed. As the size of development increases, this becomes progressively more difficult.

2 If Developer 2 deploys RTA2 on a central test system, it will lead to inconsistencies, which would be hard to track and therefore would hinder other developers in the central test system.

out losing the customer's modifications. This dilemma is solved by the Design Time Repository (DTR), which has a built-in recognition feature for such situations (conflicts between file versions), even after the files have been transported.

8.1.2 Software Logistics in the Java Development

To solve the aforementioned problems, we need mechanisms of software logistics. Under software logistics, we can combine all steps regarding the administration and transport of development objects. Many concepts of the SAP NetWeaver Java Development Infrastructure (JDI) are the results of decades of experience with the ABAP development.

Let's start with a short overview of the systems of the JDI and the relevant development process to provide an overall picture. The Design Time Repository (DTR) administers the source files; the Component Build Service (CBS) administers the archives of the development. You must consider that these objects are used in different versions in development and consolidation systems, and again in different versions in support packages and new releases. It is the administrator's responsibility to enable the developers to access the correct versions of source files and archives. This is done in the System Landscape Directory (SLD), in which products and software components—the development goals—are defined,[3] and in the Change Management Service (CMS), in which the access to objects—the source files in the DTR and the archives in the CBS—is arranged for all development tasks. In the CMS, also, the next steps leading up to the software delivery are performed after the developer has released the development.

Identical names of objects often cause errors. A *Name Service* checks the names of objects for uniqueness at the moment that they are created. Often, these names contain prefixes that define namespaces for enterprises.

Figure 8.1 shows the entire Java development process:

1. In the first step, a product is defined in the SLD. This includes name, release, and used software components.

---

3 The SLD is not an actual component of the JDI, but part of the J2EE standard installation; the JDI is installed separately. The SLD is used to administer information on the landscape and software for ABAP and Java. However, we deal with it in this context, because the use of the SLD is a prerequisite for the development process with the entire JDI.

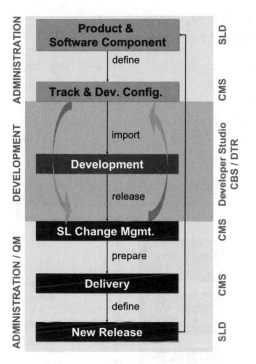

Figure 8.1 Overview of the Java Development Process Using SAP NetWeaver

2. In the next step, the logical development system is created, which defines the access to the source files and archives required for the project. The entity of all required logical development systems for one release is called a *track*.

3. The resulting development configuration is imported into every SAP NetWeaver Developer Studio of the developer group. Now the configuration of the local environment of the individual developer is finished. Development steps—such as creating and changing source files, local build, testing, checking-in into the DTR and subsequent central builds in the Component Build Service (CBS)—follow. After a successful central test, the developer releases the objects for the next steps in the Change Management Service (CMS).

4. After all steps of development and consolidation have been completed, the quality manager releases the entire software. The software is now assembled and delivered.

5. For the development of the next release, only its definition in SLD and CMS is required. All physical systems remain unchanged. The new development configurations are used to separate the different release states.

8.2 Elements of the SAP NetWeaver Java Development Infrastructure

In this section, we want to look at all elements of the SAP NetWeaver Java Development Infrastructure. These include the systems CMS, DTR, and CBS. In addition, SLD and name services are used. The developer accesses them using the Integrated Development Environment (IDE), the SAP NetWeaver Developer Studio. The development follows the SAP component model.

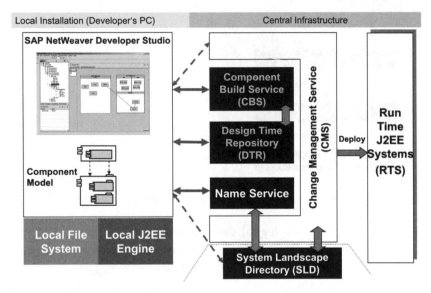

Figure 8.2 Elements of the JDI

Figure 8.2 shows all elements of the Java Development Infrastructure. The development environment consists of a local part and of the central JDI. The local part consists of the Developer Studio as the IDE, the local file system as the temporary storage for all new development objects, and usually a local installation of the J2EE Engine as a testing environment.

The Developer Studio connects the developer to the central JDI. You as a developer use the SLD to load the development configuration of the CMS into the Developer Studio. Now you can access both the source file storage in the DTR workspace you use for your work and the buildspace in the CBS. Objects you create are checked by the name service for the uniqueness of the name. The CMS is used for the deployment to the central test systems.

8.2.1   SAP Component Model

The special demands placed on SAP software deliveries require a power-   A New Way of
ful programming model. An essential feature of making software easy to   Structuring
maintain and understand is its ability to be broken down into compo-   Software
nents that can be changed almost independently of one another. After
breaking down the software into components, reusing them is the next
logical step. However, they're easier to use if two conditions apply: On
the one hand, the individual components must be uncoupled, so that
changes to one component cause no or limited changes to the other
components. To achieve this, the implementation of the individual components must be encapsulated. On the other hand, the components must
have a working relationship, with defined interfaces and established processes for using them.

The SAP component model meets these conditions. It is designed to
structure software, to allow a precise planning of the software architecture and, above all, to serve as the basis for an entirely new build process.

Component Hierarchy

The SAP component model structures software on four levels. We'll look
at these levels in descending order, because this order mirrors the creation process of software in the SAP development environment. In the
SAP NetWeaver Java Development Infrastructure, the software development process has been adapted to reflect the natural sequence of the
steps.

Initially, there is a vision of a product.[4] A product can be viewed as soft-   **Products**
ware designed to be sold to customers, which defines a particular set of
functions. A product usually takes advantage of existing software that
provides general functions. The spectrum extends from generally available libraries to developments made by the product manufacturer. The
remaining software components, which must be created, can now be
defined.

Because the nature of a product determines the kind and features of the   **Software**
software, it also determines a structure. The substructures of a product   **Components**
consisting of new and reused parts are called *software components* and

---

4   The product is actually not part of the component model. However, the use of the
    component model can be better understood if you start with the definition of the
    product, which is always the first development step in the development process—
    as it is implemented in the SLD—or must already have happened as a prerequisite
    to be able to create an SC.

represent the second level. These are larger groups of related functions. Examples are generally available Basis libraries that are combined in a software component or a framework that is shared by all applications. The new functions, which are specific for the new product, form another unit.

Software components generally function as units. The separation within a product between general and specific components provides the basis for the reusability demanded above. However, software components themselves are only a frame that is not used directly by the development, but is given by the administration layer. The inner structure must also adhere to the rules of decoupling by encapsulating elements as independent components. This is done in the development components.

Development Components

The third level, that of the *development components* (DC), lies below the software component level. Development components again are groupings of objects, but they directly define their mutual usage and thus represent the units actually worked on by the developers. Development components contain and encapsulate the development objects. They are the units that the build processor of the SAP NetWeaver JDI processes.

Development Objects

Lastly, the development objects are all kinds of objects created during development. They are the source files of the build process. They comprise files from Java development—classes, interfaces, and so forth—and specific files developed by SAP according to the component model such as Web Dynpro files or metadata.

Implementation of the Component Model

This is the order in which all objects are created in the SAP NetWeaver Development Infrastructure. Without the definition of product and software components, no development components can be created, and without development components no source files can be created.[5] The relations between the levels are determined explicitly on each level and evaluated automatically for the development processes.

Figure 8.3 shows the structuring of software according to SAP's component model. A product consists of software components (represented by the dotted lines). These software components are either used in this product and exist in read-only form after the import or, they're developed for the product and are changeable. (A software component can be used in various products). Between the software components (SCs), *use*

---

5 This is the general order of creation, however, there are exceptions: For example, an object that a Java class may have created—outside of the JDI—can be added to the DTR database at a later time.

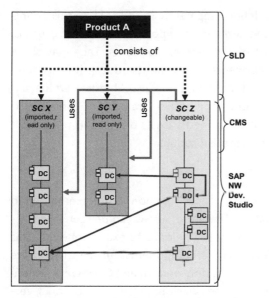

Figure 8.3 Structuring Software According to the SAP Component Model

dependencies must be defined (represented by the "uses" arrows). This is done in the System Landscape Directory (SLD).

Software components contain the development components. These always exist in only one SC. Development components contain the development objects, which always exist in only one DC. Besides the development objects, DCs can also contain other development components. You can see this kind of nesting in software component Z (SC Z). For DCs, also, use dependencies are defined (green arrows) and the dependencies to other development components are determined (represented by the arrows between the DCs).

Products

SAP products are solutions in the business environment. The management decides on new products. A new product is created in the Software Landscape Directory (SLD). The SLD stores information on the system landscape (*Technical Landscape*) and the *System Catalog*, which contains a list of all products and software components available. The definition of each product contains the name of its owner or *vendor*.[6] The development environment for the new product is created based on the information in the SLD.

---

6 This is important, because usually products are the units that are delivered to the customers.

Each release of a product is defined separately in the SLD. In this definition, the versions of the used software components and their uses are determined. Products consist of software components. They may share some of these software components with other products, for example, the software components that contain the Basis libraries, which are required in every Java-based development, or framework component. One (or more) of the software components exists only in this product. It contains the functions specific for this product.

Software Components

Structure of Software Components

SCs are groups of related functions. These functions are implemented in development components (DCs). Therefore, an SC can be seen as a container for DCs. Consequently, every DC belongs to exactly one SC. This implies that there are no development components outside of software components and that every DC exists only once in an SC. However, these two statements are valid only for the development of one product version (release). In other releases, this assignment may be changed. The reason for this fixed assignment lies in the way in which software components are used in products. A DC cannot appear twice in the same product. This implies that you aren't allowed to use software components that contain the same DC within one product.

Software Components in Development

Software components, like products, are defined in the SLD. They belong to a particular product. During development, we must distinguish between two kinds of software component usage. The software component that is specific for the product to be developed can be changed during development. Apart from this new software component, there are other software components on which you build your development. They contain, for example, basic libraries that are shared by various Java projects. These software components can only be used; they cannot (at least, they usually cannot) be changed in this context. Software components themselves don't define mutual dependencies, because they're used unchanged (in the same release) in different products. However, the administration determines such relations between software components for the current product development.

Technical Realization of Software Components

From the technical point of view, a software component is a structure of folders and files. All folders are stored in one common folder *SCs*. The SC structure consists of the *vendor* name of an SC, of the name under which the SC is developed and of a folder *_comp*. This folder contains a folder *TopLevelDCs* (top-level DCs that are not contained in other DCs) with the *.dcref* files of all top-level DCs.

The build result of an SC is a deployable *Software Component Archive* (SCA).

Development Components

Development components carry the crucial characteristics of the component model. Within them, the internal structure of the software component is determined, because the DCs contain the actual development
objects. These can be all kinds of files used in the standard Java development: Java classes and interfaces, image files for icons, or SAP-specific
files, for example, from the Web Dynpro development. DCs are the units
of the build process when you develop according to the component
model. Therefore, the structure of the software component, which you
determine in the DCs, is verified during the build. To achieve this, you use
a visibility concept along with the definition of interfaces and the explicitly declared use of other components. This combination allows and
requires a most exact planning of the development; it enables you to
replace the lengthy nightly build process of the entire development with
the build of those individual development components on its developer's
demand.[7]

Tasks of Development Components

Pure Language Visibility

- Classes, interfaces, objects (text files, icons)
- Only ordered by packages for developers' editing access

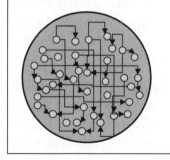

Development Components

- Unidirectional relationships
- Public Parts
- Supports automated build

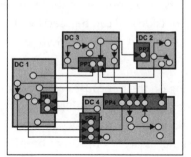

Figure 8.4 Visibility of Development Objects

The left section of Figure 8.4 shows the relationship between development objects (classes, interfaces, and so on) in the Java development: As

---

7 There are other ways of building individual parts of a software component. However, they don't include the added advantage of synchronizing the work of the
developers on the archive level.

soon as an object is marked as *public*, it can be used by any other object. Conversely, during the definition of development components, you must define objects that you want to release for use by other DCs explicitly in public parts (even if they are *public*, objects that don't lie in the public part of a DC cannot be used outside of the DC). This results in a much better organization of the software, which is evaluated in development processes such as the build process.

Nesting Development Components

Aside from development objects, DCs can contain other DCs and thus structure the software due to the hierarchical encapsulation of their modules. The visibility rules for embedded or inner DCs are the same as for the development objects. You use this nesting if a DC makes a function available in a public part that should be used by other DCs only in a special context. The limited visibility of a DC may be interesting, for example, for security-related functions.

Visibility of Objects in Development Components

We already know that DCs are containers for development objects. They limit the visibility of development objects from the outside. By default, all objects in a DC are invisible outside of this DC. Therefore, changes to the "invisible" development objects have no effects on other components. This results in a perfect decoupling of all development components, but also makes it impossible for DCs to use one another. Therefore, to allow a mutual use nevertheless, development components must have interfaces that can be used by other DCs.

Interface Concept of the Development Components

The interfaces of a development component are called *public parts*. In public parts, a DC publishes those development objects that are visible from the outside and can be used by other DCs. Objects assigned to public parts are called *public part entities*. Entities can be individual objects such as a class, as well as tree, for example, a package tree.

Depending on their purpose, we distinguish between two kinds of public parts (see Figure 8.5). A public part of type *Compilation* can be used for the development of other DCs and will be used during compilation. This is always necessary if objects of one DC are used in the compilation of another DC.

▶ A public part of type *Assembly* provides a build result that can be wrapped by other DCs. This type is required, for example, if a DC type (such as a Java DC) does not produce deployable build results. Parts of this DC can then be wrapped in a public part of this type to be uploaded to the server in the form of, for example, a J2EE Java library file.

▶ In a public part of type *Compilation*, an entire DC could be contained. However, in this case, every single object of the DC could be used, and the advantage of function encapsulation would be lost. By limiting public parts to a few entities, inner structures of a used DC can be modified without forcing the using DCs to react to this change.

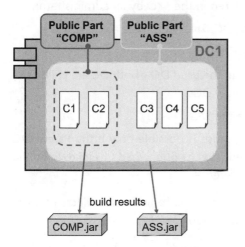

Figure 8.5 Public Parts of Type Compilation

DC 1 defines a public part **COMP** of purpose *Compilation* and a public part **ASSEMBLY** of purpose *Assembly*. **COMP** only contains the objects C1 and C2. **ASSEMBLY** contains all objects of the DC to wrap them into another DC for deployment. The build result is always a JAR file. For public parts of type *Assembly*, a ZIP file is also created.

The second part of the concept of a division into components is the *use dependency* between DCs. If you want to use objects of another DC in your DC, you have to declare this *usage* in the metadata of your DC. The new build process in the CBS checks this information, which is the basis of the build, because the knowledge of the dependencies between DCs allows the build of individual DCs instead of the entire software in the nightly build. When the use dependencies are known, dependent components can be rebuilt purposefully.

Use Dependencies Between Development Components

Whenever using DCs, you must decide in which way they shall be used. You define how DCs will be used with the relevant wizard in the SAP NetWeaver Developer Studio.

The use is limited by several restrictions that result from the attachment to the SC and from the hierarchy of the DCs due to nesting: The used DC must meet the following conditions:

Use Dependencies Between Nested DCs

▶ The used DC must lie in the same SC as the using DC. If this is not the case, in the SLD the use of the SC that contains the used DC must have been defined by the SC of the using SC. Alternatively, you can use DCs from other SCs, but only if the SC which contains your DC has a usage dependency to the SC which contains the DC you want to use. Such a usage dependency can be declared in the SLD by an administrator.

▶ It must be visible for the using DC. This is the case if:

  ▶ It lies on the same nesting level.

  ▶ It is contained as a child DC in the used DC—both DC are child-DCs of the same parent or top-level-DCs.

  ▶ The embedding DC can use the DC.

  If these conditions aren't met, a use is possible only if the Parent-DC that embeds the DC to be used adds its public parts to its own public parts by declaring an Entity-Reference.

Even if a use dependency has been defined, only those objects of a DC can be used that belong to one of its public parts.

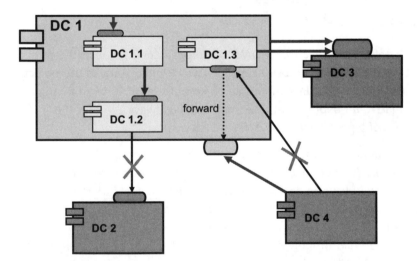

Figure 8.6 Use Dependencies Between Nested DCs

Figure 8.6 shows the use dependencies between nested DCs:

1. DC 1 contains three other DCs: DC 1.1, DC 1.2, and DC 1.3. Continuous arrows represent allowed dependencies, an X shows that these dependencies aren't allowed in the present situation.

2. DC 1 itself is allowed to use all three embedded DCs, for example, DC 1.1 in this case.

3. DCs on the same level are allowed to use one another, such as DC 1.1 uses DC 1.2 or DC 1 uses DC 3.

4. DC 4 can use DC 1.3 only if DC 1 propagates the public part of DC 1.3 in its public part.

5. DC 2 cannot use DC 1.2, because as a child DC of DC 1, DC 1.2 is not visible to DC 2.

6. In this example, DC 1 defines the visibility of particular functions and with this encapsulation structures the SC.

In addition to restrictions due to nesting, *access control lists* (ACLs) can define further restrictions. Here, you can define explicitly which DCs are allowed to access a certain DC. If DCs are named here, the use is denied to all other DCs.

Access Control Lists

Cyclic dependencies are not allowed. A cyclic dependency is, for example, a use relationship of the following kind: DC *A* uses DC *B*, which uses DC *C*, which uses DC *A*. The build process of a DC cannot prevent the definition of dependencies of this kind, but it discovers them and terminates the build process—such a dependency will never reach the active state (that is it will not be built in the CBS). In a build process as it was used up to now, dependencies of this kind have been possible. If DC *A* from our example has been built before the cyclic dependency is defined, then the build process can be executed. However, this results in inconsistent states, if in one process both DC *A* and DC *C* have been changed. In this case, the old version of DC *A* is used instead of the current one.

Cyclic Dependencies

There is a way of granting access to DCs to other components to which the nesting would usually deny access. A DC can declare a *public part entity reference* to any public part, which adds the content of that public part to the public part of this DC. This public part can then be used by other DCs. To prevent unrestricted access to certain DCs, you can use the access control list.

Entity References

When creating DCs, you must always determine their type. The type is used for the automatic control of the build process. In addition, the structure of the DC is created in accordance with its type, and type-related settings are generated. For a DC of type *Java*, this means that in addition to the usual files for a Java project, the folder *DC Meta Data* is created. The following DC types are available:

Types of Development Components

▶ **Composite Application Services DC**
A *Composite Application Services DC* contains all elements required for a Composite Application Services project. These are Dictionary ob-

jects, metadata, and Java classes. If you select a Composite Application Services DC, four projects of the types Dictionary, Metadata, EJB Module, and Enterprise are created.

The product of a Composite Application Services DC consists of three archives: These are a Software Deployment Archive (SDA) for the Dictionary project, and one Enterprise Archive (EAR) each for the Metadata and for the Enterprise project. They can be deployed on the server.

▶ **Dictionary DC**
A *Dictionary DC* defines global data structures that will be created in the database on the server where the DC will be deployed. Since the data structures will be created in a central database, it is important to use unique names. To ensure this, the name server will allow only certain prefixes for table names. To use the structures created in a Dictionary DC in another DC, you must add the simple types, structures, or tables to a public part.

The product of a Dictionary DC is a *Software Deployment Archive* (SDA) that can be deployed on the server. (To create the archive locally, use the DC build or choose **Create Archive** from the context menu on the Dictionary project in the Dictionary Explorer).

▶ **J2EE DCs**

▷ **Java Enterprise Application DC**: An *Enterprise Application DC* combines *Web Module DCs* and *EJB Module DCs* into an enterprise application. The product of an Enterprise Application DC is a deployable *EAR file* (Enterprise Application Archive). The build result is an EAR-file containing the *WAR-file(s)* from the *Web Module DCs* and the *EJB files* from the *EJB Module DCs*.

▷ **EJB Module DC**: An *EJB Module DC* contains the model classes (that is, Message-Driven Bean, Container-Managed Persistence (CMP) Bean, Bean-Managed Persistence (BMP) Bean, Stateful-Session Bean or Stateless-Session Bean) for an Enterprise Application DC. The SAP NetWeaver Developer Studio automatically creates public parts for assembly and compilation. Results of the build are compiled classes that can be used by an EJB Assembly DC.

▷ **Web Module DC**: A *Web Module DC* contains the files that belong to the view (and view controller) part of an enterprise application project, such as JSPs, Servlets, and Proxy classes for beans defined in an EJB project. The build result is also a WAR file.

- **J2EE Server Component Library DC**: A J2EE library is a special add-on for the SAP J2EE Engine. Using a J2EE Library project is easy. Refer to public parts (with purpose assembly) of Java DCs (buildtime dependency) or other J2EE Library DCs (runtime dependency). The build result is an SDA file.

- **Java DC**: A *Java DC* can contain arbitrary Java code. A Java DC does not create a deployable or installable build result. (The class files generated from the source code are stored in a temporary folder and removed after the build.) It is up to the developer to define a public part with purpose assembly, if a JAR file should be generated.

- **Web Dynpro DC**: A *Web Dynpro DC* is a container for one or more Web Dynpro components. The build result is an EAR file containing a Web Dynpro Archive (WDA).

- **Web Services**: A *Web Service Client Proxy* is a special Java DC that contains client code that accesses a Web Service. The difference between a deployable and a standalone proxy is that for a deployable proxy, the application of the Web service client must be deployed on the J2EE Engine. A standalone proxy can be executed without the J2EE Engine.

You can choose between the standard types Java and J2EE—the latter subdivided into Enterprise Application, EJB Module, and Web Module—and SAP types such as Web Dynpro or Java Dictionary. Of course, using combinations of SAP-specific and standard types is allowed and makes sense.

Using DCs in the Build Process

DCs are the units that are built in the Component Build Service (CBS). During this process, all rules of use dependencies and visibility are checked. If, for example, a method of a DC is used without being specified as a DC that is being used, the build process terminates. This ensures that the structure definition of the software component remains clear. The type of the development component defines the build process. The appropriate build script for each type is available in the build tool and is used automatically—a fact that is enabled by the evaluation of the DC metadata. This ANT-based tool is used both in the DC build of the Developer Studio and in the CBS. Therefore, the build support is available in the local, as well as in the central build, and any divergences in the build results are excluded as long as the source files and archives used are identical.

From a technical point of view, every development component—just like a software component—is a structure of folders and files (*.classpath*, *.dcdef*, and *.project*). The name of a DC defines a folder hierarchy. Via names with the same beginning, related DCs are assigned to common branches in the folder hierarchy. All DCs contain a folder *_comp*; it always contains folders for binaries (bin) and the public parts. They are stored as XML files (even though they're displayed in the Developer Studio as folders, for reasons of clarity). In addition, it contains the DC definition with used DCs—child DCs. The *gen* folder contains generated data. Here, you can view, for example, deployable build results. All other folders depend on the DC type.[8]

Help in the IDE

The SAP NetWeaver Developer Studio provides wizards for all steps in the component-based development. You create your DCs directly in the software component that you're developing and you can see all the software components that you're allowed to use. To create DCs, you use a wizard that guides you through all settings required for the DC. The structure of the DC is then created automatically. In this process, the use relationships always required for the selected type are also generated automatically.

Since the SAP NetWeaver Developer Studio is based on the Eclipse framework, which has been enhanced by SAP plug-ins, Eclipse projects must be defined for the development. A DC corresponds exactly to a project.[9]

The Eclipse user interface is organized in perspectives and views. The view to a DC in the Developer Studio depends on the selected view. To edit DCs, different views are available for the different tasks in the development process.

▶ Perspectives and views are designed only for working with the component model. Each of these perspectives shows a view of the DCs that reflects the respective task. For example, information that is not required is hidden and most actions are controlled in the context menu:

▶ *Development Configurations Perspective*: Here, you create all DCs and find the views *Inactive DCs*, *Active DCs,* and *Local DCs*. The first two views show the DCs depending on whether they have already

---

8 See Chapter 9 for figures of DCs and the tools that you will have to use.
9 For more details on Eclipse projects, see Chapter 10.

been activated (built centrally); the latter view shows all DCs available on the local PC. This perspective is useful for quick access to one's own DCs, because the other views show all DCs of all developers on the team.

Creating a DC is always done in the context of a software component. Software components and the connections to the central systems are defined in *development configurations*. They are imported in this perspective.

► *Java DC Explorer View*: You can find this view in the *Java* perspective. Here, you develop and build Java DCs. For example, you define the public parts in this view. However, you also need some of the general perspectives.

► *J2EE DC Explorer View*: This is used for J2EE projects and resembles the Java DC Explorer.

► *Activation View*: Here, as developer, you trigger the central build for your DC in the Component Build Service.

► *Transportation View*: Here, you can release activities for further processing in the Change Management Service (CMS).

There are other perspectives depending on the DC types.

► Perspectives and views that may be used with or without a component model:

► *DTR Perspective*: It shows all objects in the repository as folders and files. For example, public parts are shown as XML files.

► *Web Dynpro Perspective*: The Web Dynpro Explorer view of this perspective shows all Web Dynpro projects.

► *Java Package Explorer View*: This view shows all Java projects of this type. You need this view to create Java packages.

► *Open Activities View*: When administering changes in the DTR, use *Activities* to organize your changes.

You can configure the SAP NetWeaver Developer Studio in such a way that it mirrors your own way of working—either with or without components. In addition, you can use the Developer Studio to make settings for the development work that concerns the storage of file types in the DTR, for example.[10]

---

10 The settings may vary, depending on whether you use only the DTR or the entire JDI. A detailed explanation will follow.

In the Developer Studio, DCs are represented in the DC-specific views as folders and files. For every DC, a folder *DC Meta Data* is displayed. It contains those DC properties that go beyond an Eclipse project. Within this folder, you will always find the subfolder *DC Definition*. It contains:

▶ *Access List*: Here, you can define which DCs are allowed to access your DC. If you don't define an access list, all DCs for which your DC is visible, are allowed to access your DC.

▶ *Child DCs*: Here, the DCs embedded in this DC are listed.

▶ *Folders*: This node contains a list of the folders in this DC, for example, Java-Packages.

▶ *Used DCs*: Here, you define all *use dependencies* to DCs that you want to use. All DCs that are used by default in a particular DC type are added automatically to this list.

▶ *Public Parts*: They are displayed as folders to keep the layout clear and simple (actually, they are XML files). The folder contains the individual public parts. Each of them displays its own *Access List*, contained *Entities*, and *Entity References*.

Development Objects

In the context of the component-based Java development in the SAP environment, we use the term *development objects* for classes and interfaces, EJBs, UI icons, and so forth from the standard development, as well as tables of the Java Dictionary or Web Dynpro files. They're stored as *versioned resources* in the DTR.

8.2.2   Design Time RepositoryDesign Time Repository

The Design Time Repository (DTR) is the central source file management system of the Java Data Infrastructure (JDI).[11] The DTR is a J2EE application that runs as a service on the J2EE Engine of the SAP NetWeaver. It uses a database to store and version development objects. In this context, it performs several tasks:

▶ All versions of files must always be available.

▶ Access should always be restricted to those objects that are needed in the relevant software development project.

▶ The versioning information must be kept, even after the transport of objects into other instances of the DTR. Examples for such transports

---

11   However, the DTR can manage all kinds of files.

are the scenarios described in the introduction, which cover the delivery of source data to customers to enable modifications and the synchronization of development laboratories in different countries. For both processes, there must be a mechanism that avoids conflicts between versions during parallel developments within a product.

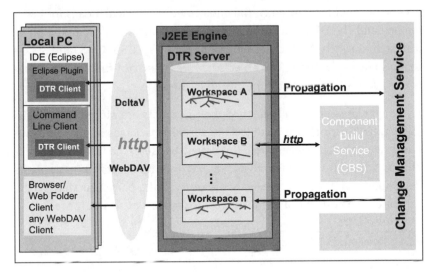

Figure 8.7 DTR Architecture

Figure 8.7 illustrates the architecture of the DTR: It consists of the server and different UIs (clients). The server stores all files as *versioned resources* in the form of *BLOBs* (Binary Large Objects) in a database (which can be shared with CBS, CMS, etc.), but presents them to the UIs in the form of files and folders. The communication is based on standards. Between clients and server, the DTR architecture uses the HTTP protocol in accordance with WebDAV and DeltaV.[12]

To access all objects in the database, you use logical storage locations, the so-called *DTR workspaces*. For the central build, source files are sent to the CBS, which again allows certain actions. Individual objects or the state of a workspace can be propagated or exported to several targets such as the CMS.

---

12 DeltaV is an enhancement of the WebDAV standard concerning versioning. Web-DAV defines a standard way of using the Web to access and manage files. DeltaV adds versioning to this concept by defining a protocol for the tasks that pertain to configuration management and version control. The DTR uses workspaces and activities to implement concepts from the DeltaV standard.

With its functions, the DTR supports the development process in the SAP NetWeaver JDI; it's embedded in such a way into this structure that it cannot be replaced by other versioning tools.

Storing Objects in the Database

The DTR stores all source files as BLOBs. All databases can be used that are supported by the SAP NetWeaver in this release. A database allows access to any object stored within and provides the ideal means for backing up data. The DTR uses its own database schema; it can share the physical database with all other development services—CBS, CMS, and SLD—that also use a database. The objects it stores need not fulfill any requirements. Basically, any file can be stored in the DTR.

All objects created for all releases of all products are stored in the DTR database.[13] This includes all objects in support packages so that continuously new objects are created for older releases. The access to these objects had to be designed in such a way that it reflects the task of the developer, giving access to exactly the objects of a particular state of the software. The concept of the DTR workspaces serves this purpose.

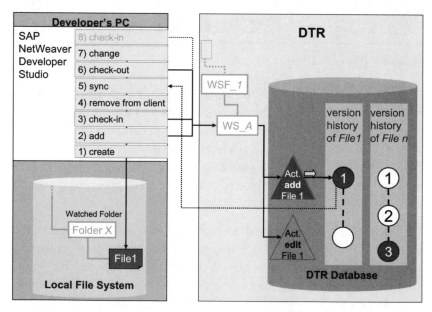

Figure 8.8 Check-In and Check-Out Mechanisms in the DTR

In Figure 8.8, you can see the check-in and check-out mechanisms of the DTR. The actions described here are integrated into most of the perspectives of the SAP NetWeaver Developer Studio. On the left side, you see

13 It is possible to use more than one database.

the PC of a developer with SAP NetWeaver Developer Studio and a local file system; on the right side, you see the DTR server whose database contains all the source files. You use the DTR client to access particular objects in the DTR database. You access all objects via the DTR workspaces. All changes are collected in activities. The total of all changes defines the workspace state.

The process flow is as follows:

1. You have created an object **File 1**.

2. You have selected the file to be inserted into the DTR database. For this, you have created an activity (add File 1). The file within the activity is open and can be changed. At this stage, it exists only in the local file system.

3. You check in **File 1** to add it to the database. Your activity is now closed and can no longer be changed. The version that was last checked in is the active version in the workspace.

4. You can now delete the local file.

5. By *synchronizing*, you can upload the file at any time from the DTR.

6. For changes, you create a new activity.

7. Make your changes.

8. Check in your changes to be stored in the database and become the new active version in the workspace.

DTR Workspaces

When all versions of all development objects of all product releases are in one database, as developer, you need a logical access mechanism that shows only those objects that you need for your task, namely, the DTR workspaces. It is only via these workspaces that you can access objects in the database.

Accessing Objects in the Database

DTR workspaces are logical views to the content of a DTR database. They work almost like folders and are created like folders. Every DTR workspace (workspace, for short) contains references to database objects. For every file, only one version can be referenced at a time in a workspace. The reason for this is that workspaces are used to define states of software components (and DCs). As we explained previously (in Section 8.2.1), every file—or even better, the function it defines—may exist only once in a software component. With every new version of a file that you create, the reference is automatically set to the new version. As soon as you create a new version of a file—in the DTR workspace in which you develop—

the reference is automatically set to the new file, which thus becomes the active version in your workspace. Every other version of this file may be the active file in other workspaces.

Note: You are able to use database objects in any number of workspaces. If one file version is required in more than one software state, several references to the same physical object are used. This saves storage space and prevents inconsistencies from occurring.

DTR Workspaces in the Development Since workspaces represent a particular collection of file versions, all major phases of the development get their own workspaces (because of the referencing, this barely increases the data volume). These phases usually are development and consolidation (*dev* and *cons*) for the development of each release.[14] We recommend this distinction for every development scenario in which the DTR is used. These phases are represented by workspaces of the same names if you use only the DTR of the entire JDI. In addition to the typical workspaces *dev* and *cons,* you can create other workspaces as required. You may create one workspace for every support package, or even several workspaces in order to recover software states (a set of particular versions of source files) as they existed at particular dates. You can then use such a workspace, for example, to find errors in a software state created at a customer site due to modifications or to recover an earlier release state.

Workspaces "inactive" and "active" If the DTR is used together with CBS and CMS,[15] for each of these phases two workspaces are created to separate objects checked by a successful central build from those that have not yet undergone this step. These workspaces are called *inactive* and *active*. The reason for this separation is that the central build is an additional check for the objects. If you use objects from other developers from the *active* workspace, you can ensure that you use the most up-to-date versions, which have been matched with all other versions. To create new objects, you always use the *inactive* workspace. For more details, see Section 8.2.3. The development phases *dev* and *cons*, which are required here as well, are represented by another level of workspace folders that contains workspaces.

Workspace Folders Organize Workspaces Typically, there are always several interrelated workspaces. The names of these workspaces are the same in every release and for every development object. To organize these workspaces more clearly, there are addi-

---

14 For details on workspaces, see Section 8.4.2. If you use only the DTR for your development, you can define the workspaces individually.

15 This is the typical usage of the DTR. Other usages are possible, but they won't be described here in detail, because this book focuses on the use of the entire JDI. Another usage would be versioning of any kind of files.

tional folders that contain the information on project and release, namely, the workspace folders. They form a hierarchy. For example, for every project one workspace folder exists, which contains one other workspace folder for all releases, which again contains the different workspaces depending on the development scenario. If the DTR is used with CBS and CMS, the lowest workspace folder level always consists of the workspace folders *dev* and *cons*, each of which contains two workspaces *inactive* and *active*. This is the scenario used by SAP and the one recommended to the customers. In this scenario, workspace folders and workspaces are no longer created manually by the administrator, but are defined and then automatically generated in the Change Management Service when creating a track (a logical development system for a new release). This results in a direct relation between the software project and the folder structure in the development system.

Development environments based on the Eclipse framework also use the term *workspace*. Don't mistake the Eclipse workspace for the DTR workspace. The Eclipse workspace is a folder in the local file system, which is controlled by the development environment. This concept is also used in the SAP NetWeaver Developer Studio. You use Eclipse workspaces for the local management of file versions that you can access using DTR workspaces.[16]

DTR Workspace and Eclipse Workspace

Activities

We have seen that all source files are stored in the database and that they're accessed in the context of workspaces, which have been defined according to the task of the development team. Now the questions arise, "How can objects be created or changed? How are new file versions managed?" The answer is that the DTR uses lists of changes—the *activities*. Activities organize related changes. Every time you create a new file (that is, its first version) or change a file, you use an activity to perform these changes. If you're familiar with the development in ABAP, you know the concept of the transport requests—activities are based on a similar concept. They contain all changes and form the (smallest) units for the transport.

Changes to the Database Content

Activities are *open* as long as they have not been checked in. You change open activities by adding or deleting files, by renaming the activity or by deleting empty activities. Open activities contain new versions in the local file system, which implies that files must be available locally in order to be changed. New files are created locally; to change files that already

Open and Closed Activities

---

16   For more information, see Section 2.2

exist on the server, synchronize them into the local file system and check them out to flag them as changeable. After changing the file, you check in the content of an activity—that is, all new file versions—onto the server to make the changes generally available. The new version automatically becomes the active version in the DTR workspace in which the activity has been created and checked in.

As soon as an activity has been checked in, it is *closed* and can no longer be changed. Closed activities can be transported or activated by a central build. This kind of transport is performed, for example, into the consolidation workspace after a file has been released in the development workspace.

Assigning Files to Activities As far as the assignment of objects to activities is concerned, there are a few cases to which we want to draw your attention.

▶ When you create a new development component, you always create several files. Since these files are related and should therefore also be transported together, you will assign all files—both the elements automatically created and every class created in the first version of the DC—to a new DC in the same activity.

▶ If, at a later time, you want to add another class to the DC or change one of the existing classes, you can use a new activity (you can also use the same activity in which the DC was created, provided that it has not yet been checked in). If several changes are related, they should be transported together to create a new working version of the DC with one single transport.

▶ If two DCs are strongly related, you can include them both into one activity. This may happen, for example, if a Java J2EE library DC—without any coding of its own—wraps a particular Java DC.

Activities contain individual or many file versions from one or more DCs. Note that objects from one activity can no longer be transported individually. Easy handling of objects therefore requires a well-considered assignment. If at a later time a separate transport should become necessary, you can still create dummy versions without making actual changes in a new activity, which then contains only a subset of the former objects.

Deleting Files in Workspaces Deleting references to files in workspaces is a special case. In the database of the DTR, no versions are ever lost that have been stored there once. However, it is frequently necessary to delete files from workspaces. To do this, you create a deletion version of a file that you also store in an activity. When you check in this activity, the reference to this file is deleted

346 SAP NetWeaver Java Development Infrastructure: Component Model and Services and it will no longer be used in this state of the software component. You can use this procedure for individual files or folders and for entire sub-trees.

All new versions are contained in activities. Activities are always created in the context of a particular workspace, and at first they take effect in this workspace only. Other states—or workspaces—of the same software component are not involved. Therefore, the state of a workspace and the state of the software component are defined by the activities it contains. To make these changes available in other systems, you use transports. The sequence in which the transports are executed are of no consequence. The name of an activity contains a GUID and a timestamp. With this information, the versions contained can always be appended at the correct position in the version tree. This implies that the most recent version of a file available in a workspace is the active version. The integration of activities changes the state of a workspace. The development is always directed forward. You can synchronize any version that is or was active in the workspace; however, older versions can no longer become active versions in this workspace.

Defining Workspace States

Copying Changes to Other Workspaces

Often, changes must be copied from one workspace (that is, software state) into another. One example is the integration of development objects from the development state into the consolidation state. The organization of copied objects is determined by the activities. You copy the activities into other workspaces. Copying files into a workspace—which is setting a reference in the workspace to the object in the data-base—is called *integration*. If source and target workspace lie in the same repository, the integration is possible without a physical transport, because every workspace consists of nothing but references. If they lie in different repositories, for example, one DTR at SAP and the other one at the customer, then the first step is the export of the objects into a result-ing file, the second step is the import of this file into the database of the target DTR, and the third and last step is the integration into one or more workspaces.

Integrating Activities into Workspaces

If you want to transport several activities—for example, an entire state of a workspace—at once, you can combine several activities in propagation lists that can then be transported. There are various options for creating propagation lists. For example, you may export a workspace state of a certain moment afterward in a propagation list. By integrating this state into a new workspace, you may be able to recover an older state.

Propagation Lists

Conflicts

At the beginning of this chapter, we mentioned the three prerequisites that the development process at SAP has to meet: Maintenance of the software over a long period of time, the possibility of developing simultaneously at different locations, and modifications at the customer site. All these processes share one characteristic: They use source files in various states. It may happen that versions are changed concurrently, that is, one version is changed at two locations so that two new versions are created that now exist in parallel.[17] This is not allowed in the same workspace, because a workspace can contain only one version of any file.

How Conflicts Arise
Parallel development can result from checking out the version in a workspace more than once, or from integrating two versions into the same workspace (of course, simultaneously created versions of one file in different workspaces don't cause a conflict, because each of them belongs to a different state of the software and they will not be installed together):

Check-In Conflict
▶ The first case occurs if a second user checks out the same file version as the first user, and does so before the first user has checked it in again.[18] Checking in the first parallel version does not cause any problems. The check-in trial of the second user or developer results in a check-in conflict (it is immaterial who checked out first; it is only important who checks in last). As the second user or developer, you must then choose one of the following options:

  ▶ To accept the currently active version and to discard your own version

  ▶ To set your version as the new active version in the workplace

  ▶ To merge the two versions into one common version
    The SAP NetWeaver Developer Studio supports this action by showing the differences between the two file versions and thus facilitating the creation of the new version, which will contain the changes from both versions.

Integration Conflict and Modifications
▶ The second case occurs if the two versions have been created in different workspaces, but are then brought together into the same workspace. This may happen within an enterprise, if, for example, changes

---

17 Existing in parallel implies that both versions are based on the same *root version*, but none of them is the predecessor of the other; if this was the case, the newer version would simply replace the older version.

18 You can avoid this by using the check-out option *Exclusive Check-Out*. However, this is not always the optimal choice.

have been carried out simultaneously in the development and the consolidation workspace or if changes from support packages are copied into a subsequent release in which these objects have also been changed.

The most important cause for this kind of conflict is the modification at the customer site. The customer creates a workspace for modifications, which will usually be updated with changes in support packages, for example, from SAP. If the same files are affected by the changes, an integration conflict occurs. In this case, the same mechanisms that were used for solving check-in conflicts are available here and no changes will be automatically overwritten.

If you want to synchronize several development locations—within an enterprise or between a software company and the modified customer system—the information that enables conflict recognition must be kept during transport. When you use the DTR to *move* objects, this is always the case, independent of whether files are integrated within the same DTR into other workspaces or whether they are exported and re-imported into other installations of the DTR. Therefore, we refer to the *Global Version History*.

Global Version History

DTR User Interfaces (UIs)

To access the DTR, you can use different user interfaces (or *clients*), but please don't confuse them with the DTR client, which determines the DTR that a DTR UI accesses. For the communication, the HTTP protocol is used. The choice of the UI depends on the task and role of the user:

▶ *DTR Perspective in the SAP NetWeaver Developer Studio*: This is the user interface that you as a developer use. In the *Repository Browser*, you display the objects on the server and in that part of the local file system that is used by the DTR. Icons represent the respective state of any object, whether it is checked out, available *only* locally or *only* on the server, or whether it has been checked out by another user, and so forth. In addition, the default layout of this perspective shows the open and closed activities of the DTR console. You can, for example, display the *Version Graph* view, which shows a version history of the selected object and allows access such as the synchronization of particular versions or the check of its content.

SAP NetWeaver Developer Studio

▶ *DTR Administrator Plug-In*: All views and perspectives in the SAP NetWeaver Developer Studio are plug-ins. The DTR Admin plug-in enables you to perform a number of administrative tasks such as creat-

DTR Administrator Plug-In

ing workspaces and integrating activities and, above all, granting access permissions to objects in the DTR database.

DTR Command-Line Client
▶ *DTR Command-Line Client*: This client is called in the command-line editor. It is used exclusively for DTR administration. It allows you as an administrator to create workspace folders and workspaces, but also to create propagation lists and to start exports. You can use it to start tasks as batch jobs. You cannot use it to maintain permissions.

Creating DTR Clients
You can use any of the aforementioned user interfaces to access various DTR instances, which is why you must restrict the access to one particular DTR. You do this by creating a *DTR client*. From a technical point of view, the definition of a DTR client is an XML file. It contains a name, the URL of the DTR server, and the *local root*. This is a folder you create or select. This folder stores all the files that you are working with, which means that all files you are synchronizing are copied to this folder and that you use this folder to create new files that you will later store in the DTR. The DTR monitors the local root: Any objects you create here are also visible in the Repository Browser. To facilitate the assignment to particular development projects and versions, during file synchronization the DTR creates a folder structure that corresponds to the structure of the workspace folders and workspaces. In addition, a DTR client usually contains a filter definition that restricts the access to special workspaces. Furthermore, access can be restricted to read-only.

DTR Client and Development Scenario
Clients are created depending on the selected development scenario. If you use only the DTR, then every developer creates his or her client in the DTR. If you use the Change Management Service (CMS), *development configurations* are used for development. They determine the access for all systems, and therefore include the DTR client into the development configuration definition.[19] In these DTR client definitions, write access is restricted to the *inactive* workspace, and read access is restricted to the *active* workspace. This is the technical basis that ensures that only in the *active* workspace are those files that have been checked by a central build available.

Integration of the DTR in the JDI
Besides the UIs that directly belong to the DTR, the other systems of the JDI also access the DTR. These include the CMS, in which the workspace folders and workspaces are created, and the Component Build Service (CBS), which for the central build process directly fetches source files from the DTR and triggers the activation of the source files after a successful build process.

---

19 For more information, see Section 8.4.2.

Authorization Concept in the DTR

In the DTR, there is a distinction between authentication and authorization. The authentication determines whether you're allowed to access the DTR. This is ensured by checking the user/password combination with the *User Management Engine* of the SAP NetWeaver or against another SAP system. The authorization enables a very fine-tuned check: The administrator can control the access explicitly for every object in the DTR. This allows you to determine that critical objects can be changed by only certain developers but still remain visible for all.

Authentication and Authorization in the DTR

For this fine-tuning, you use *access control lists* (ACLs). An access control list defines the privileges that each user or group has for a particular resource. Technically speaking, an ACL consists of *access control entities* (ACEs), which, in turn, assign one or more privileges to a user or a group. These privileges contain basic permissions, such as read and write access to files or for check-in, which are required by all developers. Privileges also contain permissions that are usually reserved for administrators, such as exporting, importing and integrating activities, and creating users and workspaces.

Access Control Lists

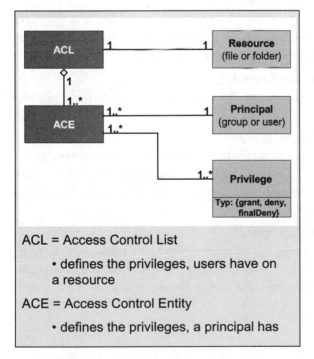

Figure 8.9 ACL Class Diagram

Access Control Lists (ACLs) and Access Control Entitities (ACEs) define how users and groups can access objects in the DTR.

Inheriting
Permissions The file path is used to determine the permissions. The permissions don't need to be defined for all files. A file of a child hierarchy level inherits all permissions granted to a parent folder, unless permissions are granted to the child file directly.

You can define ACEs that exclude one another for the same resource. This need not be an accident: Think of giving a group a write permission on a high level folder, which is inherited by lower-level folders. There you give only read permissions to some users belonging to this group. These settings are contradictory. To get a valid permission, even in the case of contradicting ACEs, privileges are interpreted according to a set of rules applicable for all permissions, independent of one another but always in the sequence of their numbering.

Hierarchy of the
Permission Rules

▶ **Rule 1—"finalDeny" before all "children"**
A privilege granted with *finalDeny* undoes all other ACEs that this privilege grants to this resource or a child resource.[20]

▶ **Rule 2—"inheritance ignore"**
This rule allows you to interrupt the inheritance hierarchy. A resource, for which an ACL—labeled as *ignore inheritance*—is defined, does not inherit any authorizations from superior folders.

▶ **Rule 3—"child" before "parent"**
This rule allows you to refine the permissions for resources in lower-level folders.

▶ **Rule 4—"user" before "group"**
This rule defines the priority for contradicting ACEs that are defined for the same resource. Because this rule is defined after Rule 3, it can affect only the same resource. This rule gives the user entry priority over the group entry.

▶ **Rule 5—"deny" before "grant"**
If there is a *grant* as well as a *deny* permission for a privilege, *deny* takes priority. Because this rule is applied after Rule 4, it can affect only colliding permissions for the same user or for user groups with a common member.

---

20 You can use this rule to set a DTR workspace temporarily into a *read-only* state, without having to explicitly change every granted privilege.

8.2.3 Component Build Service (CBS)

The Component Build Service (CBS) is a J2EE application based on the SAP component model. It contains a build tool and uses a database system to manage archives. The CBS is the central build environment of the SAP NetWeaver Java Development Infrastructure. The build process is component-based and is triggered for individual components on demand of a developer. Figure 8.10 shows the CBS architecture.

Architecture and Task of the CBS

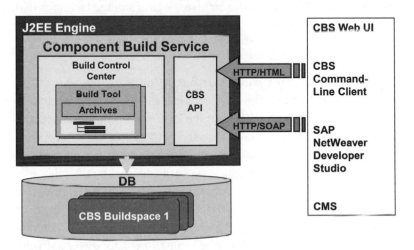

Figure 8.10 Architecture of the Component Build Service (CBS)

Like the DTR, the CBS runs on the J2EE Engine and uses a database to store archives. The archives are organized in buildspaces. For the communication, the HTTP protocol is used. As UIs, the CBS Web UI and the Activation view are available in the SAP NetWeaver Developer Studio. There is also a command-line tool for special administrative tasks. You should think of the Change Management Service (CMS) as a kind of CBS user interface, because you can use it to control important actions in the Component Build Service, such as creating buildspaces.

Apart from building archives, the CBS manages all archives that are required during development. These archives include the build results of the source files, which are created by building the source files, and the archives that already exist for the development. Archive management involves keeping them up to date, which is achieved by rebuilding all DCs that depend on a particular DC whenever that DC is built. If the build of the dependent DC fails—due to a change in the interface of the used DCs—the DC receives the status *broken*, which is displayed in the CBS Web UI and must be corrected by the respective developer.

The CBS build process is based on the component model. The built units are the development components. During the build, the relations between DCs are checked; use dependencies to all used database components must be defined and made available in a usable software component. Cyclic dependencies are not allowed and will be detected.

The CBS provides the build environment according to the development tasks. The choice of the software components matches the product version to be developed. To access the archives, logical storage locations that is, the buildspaces, are used.

Buildspace

Buildspace Tasks Because the CBS allows the parallel development of various versions of software components, the archive versions in the CBS must be separated. You achieve this by defining logical storage locations on the database, the *buildspaces*. They serve as virtual build servers. A buildspace always contains all newly built archives and all used archives from one part of the track, either *dev* or *cons*.[21] Such a state is usually defined by the release of a product and by the development phase. For every product release, one development state and one consolidation state are created, both of which are represented by one buildspace. A product consists of software components; a buildspace contains one *compartment* for every software component. Software components can be used in two ways.

▶ Used software components: They contain, for example, Basis libraries. They exist only in archive state and cannot be changed.

▶ Software components that are developed in this product version: For these SCs, there are source files in the DTR and archives in the CBS. The archives are generated by building development components that have been created in this software component.

Therefore, a buildspace usually contains several compartments. Between the software components, use dependencies are defined in the SLD.

Workspaces and Buildspaces For every buildspace, there is a pair of workspaces in the DTR. This pair of workspaces is called *inactive* and *active*, as described in Section 8.2.2. These workspaces are tightly connected with the build process in the CBS.

---

21 This can also be a state of a selection of SCs that together form a product.

Build Process—Activating Changes

The build process in the CBS is not a build that tries to build the entire product. Instead, every developer decides when to build his or her changes, based on that developer's respective activities. Activating an activity starts the build process for the relevant DCs. This is possible because, due to the metadata of every DC, the use dependencies to other DCs are known. Based on this information, the dependent DCs of any DC can be determined and updated by an automatic build whenever the using DC has been changed. The nightly build is no longer necessary, as it was when one could build the dependent DCs only by building all DCs, because the dependencies were not transparent. The component-based process has the following advantage: You can build every section of the entire software individually. This is the technical prerequisite for the build on demand of the developer. This optimizes the waiting period of the individual developer for the results of the central build of his or her DCs and has another important effect: A failed central build of one component hardly affects the other developers in the same software project. Until the build is successful, the latest archive versions—and, due to the activation concept, also the latest source file versions—remain active for all users. If required by the development situation, you can also start all DCs together in the CBS.

Tasks of the Build Process in the CBS

The CBS build process performs three essential tasks. To achieve this, it uses the development component concept.

▶ It creates the runtime objects. An essential advantage for the developer is that manual build scripts are no longer necessary. They're already available in the build tool and are used according to the type of the DC to be built.

Build Scripts

▶ It introduces an extra check of the development. This is important because the build process determines whether the rules of the component model are kept. This also occurs in the *DC Build* in the SAP NetWeaver Developer Studio, which uses the same build tool as the CBS.

DC Check

▶ The biggest difference to the local build is that the objects required for the build process are retrieved exclusively from the central systems DTR and CBS.[22] This implies that there is always a check to determine whether the most up-to-date versions of all objects—source files and archives—are used.

Synchronizing the Developer Team

---

22 The difference with the local build is that the archives (or runtime objects) that a developer has copied to his or her local file system can be changed during his or her work (provided that they lie in a changeable SC).

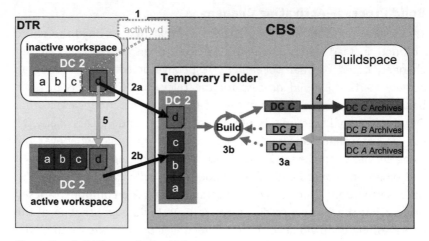

Figure 8.11 Build Process in the CBS

Let's look at an example for a build process (see also Figure 8.11). Assume that you want to build a DC *C*, which depends on the DCs DC *A* and DC *B*. DC *C* consists of four development objects, a, b, c, and d, and has already been built successfully once before (this is why it exists in both workspaces, *inactive* and *active*). You have an activity **d**, which contains changes to the development object d.

The build process is as follows:

1. You choose **Activate** for activity **d**.

2. A temporary folder for the build task is created.

3. Object d is fetched from workspace *inactive*.

4. Objects a, b and c are fetched from workspace *active*.

5. Archives of the DCs *A* and *B* are fetched from the buildspace.

6. The build process builds the new archive for DC *C*.

7. The archives in the buildspace are updated.

8. After the successful build, the CBS automatically triggers the integration of activity **d** into workspace *active*.

The example in the figure shows the meaning of the activation. By fetching all unchanged objects from the *active* workspace, it is guaranteed that these objects have already been built successfully. Only the new versions in the activated activity are added. All used DCs, which are used as archives, are included from the *Archive Pool* in the buildspace. With this procedure, the latest versions of all archives are used automatically. All things considered, the build process in the temporary folder of the build tasks provides a *preview* to the new state of the buildspace. Only if it executes without error, will this state be actually written to the database.

Now only one step is missing in the activation process,[23] which is the activation of the source files. You know that for every buildspace there are two workspaces in the DTR—*inactive* and *active*. New objects are always created in the *inactive* workspace. After these objects have been built successfully in an activity, they are automatically integrated into the *active* workspace. Because you primarily use source files from this workspace, you can ensure that this state is consistent with the latest version of the entire software project. Therefore, a synchronization of all development is performed both on the source file level and on the archive level.

Activating the Source Files

A few questions arise that pertain to the size of the developer teams.

Provision for Large Teams

▶ Build processes are costly. What happens if several developers want to activate their changes? The CBS can form clusters. For very large teams, several instances of the CBS that serve a common buildspace can be called via a dispatcher, which balances the load.

▶ What happens if during my build process a used DC is changed? The CBS automatically deals with this situation. It discovers the change, builds the used DC first, and then restarts the build process of the dependent DC.

Build Variants

The CBS can generate a number of variants from the sources of a compartment (however, for every compartment, at least one variant must be defined).

Tasks of Build Variants

▶ Variants that differ in the choice of special parameters for the used compilers, for example, one *optimized* and one *debugging* variant

▶ Variants that are designed for different operating systems or runtime environments

▶ Variants that consider country-specific or language-specific peculiarities

For every compartment, the development configuration defines a list of variants and at least one variant must exist. Not all compartments offer the same variants. If variants are defined for a compartment, the compartment provides specific libraries and deployable archives for every

---

23 In special cases and with the appropriate authorization, the activation can be carried out even if the build process fails.

component and every variant (build variants). For a detailed discussion of the development configurations, see Section 8.2.4, explaining the *Change Management Service*.

Examples for Build Variants Let's look at an example. A compartment determines that a software component SC *X* creates a *debugging* and an *optimized* variant. The variants differ only in that the compilers and generators are called with different options. The variants have the identifiers *dbg* and *opt*. The component is designed to support two different operating systems so that overall four variants must be built: *linux/dbg*, *linux/opt*, *win/dbg*, and *win/opt*. Lastly, the component is translated into different languages so that the number of variants must be multiplied with the number of supported languages: *de/linux/dbg*, *en/linux/dbg*, *de/linux/opt* and so on.

Required Variants When activating changes in the build service, all variants defined for a compartment of a component are built. However, it may not be necessary for a successful activation that all variants are built without errors.

UIs of the Component Build Service

For CBS users, different clients are available.

▶ Developers use views in the SAP NetWeaver Developer Studio:

  ▶ The *Activation View* shows the changes that can be built. Here, you can directly start the build process for all activities. Since changes become generally available only after the activation, you're prompted to start the activation when you check in an activity (however, you can postpone that).

  ▶ In the *Request View*, you can monitor the build process.

▶ CBS Web UI: In a Web browser, you can perform administrative tasks in the CBS. You see all available buildspaces and find details on the following objects:

  ▶ Buildspaces: You see all compartments and their states (readiness to accept input, building of build requests activated, and so on). Here, you can change the specified buildspace and compartment settings or delete buildspaces.[24] In the details, you see information on the DCs, such as top-level DCs, broken DCs,[25] and so forth.

  ▶ Development components: Here, you can search DCs for certain criteria such as name, buildspace, or vendor. You see details on the

---

24 If required, you usually do this by deleting a track in the CMS.
25 This information is important, because incompatible changes to interfaces in the CBS also cause problems in the build process.

selected DCs, such as build status, child DCs, public parts, used DCs, and you can build the DCs.

▶ Activities: Here, you can search activities for certain criteria such as their timestamps, and activate any not-yet-activated activities. You can also enforce activation, even if the build fails.

▶ Request: Here, you find the build requests.

▶ Compartments: Here, you find information on the compartments of build requests.

▶ Development components: Here, you can search DCs for various criteria.

▶ CMS Command-Line Client: This UI is used by administrators only. Here, you can create buildspaces or build all DCs of a compartment. However, most of these functions are usually performed in the CBS Web UI or in the CMS.[26]

▶ Change Management Service (CMS): You can regard the CMS as a client of the CBS, because it is used by administrators to create buildspaces, which may then be filled by imports.

8.2.4   Change Management Service (CMS)

The Change Management Service (CMS) is the environment for administrators and quality managers of the JDI, who look after the development work in the JDI. We have seen that the management mechanisms are available both for the source files and the archives and that they are tailored to meet the needs of the respective development task. The required workspaces and buildspaces for the development phases *Development* and *Consolidation* must be created and the buildspaces must be filled. For both phases, additional test systems are defined, which allow extensive testing of the entire application at a very early stage. Like DTR and CBS, the CMS is a J2EE application that runs in the J2EE Engine of SAP NetWeaver. CMS also uses its own database schema, which can run on the same physical database with DTR and CBS.

Architecture and Tasks of the CMS

As Figure 8.12 shows, the CMS runs on the J2EE Engine—like DTR and CBS—and uses a database to store development configurations and transport requests. For the communication, the HTTP protocol is used. The UIs are the CMS Web UI and the Transport View in the SAP NetWeaver Developer Studio.

---

26 In particular, this includes the creation of buildspaces, which occurs automatically when a track is created.

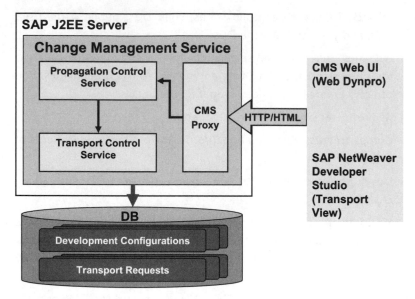

Figure 8.12 Architecture of the CMS

All objects for every development phase of a product release (as a typical application example) collectively are called *logical systems.* We refer to them as *logical* because no physical system is required for each of these systems, since the workspaces and buildspaces of many development versions can lie in the same DTR or CBS. Because the systems for development and consolidation always belong together, we refer to these combined systems as a *track*. Tracks are organized in *domains*. For every vendor, a domain is created and managed in the CMS of this vendor; therefore, each CMS manages one domain. A domain organizes tracks. It contains the data required for the environment of the track management: which SLD is used, and on which server the CMS runs.

It is the administrators' task to define these logical systems and to manage the transports into and between these systems. We can distinguish two large task complexes.

▶ One complex comprises the creation of the logical development systems. They provide the development landscape for the respective development tasks and consist of the DTR workspaces, the buildspaces with the appropriate archives, and the related test systems. For these tasks, you use the *Landscape Configurator* of the CMS.

▶ The second large complex consists of the transports and processes of the software logistics. For these tasks, you use the *Transport Studio* on the CMS.

Before we discuss the individual tasks in detail, we'll look at the software logistics process as a whole (see Figure 8.13).

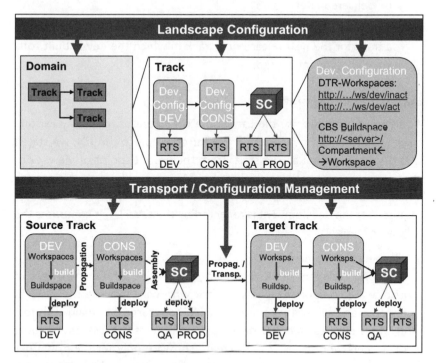

Figure 8.13 Processes of the Software Logistics

Figure 8.13 shows the structure of the logical development systems and the transport tasks in the development process. We begin in the Landscape Configurator.

1. You start with the definition of a domain for the development.

2. In the domain, you define a track for every product release.

3. Tracks contain logical development systems for development and consolidation. Each of these systems is laid down in a development configuration. The development configuration lays down workspaces, buildspaces, and the used runtime systems.

   ▶ After the track definition, the tasks in the Transport Studio follow: Used software components (SCs) are checked in and imported into the buildspaces as archives.

   ▶ During the development of the new SC, the consolidation version is supplied from the development version.

- The result of a track after approval and assembly is an SC archive that is deployed into runtime systems for testing purposes and will be delivered later.

- From one (source) track, other tracks can be supplied. This may be a track for the next release or a track in which the newly built software component is used.

Landscape Configurator

As administrator, you use the Landscape Configurator to display existing tracks and to create new ones. In the introduction to the JDI, we stated that the development always starts from the product point-of-view. Consequently, the software logistics in the CMS also adhere to this model. You create a new track for every new product release. The process required for the development is reflected by the CMS UI. It comprises the following steps:

Step 1   1. **Creating the Domain**

The domain defines the CMS area of the vendor, who is the owner of a software component. Every vendor who wants to use the CMS to produce and sell software must ask SAP to reserve a domain. This reservation ensures that the development objects are globally unique. Customers who use a CMS to create software only for their own use can choose a name at will. They can also use a number of domains, however, the names of these domains must be unique. A domain definition contains the following elements:

- **Domain Name**: It consists of four digits for customers who want to sell the software created in the CMS and three digits for customers who use their software only internally.

- CMS Name, Description, and URL

- **CMS User and Password**: The CMS user is required for the communication between the individual JDI components; with this CMS user, the logged-on user connects to DTR, CBS, and CMS. To be able to do this, the user needs the configuration authorization in the User Management Engine.

- **Transport Directory**: Here, files for the import into a track are stored.

Per the domain definition, you also load the information on the existing software components. You need this information in order to choose a unique name and receive data on the available (usable) software components. You need this information when you create the track.

2. **Defining the Track** Step 2

As an administrator, you define the logical systems for the development and consolidation of a release as follows:

▶ **Track Name and Description**

▶ **Repository Type**: You can choose between DTR and SAP Exchange Infrastructure (XI) repository.

▶ **URL of DTR and CBS**. With the specifications made here, the workspace folders, workspaces, and buildspaces are generated automatically. The DTR client is created accordingly; it has the same name as the track with the extension _D for *Development* and _C for *Consolidation*. It contains a filter that displays only the workspaces *inactive* and *active* that belong to this development phase. The Write permission is valid only for workspace *inactive*. The workspaces— always *inactive* and *active*—lie in a hierarchy of workspace folders with the a) name of the track, b) name of the SC to be developed, and c) name of the development phase. The buildspaces carry names that are composed of a) the track ID, b) the track name, and c) the identifier of the development phase that can extend the name.

Now you define the SCs that compose the product release. You use two tables to do this:

▶ The table of the software components for the development: Here, you select the SCs that contain the functions that are specific to this product. These SCs with the release specification can be selected from only the SCs that have been loaded from the SLD. In addition, you determine the delivery format: archives, source files, or source files plus archives.

▶ The table for the used (required) SCs: The dependencies are defined in the SLD and read from there. Only in special cases are you allowed to select the available SC releases from a list of existing software components. In this case, the defining XML file must be adapted manually.

3. **Determining the Runtime Systems** Step 3

You can determine runtime systems for all four development phases: development, consolidation, test, and production. You define the systems by entering the following information:

- **SDM Host Name and Port Number**: The SDM is the Software Deployment Manager, which deploys the runtime objects (archives) into the runtime systems.

- **Password**: Not all users are allowed to deploy into all systems.

Step 4 4. **Defining the Track Connections**

Two different states of software components have been introduced in the development: the used SCs and the newly created SCs. There are two cases, in which newly created SCs are used in a different track:

- The product extends into the next release. Still the same SC is developed and the same SCs are used.

- The newly created SC becomes a used SC in another track that is developed in parallel. During the development phase, versions of the SC developed in the source track are constantly imported as used SCs into the target track.

Transport Studio

After the definition of the logical development systems, you switch to the Transport Studio, because your next task is to provide the used objects centrally to all developers on the team that develops this product release. In this studio, the UI again reflects the order in which the required steps must be executed:

1. **Check-In**

Check in all used software components as archives. They will not be changed. You specify the name of the Software Component Archive (SCA) file of every used SC. The archives must be available in the transport directory of the CMS. You select them from a list. The details of each SC contain the following information:

- Component: The name of the software component.

- Release: The release is determined by the information in the track definition.

- Patch level, support package number, and version of the archive.

2. **Development**

The selected archives are now listed for the development system — you can import the archives that you checked in the last step. They are now available in the buildspace for the development phase.

3. **Consolidation**

You repeat this step for the consolidation system. However, you import[27] the newly developed SC—in addition to the used SCs as a source file—into the consolidation system. The archives are created in the Component Build Service. You can perform extensive tests in the consolidation system.

4. **Assembly**

After the testing, the delivery version is created. From the imported and the new archives—and, depending on the management decisions also from the source files   the new delivery version is created. Delivering source files is a prerequisite for modifications at the customer site. The respective setting in the CMS enables or disables these modifications. The build result of the assembly is a deployable *Software Component Archive* (SCA).

5. **Approval**

Now the results of the assembly must be approved. The approval for the delivery will, of course, depend on the test results of the SCAs.

6. **System State**

With this extra option, you can check the current state in the development system at any time. Here you can determine which software components are available in which versions in the different systems.

With these steps, the development cycle is completed. For the support packages, the next release, or a new product, no new physical systems need to be created; all you have to do is to define them in the SLD and create new tracks in the CMS.

Development Configurations

Creating a new track produces two development configurations that describe the development and consolidation system. Every development configuration has an XML file. It contains all the information that you specified when creating the track, but also information that you provided in the product release definition in the SLD.

▶ **Information from the SLD**

This includes use dependencies between the SCs. As you may recall from the section on the component model, you can use another SC only if this particular use has been defined.

---

27   In the DTR, this step is the integration of workspace *dev active* and *cons inactive*.

▶ **Information from the CMS**

As described above, this includes specifications on the workspaces to be used, the related buildspace, CMS, and test systems.

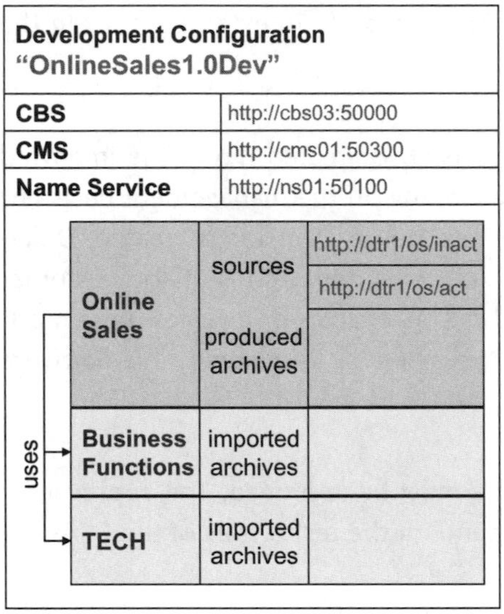

Development Configuration "OnlineSales1.0Dev"	
CBS	http://cbs03:50000
CMS	http://cms01:50300
Name Service	http://ns01:50100

uses			
	Online Sales	sources	http://dtr1/os/inact
			http://dtr1/os/act
		produced archives	
	Business Functions	imported archives	
	TECH	imported archives	

Figure 8.14 Development Configuration "Online Sales"

Figure 8.14 shows an example of a development configuration for a product *Online Sales* Version 1.0 in the development state. You can see the following information that defines the access of the developer—who uses the SAP NetWeaver Developer Studio—to the JDI and the objects managed within: the URL of the used CBS, CMS, and Name Service. You can see that the SC *Online Sales* uses the SCs *Business Functions* and *TECH*, and which DTR workspaces are used.

The developer imports the XML file of every development configuration into the SAP NetWeaver Developer Studio. This configures the Developer Studio in such a way that it accesses only those objects that are required for the relevant development task. As described in the section on DTR, the development configuration defines the DTR clients used to develop the product release.

8.2.5 Software Logistics in the Development Process with the SAP NetWeaver Java Data Infrastructure

Let's look at the entire development process as you find it when using SAP NetWeaver Developer Studio and Java Development Infrastructure.

We want to focus on the effects of the described concepts on the processes controlled by the developer, which we have not yet discussed in detail.

A product release has been defined with the related SCs and stored in the CMS track. The development process starts with the importing of one of the development configurations into the SAP NetWeaver Developer Studio:

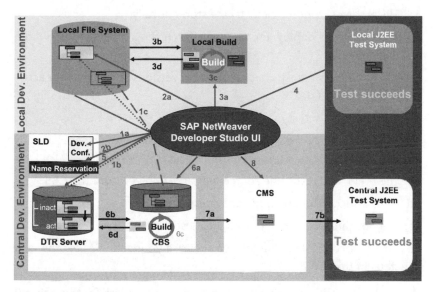

Figure 8.15 Development Process with SAP NetWeaver Developer Studio and JDI

In Figure 8.15, you see the local development environment with the SAP NetWeaver Developer Studio UI (this is important, because even though the installation is local, the UI shows a combined view of local and central objects) and the central JDI.

For the developer, the development process includes these steps:

1a. Use the SLD to import a development configuration. To be able to start, all you need is its URL and the name of the configuration.

1b. Download (synchronize) the source files from the DTR.

1c. Download (synchronize) the archives from the CBS.

2a. Create new objects or check out existing ones and change them.[28]

---

28 When you synchronize existing database components in order to change them, you need a project. You can use **Create Project** in the Developer Studio to execute both simultaneously.

2b. When creating new objects (DCs or packages), the name service is called to guarantee the uniqueness of names.

3a. Start the local build of the DC in the SAP NetWeaver Developer Studio.

3b. Source files and archives are retrieved from the file system.

3c. The new archives are built—the build tool is the same as the one in the CBS—and the same checks are performed to build the DCs.

3d. The archives (runtime objects) are stored locally.

4. You can now deploy the archives for testing into the local J2EE Engine.

5. After a successful test, check in the new versions (stored in your activities) into the DTR.

6a. Activate your activity.

6b. The new objects are retrieved from the *inactive* workspace, already built source files are retrieved from the *active* workspace.

6c. The build starts with the source files and archives from the CBS.

6d. After a successful build, the activation is triggered.

7a. The new archives are deployed into test systems.

7b. After a successful central test, you release your activities for the next steps in the CMS.

With the release of your objects, your development work for this phase is complete. New steps follow in the CMS for the consolidation—the import into the consolidation system and the appropriate tests.

The last phase of the process comprises assembly and approval. Now a release cycle is complete. The next release cycle begins with the definition of the next release in the SLD.

Summary

The outstanding characteristic of the development process with the JDI is that the entire lifecycle of the software is reflected in an integrated development environment. This new way of structuring software in the component model—from the product to the development objects—forms the basis of this process. The exact definition of interfaces and their use in the development components permit a build process on the component level and improve the maintainability and reusability of software. Arranging development components in software components facilitates the definition of dependencies between functions within a product release.

You define a product in the SLD by describing name, vendor, and release. Then you define the used and new software components, including the relationships between them.

The definition of the new product release is copied into the CMS. Here, you define the track for the development, which consists of the logical development systems for development and the consolidation phases of the new release. With this, you automatically create the buildspaces and workspaces in CBS and DTR, trigger the name service and determine the test systems for the individual development phases. The track definition results in two development configurations, each one represented by an XML file. This defines the access for all members of the development groups to the correct objects in the JDI.

The new way of managing the source files with a global version history in the DTR permits the synchronization of development locations for a distributed development. Without such synchronization, the common work on one consistent code basis would not be possible, unless you're willing to accept immensely long waiting periods when using one single central system. With this process, the implementation of a joint project, for example, between India and the US, becomes possible. These same mechanisms permit a real modification concept for the customers that allows you to apply support packages to your development system without overwriting the modifications that you made. All source files are stored in a database, and access to the objects is based on a concept of logical storage locations, the workspaces, which are defined according to the development task.

Consistency is also the keyword for the archives: You find build and archive management centrally in the CBS. For the first time, this ensures that archives are always kept up-to-date. In the CBS, too, the storage is organized according to the development tasks in logical storage locations, the buildspaces. Even if an inconsistency occurs with locally downloaded archives, because used DCs have been changed by their owners, the central build recognizes it and doesn't write inconsistent states into the CBS database. The activation concept linked to the central build represents an additional check of all objects and provides security when using source files and archives of other developers.

Consistency and availability of source files and archives are ensured. Storing all objects in databases provides the perfect basis for scaling and backup. The communication between the systems of the JDI follows the SAP principle of supporting open standards. This is also emphasized by

SAP's choice of the Eclipse framework as the basis for the SAP NetWeaver Developer Studio.

As developer, you have access to all objects defined in Java and J2EE, as well as access to the objects developed by SAP such as Web Dynpro and Java Dictionary. Check-in and check-out are performed in a consistent environment. The local part of the development environment uses the efficiency and flexibility of the PCs. Waiting for the results of the nightly build is no longer necessary. By activating and releasing your objects, you decide when they will be built and when they will become available for use by other developers.

After the release by the developer, the quality manager can use the utilities and test systems defined in the CMS, which are required for a secure and timely delivery.

Thus SAP NetWeaver Developer Studio and Java Development Infrastructure provide new ways for a more efficient software development in global development and delivery scenarios, both at SAP and at customers and partners. Advantages of the new processes are: The consistent environment for all development groups covering the entire software lifecycle from product definition to maintenance; the possibility of synchronizing distributed development; and the opportunity for modification management. Some of these possibilities are especially essential for large user groups; others are independent of the size of the development groups.

9 SAP NetWeaver Java Development Infrastructure: Step by Step to the Example Application

You already know the SAP NetWeaver Developer Studio from the example in Chapter 3, the Employee Application. We will now use this example—as we did in many other sections—to illustrate the development with the Java Development Infrastructure (JDI) according to the component model. You will create the same development objects as before. However, this time, you'll use software components (SCs) and development components (DCs), and define public parts and use dependencies of DCs. Then, you'll check in your components into the Design Time Repository (DTR) and activate them in the Component Build Service (CBS) to make them centrally available. Last, you'll release your components in the Change Management Service (CMS) to complete the development.

In order to work with this chapter, you should know Java and J2EE. However, more importantly, you should understand the concepts of the component model and its use in the Developer Studio, as well as the interaction between the Developer Studio and the central Java Development Infrastructure (JDI). Therefore, to gain the most benefit from this exercise, you should have read and understood the sections on the JDI—Design Time Repository (DTR), Component Build Service (CBS), and Change Management Service (CMS).

Prerequisites

Before you can perform your steps as developer, you must have executed the administrative steps of creating a user and a track. For more details, see Section 9.2.

This exercise is designed to give you a feeling for modularizing the software purposefully into development components (DCs) and to familiarize yourself with working in the central SAP NetWeaver Java Development Infrastructure. You will learn that by simply selecting a development component, you can configure your development environment—the Developer Studio—for your development task, which in our case is the Employee application. All other steps will then be carried out in this configuration. Source files and archives are managed in the JDI. You can access only those objects that have been defined in the development configuration by using the DTR workspaces and buildspaces.

Objectives

The development process with Developer Studio and JDI has been discussed in detail in Chapter 8. Therefore, you already know that even
though you use the JDI, the local PC still plays a vital role. All existing
source files and archives of the runtime objects are stored in the central
systems of DTR and CBS. If you want to change them, you must download them to your local file system, check them out, and then make your
changes locally. These changes are gathered in activities. Only after a successful local DC build (it corresponds exactly to the build in the CBS) and
test in the local J2EE Engine should you make your changes generally
available on the DTR server by checking in your activities. The central
build now activates your source files, which implies that they have been
tested and can safely be used by other developers. (By default, outside of
the group that develops a DC, only the activated versions should be
used.) After a successful test of the centrally built archives, you release
your activities in the CMS. The SAP NetWeaver Developer Studio provides the user interface for all these steps.

9.1   The Employee Example Application

We want to emphasize again that using the JDI does not result in a different basic structure of the development objects. However, some objects
are added due to the component model. All features of the SAP *component model*—such as *public parts* and *use dependencies*—are added
through the metadata of the database component. EJBs, JSPs, Java
classes, and so forth are not involved. For our example application, this
means that you can copy all specifications on the data model, persistency,
business logic, presentation layer, and Web service without changes.
With the JDI, you will import the required development configurations
and create all elements with unchanged source code. You still use the
Developer Studio to do so. However, it is now important that you create
all projects as DCs. The steps that follow are basically new: You define the
DC-specific properties, which are the public parts and the use dependencies. Then you perform the steps that make your objects centrally available. You store them centrally in the DTR, create the runtime objects in
the CBS, and release them in the CMS.

Using DCs results in the structure shown in Figure 9.1. There, you see the
SC *EMPLOYEE* with 4 DCs displayed with their names and types. As components of the DCs you see their public parts and the use dependencies
between the DCs and SCs according to the SAP component model. For
the SC *EMPLOYEE*, you see the use dependencies to the imported SCs
SAP_BUILDT, SAP_JTECHS, and *SAP-JEE.*

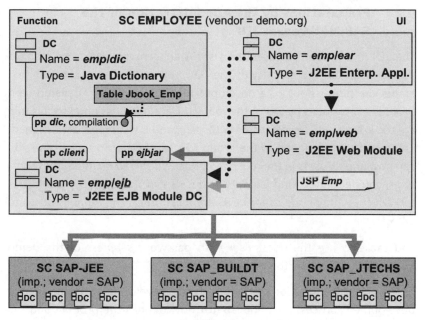

Figure 9.1 Structure of the Employee Application in the Component Model

9.2 First Steps with the SAP NetWeaver JDI

As specified before, this example adheres very closely to the known Employee application.[1] For this reason, the steps that do not change—because of using the component-based development with the JDI—will only be named and not described again. Any changed or new steps will, of course, be explained in detail. Therefore, it makes sense at this point to run through the example again without using DCs, just to familiarize you with the concepts of this development task and with the Developer Studio. In addition, this helps to emphasize the differences between the two development processes. If you want to learn only about the DC-based development, you can look up any details in the non-DC-based example, because the classes, tables, and so forth will be copied unchanged.[2]

---

1 For more step-by-step descriptions of how to use the SAP NetWeaver JDI for development, see the SAP NetWeaver Developer Studio help: Choose **Help • Help Contents • SAP NetWeaver Developer Studio • Web AS**. For the tutorials on the JDI in the different development scenarios, in the section **Development Manual** choose **Working with the SAP NW Development Infrastructure • Getting Started – Development Infrastructure**.

2 In many cases, you can use copy & paste, for example, in the Dictionary Explorer; however, make sure that table names are unique.

9.2.1 Preparations by the Administration of the SAP NetWeaver JDI

User Management

The JDI in our example uses the User Management Engine to manage users. To be able to work with the JDI, you need a user account that grants the permissions of a developer for the JDI. In the development process as proposed by SAP is the role *JDI.Developer*. Assigned to this role are the *actions CBS.Developer*, *CMS.Display*, and *CMS.Import* are assigned. The role itself is assigned to the group *JDI.Developers*. To this group, you can now add all users in the role of a JDI developer. To maintain these settings, you need the group *JDI.Administrators* with the role *JDI.Administrator*, which contains the *actions CBS.Administrator*, *CMS.Administrate* and *CMS.Display*.[3]

You can also use the *Guest* user with password *sappress* of the demo installation, which has the role *JDI.Developer*.

Preparing the Development Project

To create the context for the new software development, in the regular development process an administrator now defines the product and the software component and the dependencies between the SCs in the SLD. For this example, an SC *LBOOK_EMPLOYEE* has been defined, which uses the SCs *SAP-JEE*, *SAP_BUILDT*, and *SAP_JTECHS*.

Tracks and Development Configurations

Based on these prerequisites, at least one track must be created in the CMS, which generates the development configurations for the development phases. To create a new track including the development configuration, you can use **Save As** in the Landscape Configurator of the CMS to save one of the delivered tracks under a new name. Then, enter the used software components as SCAs on the **Check-in** tab page *(SAP_JEE.SCA, SAP_JBUILDT.SCA, SAP_JTECHS.SCA)*, check them in, and select and import them onto the **Development** tab page (and onto **Consolidation**, if required).

For this example, the tracks *Development* and *Maintenance* have been created, each of which contains the development configurations for development and consolidation (*dev* and *cons*). You can copy and prepare them for development by checking them in and importing them. In the example, we use the track *JBookEmp*.

---

3 For the roles *JDI.Administrator* and *JDI.Developer*, you must additionally assign the settings *LCRLcrInstanceWriterAll* and *LcrInstanceWriterNR* in the Visual Administrator.

Configuring the Developer Studio

Start the SAP NetWeaver Developer Studio as usual. You still need an Eclipse workspace. However, now you must make or check a few settings that are specific for developing in the JDI.

Start Parameters

Settings for working with the JDI are made in the menu **Window · Preferences**:

▶ The first important setting is for the files that you want to store in the DTR.[4] It varies in the different development scenarios. In our example, we use the entire JDI and must set the Developer Studio accordingly. Ensure that all listed types including *.project* and *.classpath* are marked under **Window · Preferences · Team · Ignored Resources**. This means that they will not be stored in the DTR.

▶ The second setting defines the system from which you retrieve the development configurations. Under **Window · Preferences · Java Development Infrastructure · Development Configuration Pool** enter the address of the System Landscape Directory (SLD) of your JDI. This system defines the connection to the Change Management Service (CMS) in your landscape, from which the list of available development configurations will be retrieved. Here, enter server and port of your SLD *(http://<server>:port)*: In our example, it is *http://localhost:50000*.

Even though you use a JDI, you frequently test your objects locally. Therefore, make the settings for the local J2EE Engine.

9.2.2 Importing the Development Configuration

The work of a developer with the JDI always starts with importing the development configuration. It determines the developer's access to the correct logical systems (that is, the DTR workspaces and buildspaces). You can create DCs outside of a development configuration, but you will then have to invest an extraordinary amount of manual work to migrate them into the JDI. In addition, you can execute the required check for uniqueness of name of a DC or a package only in connection with the JDI.

Figure 9.2 shows the Development Configurations perspective. No development configuration has been imported; *Local Development* is a

---

4 You will remember that in the standard development process, only source files are stored in the DTR. These include files that contain coding and files that contain metadata such as public parts or DC definitions. In addition, there are files with information on the class path and the project. Whether these are stored depends on the development scenario. When using the entire JDI, the latter two files types must not be stored.

genuine *test configuration* that does not create a connection to central systems.[5] The cursor is already positioned on the icon for importing a development configuration.

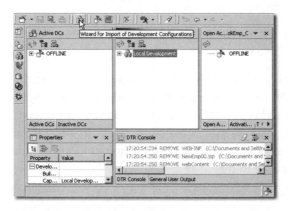

Figure 9.2 Development Configurations Perspective

Open the *Development Configurations* perspective in the Developer Studio. In the top function bar, choose **Wizard for Import of Development Configurations** . On the **Development Configuration Import** wizard, choose **remote**. You get a list of the available development configurations of the JDI, who's SLD you have specified in the preferences. Log on to the central systems and select the development configuration for your tasks. In our example, use the development configuration *JBookEmp_dev* (see Figure 9.3). Choose **Next** and **Finish** to complete the import.

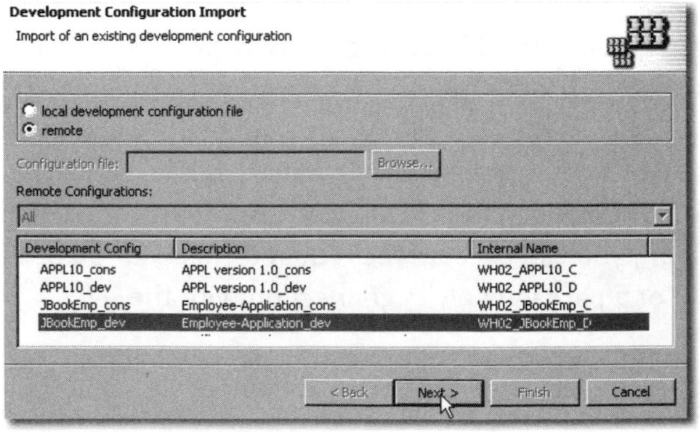

Figure 9.3 List of the Development Configurations[6]

---

5 A migration at a later time is not supported.
6 The figures may differ in individual details of the object names from the text of the tutorial.

The import automatically creates a folder in which the files created in this configuration are stored. By default, you find this folder under *<drive>:\ Documents and Settings\<user>\.dtc\<development configuration name>.*[7]

9.3   Defining a Data Model

Compared to the non-component-based procedure, the data model of the Employee application remains unchanged, which means that you will use the Java Dictionary to create the table for the management of persistent Employee data and then add the desired columns in the related editor. To do this, however, you will now create a DC project that will result in the related archive, which you will deploy from the Developer Studio to convert your locally existing table definition into a physical representation on the database instance.

9.3.1   Creating a Dictionary DC Project

Dictionary projects are designed for creating tables that during design time serve as containers for both Dictionary data types and data structures and tables. You use a DC wizard to create an initial project frame for the new Dictionary DC project.

After reading the sections on DTR and CBS (see Sections 8.2.2 and 8.2.3), you should be familiar with the activation concept and understand that new development objects are always created in the **inactive** state. In the *Development Configurations* perspective, choose the **Inactive DCs** tab page. You see the compartment that contains your changeable SC; vendor[8] and name. In this example, vendor and name are *demo.org.JBOOK_EMP*.

Creating DCs

To start the DC wizard, in the context menu of your SC, choose **Create New DC ...** (see Figure 9.4). The **New Development Component project wizard appears.**[9]

Here, you determine all important settings of your DC. Now set the following parameters (see also Figure 9.5):

---

7   The Eclipse workspace refers to this directory. For more details, see the section on the Developer Studio.

8   The vendor name usually corresponds to the internet domain of the vendor. For the SCs of SAP this name is *sap.com*. In the screen shots, a different vendor name is used, *example.org*.

9   You can also use the menu path **File** • **New Project** • **Development Component** • **Next** • **<Development-Configuration>** • **SC** to start this wizard.

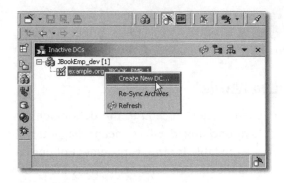

Figure 9.4 Creating a New DC

▶ **Vendor**: The owner of the DC. This value is usually preset with information from the SLD, in our example with *demo.org*.

▶ **Name**: It consists of two parts:

   ▶ **Prefix**: Is specified in the Name Service. In our example, this is *jbook*.

   ▶ **Hierarchical DC Name**: Call this Dictionary DC *employee/dic*.[10]

▶ **Caption**: Enter a description for your DC.

▶ **Language**: Determine the language for the DC. Select **American English**.

▶ **Domain**: This is not the CMS domain. Here, you can specify the business environment to which your DC belongs. Select **Basis**.

▶ **Type**: Every DC has a type according to which its structure is generated. Select the type **Dictionary**.

▶ Keep the settings for **Local Development Component** (not selected) and **Sync Used Archives** (selected).

▶ Then, click on **Next**. You will now be prompted to select an activity (see Figure 9.6).

Creating an Activity
When creating a DC project using the JDI, source files are generated that are stored in the DTR. An activities selection screen appears.[11] Since you have not yet created an activity for this DC, the list will be empty. Click on **New Activity** to create a new activity.

---

10 If more than one person executes this example on the same system, this name is reserved for the first one who creates it. In such a case, append a suffix such as your initials directly to the *dic* name part.

11 You probably remember that all changes to objects in the DTR are organized in activities.

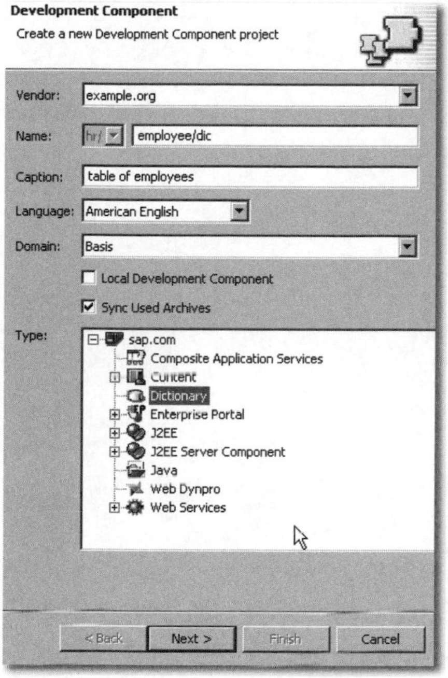

Figure 9.5 Properties of a new DC in the New DC Project Wizard

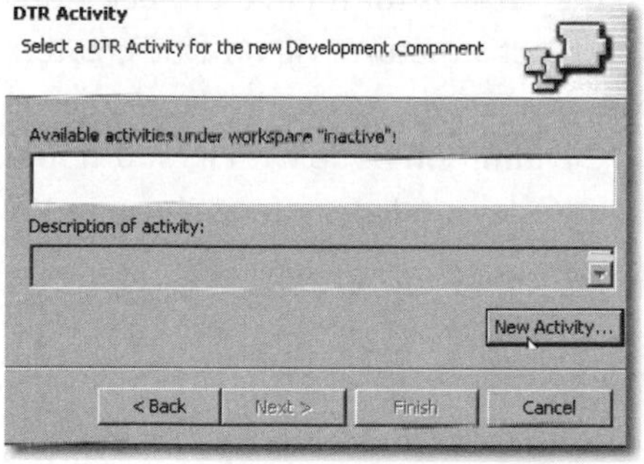

Figure 9.6 Creating an Activity

Enter the name **New Java Dictionary DC**[12] and a description (to be able to identify the DC) and confirm with **OK**. The activity is now available in the list. You will use this activity for all changes to this DC—right up to checking it in for the first time after a successful local test. This guarantees that all DC elements are in one group and can later be activated and transported together (see Figure 9.7).

---

12   If more than one person executes this example, you may add your initials as a suffix.

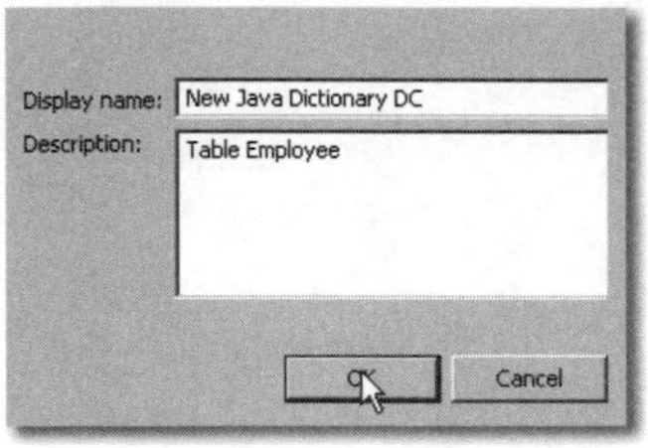

Figure 9.7 Properties of an Activity

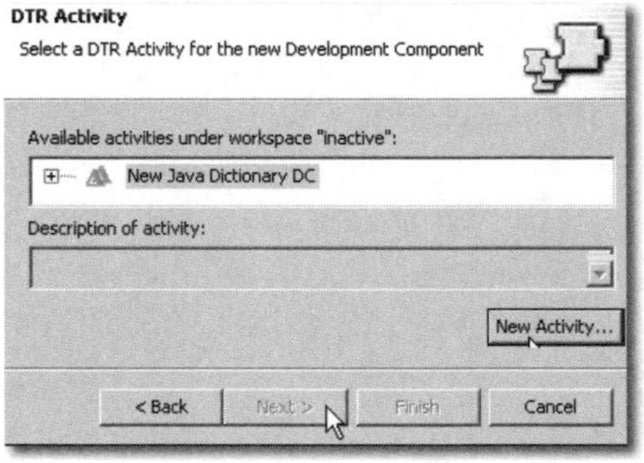

Figure 9.8 Selecting an Activity

Now select the new activity from the list (see Figure 9.8). Confirm your entries by clicking on **Next**. You see the settings for the DC project. Copy them by clicking on **Finish**. The DC project structure will now be created; the appropriate perspective for the new DC is automatically displayed (see Figure 9.9). All DCs share the **DC Definition** node with its sub-nodes and the **Public Parts** node. The other nodes are the same as those in the non-DC project.

Figure 9.9 Structure of the Dictionary DC

9.3.2 Defining the Employee Table

Now create the table for the employee data as part of the newly created DC project. Then add the required table fields as columns.

Open the DC *employee/dic* in the Dictionary Explorer and create a table named **JBOOK_EMPLOYEE**.[13] Select the same activity for all changes to your Dictionary DC in order to be able to check them in, activate them, and transport all changes as a whole later.

Create the table fields according to the information in Chapter 3.

Create the table fields as described in *Getting Started:*

Table Fields

▶ ID

▶ LASTNAME

▶ FIRSTNAME

▶ DEPARTMENT

Remember to set up secondary indexes and buffering as explained in Chapter 3. During the aforementioned procedure, metadata has been generated.

Secondary Indexes and Buffering

Save your data. Now our table is completely defined and currently exists as a local project resource in the form of an XML file. We record an important result: Our table, as part of the Java Dictionary, has a database-independent definition.

Saving the Entries

9.3.3 Defining Public Parts of the Development Components

You know that you have to declare the use of another component explicitly when working according to SAP's component model. As a reminder: The use dependencies between software components (SCs) are defined in the SLD by the administrator. Use dependencies are (optional) parts of the metadata of every DC. For a valid use of a development object, this data must be part of a public part of the DC to which it belongs. Depending on the purpose of the public part, we distinguish between the types *Compilation* and *Assembly*.

Public Parts

---

13   The *JBOOK_* prefix must be defined for database objects in the Name Service of the SLD. If this has not been done, start the SLD UI, choose **Name Reservation · Define Namespace Prefix, Name Category = DB Object Name** and enter the *Namespace Prefix*.

You now define a public part of the DC: In the DC structure, open the **DC Metadata node**.[14] You see the nodes **DC Definition** and **Public Parts**. In the context menu of the **Public Parts** node, choose **New Public Part ...** (see Figure 9.10).

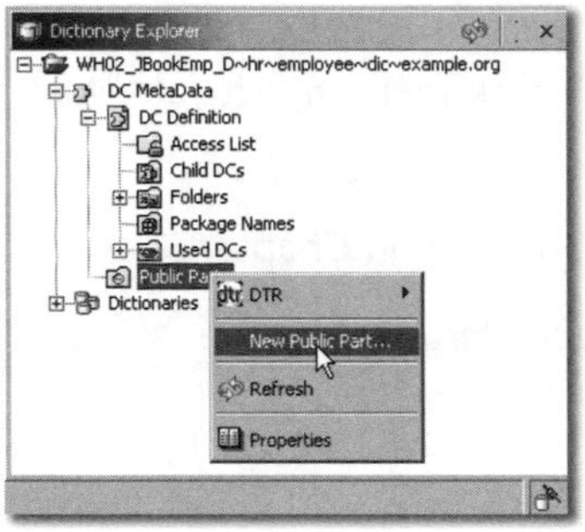

Figure 9.10 Creating a Public Part

In the **Add Public Part** wizard, enter the following parameters (see also Figure 9.11):

▶ **Name**: emp

▶ **The exposed items can be used as a library that**: Provides an API for developing/compiling other DCs

▶ **Caption:** Enter a description for the public part.

▶ **Description**: Here, you can specify details on the public part.

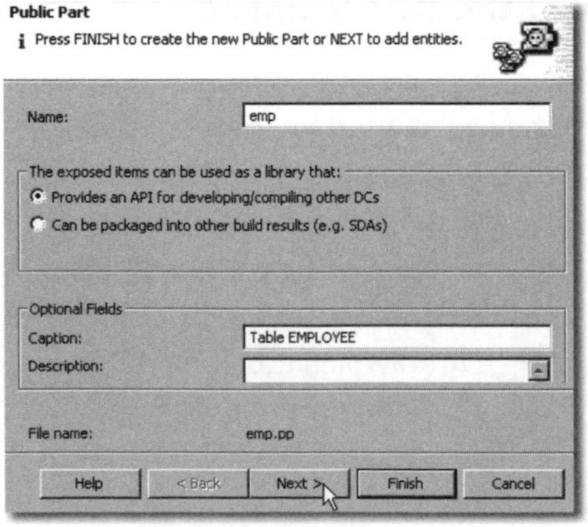

Figure 9.11 Public Part Properties

---

14   This public part is not explicitly required for this example application. However, it could be important for other uses and, in addition, shows you how to create a public part manually.

To add entities to the public part, click on **Next**. On this page of the Public Parts wizard, under **Select Entity Type**,[15] select the types of objects that you want to propagate in the public part; then, select these objects under **Select Entities**.

In this example, select the type **Dictionary Database Table;** and in the hierarchical representation of the entities, select your new table **JBOOK_ EMPLOYEE** (see Figure 9.12).

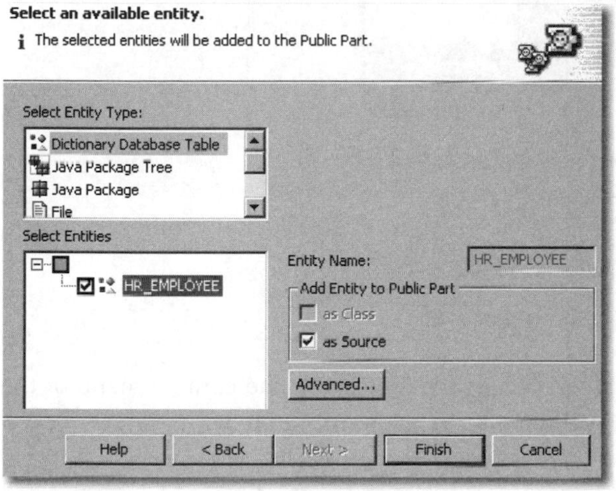

Figure 9.12 Public Part Entities

Include these changes to the DTR into the activity that you created for your Dictionary DC.

9.3.4 Building and Deploying Development Components

Similar to creating an archive from a local project, you must use the build process to create an archive from a DC project to receive a deployable result.

Creating a
Dictionary Archive

To do this, from the context menu of the DC, choose **Development Component · Build.** The archives for DC and public part are created locally (see Figure 9.13). Confirm the build on the next screen with **OK.**

---

15 You can maintain the public part entities at any time: Every public part contains an *Entities* node. To navigate to the editor for the public part entities, from the context menu of this node choose **Edit Entities ...** Since this is a change to the source files, at least one public part must be checked out and you need an activity for the changes.

Preparing the Deployment

Since you must test your objects locally before making them centrally available, start the local J2EE server and the related SDM server process[16] as well as the database.

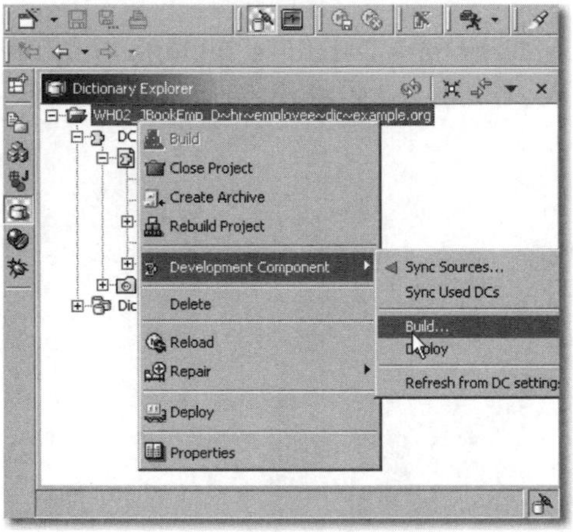

Figure 9.13 Build and Deployment of a DC

To deploy the DC, in the Dictionary Explorer in the context menu of the DC node, choose **Development Component • Deploy**.

9.4 Providing Access to Table Data and Business Logic

9.4.1 Creating an EJB Module DC

Create another DC with the following parameters. Then, perform the steps described in Chapter 3:

- **Vendor**: The owner of the DC. This value is usually preset with information from the SLD.
- **Name**: It consists of two parts:
- **Prefix**: Is assigned in the Name Service—*jbook* in this example.
- **Hierarchical DC Name**: Call this Dictionary DC *employee/ejb.*
- **Caption**: Enter a description for your DC.
- **Language**: Determine the language for the DC. Select **American English**.

16 The Software Deployment Manager (SDM) is usually started as part of a server instance of the SAP Web AS, together with the other server processes of the instance.

- **Domain**: This is not the CMS domain – here, you can specify into which business environment your DC belongs. Select **Basis**.

- **Type**: Every DC has a type according to which its structure is generated. Select the type **J2EE · EJB Module**.

- Keep the settings for **Local Development Component** (not selected) and **Sync Used Archives** (selected).

Use a new activity for this DC, which you call **New EJB Module DC**. From this point on, you use the J2EE DC Explorer as the basis for all other steps in the EJB development.

Activity

The initial project structure already contains two deployment descriptors, the standard descriptor *ejb-jar.xml* and a server-specific descriptor named *ejb-j2ec-engine.xml*. In the next step, we add an entity bean to this project.

In this DC, define the following objects as described in the example in Chapter 3, and include all these objects into the new activity for the DC:

- Define the entity bean **Employee**.
- Create the data transfer object class.
- Create the session bean **EmployeeServices**.
- Implement the bean class.
- Add the deployment descriptions.

The public parts of this DC are created automatically: You find the public parts *ejbjar* and *client* in your DC structure.

Public Parts of the EJB Module DC

At the local reference, select the *Employee Bean* from your EJB DC. Now use the activity of this DC to add your changes to the DTR. Execute the DC build. For this DC, no extra deployment is required; it will later be deployed in an Enterprise Application DC.

Local Reference

9.5 Creating a JSP-Based User Interface

To create a simple UI for the Employee application, you need another DC which contains the Web resources. Create a DC with the following parameters:

- **Vendor**: The owner of the DC. This value is usually preset with information from the SLD.
- **Name**: It consists of two parts:
- **Prefix**: Is specified in the Name Service.

- ▶ **Hierarchical DC Name**: Call this Dictionary DC *employee/web.*

- ▶ **Caption**: Enter a description for your DC.

- ▶ **Language**: Determine the language for the DC. Select **American English**.

- ▶ **Domain**: This is not the CMS domain, but rather where you can specify the business environment to which your DC belongs. Select **Basis**.

- ▶ **Type**: Every DC has a type according to which its structure is generated. Select the type **J2EE · Web Module**.

- ▶ Keep the settings for **Local Development Component** (not selected) and **Sync Used Archives** (selected).

As for the other DCs, create an activity *New Web Module* for this DC. Then execute the following steps as described in Chapter 3:

- ▶ Implement the user interface with a JSP.

- ▶ Create the JSP **New Employee**.

- ▶ Implement the JSP.

Use Dependency   The Developer Studio will now display an error message as shown in Figure 9.14. It tells you that you are not yet allowed to use the EJB DC. First, you must create a *use dependency*. Only then are you allowed to use the released objects of another DC (the public part entities).

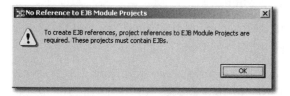

Figure 9.14 Missing Use Dependency

In the J2EE DC Explorer, open the structure of your **Web Module DC**. In the context menu, choose **DC Meta Data · DC Definition · Used DCs** and then **Add Used DC …** (see Figure 9.15).

In the **Add Dependency wizard** (see Figure 9.16), select your SC from your development configuration (up to now, it exists only in the DTR workspace **Inactive**, because it has not yet been built centrally, and thus activated). Navigate in the EJB DC *employee/ejb* to the public part *ejbjar* and declare a use dependency of dependency type *Build Time*. Save your entries. The errors should now disappear.

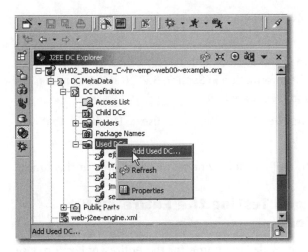

Figure 9.15 Create Use Dependency

Again, you use the activity of the DC whose metadata you change, which is the one that declares the use dependency.

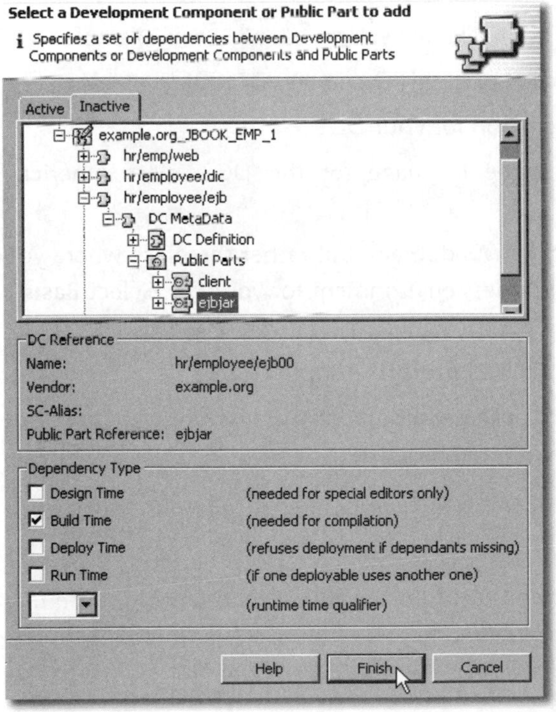

Select a Development Component or Public Part to add

i Specifies a set of dependencies between Development
Components or Development Components and Public Parts

Active | Inactive

例 example.org_JBOOK_EMP_1
  hr/emp/web
  hr/employee/dic
  hr/employee/ejb
    DC MetaData
      DC Definition
      Public Parts
        client
        ejbjar

DC Reference
Name: hr/employee/ejb00
Vendor: example.org
SC-Alias:
Public Part Reference: ejbjar

Dependency Type
☐ Design Time   (needed for special editors only)
☑ Build Time   (needed for compilation)
☐ Deploy Time   (refuses deployment if dependants missing)
☐ Run Time   (if one deployable uses another one)
☐ ▼   (runtime time qualifier)

Help | Finish | Cancel

Figure 9.16 Properties of a Use Dependency

After that, execute the following steps according to the description in Section 3.7.3:

▶ Add the description in the deployment descriptor *web.xml*: Enter your data according to the information in Section 3.7.3 (reference names for the session bean and URL mapping).

▶ Create the Web archive: To do this, you use a DC build that you already know.

Lastly, execute the DC build. A deployment is not required at this time.

9.6 Creating and Testing the Entire J2EE Application

Now create a DC that provides the frame for the entire application. Use the following parameters:

▶ **Vendor**: The owner of the DC. This value is usually preset with information from the SLD.

▶ **Name**: It consists of two parts:

    ▶ **Prefix**: Is assigned in the Name Service—*jbook* in this example.

    ▶ **Hierarchical DC Name**: Call this Dictionary DC *employee/ear.*

▶ **Caption**: Enter a description for your DC.

▶ **Language**: Determine the language for the DC. Select **American English**.

▶ **Domain**: This is not the CMS domain, but rather the place where you can specify the right business environment for your DC. Select **Basis**.

▶ **Type**: Every DC has a type according to which its structure is generated. Select the type **J2EE · Enterprise Application**.

▶ Keep the settings for **Local Development Component** (not selected) and **Sync Used Archives** (selected).

Use a new activity for this DC, which you call *New Enterprise Application DC.*

Execute the following steps according to the description in the *Getting Started* section: From the context menu of the DC, choose **Add Modules**. Select your two DC projects, which are offered in the display.

▶ Add descriptions to *application.xml*:

  ▷ Context Root: Usually, this is predetermined by the JDI administration; you can select it under **Get Context Root**. If there should be a conflict, choose the context root **emp** as described in *Getting Started*.

  ▷ Datasource Alias: Enter the alias *EMP_DATA* as described in *Getting Started*.

▶ Create, build, deploy and test the EAR: You do this by first building the DC and then deploying and executing the Enterprise Application DC on the local J2EE Engine, as you have done before.

Figure 9.17 Selecting the Context Root

9.7 Making Development Objects Centrally Available

After you have successfully created, built and tested the application locally, you must now make your development objects centrally available.

9.7.1 Checking in Source Files and Activating All DCs

Your activities contain all files versions that you have created. After the successful test, you know that they contain a complete version of your DCs. To store these versions in the DTR database, check in your changes as follows.[17]

Navigate to the Development Configurations perspective. By default, it contains the **Open Activities** view. In this view, you see your open (local) activities in the context of your DTR workspace.

---

17 When you work on a DC for a long time, the risk of a loss of data increases. Checking the data in stores them reliably, but nevertheless, you should check in only completed changes. For this case, there is a function *Upload of Changes*, which allows you to store changes on the server without checking them in.

In the context menu of the activity you created first, choose **Check In**[18] (see Figure 9.18). With this step, you make all versions in these activities visible in the Design Time Repository.

Figure 9.18 Open Activities—Check-In

During check-in, the Activation wizard automatically opens. To build your DC centrally in the *Component Build Service*, in the **Activation** wizard choose **Activate with all Predecessors** (see Figure 9.19). After a successful build, your DC becomes visible in the **Active DCs view**.[19] Now when you choose **Open Request view**, you can see the result of the build process and, if errors occurred, display a log file.

9.7.2 Releasing Changes

If the central build was successful, your work as a developer is finished for the time being. For the other steps (transport into the consolidation system, further tests, assembly, and so forth), controlled via the Change Management Service, the quality management is responsible.

To release your objects, in the Development Configurations perspective select the **Transport** view. Expand the node **Waiting**. You see all activated activities. In the context menu of your activities, choose **Release** (see Figure 9.20). With releasing your activities, your work as a developer is finished.

---

18 It contains no dependencies to DCs that have been created later and should therefore be checked in and activated first.
19 By default, this is the only place from which it can be used by other users than the group that develops the DC, because the central build guarantees that all objects are up to date.

Figure 9.19 Activation

Figure 9.20 Release Activity

10   SAP NetWeaver Java Development Infrastructure: Configuration and Administration

We hope that Chapters 8 and 9 have convinced you of the advantages of the SAP NetWeaver Development Infrastructure. This chapter will deal with setting up and administering the Java Development Infrastructure.

As you already know, the SAP NetWeaver Java Development Infrastructure (JDI) provides ingenious functions that support you with Java software development and maintenance.

In this chapter, we first want to show how such a Java Development Infrastructure is set up and then develop a small example project in the infrastructure that we have set up.

Because we want you to create a fully operational mini development infrastructure on your PC, we will concentrate on the procedures for setting up and configuring the Java Development Infrastructure. Any theoretical explanations are inserted in places where they will be most helpful and not interfere with the actual setup. There are a few tasks that you must execute repeatedly during the first setup and throughout your daily work. To save space, these steps are described and explained only in the section on the Java Development Infrastructure setup.

10.1   Configuration of the SAP NetWeaver Java Development Infrastructure

The SAP NetWeaver Java Development Infrastructure consists of three main building blocks: the *Change Management Service* (CMS), the *Design Time Repository* (DTR), and the *Component Build Service* (CBS). Apart from these, there is the *System Landscape Directory* (SLD), which is used as the central management system for system landscape data by many other NetWeaver components.

10.1.1   Java Development Landscape

From the viewpoint of system integration and administration, a Java development landscape consists of SAP systems, each of which realizes one or more functions of the Java Development Infrastructure building blocks (CMS, CBS, DTR, and SLD).

Building Blocks of the Java Development Infrastructure

For a minimum development landscape, you need one hardware server on which a SAP Web Application Server (SAP Web AS) runs with all building blocks of the Java Development Infrastructure.

In the Java Development Infrastructure, the Change Management Service (CMS) forms the central control unit. It is responsible for the configuration of development landscape and transport management. In every Java Development Infrastructure, there is exactly one CMS instance.

The Design Time Repository (DTR) and the Component Build Service (CBS) are responsible for the source file management and the central build of software components. In one Java Development Infrastructure, you can install any number of systems as DTR and CBS servers. All these systems are controlled by one CMS.

Note that the availability demands on the DTR systems are high. They store the source files of your development objects. Any hardware defects can result in a loss of source files. Network accessibility is another important aspect in this context. A network downtime implies that the developers cannot continue their development work during this period.

The CBS server is the one building block of a Java Development Infrastructure that requests most of the computing capacity. Whenever a developer activates an activity, a central build process is triggered. Each of these processes blocks a processor for the duration of the compilation. There are typical times during the day, for example, before the end of daily work, when the developers check in and activate their developments. In this context, the CBS server is the bottleneck in the Java Development Infrastructure. Inappropriate ratios between the number of processors and the size of the development projects result in long waiting times for the activation.

The System Landscape Directory (SLD) is used by the Java Development Infrastructure for software component information and landscape configuration. The SLD is used by many other NetWeaver components as a provider of landscape data. One IT system landscape requires exactly one SLD. If an SLD already exists in the system landscape, there is no need to install another one for the Java Development Infrastructure.

The Name Server is used in the Java Development Infrastructure to avoid name conflicts among development objects. The SAP Web AS provides a runtime environment for applications of different manufacturers. Therefore, it is possible that different manufacturers name their development objects (such as database tables or Web Applications URLs) identically, so that these objects collide when used in the same runtime environment.

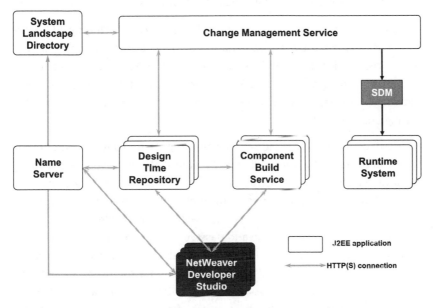

Figure 10.1 Landscape from the System Integration and Administration Viewpoint

This is why SAP has developed the namespace concept to ensure the uniqueness of names of the development objects created by different manufacturers. (By the way, this concept has been (and still is) used successfully in the ABAP development.) Every SAP customer or software development partner can reserve so-called *namespace prefixes* at SAP to guarantee their global uniqueness.

The Name Server within a Java Development Infrastructure ensures that developers can create object names and sub-namespaces only within the registered namespaces. Each object name can be used only once.

The Name Server uses the same technical entity as the SLD, that is, the same piece of software. However, it is not necessary to run the Name Server and the SLD on one Web AS. On the contrary, it is recommended that you run these two functions on different Web Application Servers.

Besides the systems that execute one or more building blocks of the Java Development Infrastructure, other runtime systems can be included into the development landscape for testing purposes or production.

Runtime Systems

Developers work at their local offices with the SAP NetWeaver Developer Studio—an integrated development environment that supports the development work in the SAP NetWeaver Java Development Infrastructure. Additionally, every developer can optionally install an SAP J2EE Engine on his or her local workplace for local tests.

As you can see in Figure 10.1, all building blocks (including SLD and Name Server) use the *Hypertext Transfer Protocol* (HTTP) for communication. If required, the *Secure Sockets Layer* (SSL) for HTTP can be activated in the relevant systems. An SAP protocol is used for communication between the Change Management Service and the runtime systems for testing and production.

Central User Management As we have seen above, the server components of a Java Development Infrastructure usually run on different systems. When developers work in the Java Development Infrastructure, they need access to all systems. This means that they need a user account in all of these systems. To facilitate the logon procedure, developers in the NetWeaver Developer Studio must enter only one user name and password to log on to the central Java Development Infrastructure. This implies that their user names and passwords must be identical in all systems. To facilitate the user data maintenance, we recommend that you set up a central user management. Such a user management can either be a central directory service (for example, LDAP) or an ABAP system. The *User Management Engine* (UME) of the SAP Web AS supports both concepts.

An Example Landscape

A system vendor wants to use the SAP NetWeaver technology platform to develop an Internet application for online sales to be used by different customers. Suppose that the core of this application consists of two software components—the catalog server for product search and the transaction server for posting orders. For the customers, the Web UI must be adapted to their respective needs. As you can see in the following figure, the CMS can be used to divide the development into different development units (*tracks*), one unit each for the software components Catalog Server and Transaction Server. Every customer project forms its own development unit as a successor of these two tracks (see Figure 10.2).

In this case, the Java Development Infrastructure consists of two DTR and CBS servers each, whose first pair is used for the standard development (catalog and transaction server). The second pair is needed for the customer projects.

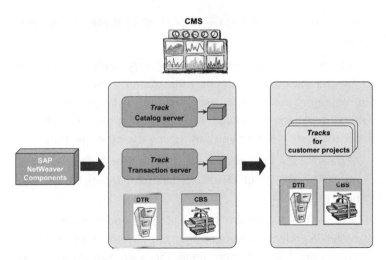

Figure 10.2 An Example Development Landscape

At the beginning of the development track for the catalog or transaction server, the CMS is used to copy any required SAP NetWeaver components into the tracks. At the end of the two projects, stable versions of the software components have been created, which are now delivered to the tracks of the customer projects under CMS control. This reduces the interweaving of development projects. Every project can be constructed on stable versions of the predecessors.

10.1.2 Setting Up a SAP NetWeaver Java Development Infrastructure

In this section, we will set up—install and configure—a SAP NetWeaver Java Development Infrastructure. Since this is just an example, we want to keep it simple by running all building blocks in one single SAP Web AS (Java), which, in reality, will rarely be the case.

Deploying the Software Packages of the Java Development Infrastructure

To install the Java Development Infrastructure, you must deploy three additional software packages into existing Java systems. Usually, you find these software packages on an installation CD of the SAP Web AS or the SAP Service Marketplace.[1] These software packages are divided into *Soft-*

---

1 To relieve you of having to search for all necessary elements, we have included a preconfigured NetWeaver Java Development Infrastructure with the installation on the accompanying CD. Nevertheless, you will have to adapt a few parameters that depend on your specific environment.

ware Component Archives, SCA files). The content of these files is organized as follows:

Software Packages of the Java Development Infrastructure

▶ The file *SAPDEVINFF.SCA* contains all primary software libraries required by the Java Development Infrastructure, which must be loaded into memory as soon as a Java system is (re)started. This is why it is an offline deployment package. After deploying this package, you must restart the system before you can deploy the other packages.

▶ The file *SAPDEVINF.SCA* contains the other part of the libraries and the applications (CMS, CBS, and DTR) and database tables of the Java Development Infrastructure.

▶ The file *SAPBUILDT.SCA* contains the build tools and libraries of the respective Web AS release. You need them to develop J2EE and Web Dynpro applications.[2] This does not mean that you must set up a new Java Development Infrastructure for every Web AS release. You can develop applications for other NetWeaver releases independent of the Web AS release on which the Java Development Infrastructure runs. All you need is the respective version of this file. You can find the different versions of this file on the SAP Service Marketplace.

You must deploy the first two files into all Java systems, in which one or more of the Java Development Infrastructure building blocks are running. The third file must be deployed only to the system in which the CMS is running. For our mini development infrastructure, we have deployed all three files into the Java system.

For the deployment, you use the *Software Deployment Manager* (SDM) of the installed Java system. You can include all three files at once into the deployment queue and start the deployment. The SDM analyzes the dependencies of the files to be deployed and deploys them in the correct order. The offline deployment is carried out first. After this phase, SDM restarts the Java system before continuing with the online deployment.[3]

The SLD is automatically installed with every Java system. To be able to use it, you must activate it. You will learn more about that later.

---

2   However, this file does not contain any other libraries you will call in your applications. You must import these libraries into your buildpsaces.

3   To facilitate work with our mini development infrastructure, you can deploy the application *sap.com~nwdi~links~ear.ear* from the accompanying CD. Use the URL *http://<host>:<port>/nwdi* to find a page with useful links.

Configuring the Java Development Infrastructure

After deploying the required software components, other configuration steps are required before the Java Development Infrastructure is up and running. You can organize these steps in the following categories:

▶ Creating global system parameters

▶ Setting up user authentication and authorization

▶ Putting into operation the SLD server, the Name Server, and the data supplier of the SLD

▶ Configuring the DTR server

▶ Configuring the CBS server

▶ Defining a CMS domain and setting up a transport directory

The global settings include parameters of the *Java Virtual Machine* (JVM), of the Web AS, and of the underlying database. These parameters are not application-specific; however, they enable the Java Development Infrastructure to operate on a more robust and efficient basis. We will discuss three important parameters below.

Global System Parameters

Every server process of a Java system runs in a JVM. The memory demand (heap memory) of the JVM depends on the applications to be executed. For the Java Development Infrastructure, we advise you to set the maximum heap size of *all* server nodes of the Java system to at least 1,024 MB using the *Config Tool* (see Figure 10.3).

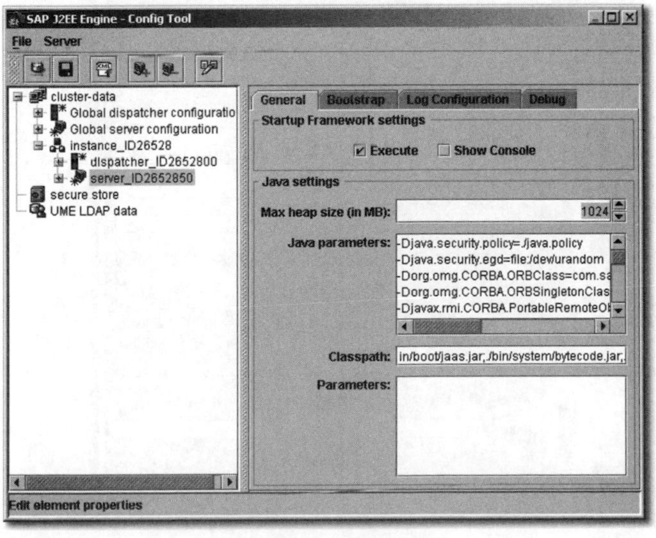

Heap Size of the JVM

Figure 10.3 Maximum Heap Size for the Java Virtual Machine

The Java Development Infrastructure uses the database underlying the SAP Web AS to store the source objects and binary archives. For certain processes (such as the build process), the Java Development Infrastructure requires a large number of simultaneous connections to the database. Use the Visual Administrator to set the Java Database Connectivity (JDBC) parameter *sysDS.maximumConnections* for every server node to a higher value. The actual value depends on two factors:

▶ **Workload of the building blocks**
Both the DTR and the CBS server trigger a significant number of database accesses during their operation. The workload depends on the scope of the development objects used in a Java Development Infrastructure.

▶ **Number of server nodes**
This workload is actually distributed to the server nodes. The more server processes that are running on a Java system, the lower the required connection pool size per server node.

You can adjust these parameters according to your experiences, once you have put the Java Development Infrastructure into operation. For our mini development infrastructure, we set the parameter in such a way that the total of all server node connections is approximately 50 (see Figure 10.4).

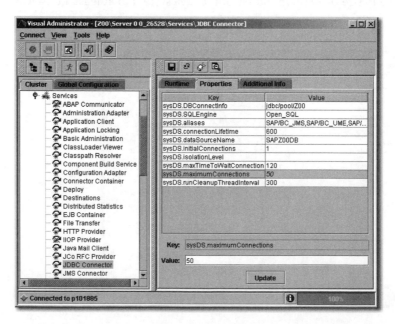

Figure 10.4 Connection Pool Size of the JDBC Driver

On the database side, you must also adapt parameters, which allow you to use the set connection pool sizes of the JDBC driver. These parameters depend on the manufacturer. For the MaxDB, for example, the value of parameter *MAXUSERTASKS* must be slightly higher than the total of all JDBC connection pool sizes.

Maximum Number of Simultaneously Allowed Accesses to the Database

Remember to restart the database and the SAP Web AS after setting these parameters to make them effective.

As previously explained, different server applications participate in the Java Development Infrastructure. These server applications can run on different systems. The users must log on to these systems to be able to call services of the Java Development Infrastructure. To facilitate the user data maintenance, we recommend that you set up a central user management. Such a central user management can be an ABAP system or an LDAP server. All Java systems participating in the Java Development Infrastructure can connect to this system to retrieve user data. Consequently, during logon, every user must specify one single user account and password for all systems in question.

Central User Management

For particular functions of the building blocks, authorizations are required. Depending on the user type (for example, developer, quality manager, and so on) each user is granted different authorizations for the building blocks, allowing him or her to perform exact tasks. To avoid the JDI administrator's having to change the authorization assignment in all relevant systems—if a new user is included or another user leaves a development project—we recommend that you set up one user group for each existing user type in the central user management. Authorizations can then be assigned once on the group level for all relevant systems. The users automatically receive the authorizations assigned to their group.

Assigning Authorizations

The SAP Web AS (Java) offers two concepts for user identification and authorization. The first concept adheres to the J2EE standard to ensure the J2EE conformity of the Web AS (Java). The other concept is called the *User Management Engine* (UME). The UME uses a multi-layer authorization model to facilitate the integration of the Java and ABAP stack. The building blocks always adopt one of these concepts.

The SLD and the Name Server use the J2EE security roles to control access, while CBS and CMS use the UME roles. Both security roles are coupled with the actions to be executed.

The DTR manages source files of the development objects. For this reason, access to these objects is controlled by *Access Control Lists* (ACLs).

ACLs work similarly to the security concepts for file systems on the operation-system level. They are coupled with the objects in the DTR.

Every building block is accompanied by a number of security roles, authorization objects, or access rights. To address all these authorizations in detail would exceed the scope of this book. For a detailed description of the individual authorizations, refer to the product documentation. We want to explain the required authorizations with the most frequent user types in the Java Development Infrastructure as an example.

Authorizations for Developers The daily work of a typical developer can contain the following activities:

▶ Creating and developing development objects

▶ Reserving object names during creation

▶ Checking source files in and out

▶ Activating changes to the source file

▶ Releasing activities for transport

These tasks result in the following authorizations that a developer needs for the building blocks (see Table 10.1).

Building Block	Authorizations
Name Server	J2EE security role *LcrInstanceWriterNR*
SLD	J2EE security role *LcrUser*
CBS	UME action *CBS.Developer*
CMS	UME actions *CMS.Display* and *CMS.Export*
DTR	Root directory: *read*, *write*, and *checkin* Project-relevant workspaces: *access*, *read*, *write* and *checkin*

Table 10.1 Authorizations for Developers

Authorizations for Project Leaders A project leader is typically responsible for the following tasks:

▶ Entering products to be developed in the SLD

▶ Entering namespace prefixes reserved at SAP in the Name Server

▶ Defining and changing tracks for relevant projects in the CMS

▶ Administering project-relevant tracks in the CMS

A project leader needs the authorizations shown in Table 10.2.

Building Block	Authorizations
Name Server	J2EE security roles *LcrInstanceWriterNR* and *LcrInstanceWriterCR*
SLD	J2EE security roles *LcrInstanceWriterCR* and *LcrInstanceWriterLD*
CBS	UME actions *CBS.Developer* and *CBS.QM*
CMS	UME action *CMS.Administrate*
DTR	Root directory: *read*, *write*, and *checkin* Project-relevant workspaces: All access rights

Table 10.2 Authorizations for Project Leaders

Administrators of the Java Development Infrastructure need the authorizations shown in Table 10.3.

Administrator of the Java Development Infrastructure

Building Block	Authorizations
Name Server	J2EE security role *LcrAdministrator*
SLD	J2EE security role *LcrAdministrator*
CBS	UME action *CBS.Administrator*
CMS	UME action *CMS.Administrate*
DTR	All access rights for all directory levels

Table 10.3 Authorizations for Administrators of a Java Development Infrastructure

In contrast to the latter three user types, the so-called *CMS User* represents a single user. The CMS uses this user for authentication in SLD, DTR, and CBS to create workspaces in the DTR and buildspaces in the CBS during track definitions, and to transport changes to source files through the landscape at a later time. The CMS user needs the authorizations shown in Table 10.4.

CMS User

Building Block	Authorizations
Name Server	None
SLD	J2EE security role *LcrInstanceWriterLD*
CBS	UME action *CBS.Administrator*

Table 10.4 Authorizations for the CMS User

Building Block	Authorizations
CMS	UME action *CMS.Administrate*
DTR	All access rights except *adminX* for all directory levels

Table 10.4 Authorizations for the CMS User (cont.)

Assigning Authorizations Here, we will set up the user types of *Administrator* and *CMS User* for our mini development infrastructure to be able to perform administrative tasks. The procedure for other user types is similar. Follow the procedure below:

1. Log on as a J2EE administrator to the user management (*http://<host>:<port>/useradmin*).

2. On the left side, choose **Create User** to create the two users *nwdi_admin* and *cms_user*.

   Use a different Web browser to log on with the newly created users and change their passwords. The user management expects a user who logs on the first time to change his or her initial password. However, this can be done only in the Web browser. This step is very important. Otherwise, the applications trigger unexpected errors if the user tries to log on to the system in the background with this user name.

3. On the left side, choose **Groups** and on the right side, choose ⬚. Enter the group name "NWDI.Administrators" on the next page.

4. Assign the user *nwdi_admin* to the group by choosing ⬚. Use ➕ to add the user to the group.

5. On the left side, choose **Roles** and on the right side, choose ⬚ to create the UME role *NWDI.Administrator*.

   On the next page, enter the role name *NWDI.Administrator*. Then add the UME actions *CBS.Administrator* and *CMS.Administrate* at the bottom.

6. After saving the new role, select this role on the main page of the role management. Use ⬚ to assign this role to the user group *NWDI.Administrators*, so that all users of this group (and of course of *nwdi_admin*) receive all authorizations granted for CBS and CMS.

7. Use ⬚ to assign this role to the single user *cms_user*.

We have now granted the required authorizations for CBS and CMS to our two users. Next, we must grant them the authorizations for the SLD and the Name Server. Since these two building blocks use J2EE security roles, we will perform the following steps in the *Visual Administrator*. Due to the fact that SLD and Name Server of our mini development infrastructure run in one system, we must grant authorizations for the SLD only once to the users or user groups, because SLD and Name Server use the same piece of software in the system.

Log on to the Visual Administrator as an administrator. Follow the path **Cluster · Server * · Services · Security Provider · Runtime · Policy Configurations · Security Roles.** In the **Components** area, select the component *sap.com/com.sap.lcr*sld* and assign the role *LcrAdministrator* to group *NWDI.Administrators* and the role *LcrInstanceWriterLD* to user *cms_user*.

We have now assigned authorizations to the users *nwdi_admin* and *cms_user* in our mini development infrastructure.

The SAP System Landscape Directory (SLD) provides the central storage unit for system landscape data of the NetWeaver platform. It is increasingly used by various SAP tools for system management.[4] The basic concept of the SLD is to provide a central unit for the entire system landscape to reduce data redundancy as it would result from distributed data management. Different applications can share the data in the SLD and even store their data there to make it available to other applications. In the SAP NetWeaver Java Development Infrastructure, the SLD is used at several places. We will discuss these functions in the appropriate sections. Now we will focus on setting up a working SLD.

SLD Server and Data Supplier of the SLD

If you already have an operational SLD, there is *no need* to set up an additional SLD for the Java Development Infrastructure. For our mini development infrastructure, we assume that it is an island landscape (that is, decoupled from its network neighbors). Consequently, in this case, we need our own SLD.

The SLD application is installed with every SAP Web AS Java. However, it is not activated automatically. You should activate it only in the system that acts as the SLD in the system landscape. We use the system of our mini development infrastructure as the SLD server. In the first step of activating the SLD, we set a few server parameters. To do this, call the Web UI of the SLD (*http://<host>:<port>/sld*) and on the initial page of the SLD follow the **Administration** link. On the next **Administration** page, you see that the SLD is stopped. Choose the **Server Settings** link to set the server parameters. The *Object Server* parameter must be a globally

Server Parameters of the SLD

---

4 This includes the SAP Exchange Infrastructure (XI) and the SAP Solution Manager.

unique name. SAP recommends that you reserve a namespace prefix at SAP (on the SAP Service Marketplace *http://service.sap.com/namespaces*) to guarantee this uniqueness. You can use this namespace prefix later as the namespace for your development objects. Learn more about that later. For our mini development infrastructure, we assume that we have reserved the prefix *JBOOK* at SAP. We use this prefix as our object server name (see Figure 10.5). We leave the other parameters on this page as they are. After saving the parameters, return to the **Administration** page and start the SLD server.

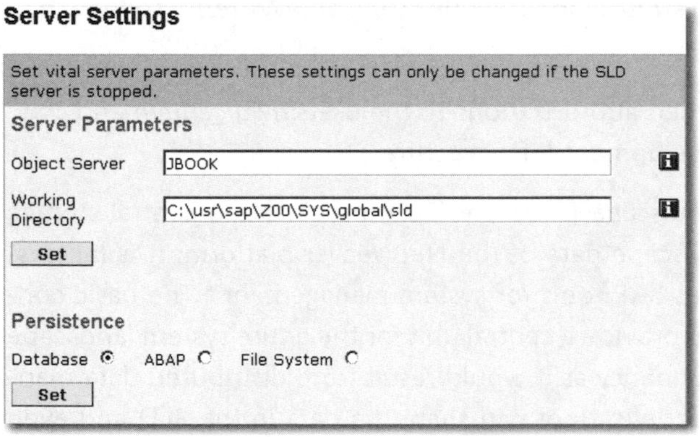

Server Settings

Set vital server parameters. These settings can only be changed if the SLD server is stopped.

Server Parameters

Object Server	JBOOK
Working Directory	C:\usr\sap\Z00\SYS\global\sld

Set

Persistence

Database ⦿ ABAP ○ File System ○

Set

Figure 10.5 Server Parameters of the SLD

Initial Data Import in the SLD

In the next step, we import data of the *SAP Master Component Repository*. This data includes information on all products and support packages that were ever delivered by SAP. On the **Administration** page, choose **Import**. On the **Import Selection** page, choose **Import CR Content from Server**. The import procedure may take up to 30 minutes.

This imported data represents only a snapshot of the SAP products at a particular point in time. SAP provides information on products delivered after this point in time via incremental updates of the *master component repository data*. You can download these updates from the SAP Service Marketplace and import them into your SLD to update the data stored there (see Figure 10.6). You should make these updates at regular intervals to keep the data in your SLD current. For the mini development infrastructure, already we have downloaded the updates from the SAP Service Marketplace and imported them into the SLD. You usually specify and import the updates on the **Import Selection** page.

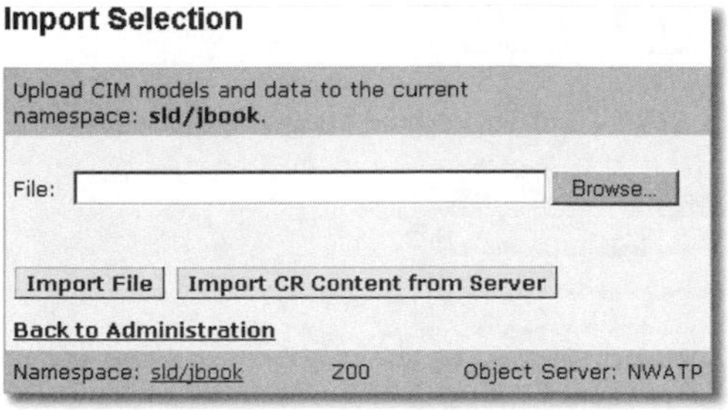

Import Selection

Upload CIM models and data to the current namespace: **sld/jbook**.

File: [ ] [Browse...]

[Import File] [Import CR Content from Server]

Back to Administration

Namespace: sld/jbook   Z00   Object Server: NWATP

Figure 10.6 Initial Data Import for the SLD

An essential feature of the SLD is that the systems in a system landscape automatically provide the SLD with current system data at regular intervals. Therefore, the SLD always contains a current picture of the entire landscape. The individual systems report their system data using the *Data Supplier*. The Data Supplier in every system is configured in such a way that it provides the SLD with data at regular intervals. On the server side of the SLD the *Data Supplier Bridge* receives this data, converts it to the correct format, and inserts it into the SLD.

Data Supplier and Data Supplier Bridge of the SLD

To set the Data Supplier Bridge for our mini development landscape, we choose **Data Supplier Bridge** on the **Administration** page. There, we set the parameter *Update Local SLD (sld/active)* to **true** and start the bridge.

Now we can set the Data Supplier in our system. To do this, call the Visual Administrator of the Java system. Choose **Cluster · Server · Services · SLD Data Supplier**. On the **HTTP Settings** tab page, enter host, port, and logon data (see Figure 10.7). The host is the machine name or the Internet address of the SLD server. The port is the HTTP port of the Java system. For using the Data Supplier, you should create a new user. This user must have the J2EE role *LcrInstanceWriterLD* for the application component *sap.com/com.sap.lcr*sld*. After saving the setting, you can start a data transfer to the SLD server manually by choosing ⚡. After a few seconds, a message should appear telling you that the data transfer has been completed successfully. Now you can check whether the data has really reached the SLD. On the SLD start page, choose **Technical Landscape**. Specify "Web AS Java" as the **Technical System Type**.

The last step consists of registering our SLD server in the SLD. This means that you must enter the Java system on which the SLD server is running in the SLD. On the SLD start page, choose **Technical Landscape**. On the next page, in the **Technical System Browser, choose New Technical System**. In the wizard that opens, choose **System Landscape Directory** and

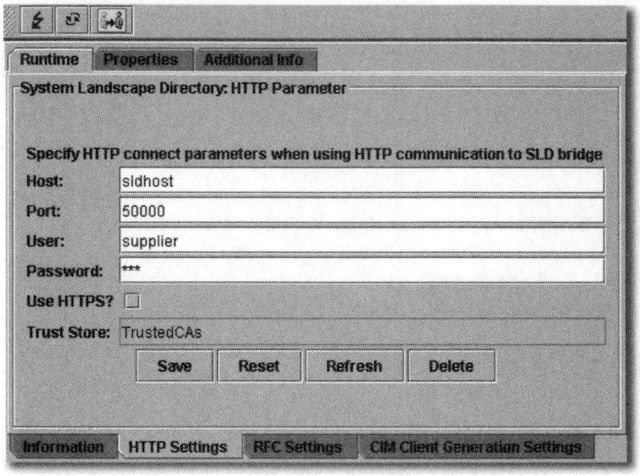

Figure 10.7 SLD Data Supplier for a Java System

continue. On the next screen, select the system of our mini development infrastructure. Since we later want to use this SLD server in our mini infrastructure both as the SLD and as the Name Server, check both options as **Roles**—**Landscape Server** and **Name Server**. To save your setting, click on **Finish** (see Figure 10.8).

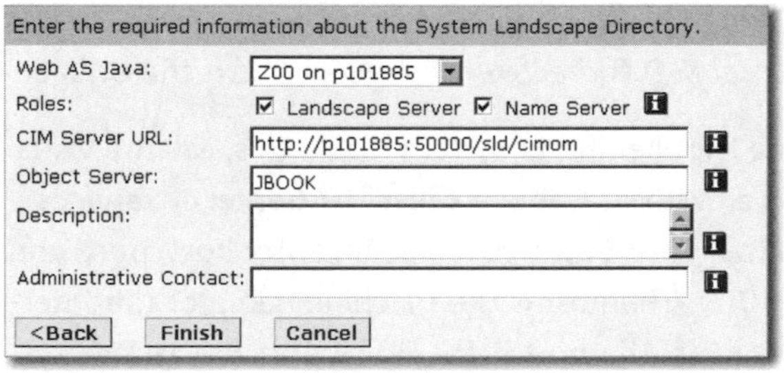

Figure 10.8 Registering the SLD Server and Name Server in the SLD

Using the
Name Server

The Name Server is used in the Java Development Infrastructure to avoid name conflicts of development objects. Assume that you develop your own additional applications based on the SAP NetWeaver platform. In addition, you want to use third-party software. It is quite likely that the applications of different manufacturers contain development objects (for example, database tables) with identical names. If you use both your own and third-party software in the same runtime environment, the object that has been deployed first is overwritten. Such name conflicts are even likely in the same development team.

SAP had originally introduced the name reservation concept for the ABAP development. All you have to do is reserve the desired namespace prefix at SAP. SAP guarantees the global uniqueness of the reserved namespace prefixes. You enter these prefixes in your Name Server. In the namespaces provided by these prefixes, you can create your development objects unquestioningly.

The Name Server uses the same technical basis as the SLD, that is, the same piece of software. Due to this, you can operate the SLD and the Name Server both in the same and in separate systems. SAP recommends that you operate these two functions in separate systems in order to reduce maintenance effort and improve performance.

However, for our mini development landscape, we will operate the two functions in the same system. We have already provided the basis for this when registering the SLD server.

Setting up the DTR server consists of two actions: Setting the URL for the Name Server and setting the initial access rights.

Setting Up the DTR Server

As we already explained, the names of the newly created development objects are entered in the Name Server so that they can never be used again so as to avoid name conflicts. When creating a new development object (for example, a new database), the developer uses the SAP NetWeaver Developer Studio to provisionally reserve the name of the object in the Name Server. When the developer activates the new object, the DTR server finally reserves the name in the Name Server. To be able to do this, the DTR server must know the address of the Name Server. To specify the Name Server and the logon data on the **Name Server Configuration** page, use the URL *http://<host>:<port>/dtr/sysconfig* and then choose **Support • Name Server Configuration**. The host and the port in the URL must be identical to the data you registered for the Name Server in the SLD. The user used by the DTR server to log on to the Name Server needs the J2EE security role *LcrInstanceWriterNR* in the Name Server for the application *sap.com/com.sap.lcr*sld*. For our mini development infrastructure, specify *nwdi_admin* with its password, because this user has the superior authorization *LcrAdministrator*.

Before we focus on setting the initial access rights in the DTR, we will have a closer look at the concept of the *access control list* (ACL).

Access Control List

The development objects in the DTR are stored as files in the database underlying the SAP Web AS. The DTR organizes these objects hierarchically according to functional relations and displays them in the UI in a directory structure similar to the file structure on operating-system level. Unlike the case with CMS and CBS, access to these objects is not controlled by authorizations for particular actions but by access rights attached directly to the objects. For every object or group of objects—a directory—nine kinds of access are defined. (These kinds of access are *access*, *read*, *write*, *checkin*, *import*, *export*, *integrate*, *adminA*, and *adminX*. For a description of the individual types of access, refer to the product documentation.) You can *grant* or *deny* access rights for a certain object or directory to a particular *principal* (either a user or a user group). For example, you can grant *read* access for an object to a user, but deny *write* access for the same object.

To facilitate the work of administrators, access rights on a superior directory level are inherited by the inferior directory levels. This means that the subdirectories copy the access definitions of the superior directory levels unless there are extra access definitions on inferior levels. This relieves the administrator of having to define access rights on all directory levels (whose depth cannot be foreseen).

As of Support Package Stack 9 of the NetWeaver platform, it is possible to terminate the inheritance of ACLs on any subdirectory level. This extra feature may be very helpful, as we will see when setting up ACLs for our mini development infrastructure.

Apart from the two types of granting access rights we discussed—*grant* and *deny*—there is another type, *FinalDeny*. You can set the FinalDeny access rights for particular principals on a superior directory level in order to permanently deny these users or user groups access rights that may be granted to them on the subdirectory levels of the structure. If, for example, you want to perform a database backup for the Web AS of the DTR server, you can temporarily set the FinalDeny of the write access for all workspace folders for all developer groups to ensure that no one modifies the database content during the backup. Remember to revoke the FinalDeny after the backup. Never set FinalDeny for all users (this would include the administrator), or for the root directory or the subdirectory */ws/system*. If you do, no one may be allowed to revoke the FinalDeny.

Four Priority Rules You may have noticed that you can contradict access rights. What happens if you grant read access to a user on the root level but deny this same right for a subdirectory? Does this user have read access to the subdirectory? To resolve these kinds of conflicts, there are four priority rules that the DTR server uses in its evaluation:

1. **FinalDeny before subdirectories**

   You already know this rule. A FinalDeny of an access right on a superior directory level overrules the granted right on the respective subdirectory level. For example, a user can have read access for the .../projects/app1 directory. However, this read access is no longer valid if a FinalDeny of the read access is set for directory .../projects.

2. **Subdirectories before superior directories**

   This rule states that the definition of rights granted for subdirectories takes priority over contradicting definitions on superior directories. For example, you can deny write access for directory .../projects to a user and, simultaneously, grant write access for directory .../projects/app1 to the same user. This allows the user to write to this subdirectory and to all levels below it, but not to the superior directories. This rule enables you to restrict the developer's work to exactly his or her project directory.

3. **User before group**

   A right explicitly granted or denied to a single user always takes priority over the rights defined for the user's group on the same directory level or for the same object. For example, you can deny write access for directory .../project to a group but grant this right to a particular member of this group. This member is then allowed to write into this directory.

4. **Deny before grant**

   Denying a right takes priority over granting the same right. For example, a user is a member in two different groups. If read access for directory .../project is granted to one group and denied to the other, then the user has no read access to this directory.

These four rules are checked—one after the other—in this order until one of these rules applies.

After the deployment, only one access right is set in the DTR, which grants all kinds of access to all users starting from the root directory. For a productive Java Development Infrastructure, this is *by no means* sufficient. On the one hand, developers don't need administrator rights or rights starting from the top directory level. On the other hand, there are some critical subdirectories to which every user should have access. For this reason, you should set at least the following access rights for every DTR server immediately after the deployment:

Initial Access Rights for the DTR

► **Root directory**

This is the highest directory level. All access rights set here are inherited by the subdirectories unless other access rights are set there explicitly.

1. Grant these kinds of access rights (*access*, *read*, *write*, and *checkin*) to all users. For their work in the Java Development Infrastructure, developers usually need these types of access rights to their project directories. Due to the access right inheritance, the project directories automatically receive these rights.

2. Grant all kinds of access to the root directory (including every directory below) to the group of Development Infrastructure administrators.

3. Grant all kinds of access except *adminX* to the CMS user.

► **System directory /ws/system**

This directory contains the system settings, such as the Name Server configuration. Only administrators should be allowed to access it.

1. Deny all kinds of access to all users, but

2. Grant all kinds of access to at least one administrator (as a single user, not as a group).

   For all users, the DTR server provides an implicit user group *<All Users>*. If you grant the access rights to the administrators as a group (they also belong to the *<All Users>* group), then the fourth priority rule (deny before grant) applies, which would deny these rights to the administrators as a group.

► **DTR configuration directory /sysconfig**

This directory contains all administration tools for the DTR server. Set the same access rights as you would for directory */ws/system*.

Now we want to apply these initial access rights to our mini development infrastructure. We use the SAP NetWeaver Developer Studio to do so.

DTR Administration Plug-In
The Developer Studio contains a DTR Administration plug-in. Because not all users need this plug-in, it is deactivated after the installation of the Developer Studio. To activate the plug-in, rename the file *plugin.xml.disabled* in the directory *<dev-studio-install-dir>/plugins/com.tssap.dtr.client.eclipse.admin* to *plugin.xml*. Restart the Developer Studio to activate the plug-in.

DTR Perspective
In the Developer Studio, choose **Window · Open Perspective · Other · Design Time Repository** to open the *DTR perspective*.

To connect to a particular DTR server, you need a DTR client. You can create any number of DTR clients to various servers in the DTR perspective to be able to administer different servers from one IDE instance. In the DTR perspective, choose **DTR · Create Client.** In the **New DTR Client** dialog window, enter information on the new client as shown in Figure 10.9. **Local Root** is the directory on the local PC in which the client stores the data downloaded from the server.

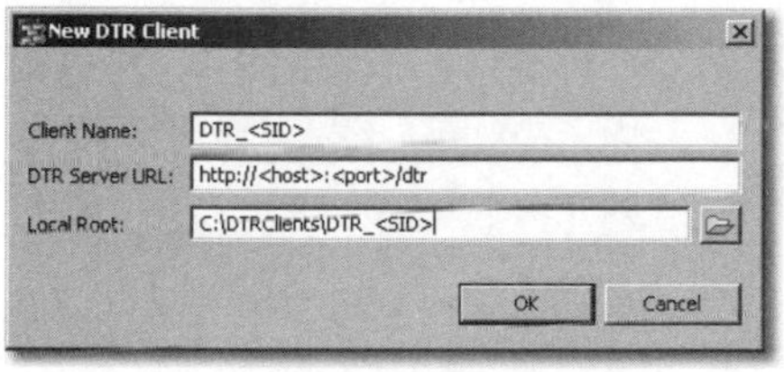

Figure 10.9 Creating a New DTR Client in the Developer Studio

It is good practice to name the client and the local directory after the Server name or system ID of the server system.

After creating the DTR client, you can log on to the DTR as *nwdi_admin* by choosing **Log On** 🖳 from the toolbar. The node **DTR_<SID>** now appears in the *Repository Browser*. This node is linked to the directory of the workspaces in the DTR *http://<host>:<port>/dtr/ws*. In the context menu of this node, you can use **View Permissions** 🔲 to open the view for access rights. To reach the access rights on any directory level, it is preferable that you use the menu entry **View Permissions for URL** under the ▼ pushbutton in the title bar of the **Permissions** view (see Figure 10.10). Besides, in the title bar of the **Permissions** view, you can see the path of the directory currently displayed in the view. This is especially helpful when setting access rights, because you can get lost easily in the directory structure and may set access rights for wrong directories, which could have serious consequences.

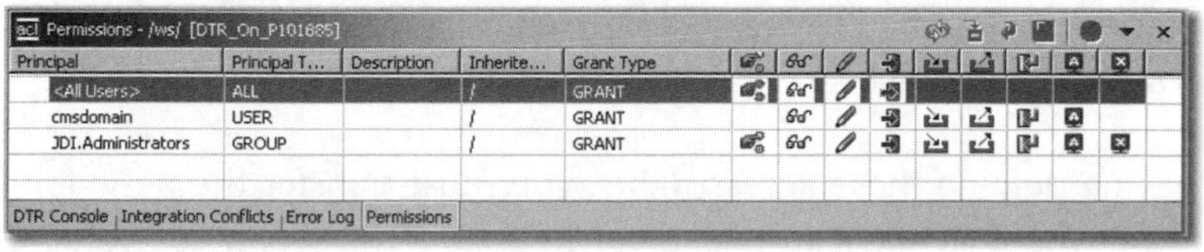

Figure 10.10 Permissions View of the DTR Administration Plug-In

We now use the menu entry **View Permissions for URL** in the **Permissions** view to switch to the root directory. For the URL, we specify *http://<host>:<port>/dtr*. Set the access rights as specified in Table 10.5. In the context menu of the entries for access rights, you find the items **Add Principal** 📄, **Edit Principal,** and **Delete Principal** 📄, all of which we need to set the access rights. You can modify and delete entries only if the relevant rights are set exactly for the current directory and have not been inherited from superior directory levels. You can determine this by looking at the **Inherited from** column in Figure 10.10.

Principal	Principal Type	Grant Type	Access	Read	Write	Check-in	Import	Export	Integrate	Admin A	Admin X
<All Users>	All	Grant	✓	✓	✓	✓					
NWDI. Admini- strators	Group	Grant	✓	✓	✓	✓	✓	✓	✓	✓	✓
cms_user	User	Grant	✓	✓	✓	✓	✓	✓	✓		

Table 10.5 Access Rights for the Root Directory of the DTR

We execute the same procedure for the directories */ws/system* and */sysconfig* according to the specifications in Table 10.6. Make sure that you explicitly grant all rights to user *nwdi_admin* in any case. You already know the reason why. As of Web AS Support Package Stack 9 (NetWeaver 04, SR 1), there is a better way of setting access rights on subdirectory levels. As of this Support Package, the DTR Administration plug-in provides an extra feature that allows you to stop the inheritance of rights from superior directories. You'll find the **Ignore Inheritance** 📄 pushbutton in the title bar of the **Permissions** view.

Principal	Principal Type	Grant Type	access	read	write	checkin	import	export	integrate	Admin A	Admin X
<All Users>	All	Deny	✗	✗	✗	✗					
nwdi_admin	User	Grant	✓	✓	✓	✓	✓	✓	✓	✓	✓

Table 10.6 Access Rights to the /ws/system and /sysconfig Directories of the DTR

After having defined these access rights, you must transfer the new definition from the DTR client to the server to enable the server to evaluate them. The title bar of the **Permissions** view contains the **Activate All Changes** ⬤ pushbutton, which you use to transfer the changes to the server.

On the other hand, the DTR server reads the definition of the access rights only in intervals. This means that the changes transferred to the server apply only after the next synchronization of the access right definitions by the server. However, you can enforce the synchronization on the server side: Navigate in the Web browser to the *http://<host>:<port>/dtr/* site, follow the path **sysconfig · support · AclRefresh,** and click on **Refresh**.

Now you can ensure that the access rights are set correctly and that you can, for example, in the Web browser log on as *nwdi_admin* and *cms_user* to the DTR server and navigate to the directories for which the access rights have been set.

If you have inadvertently excluded all users (including *nwdi_admin*), don't panic. SAP has made provisions to remedy this situation. Use the UME to create a user with the ID *superadmin* (remember to switch to another browser to change the password for the new user before you continue) and log on as this user in the Developer Studio. This loophole user has all rights in the DTR so that you can delete your fatally set access rights.

A Backdoor

Now let's look at the configurations that we must make for the CBS server. There are a few parameters that must be set for the CBS server for each server node of the system. You must explicitly set four of these parameters before putting the CBS server into operation:

Configuration for the CBS Server

▶ *idleStart*: This parameter tells you whether the Component Build Service shall be started in the respective server node. After the deployment, it has the value **true**. If you set the value to **false**, the CBS in the respective node is started whenever the system is launched.

As you already know, when deploying the SCA files, all building blocks of the Java Development Infrastructure are deployed to all systems. Set this parameter to **false** only in those systems that you want to act as CBS servers in order to activate the CBS.

▶ *threadPoolSize*: These parameters set the maximum number of the build processes that can run in parallel.

The build processes use a great deal of the computing capacity (CPU and memory). Despite multitasking, a running build process *de facto* blocks a processor. Therefore, set this parameter in such a way that the total of these parameters—of all server nodes in one system instance—does not exceed the number of available processors in order to allow the computer to still execute other processes (such as monitoring the server) during the build processes.

▶ *BUILD_TOOL_JDK_HOME*: This parameter specifies which JDK version the CBS will use to run the build tools.

You can install a number of JDK versions on operating-system level. The CBS uses the version specified here to start the build tools.

▶ *JDK_HOME_PATHS*: This parameter specifies all available JDK versions that are required by the build tools to build software. Separate these versions with a semicolon (;).

Remember that contrary to the previous parameter, the JDK versions here are called by the tools. For example, here, you want to compile a particular software component using a particular Java compiler version (*javac*), which can differ from the version of the JDK for starting the build tool.

Now we want to set these parameters for our mini development infrastructure In the Web browser call the URL *http://<host>:<por>/tc.CBS. Appl/properties*. Set the four parameters according to your actual system environment (such as paths of the JDK versions) for all server nodes and then start the nodes (see Figure 10.11).

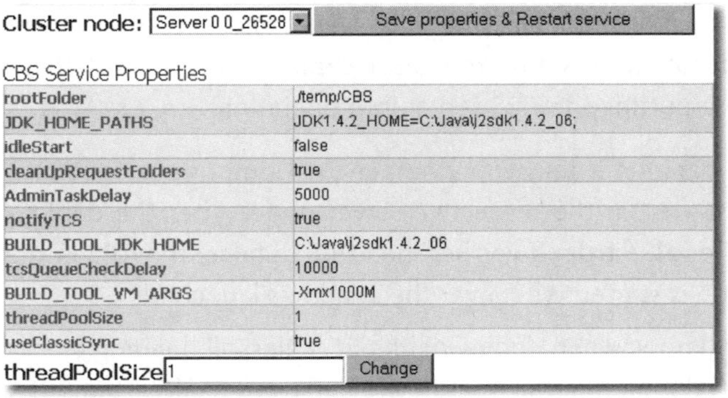

Cluster node: Server 0 0_26528 ▼	Save properties & Restart service
CBS Service Properties	
rootFolder	./temp/CBS
JDK_HOME_PATHS	JDK1.4.2_HOME=C:\Java\j2sdk1.4.2_06;
idleStart	false
cleanUpRequestFolders	true
AdminTaskDelay	5000
notifyTCS	true
BUILD_TOOL_JDK_HOME	C:\Java\j2sdk1.4.2_06
tcsQueueCheckDelay	10000
BUILD_TOOL_VM_ARGS	-Xmx1000M
threadPoolSize	1
useClassicSync	true
threadPoolSize 1	Change

Figure 10.11 CBS Parameters

CMS Domain
Now we discuss the heart of the Java Development Infrastructure, the Change Management Service. The CMS is responsible for the configuration of the development landscape and the management of all building blocks.

The configuration task mainly consists of defining a CMS domain. If after the deployment of the SCA files of the Java Development Infrastructure, you call the Web UI of the CMS for the first time (*http://<host>:<port>/ webdynpro/dispatcher/sap.com/tc~SL~CMS~WebUI/Cms*), the page for the domain definition automatically appears. A *domain* represents a transport landscape. It consists of all tracks that are related by one transport route.

To transport *Software Component Archives* (SCA files) between tracks, the CMS uses a transport directory. This directory stores the SCA files to be transported and, during the import, moves them into the follow-up tracks. If you intend to use a network drive as a transport directory, make sure that this network drive is available at any time to the CMS server and that the service user (*SAPService<SID>*) of the CMS system has write access to this drive.

Transport Directory

This is where the CMS user comes in. The CMS uses this user ID to communicate with all building blocks.

As explained earlier, the Java Development Infrastructure uses the SLD server in the system landscape to retrieve and store information. When creating a CMS domain, the SLD address is specified for later use.

The domain ID identifies a CMS domain and, if you want to accommodate several CMS domains in your system landscape, it must be unique throughout the system landscape. This ID is stored in the SLD. It may be up to three alphanumerical characters long. We call our CMS domain *ATP*.

After these explanations, the configuration of a CMS domain in our mini development infrastructure shouldn't pose a problem. The URLs of CMS and SLD server have the form of *http://<host>:<port>*. For the transport directory, we simply use *<sap-dir>/jtrans*.

After saving the domain definition, switch to the operating-system level and look into the SAP directory *<sap-dir>*. There, the transport directory *jtrans* is created with the subdirectory *CMS/inbox* (see Figure 10.12).

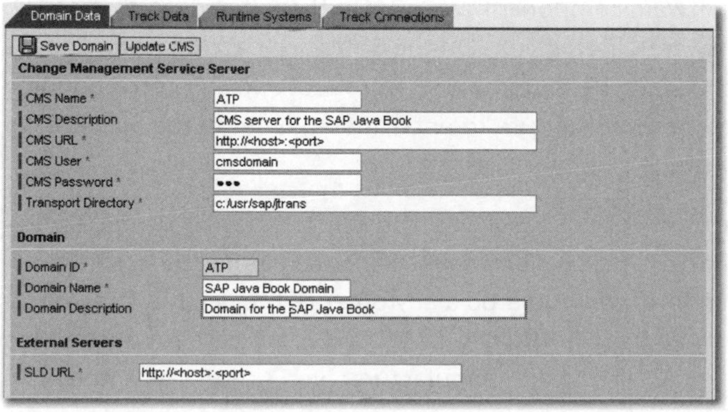

Figure 10.12 Definition of a CMS Domain

On the Web UI of the CMS, you can find the **Update CMS** pushbutton at various places. You can use this function to enforce an update of the temporarily stored SLD data (for example, software component data).

10.2 Administration of the SAP NetWeaver Java Development Infrastructure

We trust that so far setting up a mini development infrastructure was not problematic for you. In this section, we want to look at the administrative tasks in the Java Development Infrastructure. As in the previous section, we'll combine theoretical explanations with practical administrative steps in our mini development infrastructure.

10.2.1 Product Definition in the SLD

Before you can start a software development in the Java Development Infrastructure, you must define the software to be developed in the System Landscape Directory. The purpose is to register information on software products, such as version numbers and support packages, in the SLD. If these products are deployed later in the system landscape, not only does the SLD contain information on the systems in which the software is installed, but also information on the software itself. This allows you to organize the software lifecycle management more methodically and with greater flexibility.

We will not develop any new software in this chapter, but copy the Employee example from the previous chapters. In the SLD we define a software product *JBook*, which contains a software component **JBOOK_ EMPLOYEE**. The vendor name is *demo.org* (as if we are a new software manufacturer on the market named *demo.org*) and the versions for both product and software component are *1.0*. On the initial page of the SLD, follow the **Software Catalog** link. On the **Software Catalog** page, choose **New Product** to start the definition of a product and the corresponding software component. Make sure to enter these names in the SLD exactly as specified above.

If you find this too complicated, you can import the file *ProductDefinition.zip* and the *SAP Master Component Repository* from the accompanying DVD.[5] Therefore, we would be a customer of the *demo.org* manufacturer who wants to use the **JBOOK_EMPLOYEE** software product with a few adaptations. As a software manufacturer, you use this as a means to

---

5 Just ignore the warnings that come up during the import process.

deliver the product definitions to your customers. Your customers must import this information into their SLD in order to modify and use them.

During software development, it is almost an absolute rule that one component needs other components. For the development of our software component **JBOOK_EMPLOYEE**, we need three SAP software components that offer basic libraries and tools for J2EE applications. We call the use relationship between components *usage dependency*. Independent of whether you have defined the product and the related software component yourself in the SLD or whether you have simply imported the definition as a file into the SLD, use the Software Catalog to find the software component **JBOOK_EMPLOYEE** Version *1.0* and on the **Details** page of this software component Version, choose **Usage Dependencies**. Choose **Define Dependencies** and select the following software component versions as used software component versions (see Table 10.7). Now we have completed the product definition for our development.

Software Component Name	Technical Name	Version
IDI BUILD TOOL	*SAP_BUILDT*	6.40
SAP J2EE ENGINE	*SAP-JEE*	6.40
SAP JAVA TECH SERVICES	*SAP_ITECHS*	6.40

Table 10.7 Used Software Component Versions

10.2.2 Namespace Prefix

You have learned in detail the purpose of the namespace prefixes. Now we must reserve such a prefix and register it in the Name Server.

Global uniqueness of development object names can be guaranteed only if an assigned object name is registered as such—reserved, to be more precise—somewhere in a global instance so that this name cannot be re-assigned to another object. Suppose that someone volunteered to play the role of this global instance for a name reservation. Could you imagine having to go through an entire name-reservation process for every object created in your daily development work? Besides, you must also consider that a desired name could have been assigned, and therefore you may have to run through the name reservation process several times just for one single object before you can finally create this object.

To avoid such inconveniences, SAP has developed a two-level concept. SAP assumes the role of the global reservation instance for all SAP customers and partners. However, SAP provides only namespace prefixes. A namespace prefix opens a theoretically unlimited space for sub-namespaces and object names. All the users have to do is register the reserved prefixes in their Name Servers. The Name Server then deals with the name reservation within the reserved namespace. With this procedure, neither SAP nor the SAP user must invest much time or effort in name reservation.

Reserving Namespace Prefixes on the SAP Service Marketplace

On the first level of the two-level concept, you request a namespace prefix on the SAP Service Marketplace . The quicklink */namespaces* leads you to the name reservation page on the SMP.[6] A namespace prefix can be up to eight alphanumerical characters long. Enter the prefix you want to request in the **Namespace** field. Then activate the option **SAP NetWeaver Name Server**, which means that you want to reserve the namespace for objects of the NetWeaver platform. In the **Name of Name Server** field, enter the Object Server Name of your Name Server. If you want to use the name to be reserved as the Object Server name of a new SLD server or Name Server, enter this name in both **Namespace** *and* **Name of Name Server fields**. You can also use the prefix you reserved for the Object Server Name for development objects (see Figure 10.13).

After you have sent the request for a prefix, behind the scenes an asynchronous process is started. Up to three work days may pass before you get a positive reply. (A negative reply, for example, if the name has already been assigned, usually arrives faster, because the process is terminated immediately as soon as one condition is not met). A positive reply indicates that the desired prefix has not yet been assigned and that all other conditions for a reservation are met. You must now confirm the reservation and the prefix is yours.

You can also use a previously reserved ABAP name prefix for NetWeaver development projects. All you need to do is declare the reserved prefix on the SAP Service Marketplace for the SAP NetWeaver Name Server.

---

6 For ABAP development, this page has existed for quite some time. It has now been enhanced for development for the SAP NetWeaver platform and SAP Business One.

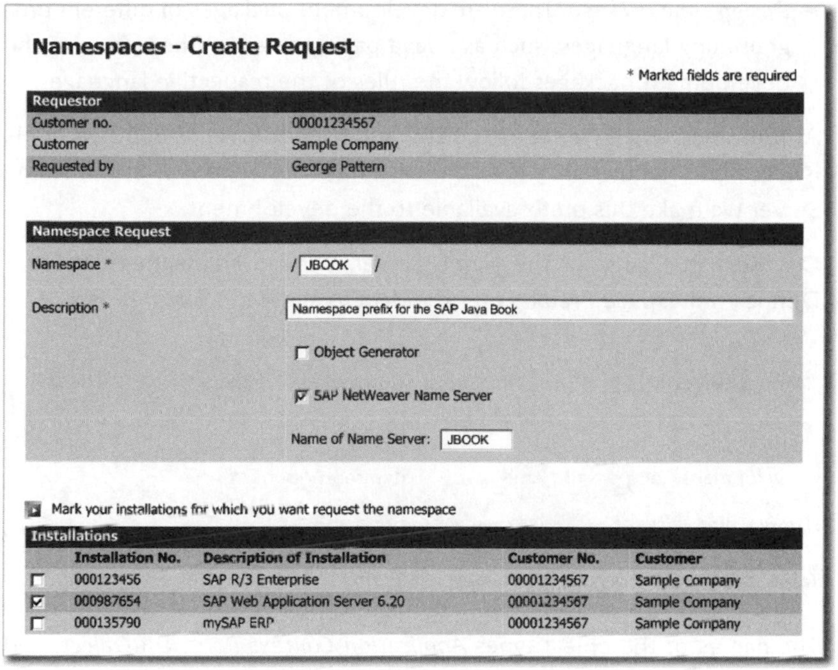

Figure 10.13 Request of a Namespace Prefix in the SAP Service Marketplace

Registering Reserved Namespace Prefixes in the Name Server

The second level of the name reservation concept is to register the reserved namespace prefixes in your Name Server, so that your developers can start to create new development objects in the reserved namespaces.

The SAP NetWeaver Java Development Infrastructure knows eight development object types. We will now look at the most important types; the *X* in the examples represents a reserved namespace prefix:

▶ *Application Context Root*: This is the relative path under which Web applications in a SAP Web AS can be called, for example, *http://<host>:<port>/x/myapp*.

▶ *DB Object*: Database objects are database tables and database indexes, such as *X_MYTAB*.

▶ *DB Pool*: These are the aliases for the database connection pool. Such an alias has the form *X/P_MYPOOL*.

▶ *Development Component*: Development components are the smallest units that can be built. Names of the development components have the form *<vendor>/x/mydc*.

▶ *Design Time Package*: These are development packages of different programming languages, such as a Java package name. The names of the development packages follow the rules of the respective languages.

As presumed when we set up the SLD and Name Server, the *JBOOK* prefix is reserved for our mini development infrastructure. Now, in the Name Server we make this prefix available to the development.

On the initial page of the Name Server, choose **Name Reservation** · **Define Namespace Prefix**. Enter the data as shown in Table 10.8.

Name Category	Namespace Prefix
By Convention	JBOOK
Development Component Name	demo.org/jbook/*
Design Time Package	org.demo.*

Table 10.8 Name Category and Namespace Prefix

The names of the object types *Application Context Root*, *DB Object*, and *DB Pool* follow certain conventions. Therefore, simply select "By convention" as the **Name Category**, instead of selecting each one separately. In accordance with the specified prefix, the Name Server generates the correct namespaces of the individual object types (see Figure 10.14).

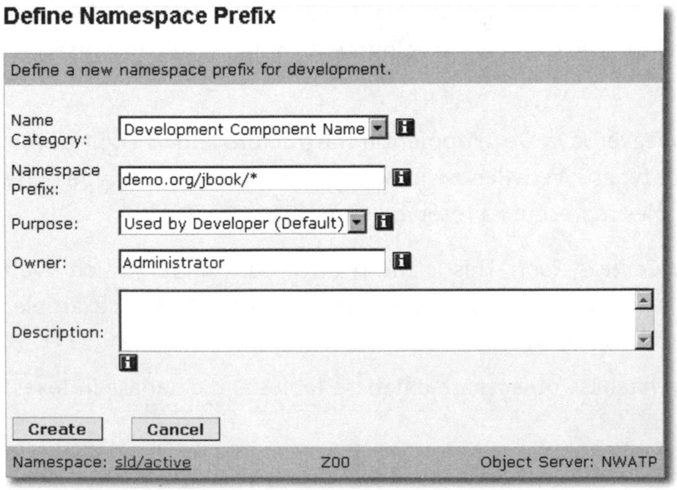

Define Namespace Prefix

Define a new namespace prefix for development.

Name Category:	Development Component Name ▾ ℹ
Namespace Prefix:	demo.org/jbook/* ℹ
Purpose:	Used by Developer (Default) ▾ ℹ
Owner:	Administrator ℹ
Description:	ℹ

Create   Cancel

Namespace: sld/active   Z00   Object Server: NWATP

Figure 10.14 Registering Reserved Namespace Prefixes in the Name Server

10.2.3 Preparing a Track

Defining Track and Transport Route

A *track* is a development environment in which one software component version or versions of several software components can be developed. A track includes up to four project phases: development, consolidation, quality assurance, and production. In the first two phases, program codes are written and changed. The program codes are stored in the appropriate workspaces in the DTR and built in the appropriate buildspaces in the CBS. To relieve the developers of having to deal with the access data of these workspaces and buildspaces, the architects of the Java Development Infrastructure constructed the *development configuration*. A development configuration contains the access information for workspaces and buildpaces of each project phase and the software components included. As we will see later, all a developer has to do in the Development Studio is to import a development configuration for the project phase in which he or she intends to work. The developer's development environment is then automatically connected to the correct workspaces and buildspaces. This ensures that every developer always accesses the correct versions of the source files and used library versions. For every track, there are two development configurations, one for development and one for consolidation.

Project Phases of a Track

When you define a track, you specify the DTR and CBS server to be used and the software component versions to be developed. The CMS creates workspaces and buildspaces accordingly. At the same time, these configurations are stored in the CMS and entered in the SLD as a development configuration. Developers can use the IDE in the SLD to search for the relevant configuration and then load this configuration from the CMS into the IDE to create a real development context in the IDE (see Figure 10.15).

Defining a Track

For every project phase in a track, you can choose to include a runtime system to serve as a test system for the respective phase. In the CMS, you must specify the logon data of the *Software Deployment Manager* (SDM) of the runtime system. Whenever new versions of development components are created by activation or transport, they are deployed into the runtime systems to be available for testing by the developers or quality managers. If a production system is part of a track (as a runtime system for the production phase), this production system is immediately supplied with the software component versions released for delivery after the test phase.

Runtime Systems

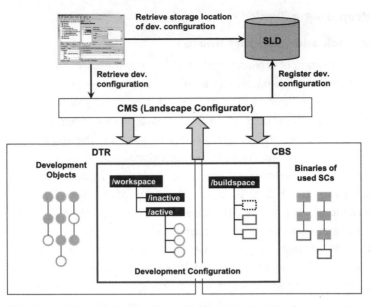

Figure 10.15 When Defining a Track, Two Development Configurations Are Generated.

Transport Route Up to now, we have seen the configuration of a track. Besides development in a track, the Java Development Infrastructure supports layered developments. This implies that a CMS domain represents a transport landscape. Tracks in a domain are interconnected according to supply dependencies. We call these connections between tracks transport routes, because they are used to deliver the released software component versions of one track—the results of this track—to the follow-up tracks.

There are two types of transport routes: The first type is simply called *transport*. This type connects two tracks according to the supply dependency of these tracks. For example, the development in track B uses components developed in track A. Then the transport route from A to B is of type *Transport*.

Maintenance Tracks and Backward Transport There is a different situation if track B is a maintenance track of track A. In track A, the development of software continues. In track B, a particular release state of track A is kept in order to correct any errors that are found only after the released version has been delivered. In track B, support packages of this version are developed. In this case, it is not sufficient to connect from A to B using a transport route of type *Transport* to transport the release state into track B. We need an additional transport route of type *Repair*, which connects the two tracks from B to A. This is the way in which error corrections can (but don't necessarily have to) be integrated from the maintenance track backwards into the original track. If you release an error correction in the maintenance track for transport, the transport request is not only included into the import queue of the next phase as usual, but the transport request is additionally added to the import queue of the development phase of the original track. The decision regarding whether to integrate such error corrections is up to the project leader.

A backward transport of error corrections is not only carried out between two tracks connected via a *Repair* transport route. Backward transports also occur within a track between the consolidation and development phases. Errors detected early—that is, before delivery—can still be eliminated in the consolidation phase. These error corrections can be integrated into the development phase via backward transports. Figure 10.16 illustrates both kinds of backward transports.

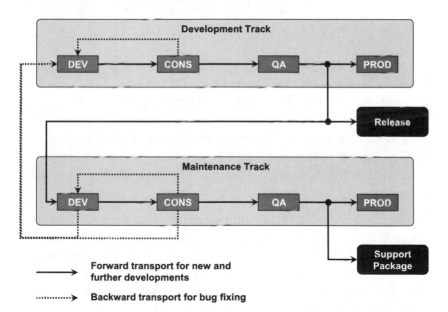

Figure 10.16 Transport Directions Within a Track and Between a Development Track and a Maintenance Track

Let's return to our mini development infrastructure and create two tracks for development and maintenance. To do this, we switch to the **Landscape Configurator** of the CMS and select the **Track Data** tab page. If a track already exists, choose **New** to reset the input fields.Then, fill in the fields as shown in Table 10.9.

Repository Type	DTR
Track ID	Develop
Track Name	Development
Track Description	Development Track
Development Configuration Path	JBOOK (or as you choose)
Design Time Repository URL	http://<host>:<port>/dtr
Component Build Service URL	http://<host>:<port>
Software Component for Development	JBOOK_EMPLOYEE, Release 1.0, Package Type Source and Archive
Required Software Components	SAP-JEE, Release 6.40
	SAP_BUILDT, Release 6.40
	SAP_JTECHS, Release 6.40

Table 10.9 Data for the Development Track

The three software components required for the development (**Required Software Components**) are inserted automatically, because in the SLD we have declared that our component **JBOOK_EMPLOYEE** depends on them. The CMS retrieves this dependency information from the SLD as soon as we have specified the component that we want to develop. The **Package Type** of the component to be developed specifies whether the component will be delivered with the source files, or only with binary archives.

By saving the track definition, you trigger the track generation process. The CMS now tries to create workspaces and buildspaces and to register the development configuration in the SLD. The process can take several minutes. After we have finished creating our first track, use the Web browser to look into DTR and CBS to see whether new workspaces and buildspaces have been created there for our track.

For our mini development infrastructure, we don't use any runtime systems. Otherwise, you could now assign a runtime system to each of the four project phases of the new track.

Next, we want to create a maintenance track. Basically, there is no difference between the maintenance track and the development track, except, of course, that the track ID differs. So, all we have to do is copy the definition of the development track. To do this, choose **Save As** and enter "Maintain" as the **New Track ID** and "Maintenance" as the **New Track**

Name. The **Track Description** is not mandatory but you should still enter a descriptive text such as "Maintenance Track for ...". Such descriptions can be very helpful in your daily work. Save your entries to create a second track as a maintenance track.

After we've created the two tracks, we want to connect them via transport routes. We switch to the **Track Connections** tab page and create two transport routes as described in Table 10.10. Now we have completed the definition of two tracks and the transport relationship that exists between them.

Source Track	Target Track	Connection Type
Development	Maintenance	Transport
Maintenance	Development	Repair

Table 10.10 Transport Routes Between the Development Track and the Maintenance Track

Importing Required Software Components into the Track

When you create a track, workspaces and buildspaces are created in DTR and CBS for this track, but they are still empty.

In the workspace, source files are stored. Depending on whether a track will be used for a new or a further development, the development starts either with completely empty workspaces, or with workspaces filled with the source files of the previous version.

The buildspaces are usually filled with the required software components. The software component **SAP_BUILDT** is required for every component type, because it contains the required build tools for all supported component types.

This is why the used software components, and maybe even the previous version of the software component to be developed, must be imported into the track before the actual development work can begin. The three used software components can be found in the *<sap-dir>/<SID>/<SYS>/global/CMS_CBS/plugins* directory. When the SCA file *SAPBUILDT.SCA is deployed*, the components are copied into the file system; the version of the files there corresponds to the version state of the Java system. If you use this Java Development Infrastructure but want to develop software for Web AS with other version states, you must download the respective versions of the used software components from the SAP Service Marketplace.

**Checking-In
the Software
Components
into a Track**

In our mini development infrastructure, there are only two tracks, where the first track *Development* is located at the beginning of the transport landscape. This implies that it is not automatically supplied by other tracks. We must check in the required components into the import queue for the development phase of this track. In addition, we don't want to start a new development but rather to continue developing the Employee example from the previous chapters, so we also must include this component with the source files into the import queue. Copy the file *demo.org~JBOOK_EMPLOYEE.sca* from the included CD and the three usually required components from the directory *<sap-dir>/<SID>/<SYS>/ global/CMS_CBS/plugins* into the subdirectory *CMS/inbox* of the transport directory. Then, on the left side of the Transport Studio in the CMS, select the track Development and on the right side select the **Check-In** tab page. In the **Archive Name** field, enter each of the file names individually and then choose **Check-In**.

After you have inserted all four packages into the import queue of the track, switch to the **Development** tab page. There, you should see four transport requests for the four packages. Select all requests and choose **Import** to start the import. It takes a few minutes to complete this process. After the import into the development phase, switch to the **Consolidation** tab page. You should see four transport requests as well. As described for the development phase, proceed to import the packages into the consolidation phase.

You may want to know what exactly happens during the import. Importing SCA files consists of three steps that are executed consecutively:

1. **Repository Import**
   If an SCA file does not contain source files from the respective software component, these source files are first loaded into the inactive workspace of the DTR.

2. **Build**
   The source files loaded in the previous step are now built into the CBS. If the build is successful, they are activated, that is, integrated into the active workspace. The build creates binary build and deploy archives.

   If a package does not contain any source files but only binary archives, these archives are loaded into the respective buildspace.

3. **Deployment**
   The deploy archives contained in the SCA file, or the deploy archives created in the build in the last step, are deployed into the runtime system, provided that a runtime system exists for the relevant project phase.

The import terminates immediately if one of these steps fails. After the import for the consolidation is complete, use the Web browser to look at DTR and CBS again. Are the workspaces and buildspaces of the *Development* track filled with the correct content? If they are, we can begin our actual development work.

10.2.4 Development in the Java Development Infrastructure

Before we can continue to develop our Employee example in the mini development infrastructure, we must perform two preparatory steps in the Developer Studio.

First, we open two perspectives, the *J2EE Development perspective* and the *Development Configurations perspective*. To do this, choose **Window** • **Open Perspective** • **Other** and select these two perspectives.

Then we want to inform the Developer Studio of where to find the SLD. (Do you still know what this is for? We will return to it later.) Choose **Window** • **Preferences** • **Java Development Infrastructure** • **Development Configuration Pool** and in the **URL** field enter the address of the SLD in the form *http://<host>:<port>*.

Now switch to the *Development Configurations* perspective and use the icon in the toolbar to log on as *nwdi_admin*. As you know, we need a development configuration to set the context for the development. Choose the icon to open the **Development Configuration Import** wizard and activate the **remote** option. A list of the existing development configurations appears in the bottom half of the dialog window. This list has been downloaded from the SLD, which we have just specified in the Developer Studio as the development configuration pool. From this list, select the development configuration *Development_dev* and click on **Next**. On the next screen, details for this development configuration are displayed such as addresses of CBS, DTR, and Name Server. Click on **Finish** to import the development configuration.

Importing the Development Configuration into the IDE

If you expand the node **Development_dev** in the **Inactive DCs** view of the *Development Configurations* perspective, you see the software component **demo.org/JBOOK_EMPLOYEE** with the four development components that we want to modify in this track. If you expand the same node in the **Active DCs** view, in addition to the component to be developed, you will see the three standard required components used by the development of our component. Again, each of these components contains numerous development components (DCs).

We now want to tailor the Web UI of the Employee example to our liking. To do this, we must load the DC *jbook/employee/web* for the Web UI and the DC *jbook/employee/ear*, which composes a deployable and executable J2EE application of all the individual DCs, as development projects into the Developer Studio. First, from the context menu of *jbook/employee/web*, choose **Create Project**. In the dialog window (see Figure 10.17), you see the DC *jbook/employee/web* at the top of the list; its source files are synchronized to the local PC because we want to change this DC. The other DCs in the list, among them two DCs *jbook/employee/dic* and *jbook/employee/ejb* that belong to the **demo.org/JBOOK_EMPLOYEE** software component, are synchronized to the local PC as binary build archives to be used by *jbook/employee/web*. Simply click on **OK** and the correct versions of the source files and build archives will be downloaded.

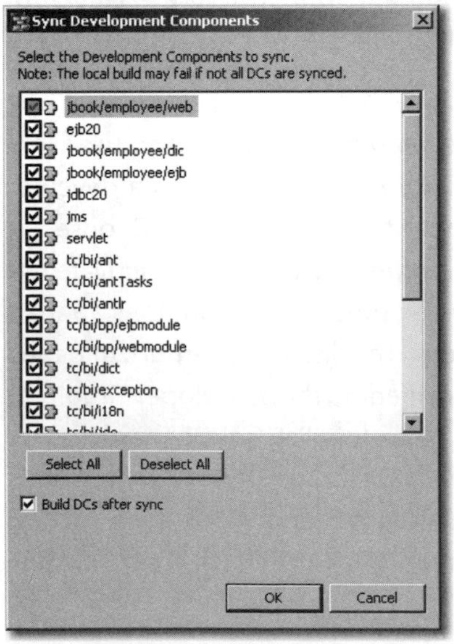

Figure 10.17 When Generating a DC Project in the Developer Studio, the Source Files of the DC and the Binary Archives of the Used DC Are Synchronized to the Local PC.

Repeat the same steps for the DC *jbook/employee/ear* to generate the second DC project. (Can you detect any differences in the synchronization dialog window as compared to the last time?) After the synchronization of the second DC, you can see in the **Inactive DCs** view that the DCs are either accompanied by a light green arrow or a dark green arrow. A light green arrow indicates that the inactive versions of the source files of the relevant DC are available for modifications on the local PC. It applies to the two DCs for which we explicitly generated DC projects. A dark green arrow indicates that the active versions of the binary archives of the DC are available on the local PC. This applies to the other two DCs, which have automatically been synchronized due to the use dependencies.

You see how straightforward a process it is to find the correct versions of source files and binary archives in the Java Development Infrastructure. All you actually did was set the SLD address in the Developer Studio. In the SLD you'll find the development configurations that describe the development contexts. You import one of these development contexts into the IDE, and the IDE then finds and collects the correct file versions.

Now we finally want to modify our Web UI. Switch to the **J2EE Development** perspective. In the **J2EE DC Explorer** view, expand the node for the Web project. In the **WebContent** subfolder, you'll find the JSP file *NewEmployee.jsp*. In the context menu of this file, choose **DTR • Edit** and then create an activity. The activity name can be any text, for example "Change Web Interface." Open the file and display its source file in the **Source** view. We'll change the background color of this Web page. (We find the current color an eyesore.) In the third line, overwrite the value of the *bgcolor* attribute with *EFEFEF*. In the **Preview** view, look at the new background color—do you like it better?

```
<body style= "font-family:Arial;"  bgcolor="EFEFEF">
```

If you are content with the preview, we can now build a deployable and executable application from the Employee example. In the context menu of the *jbook/employee/ear* DC project, choose **Development Component • Build**. The **Build Development Components** wizard that is displayed automatically proposes that all DC projects that have been modified since the last build—and on which the DC *jbook/employee/ear* depends—must be rebuilt. Rely on the proposals and allow the Enterprise Application DC to be built. The wizard works perfectly. (How fortunate that there are such intelligent tools!) The result of the build is that you get an enterprise archive for the Enterprise Application DC (see Figure 10.18).

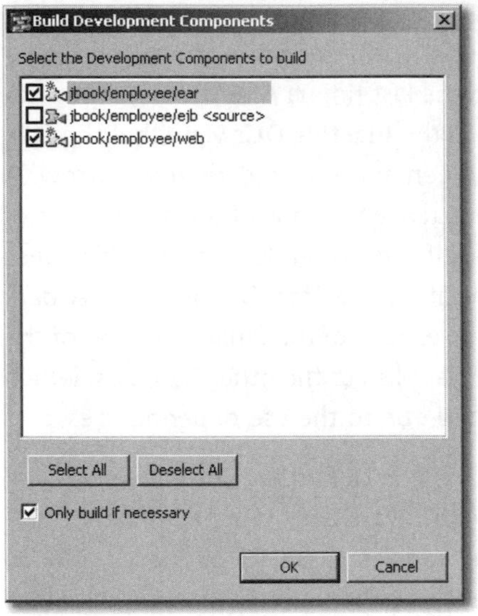

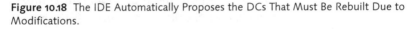

Figure 10.18 The IDE Automatically Proposes the DCs That Must Be Rebuilt Due to Modifications.

After the successful build we can now start the deployment. Remember to first deploy the Dictionary DC *jbook/employee/dic*, because our application uses the database table in the Dictionary DC. To deploy the Dictionary DC, use the **Inactive DC** view in the Development Configurations perspective.[7] Choose **Deploy** from the context menu of this DC. Then you can use the same procedure to deploy the Enterprise Application DC. If everything went as it should, you ought to be able to call the application in the Web browser, replete with the new background color! Note that the namespace concept provided the URL with a prefix in the path. The URL is now *http://<host>:<port>/jbook/employee/view*.

We hope that you're content with the modification, because then we can check in our change and activate it. Switch to the **Open Activities** view in the *Development Configurations* perspective. Under our workspace node, you find the activity you created to check out the JSP file. This file is contained in the activity and it will probably be the only file unless you edited other files. To check in the activity, choose **Checkin** from the context menu of the activity and confirm the subsequent prompt. Usually you will want to activate the changes to the source files directly after checking

---

7 Deploying the Dictionary DC in the *Dictionary perspective*, as done in the previous chapters, should not be necessary here. We did not have to change this DC for our purposes. Therefore, only the binary archives of this DC have been synchronized to our PC. In the *Dictionary* perspective, you would not find a DC project.

them in. For this reason, the IDE offers an activation option. This is what we want to do now. Choose **Activate** in the **Activation** wizard to confirm the activation. For the activation, you receive an *activation request ID*. Write down this number, because we will need it later on. You know that the activation of changes triggers a build process in the CBS. The CBS uses this number to identify the build process.

You can monitor the status of the activation/build process either directly in the IDE or on the Web UI of the CBS. If you want to monitor it in the IDE, choose **Window** • **Show View** • **Other** to open the **Activation Requests** view. You'll find the view under **CBS Activation** in the **Show View** dialog window. In the **Activation Requests** view, you find the activation ID on the left side. To query the current status, choose 🔄 in the view title bar. For every activation request, the progress of the activation (in the ♣ column) and of the deployment (in the ↩ column) is displayed. On the right side, you can call the build log after the activation process has finished.

However, in the **Activation Requests** view you cannot observe the phenomenon of the so-called *follow-up requests*. What is a follow-up request? If a changed DC is activated, it is rebuilt. You already know this much. What happens to the DCs that depend on this DC? The changes may have serious effects on syntax and semantics of these dependent DCs. Therefore, they should be rebuilt based on the new build archives of the used DC. This is the only way to ensure that all DCs of a software component remain consistent. Therefore, the CBS triggers internal requests for all DCs that depend on a changed DC.

Follow-Up Requests

To track these follow-up requests, we must switch to the Web UI of the CBS (*http://<host>:<port>/tc.CBS.Appl/* • *CBS WebUI*). Here, choose the **Requests** link with the 🔧 icon. On the subsequent page, **CBS Request Information**, you can search for the build requests assigned to a particular buildspace. Select the buildspace *ATP_Develop_D*, which is the one of interest for us. If required, adapt the time interval for the search to include the activation time of our activity. Choose **Search** to start the search. The search result will contain a build request with the request ID you wrote down during the activation. However, this build request will not be the last, but probably the next to last, even though you didn't trigger any other activation. The request type of the last request is *INTERNAL_BUILD*. The owner *TC.CBS.SERVICE* is specified. This is a follow-up request for our activation. We have changed and activated the Web DC *jbook/employee/web*. Our activation request refers to this particular DC. The Enterprise Application DC *jbook/employee/ear* uses the Web DC, which is why it must be rebuilt by an internal build request and then deployed.

As Project Manager, you must monitor the statuses of the follow-up requests in this way to find out whether the dependent DCs are still syntactically correct despite changes to their using DCs and whether they can still be compiled. If they are syntactically correct, you must test the newly built application in the runtime system to exclude any semantic inconsistencies.

You may ask yourself why you can't track follow-up requests in the IDE. The answer is quite simple: An activation is successful if all DCs to be activated have been built successfully and the changes to the source files have been integrated into the active workspace. Follow-up requests for dependent DCs are irrelevant here. Suppose you're a developer of a basic DC (for example a *logging* DC). Because of new demands, you have to make incompatible changes to the programming interface (API) of this DC. You could never complete your work, because the follow-up requests for the dependent DC would inevitably fail due to the API modifications. You would be made responsible for the failure of the dependent DCs. To exclude such cases, the build results of the follow-up requests are not considered for the activation. The task of periodically checking on the Web UI—whether their DCs are still syntactically and semantically correct despite modifications in used DCs—belongs to the person responsible for the development.

Release for Transport The last step we perform in the IDE is to release the activity for transport. Transports import changes into the next project phase (for example, consolidation). Activities are placed as transport requests into the import queue of the next phase. However, a successful activation of the activity does not automatically release it for transport. Sometimes, several activities are required for one large change project. To be able to transport the related changes together and therefore synchronously, you can release the respective activities collectively and create a single common transport request.

We now release our activity for transport to finally complete our development work. In the **Transport** view, expand the structure for the build-space *ATP_Develop_D*. The substructure **Waiting** contains our activity. From the context menu of the activity, choose **Release** to release it for transport. The activity now moves to the substructure **Released**.

10.2.5 Consolidation Phase

Consolidation is the second project phase in a track. After the developers have released their activities in the development phase for transport, the respective transport requests are waiting in the import queue of the consolidation phase.

Why has the consolidation phase been introduced? The activation concept can guarantee that activated changes are always syntactically correct. But how can you ensure that the changes made by different developers match semantically? Before a software development is passed on to quality management, its functions are tested. At the same time, the development may continue. To avoid the problem of new changes constantly invalidating the tests, you must save a particular state of the software and decouple the testing from the continuing development. This is where the consolidation phase comes in.

What happens with the errors detected during the tests in the consolidation state? Generally, there are two ways of correcting them. The first way is to correct the errors in the development state and integrate the new version into the consolidation state. However, due to the continuing development, an error may have become irrelevant in the development state or its correction may have become impossible. In this case, you must use the second way and correct the error directly in the consolidation state. The error corrections in the consolidation state are included backwards into the import queue of the development phase as soon as they have been released. Whether you want to integrate them into the development state is up to your discretion.

For our little development example in the mini development infrastructure, we will do nothing in the consolidation phase. Besides, we didn't make any errors. So, simply import the activity that you released in the development phase. After the import, ensure that our change has really reached the active workspace in the consolidation.

10.2.6 Assembling the Software and Quality Assurance

After the consolidation phase, the software is assembled and passed on to quality assurance. The difference from the two previous phases is that here the software components are really packed together as such. The results of the software assembly are *Software Component Archives* (SCAs), which are deployed as packages into runtime systems. In the development and consolidation phases, only the DCs affected by changes are rebuilt and deployed. Software components, not the development components, are the delivery units sent to the customers or installed in the production systems.

The assembled software components are deployed into the runtime system for quality assurance and tested there. Generally, software products are tested by quality engineers before they are delivered.

Now we want to assemble the changed Employee example. Switch to the **Assembly** tab page. Here you find all transport requests that either have been imported from development into consolidation or have been released in consolidation. During the assembly, all changes from both phases are packed together. We'll find only one request resulting from the modification of the background color. From the drop-down list **Select Component**, you can select the software component that you want to assemble. In our case, we can accept the proposal **All Components**, because we develop only one component in this track. Choose **Assemble Component(s)** to build a new version of the selected software component into an SCA file. You can find the new SCA file in the directory *<transport-dir>/CMS/archives*.

If we had defined a runtime system for the quality assurance phase during the track definition, the Transport Studio would include a **Test** tab page, and we could now deploy our software component as an SCA into the test system and test it.

After completing the tests in the quality assurance system successfully, the software can be delivered. This means that it can be delivered to customers or be used in the developing company's own productive system. However, one formal step still has to be performed: the approval of the release for delivery. To perform this step, switch to the **Approval** tab page. Besides the version of our software component, which we just built and tested, you find the usual three required components there. It makes no sense to approve components we didn't develop. We use these components in our component. So, we have developed our component version exactly against the listed versions of the used components. Approval of the used component versions means that our component version can be used only with these used component versions. Only this one combination has been tested by quality assurance. Now select all listed components and choose **Confirm** to approve them.

10.2.7 Delivery to the Customers

Now we can deliver our software. Or can we? How do we do that? There are three kinds of delivery.

As you are already aware, the packed software components are now SCA files in the subdirectory *CMS/archives* of the transport directory. These files are delivery units. You must transfer them to the customer and install them there somehow.

If the developed software is intended for use in one's own company, you could include the production system into the track in the track definition, so that a transport request would be generated for the deployment into this system after the approval. All you would have to do is switch to the **Production** tab page and trigger the deployment.

The third kind of delivery refers to the supply of the follow-up tracks. If our component is used by other components in other follow-up tracks, then our new component version must be transported into the follow-up tracks. This also applies if a support package for a delivered software component version shall be developed in a maintenance track. Remember that we have defined such a maintenance track and connected it to the development track. After the release approval, transport requests are included into the import queue of the development phase of the follow-up tracks as well. Simply switch to the **Development** tab page of the track of *Maintain*. There, four transport requests are waiting to be imported into the track, one for our component **demo.org/JBOOK_EMPLOYEE** and one each for the three standard required components.

You can now import these components into the maintenance track. Try to change our component in this track, pretending to develop a support package. Check whether the changes in the maintenance track are really transported backwards into the original track.

Have fun and good luck!

11 The Architecture of the SAP Web Application Server

SAP Web AS 6.40 has a clear design that allows you to run numerous application server instances and efficiently distribute the load among them, thereby enabling you to handle thousands of users, while at the same time provide the reliability, availability, and scalability required by an enterprise. This chapter examines Web AS Cluster and Runtime Architecture; both form the basis for building a coherent, consistent, and scalable Java platform.

This chapter presents the architecture of the SAP Web Application Server (SAP Web AS) from two different perspectives:

▶ The SAP Web AS landscape
▶ The SAP Web AS runtime architecture

The first perspective looks at the main components and their role in an integrated cluster environment. It also discusses important production aspects for running mission-critical applications such as scalability, reliability, and availability. While the scope is clearly the landscape that executes Java and J2EE applications, many of the components and the concepts forming the Java "stack" aren't new, but adopted from R/3. Therefore, they come with a proven history in their ability to execute huge code bases and provide scalability to thousands of concurrent users.

For those of you who may have already had some experience with certain SAP products, this is a good opportunity to become familiar with the core concepts that enable the smooth operation of your company's business applications and that of many other companies. The fact that SAP is the first company to deliver what is known today as an "application server" is not well-known since SAP never sold it as a separate product. But now you can benefit from this latest server offer as well: To be able to use it not just in a ready, prepackaged form, customized to your application needs, but to use the technology and the proven environment to build your own applications.

The second part of this chapter gives more details about the internal architecture of the Java (J2EE) application server. The Java execution environment is fairly new and much more dynamic, in the same way that the technology and the standards it is built for are, as well as the implementations. However, this doesn't mean that the required layering and abstraction patterns—which SAP always tries to achieve—aren't in place. Nor does it mean that the clear and extendable design for coping with the dynamic, open standards environment is not available.

11.1 SAP Web Application Server Landscape

Cluster Landscape

The SAP Web AS cluster is a homogeneous environment that consists of:

▶ A global load balancer (for example, *SAP Web Dispatcher*)

▶ *A system database* and a central instance where central services like the message server, locking server, and the Software Delivery Manager (SDM) are located

▶ One or more dialog instances with two kinds of nodes: *dispatcher* (local load balancer) and *server* (application server)

It also contains the set of tools required for support, console and visual administration, application development, assembly, and deployment.

The overall cluster picture is depicted in Figure 11.1. The major cluster concepts and cluster participants are described below.

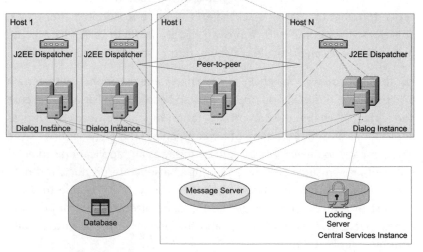

Figure 11.1 Cluster Landscape

11.1.1 Cluster Design Concepts

The SAP Web AS 6.40 cluster has a clear design that allows you to run numerous application server instances, efficiently distribute the load among them, and handle thousands of users—thereby providing the reliability, availability, and scalability needed by an enterprise.

Scalability

The scalability features are discussed in more detail later in this chapter.

The SAP Web AS cluster is completely transparent to the application developer and deployer. Porting a standalone application to a clustered environment does not require—in most cases[1]—any code or configuration changes from the developer. The support of central deployment makes the process of deploying an application in the cluster the same as deploying it on a standalone environment.

Transparency

The SAP Web AS provides a homogeneous cluster infrastructure that requires minimal administration effort. Having a central storage for all binary and configuration data ensures the consistency of deployed applications.

Homogeneous Environment

One important point of the cluster architecture that you should note is the ease of dynamic cluster administration. Adding a new cluster node to cope with increased load or removing an existing cluster node is as easy as pressing a button. Everything else is handled internally by the infrastructure, ensuring consistency and cluster-wide distribution of the deployed applications.

Self-Organizing Feature

The ability to run on a 7/24 basis with greatly reduced planned and unplanned downtimes is not simply a feature of the SAP cluster infrastructure alone. The application developer benefits from the same quality of transparent failover services, which don't require any changes to his or her applications. The fault tolerance features are discussed in more detail later in this chapter.

High Availability

The "star" cluster architecture features minimize the number of internal connections while avoiding communication bottlenecks.

"Star" Architecture

---

1 Assuming common application blueprints are followed, for example:
   - Configuration and other persistent data is stored in the central database, not on a local file system.
   - The application does not rely on critical system-wide singletons that are initialized and stored in static variables (hence, accessible only in the JVM where initialization took place).

Supportability	Debugging in the productive environment without affecting user sessions is part of the state-of-the-art support solution. The SAP Web AS cluster is designed in such a way that you can execute full-range debugging of live applications without interrupting the user's work.
	Central lifecycle management of the cluster through the startup and control framework (explained in more detail later), the central administration and remote administration functions (available also through http/https tunneling), and the central log viewer are just a few of the many features that make support at the customer's site easier.
Security	In addition to application programming security, support of the latest standards, and the internal security infrastructure (LDAP as well as R/3 and Java RDBMS user stores), the security of the SAP Web AS cluster is also ensured by the many options available for setting up and configuring a secure network infrastructure and secure remote administration via *https* tunneling.
Manageability	The SAP Web AS Java stack provides a framework that integrates the life-cycle management of a Java instance into the existing SAP instance management solution. This framework inherits the tried-and-true process management concepts from the ABAP stack. The startup and control framework is one of the key solutions used in the SAP Web AS Java stack to ensure reliability and trouble-free administration of the infrastructure.
	A short outline of the role of each participant in the cluster is given below.

11.1.2 Components of the Cluster

SAP Web Dispatcher	The *SAP Web Dispatcher* is a central load balancer for distributing the load onto different hardware boxes. It is a central entry point for all user requests whenever other mechanisms, for example, the hardware load balancer, are not already in place.
J2EE Dispatcher and Application Server Nodes	Two kinds of nodes form the basis for scaling in big clusters: the *SAP J2EE Dispatcher* and the *SAP J2EE Application Server*. A dispatcher node is a local entry point, in a hardware box, to all client requests—HTTP/HTTPS, Web Services, RMI/IIOP, and JMS for example. It parses the requests, distributes them locally among the application server nodes, and returns the replies to the client through the other front-end/proxy modules, for example, the central load balancer. The application server node processes client requests, implements the J2EE container functions, and executes the connection to external systems. There are many ways in which you

can set up the architecture for a multi-tier application—possible solutions ranging from those based entirely on the SAP infrastructure to those integrated with different Web server vendors (for example, IIS and Apache), database vendors, external legacy systems, hardware load balancers, and so on.

The communication between *Dispatcher* and *Server* regarding the client request/response is always direct (point to point). More information on how the request/response cycle works can be found later in this chapter.

System Database

The database is a central storage location for all kinds of configuration and binary data. This enables central administration of the cluster, central deployment, central installation, and upgrading.

By default, SAP Web AS is supplied with MaxDB, the successor of SAP DB, but it also supports the full range of commercial databases (Oracle, MS SQL, DB2, and so on). For the complete list of supported databases, refer to the most recent product availability matrix.

It is also possible for the database used by the deployed applications to come from one and the same vendor or from different vendors (and even different versions of the same vendor). These scenarios are supported if you are using standard technologies like JDBC. However, they are not supported when the database portability (OpenSQL from SAP) abstraction layer is used.

Open SQL

When we look at database persistence, one of the most important aspects is the Open SQL infrastructure that is delivered with SAP Web AS. There is an entire chapter dedicated to persistency. Therefore, we will only briefly outline the concepts of this important layer. The design requirements for the Open SQL layer are to ensure the enterprise level of supportability, performance, and most importantly portability of the modules that implement database persistency. This concept is not new. It was developed and proven very valuable for the application developers during the many years of ABAP development (no ABAP developer has ever changed even a single line of code for the purpose of supporting yet another database).

Figure 11.2 shows the main building blocks in the Open SQL architecture.

SDM

The Software Deployment Manager (SDM) is a central component that consists of a server part and a client part. The server part manages the consistency of all deployed content, based on version, unique provider, and component name. The client part is designed for:

- ▶ Applying single patches (software development archives) to the system using the GUI tool

- ▶ Applying upgrades to the system in this scenario—it is used internally by the SAP installation

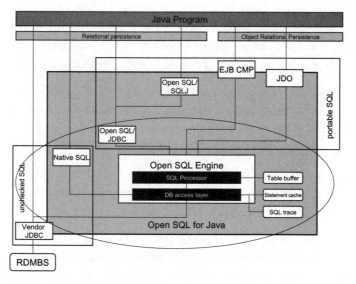

Figure 11.2 Open SQL Architecture

Locking Server Concurrent access to a common resource is achieved in the following manner, depending on the scenario in question:

- ▶ Inside one JVM synchronizing the thread access to the common resources is achieved by using language constructions. These are also extended in Java 2 Standard Edition (J2SE) by further data structures and utilities, in particular, in J2SE 1.5 by the concurrency utilities package.[2]

- ▶ In the cluster environment, locking is implemented using the *Enqueue server*. This applies to servers running on the same physical hosts as well as on different physical hosts.

A shared resource in a cluster is accessed in the following sequence: First set a lock in the Enqueue Server, then work with the resource, and finally, remove the lock.

There is a difference between resources shared in one JVM and cluster-wide resources. The former can be implemented efficiently using lan-

---

2 However, currently, at the time of unrestricted shipment, Web AS 6.40 supports J2SE 1.4 only.

guage-specific Java mechanisms, while the latter requires network or, for a single host, shared-memory communication. The design goal is to reduce the number of scenarios where cluster-wide locking is used.

Some of the scenarios where cluster-wide locking is used internally include: Starting/stopping server or dispatcher nodes; working with configuration data in the database; working with data in the EJB-CMP container, and so on.

When shared resources are used wisely and safely, the end result is a scalable architecture for both horizontal and vertical scaling. We'll discuss the fault tolerance aspects of the locking server later in this chapter.

The overall architecture of the Enqueue server and the lock request process are shown in Figures 11.3 and 11.4.

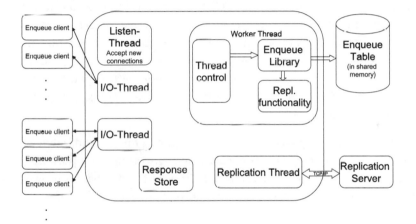

Figure 11.3 Enqueue Architecture

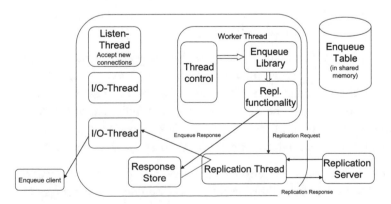

Figure 11.4 Enqueue: Locking Process

Message Server
Together with the locking process, message communication is part of the lowest layer in the cluster architecture. The central *Message Server* (MS) serves as a hub for exchanging messages and important information in a cluster environment. Information on the current state of the cluster—and each participant in it—is also stored in the message server. All communication between nodes, for example, transmitting a cluster-wide event for cache invalidation, is done using the message server. From a component perspective, this is accomplished using a predefined flexible and feature-rich API.

All nodes in the cluster are connected to the message server through a single, persistent TCP connection. This approach has many advantages as compared with the "fully connected ring" architecture where each individual application server is connected to one another in the cluster.

Appropriate mechanisms are also in place to prevent the message server from becoming a bottleneck for the system. Any time a message exceeding a given size limit has to be sent, a lazy connection is opened automatically. By default, this connection is closed after a 30 second timeout since the last data transmission. This differentiation with regard to message size is transparent in the upper component layer, that is, it is visible to services and applications.

The common scalability goal is to have message communication between nodes take place primarily for notification and synchronization purposes, and for any kind of data distribution where the central database is used—application deployment, configuration, and session failover, for example.

11.1.3 Cluster Landscape Options

The SAP Web AS may also work in different cluster scenarios, such as the *SAP integrated scenario*—bundled with the *SAP Internet Communication Manager*—as well as with other third-party Web servers.

SAP Integrated Scenario
In general, the entire static content of this scenario is handled and returned to the user through the *Internet Communication Manager* (ICM). For serving the dynamic content and executing the business logic, there are two stacks available: the ABAP stack with the full range of R/3 ABAP functions and BSP support, and the J2EE stack with J2EE 1.3-compliant implementation (JSP/servlet support, EJB, Web Services, and so on).

Because the J2EE dispatcher also includes a Web server, good integration between the ICM and the J2EE Dispatcher is essential. This is achieved in the areas of caching static content, load distribution, and handling secure communication.

The overall picture of such integrated scenarios is shown in Figures 11.5 and 11.6.

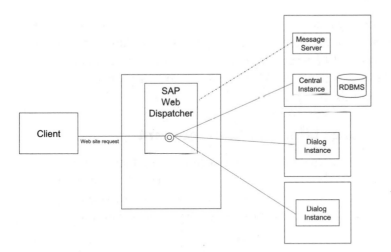

Figure 11.5 Integrated Scenario with SAP Web Dispatcher

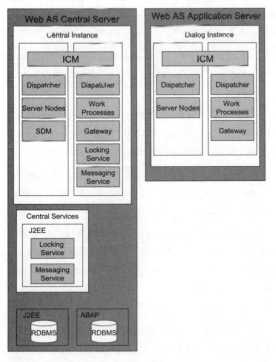

Figure 11.6 Integrated Scenario: Java and ABAP Together

Bundling with Third-Party Web Servers

Many of the Internet Web sites that run J2EE technology choose the three-tier-model: In the upper tier, a common Web server is used—mostly Apache or Microsoft IIS; in the middle tier, an application server executes the business logic; in the lower tier, there is a persistency layer that includes a database.

SAP supports this scenario with vendor-proprietary solutions for different Web servers. For example, the default installation includes an ISAPI filter for the Microsoft Internet Information server, which forwards all servlets and JSP requests to the back-end application server, while all the static content is processed by the IIS.

11.2 Cluster Lifecycle Management

The SAP Web AS Java provides a framework that integrates the lifecycle management of a Java instance into the existing SAP instance management solution. This framework inherits the tried-and-true process management concepts from the ABAP stack, and comes with the following features:

Cluster Startup and Control Framework

▶ It offers operating-system independent management of the entire cluster landscape. In a cluster setup consisting of many physical hosts, this is one of the most valuable and time-saving administration features.

▶ It strictly defines the sequence for starting Java processes for the Java instance—bootstrapping, starting a separate Java dispatcher, and server processes.

▶ It serves as a "watchdog," that is, it controls the Java processes that run in a Java instance and restarts them if necessary. This eliminates the possibility of hanging elements that interrupt cluster operations.

▶ It provides for remote control of all Java instances in the cluster. It allows cluster-wide lifecycle management activities such as starting, restarting, or shutting down the Java processes.

▶ It includes a startup framework client that can be easily integrated into other software elements that need control over the Java instance's lifecycle, for example, integration into the SAP NetWeaver Developer Studio (NWDS) to enable instance restart.

▶ It allows the binding of native functions into the Java processes that run within Java instances (for example, SAP Basis functions like jRFC).

▶ It includes management functions for remote debugging to improve supportability.

After installation, the administrator uses the startup framework as a central place for lifecycle management of the elements in the application server cluster. The administrator's view—using Microsoft Management Console technology on Windows platforms—is shown in Figure 9.7. Equipped with an intuitive interface, the startup and control framework enables easy monitoring of the state—**stopped**, **initial**, **starting**, and **running**—of each cluster participant. It also allows you to explicitly enable or disable the entire cluster, particular instances, or specific dispatcher or server nodes.

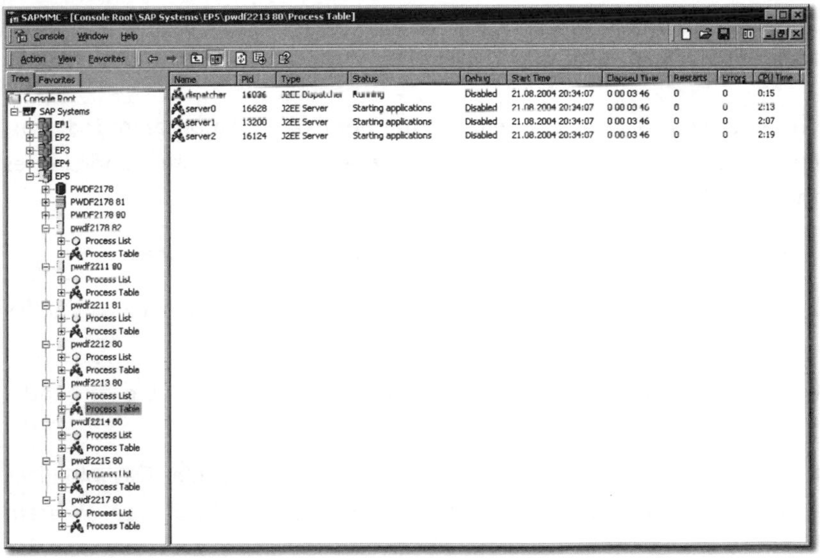

Figure 11.7 Example Cluster Landscape—Six Physical Hosts with 35 Application Servers in Total, Managed Centrally.

The management console (on Windows) is merely a GUI to the Java startup and control framework. It consists of the JControl and JLaunch programs. JControl is the master program for the Java instance and starts all necessary JLaunch programs in the right order and later controls them. **JControl and JLaunch**

The overall architecture is outlined in Figure 11.8.

The JLaunch program can execute any Java program, similar to the standard *java.exe* program. Specifically, it loads the JVM into its own address space and then into the required cluster element. The program can receive notification from the JControl process—through named pipes—for example, to stop the cluster element and then terminate it if JControl stops running.

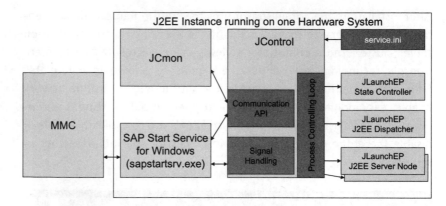

Figure 11.8 Startup Framework Architecture

The JLaunch program also executes the bootstrap Java program that synchronizes the binaries from the database with the file system and creates the property files that describe the Java instance.

The following steps are involved in starting the Java instance:

▶ JControl is started, on Windows, by the SAP start service; on UNIX platforms, by the *startsap* script.

▶ JControl initializes SAP signal handling in order to be able to handle signals received.

▶ JControl starts JLaunch with the *bootstrap.properties* file. This initializes and starts JVM with the bootstrap program; the bootstrap program synchronizes the binary data of the Java database with the local file system.

▶ JControl reads and creates a list of the Java cluster elements to be started.

▶ JControl starts a JLaunch process for each cluster element. The JLaunch loads the JVM into its own process, initializes it, and starts the Java cluster element.

Dump Stack Trace in Cluster One of the many additional and useful features of the Java control framework is its ability to trigger an internal JVM thread dump for server nodes that may be located on different (remote) machines.

As shown in the Figure 11.9, you can select an arbitrary Java node in a distributed environment, and get information about the threads currently running there. This is often used by the developers to analyze cluster-wide "hangs" caused by a cluster-wide resource, performance bottlenecks, and JVM deadlocks.

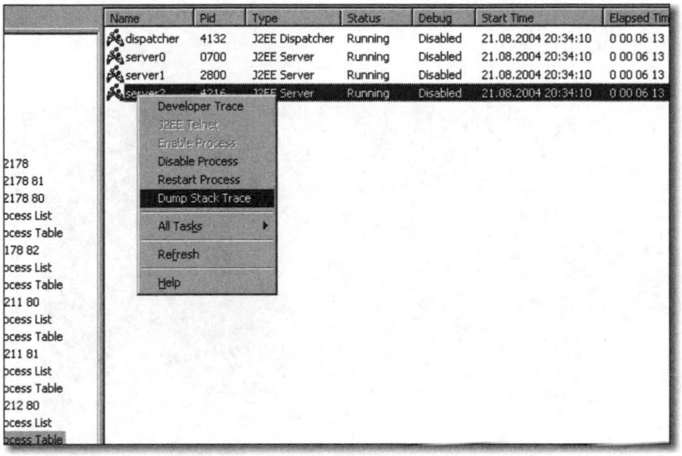

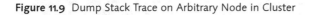

Figure 11.9 Dump Stack Trace on Arbitrary Node in Cluster

Visual tools are available that make this analysis even easier. Once you trigger the stack trace, the result is written to the work folder of the JControl. This is located in

/usr/sap/<SAP System ID>/J<SAP Instance Number>/work/
std_server<n>.out

For example:

/usr/sap/EP5/J82/work/std_server2.out

Whenever you trigger the stack trace on the remote host, you must access the corresponding folder in this remote host. The easiest way to do this is remotely—simply use the default "saploc" share of the \usr\sap folder.

Another useful feature that can be started from the management console is the J2EE Telnet. J2EE Telnet is generally recommended for company "hackers" only, because this tool exposes many of the administration functions of the server, which are otherwise available through the Visual and Web Administration tools, but in a text-based, shell-like way. Also, you should bear in mind that although the login through Telnet is authenticated, the console uses just the simple Telnet protocol, thereby making it dangerous in insecure environments. For secure remote administration, you should always use the Visual Administrator, or one of the Web-based tools.

J2EE Telnet

Right-clicking a dispatcher node allows you to launch the Telnet console for cluster administration. After successful login, you can use the UNIX-like console administration tool, which comes with hundreds of low-level administration capabilities.

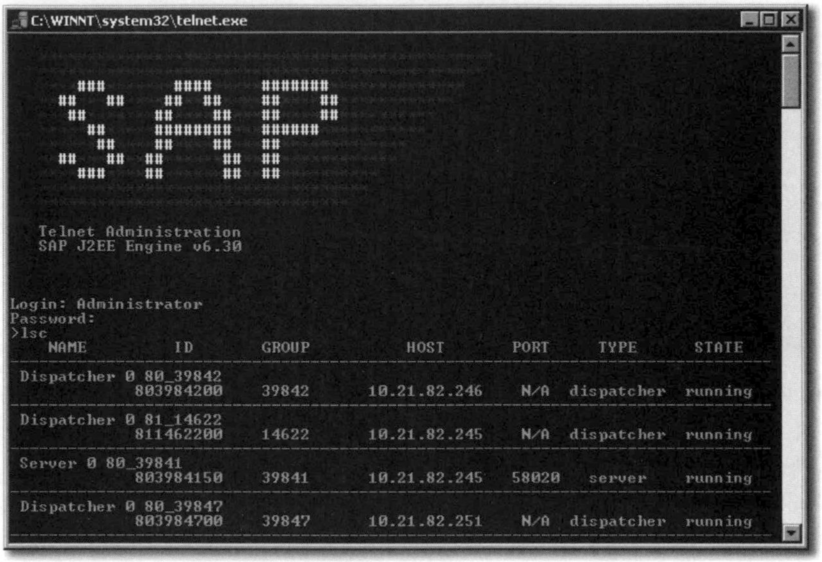

Figure 11.10 Telnet—Login and Listing Cluster Elements (lsc)

Jump After the very first element, you are on the dispatcher where the Telnet was started. Listing the available cluster elements allows you to "jump" to a node of your choice (see Figure 11.11).

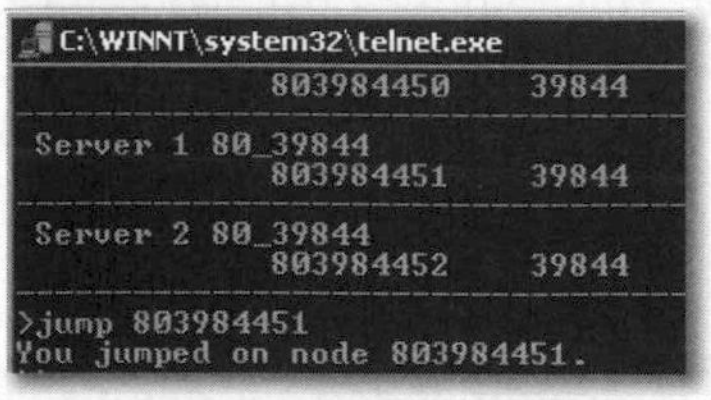

Figure 11.11 Jump to A Particular Server Node

We won't go into the details of every single command in the J2EE Telnet. Instead, we'll review the two primary commands:

"Add" and "Man"
- man: Those people with UNIX experience will easily guess what this means: It displays help for a specified shell command. When executed without parameters, it displays all currently available commands.
- add ⟨group⟩: This command adds a new group of commands to the list of existing ones. If executed without parameters, it displays all available groups of commands.

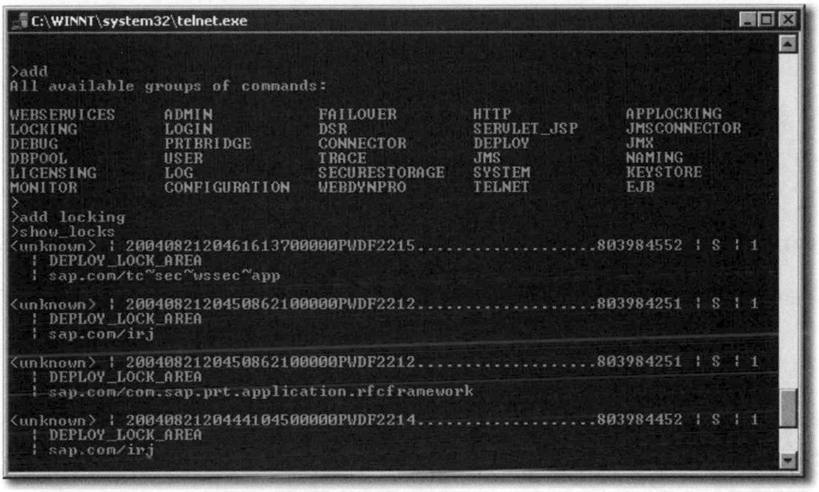

Figure 11.12 Example: Listing All Available Groups, Adding the "Locking" Group, and Listing All Set Cluster-wide Locks.

With these two commands, you can easily discover the details for each single command available, either by executing it with the -h option (provides a short help), or by looking at the additional documentation.

Finally, on all UNIX platforms where the Microsoft Management Console (MMC) is not available, there is another central console wrapper belonging to the startup framework functions called JCMon. It's also available on Windows platforms, next to the MMC.

JCMon

You can start the JCMon from the *os_libs* folder after the */usr/sap/<SAP System ID>/J<SAP Instance Number>*, specifying the instance profile (in the SYS/profile folder):

```
bash-2.05$ /usr/sap/E00/J02/j2ee/os_libs/jcmon
pf=/usr/sap/E00/SYS/profile/E00_J02_us7214
```

Once it is running, you will get a simple console to the same functions available from the MMC.

For example, you can start a server as shown in the other cluster example in Figure 11.14.

The state of the different elements on the selected instance is displayed; however, you must trigger the refresh function manually.

Figure 11.13 JCMon

```
Telnet us7214                                                    _ □ X

SAP System Name    : E00
SAP System         : 02
MS Host            : us4195
MS Port            : 6390
Process Count      : 3
PID of JControl    : 26746
State of JControl  : Some processes running
State inside MS    : Some processes running
Admin URL          :

 Idx Name                    PID        State           Erro

  0 dispatcher              19613 Running
  1 server0                 21905 Running
  2 server1                     0 Stopped



JControl Monitor Program - Administration Menue (Local)
Instance : JC_us7214_E00_02

0  : exit
1  : Refresh list
2  : Shutdown instance
3  : Enable process
4  : Disable process
5  : Restart process
6  : Enable bootstrapping on restart
7  : Disable bootstrapping on restart
8  : Enable debugging
9  : Disable debugging
10 : Dump stacktrace
11 : Process list
12 : Port list
13 : Activate debug session
14 : Deactivate debug session
15 : Increment trace level
16 : Decrement trace level
17 : Enable process restart
18 : Disable process restart

98 : Synchronize instance properties
99 : Extended process list on/off

command => 3

Process Index : 2
    Do you want to enable the process [2/server1] ? (y/n
    [enable process] successfully done
```

Figure 11.14 Command 3—Enable (Start) Process

Cluster Monitor Application

Yet another simple, Web-based view of the cluster is available through one of the default applications that run on the Web Application Server. With only very limited functions, this application offers a simple interface for fast viewing of the cluster status in cases where no other management tool is available.[3]

---

3 As of SPS 12 of Web AS 6.40, a full range of Web-based administration and sup-portability tools is available.

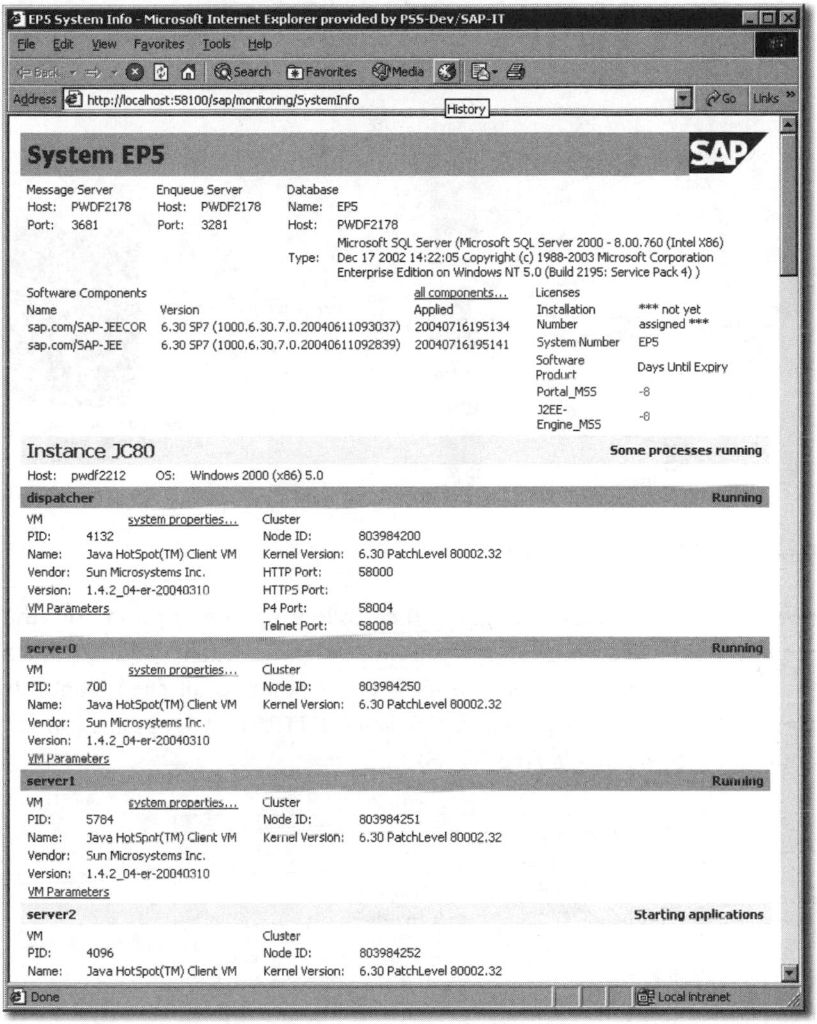

Figure 11.15 Web-Based Cluster View

11.3 Scalability and High Availability

In this section, we'll discuss some of the most important non-functional aspects of the application server: scalability and load balancing, as well as high availability and fault tolerance of the SAP Web Application Server.

11.3.1 Request Processing and Load Balancing

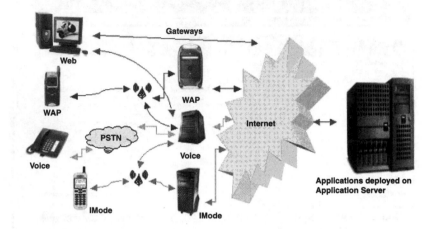

Figure 11.16 Standard Web-Based Access to Server-Side Applications

Request/Response Cycle

Both server-side handling and the follow-up description of the request/response cycle start at the point where the client requests reach the J2EE dispatcher, that is, the local entry point to all client requests (Servlet/JSP/Web Services request through HTTP/HTTPS, application client request through RMI/IIOP, JMS).

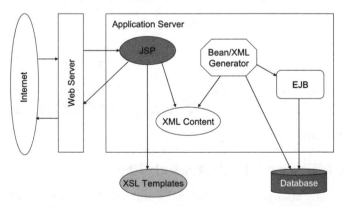

Figure 11.17 Simple View of Request Flow Along Different Layers of a J2EE Application

Entry Points

For each protocol provider, there is a part of it that runs on the dispatcher. This is called the HTTP dispatcher "frame," RMI/IIOP dispatcher "frame," and so on. The role of these components is to parse the incoming request according to the specific protocol, to re-dispatch the request for processing to a dedicated application server, to get the response from the application server, and to return it to the client.

SAP Web Dispatcher

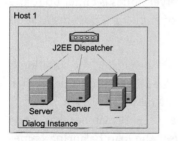

Host 1

J2EE Dispatcher

Server   Server

Dialog Instance

Figure 11.18 Local Load Distribution

Connection handling and pooling as well as load balancing and resource management are implemented centrally in the J2EE dispatcher, and all different protocol providers use this framework function.

When the server processes client requests, the ultimate goal is to have them, and hence the load, distributed evenly among the cluster nodes. The SAP Web AS by default supports two load balancing algorithms: the Round Robin and the Weighted Round Robin algorithm. SAP Web AS is also delivered with a pluggable load balancing framework, which offers easy extensions to and customization of the load distribution function.

Load Balancing

The Round Robin algorithm—executed on the J2EE dispatcher node—distributes the load to all server nodes participating in an *Instance* (usually a hardware box), one by one. However, this is an extension of the simplest and most straightforward approach where the distribution sequence is fixed (such an approach often fails in scenarios where one user transaction consists of a fixed sequence of steps that aren't bound to a session).

Round Robin

Although this algorithm achieves fairly good performance for one hardware box, it is not the optimum load distribution among the different hardware boxes. Often, these boxes are not equal in terms of processing power, memory, and so on.

In such cases, a second load balancing algorithm is implemented in the SAP Web Dispatcher—the Weighted Round Robin. The general idea behind this is the following: There is an assigned number or weight for each instance (hardware box). This denotes the approximate "power" of this box. For example, if you have two boxes, and the first box is a 2xCPU Pentium III, while the second box is a single CPU Pentium III, you can have two for the first and one for the second. The request distribution will then be in a 2:1 ratio, that is, the first box will get twice as many requests

Weighted Round Robin

as the second one. In the SAP Web Dispatcher, the right numbers are determined exactly by the number of application server nodes running on the box. Configuring the number of these server nodes is either up to the user or the administrator, or it is the result of applying a post-installation template for the given hardware.

In cases where a remote client is connected to the cluster, the situation is similar. In the SAP Web AS, remote client load-balancing is performed during the creation of a new remote client or a new `InitialContext()` call. After the remote connection to the J2EE dispatcher has been achieved, the RMI/IIOP dispatcher frame uses the load balancing framework to select the right node. The request is then redirected.

Session Management

Whenever a session is created on a particular server node, for example, after a servlet/jsp request, it is important that all follow-up requests from the same user go to the same server node. This is referred to as *session stickiness*. The HTTP is a stateless protocol, so an additional mechanism is required to ensure session persistency. The SAP Web AS comes with two methods for session demarcation: cookie-based and URL rewriting (the browser doesn't support cookies). When the first user request comes, the dispatcher uses the load-balancing algorithm to distribute it to a server node where the session is created. The corresponding server ID of the selected server is added to the cookie, and, for URL rewriting, it is appended to the URL. The next time a request comes in from the same user, the HTTP protocol dispatcher checks whether the incoming request is already in session and the request is forwarded to the designated server node—load balancing is no longer applied.

Heterogeneous Load Balancing

An additional option exists for heterogeneous Web load-balancing. Whenever an application is deployed in a cluster, it is deployed on every server node in the cluster. However, there is an option that allows the application to run after deployment on only some of the nodes. This approach of partitioning the applications has a few main advantages:

▶ **Isolation of the applications**: If one application crashes the JVM more often, it can be isolated from the other applications. This promotes stability.

▶ **Better resource utilization**: For example, caches that are usually dynamic and bound to specific applications are separated for better memory utilization and a higher hit-rate.

▶ **Better and more accurate sizing** on the basis of how much the different applications are loaded on a complex system.

For more details on the support of this feature,[4] refer to the appropriate product documentation.

Coping with Increased Load

It is often necessary to add more processing power to the cluster and applications that are already running productively. The SAP Web AS is designed in a way that you can easily increase the processing power by adding new server nodes or new dialog instances on additional hardware boxes. All the deployed applications are synchronized automatically; the newly created server nodes are automatically registered in the load balancing framework, and they can immediately start to participate in the load-balancing "game."

11.3.2 High Availability

Transparent failover mechanisms are provided to the enterprise applications. They ensure high availability to the end user.

In the SAP Web AS cluster, there are three central instances, each of which represents a potential *Single Point of Failure* (SPOF). A short description of which fault tolerance mechanisms are available and how each of these systems and their "users" react in the case of failure—thereby preserving the consistency of the cluster and the correct execution of the hosted applications—is given below.

Furthermore, there will be a description of the fault tolerance of the dispatcher and server nodes as well as the fault tolerance from a J2EE perspective, including transparent mechanisms that an application benefits from without any additional development effort.

There are two aspects that we need to consider when thinking about the locking server failures. The first aspect is the behavior of the components that use the locking-client API in situations where the locking server is

Enqueue Server

---

4 In addition to application-based load balancing, some NetWeaver components that run on the SAP Web Application Server support role- and user-based load balancing.

not available, for example, due to a crash. In these cases, requests for locking resources are denied. The behavior is the same as if the resource were already used. Hence, the aforementioned components don't require special care in this situation.

Similarly, requests for unlocking resources—whenever the *enqueue* function is not available—don't require any attention from the component layers above. The request is blocked until the locking server is running again.

The second aspect that we need to consider is the behavior of the locking server itself. The scenario for coping with a locking server crash and preserving the active locks is shown below.

Refer to the appropriate product documentation for information on how to set up the *enqueue* server in replication mode.

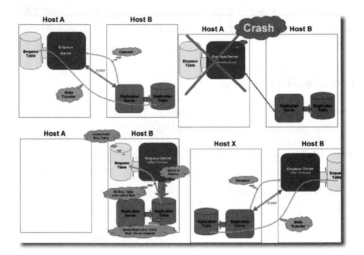

Figure 11.19 Enqueue Failover

Message Server With the message server being a central instance for cluster-wide communication, any message server crash could affect the work of the entire cluster. Because request/response communication is implemented via the direct TCP connection between the server and the dispatcher node, the workflow of client requests won't be interrupted, that is, serving static data, executing JSP/EJB requests. During the crash, all threads requesting any cluster communication or cluster state are blocked. As the message server is a very lightweight process, its restart—which is performed automatically—is very fast, and both the reconstruction of the cluster information and the return to normal work take only a few seconds.

There are no inconsistent scenarios or special aspects that a server component or the administrator should care about in cases where the message server crashes. Restarting the message server—due to a software error—is transparent to the client and does not interrupt the availability of the system. Failover in the case of a hardware error on the machine where the central Web AS instance is located can be implemented through failover cluster hardware.

Although the database software is often referred to as "unbreakable," the SAP Web AS takes into account the possibility of database crash and restart.

Database

The setup of a highly-available environment that hosts a database is usually considered by the respective database and hardware vendors. However, the database clients also need to be aware of any database crashes so that they can react appropriately.

There are a few places where the actual connection to the database takes place:

▶ The Open SQL abstraction layer—part of the Web AS—handles and offers a vendor-independent view of the database.

▶ The configuration manager—part of the Web AS kernel—offers an API for transactional management of the configuration data. The Implementation of the configuration manager is based on the Open SQL layer, while all components in the system use the configuration manager for writing persistent information to the database. These include Web AS services and J2EE containers, which write the configuration and the binaries of the deployed application to the database.

▶ From the application developer's perspective, all work with the database is J2EE-specific. The Database Connection Pool service serves as a proxy to the database.

▶ The Container Managed Persistence (CMP) and Java Data Objects (JDO) implementation in the server also deal with database persistence, again using the underlying Open SQL layer.

The situation where the database is missing is considered in all crucial places, implementing either a reconnection function in the core layers or generating an appropriate reaction to this event in the function modules above.

An example scenario follows:

1. Cluster is started.

2. Some applications are deployed.

3. A database property is changed, for example, the maximum number of connections to the database. This change requires a database restart (for example, in the case of MaxDB).

4. The database is restarted without restarting the cluster (the cluster can be very big, consisting of 50 server nodes on ten different hosts for example).

5. After the database has started, the full cluster and application functions are working again.

After Step 4—when the database is stopped—it is possible that the Web AS will lose some of its functions. You can no longer change any properties, deploy new applications, or change their state. As soon as the database is called up again, all these actions will be allowed.

J2EE Dispatcher Failure

One of the good things about the dispatcher and server nodes is that—in a big cluster environment—you have many of them. However, when you're running mission-critical applications, the impact from any user sessions lost due to a hardware or software crash is costly and erodes the credibility of the application vendors.

The J2EE dispatcher is a completely stateless instance. Thus, any crash of the dispatcher node won't affect the user sessions currently running. It is also a very lightweight fault: Recovery and restart from a crash is in the seconds range, and no data can be lost when this happens. If the J2EE dispatcher cannot be started again, the Web dispatcher will notice that it is missing, and, consequently, will stop sending requests to this host. The currently running user sessions will be redirected to another host where session failover will take place.

J2EE Server Failure

Whenever one application server node crashes, this affects only the sessions running inside this application server. However, this is the worst case and, although there is no generic solution for solving the problem, there are many cases where effective failover schemes can be applied. Depending on the application and the objects stored in the user session, a session failover service can be used. The most common concept—which also comes with the SAP Web AS cluster—is session replication (persistency). In general, at the end of the request/response cycle, the HTTP session is replicated to a backup storage. If there is a system crash, the backup storage is used to restore all lost sessions. Replicating, which is done using serialization and is only possible in the JVM, has its trade-offs: performance on the one side and restrictions to the application on the other. These restrictions are discussed in more detail below.

11.3.3 Session Failover

Providing fault tolerance for the Java server processes means that a mechanism to preserve the state of the active sessions must be available. Without session failover, any information regarding the state of the user at the moment of the crash is lost. The requests are merely dispatched to another server process in the cluster where the same business objects are available.

With session failover in use, the stateful information is made persistent. This allows the state to be retrieved when the request is dispatched to an available server process.

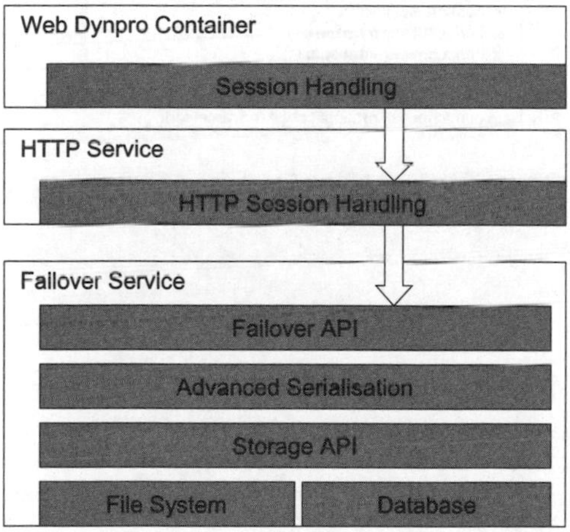

Figure 11.20 Session Failover Framework Architecture

To enable session failover, the only effort required by the application assembler and deployer is to set a Boolean flag denoting that failover is to be used. This flag is part of the extended J2EE application descriptor (*application-j2ee-engine.xml*):

```
<?xml version="1.0" encoding="UTF-8" ?>
<!DOCTYPE application-j2ee-engine SYSTEM
  'application-j2ee-engine.dtd'>
<application-j2ee-engine>
<provider-name> engine.book </provider-name>
```

```
<fail-over-enable mode="on-request"> </fail-over-enable>
</application-j2ee-engine>
```

The preference to run with or without session failover can also be switched during runtime, after the application is already deployed. Figure 11.21 shows the correct place in the Visual Administrator of the J2EE server where you can determine this preference.

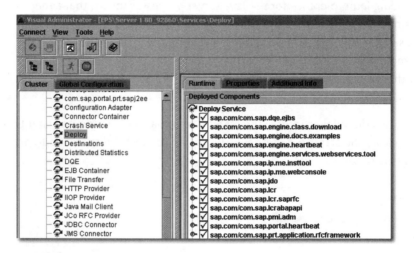

Figure 11.21 How to Navigate to the Deploy Service on Any Server and Choose Your Application

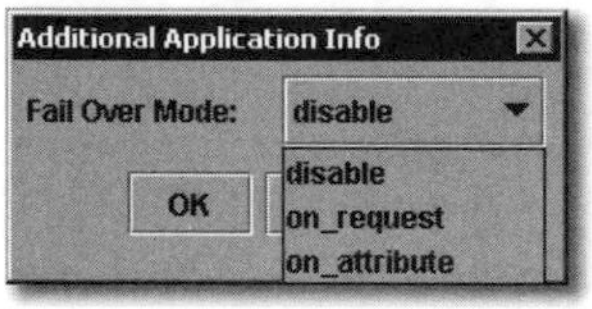

Figure 11.22 Click the Additional Info button, then choose the preferred failover type

Using session failover, however, leads to some restrictions for the application developer. The cases where failover is transparent are all stateless database components in a J2EE application:

▶ Static content

▶ Stateless jsp/servlet components

▶ Stateless session beans—the bean instance is recreated on another node, hence able to provide full recovery.

▶ Entity beans—similarly, the state of the entity beans is stored in the database; if there is a crash, they are reactivated on another node and synchronized with the database.

In a stateful component, the use of session replication is optional. If used, the servlet/jsp state—the *HttpSession* object and everything located in it—is replicated each time the request is returned to the client. The replication itself implies serialization; thus, the only possible objects that can be bound to a user session are:

► Pure data objects implementing java.io.Serializable

► Stateless session beans

► Stateful session beans

► Entity beans

► EJB Home objects

► JNDI Contexts

Finally, session failover must be used with caution as it often results in a decrease in the performance of the application. To preserve the session state in the event of a server crash, the session data is kept persistent on each request whenever a write or read action has been executed. Why does data need to be kept persistent if only a read operation is performed? Whenever a Web component developer uses only the getAttribute method of *HttpSession*, he or she often modifies the obtained objects directly, without executing the setAttribute method later. Although the modification will take place in the JVM and will remain there because the next request will come to the same JVM, there is no way for the Web Container to notice that there has been a change. The only way to ensure that the data is always persistent is to serialize it after the execution of each http request.

Another option for session serialization is also available: A given application can choose its user sessions to be serialized only when a session attribute is changed, that is, set or removed. In such cases, the application programmers have to ensure that no objects in the session are modified directly in the memory or reset in the HTTP session object afterwards.

This second option allows the Web Container to avoid unnecessary serialization operations and to serialize only those parts of the HTTP session that were modified, thereby reducing the negative performance impact to a minimum.

The failover service in the SAP Web AS comes with few configuration options. The main configuration option pertains to the data storage to be used and the options here are:

Configuration options

- The central database
- The local file system

As you might expect, the first option is often slower while the drawback of using the file system as session storage is that it is less reliable. In the case of file system failover and whenever the storage folder is not shared and accessible from all server nodes, the failover will take place only on each physical host. This is helpful in the case of a JVM crash, but not if the entire machine crashes. This option, however, is a good compromise and the performance impact can be reduced to object serialization alone.

11.4 Remote Debugging

Another important aspect of clustering that has an impact on reliability and supportability is providing a solution for remote debugging. The purpose is to provide isolated cluster elements that carry out the debugging operations without affecting the operations of the productive elements. In the SAP Web AS Java 6.40, isolation takes place at two levels: First, a debugging element is isolated from any load-balancing that occurs on the Java dispatcher; secondly, it is removed from the destinations list of addresses for transmitted messages that is kept by the message server. In this way, any productive request is prevented from being dispatched to the debugging element. Also, no internal events caused by debugging operations can be distributed among the productive elements of the cluster.[5]

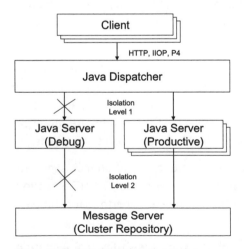

Figure 11.23 Remote Debugging Isolation

---

5 If there is only one server node running and it is in debugging mode, the system will return the error to all users who are placing non-debugging requests.

A remote debugging client and a startup framework client have been integrated into the SAP NetWeaver Developer Studio to provide central, easy-to-use control over the remote debugging process on the SAP Web AS Java. For the developer, activating the debugging process—that is, preparing a debugging cluster element and isolating it from the productive elements in the cluster—involves merely a single mouse-click. Everything else is done by the Java Startup and Control Framework.

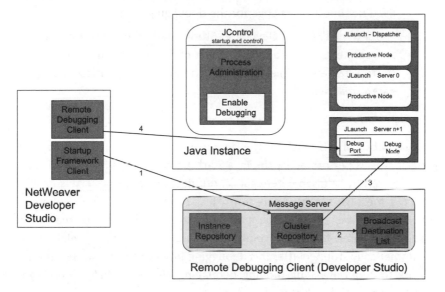

Figure 11.24 Preparing and Activating Remote Debugging

To get more details about what goes on behind the scenes, here is an outline of the process: **The process**

1. The startup framework client inside the SAP NetWeaver Developer Studio sends the "enable debugging" notification to the message server.

2. The message server forwards the notification to JControl.

3. JControl switches on the debugging mode and starts the process.

4. The debugging element uses the specified debugging port from the *instance.properties* file.

5. Isolation of the debugging element from the cluster communication:

   ▶ The startup framework client sends the activation notification to the message server.

- The message server removes the element from the transmitted destination list. After this step has been completed, the debugging element is no longer synchronized with the productive cluster elements.

- The message server sends the activation notification to the debugging element. The debugging element changes its own debugging mode from "Off" to "On." All other cluster elements will get a notification about this change for the debugging element.

- The SAP NetWeaver Developer Studio starts the debugging session and connects to the debugging port of the debugging element. The startup framework client provides the port configuration in a transparent manner.

6. Start debugging the application.

Once debugging is finished, the debugging element must be stopped.[6] Again, this is performed by the Java Startup and Control Framework, and is triggered by a "disable debugging" notification sent from SAP's NWDS to the message server. Apart from this, JControl has a pre-configured debugging timeout, for example, 10 minutes. This is the maximum debugging time from debugging activation. The debugging element is automatically stopped after this debugging timeout by the startup framework to avoid any long-running debugging elements that are not synchronized with the cluster.

11.5 Runtime Architecture Overview

While the previous sections covered the Web AS landscape, we will now focus on the runtime architecture of a Java application server or dispatcher process.

The component frameworks and layered setup of the dispatcher and the server nodes are very similar, and, from a runtime design perspective, there is no difference between a dispatcher and a server node. Although one of the goals of the J2EE programming model is to hide these low-level architectural concepts of the application server, in reality, this is rarely achieved. Therefore, understanding the architecture of the chosen application server will make the development and deployment of appli-

---

6 Also restarted. During a debugging session, whenever a new application is deployed or updated, these changes will not be visible on the "debugging" node because all cluster-wide events will not reach that node. To replicate the latest persistence and configuration changes, the note must be restarted.

cations easier and will help to avoid some of the usual pitfalls for running applications smoothly on top of it.[7]

Let's look at the "job" of the application server vendor. The development of Java/J2EE middleware is a very dynamic process: On the one hand, you have to catch up with the latest J2SE features, so that the infrastructure developers can exploit the most valuable new features of the Java language and its surrounding infrastructure; on the other hand, there is the need to implement—and also drive and design—the fast-changing, new specifications and application requirements. Hence, the only way to deliver a well-integrated and coherent infrastructure, that is, to host gigabytes of Java binaries of components and application, is to use a well-defined, modular structure for your software. A further decrease in the implicit and explicit references among the different parts of the product and building modules with clear interfaces that can be easily maintained, but are open for improvements, are the other key parts that form the core of the Web AS Runtime Architecture.

The architecture of a node, server or dispatcher, is structured in three different layers: *kernel*, *infrastructure*, and *application layers*. **Layers**

By design, the communication between these layers is always top-down. The components from the upper layers "know" the lower-level components and their interfaces, and can use them. Conversely, those components from the lower levels neither know nor have access to interfaces or implementation of the upper-layer components.

As an application developer, you are mostly concerned with the topmost layer and the APIs exposed by the previous one; these are the J2EE APIs as well as SAP's proprietary extensions to them, for example, the Web Dynpro programming model. Therefore, we'll look only briefly at the concepts of the underlying layers, and in the different places, like class-loading, we will try to emphasize the specifics of the concepts that may concern the application developer rather than describe the architecture in a completely abstract way.

---

7 There was a JCP (Java Community Process) attempt to not only standardize the concepts in the low-level building blocks, but to offer the application developers a way to extend and develop their own modules to run in the core layers of every application server. However, the corresponding JSR (JSR 111—"Java Services Framework") failed and was withdrawn in late 2003. Although understanding the architecture of an application server is important, SAP, like many other vendors, does not support the direct use of or building of low-level components by its customers.

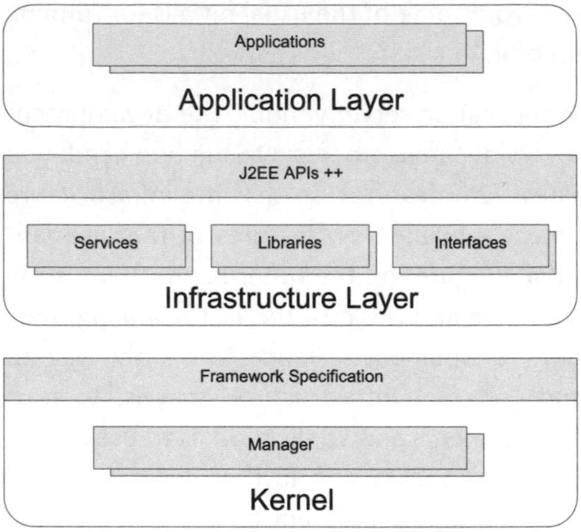

Figure 11.25 Runtime Architecture—Layers

11.5.1 The Java Kernel

The Java kernel implements the lowest-level function in the system. It provides the basic resource management and the operating-system-related functions: thread pooling and management, sockets and session communication, access to the persistent storage, cluster-wide locking, cluster-wide messaging and communication, logging and tracing, and Java proxy to some native functions (nanosecond timer and other functions that don't exist in the currently supported J2SE release). It is divided into subsystems, internally called *managers*. The activation order of these systems during startup is predefined and sequential. The only way to access and use the managers' functions from an infrastructure component is to include some manager's APIs as part of the *Services Framework*—a set of interfaces that separates the kernel from the next level. This is described later in more detail.

Framework APIs You can look at the Java kernel as a container that enables the development of the next level infrastructure components: services, libraries, and interfaces.

The building concepts of the *Service Framework* and the implementation of the Services framework, the kernel or the set of managers, are:

▶ It does not define dependencies or interfaces among the different infrastructure components in the system.

▶ It takes care of the lifecycle, deployment, and removal of these components.

- It defines the interfaces that the infrastructure components implement in order to handle the lifecycle state transitions as well as receive notification for system or component lifecycle events.

- It defines clear mechanisms for preventing runtime exceptions.

- It isolates the components from any direct access to the kernel and limits the use of the kernel by well-defined functions through a set of well-defined APIs.

- It provides an easy method for communication between the different parts of one component in a distributed environment.

- It takes care of the integrity of the entire system.

We will take another look at thread management in the J2EE server as an example of a manager that implements kernel functions.

Thread Management

One of the most important parts of the Java kernel is the implementation of thread pooling and a thread management framework.[8] These ensure better performance: Handling one user request is usually associated with the creation of Java threads, which is a costly operation; thread-related data consistency; resource distribution; resource protection and limitation; and precise kernel settings. The architecture of the internal thread system is displayed in Figure 11.26.

Two thread pools are available in the system: the *application thread pool* and the *system thread pool*. The first one is for all client-related (user request) thread uses in the system. When a client request is received, an attempt is made to find a free thread in the application thread pool. If no such free thread is available, the request is buffered into a request queue. In this way, a limit for the number of concurrently executed requests is defined. The system thread pool, on the other hand, is for system-related activities. This thread pool usually doesn't have a limit for the number of threads—or it has a sufficiently big limit—for the purpose of preventing deadlocks; the request flow in system-related activities, including any cluster activities, can lead to deadlocks if there is such a limitation.

Application Thread Pool and System Thread Pool

---

8 J2SE, Version 1.5 already includes efficient thread pool implementation (*java.util.concurrency* package); however J2SE 1.5 runtime is not supported in the 6.40 release of the Web AS. For the requirements of the application server, the implementation of the thread pool is only "half the story." Efficient monitoring, management, and integration with the thread context and resource management complete this particular kernel function.

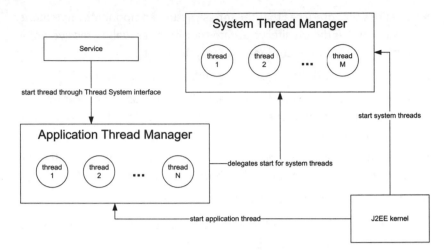

Figure 11.26 System and Application Thread Managers

Tuning system performance often includes setting the optimum number of application threads. The default in the Web AS is 40 application threads. This is a good compromise between maximum throughput— achieved with less threads—and good performance in non-CPU-bound scenarios—for example, integration scenarios where a lot of background or remote communication takes place; hence, threads are waiting for a remote response and the CPU is utilized less.

11.5.2 Infrastructure Layer

The infrastructure layer is the largest and the most important layer in the J2EE server. It consists of hundreds of components that implement the J2EE containers and other application programming model specifications, services for security, local and distributed naming system, landscape, configuration, remote management, and many more.

There are three different types of components available in this layer: *interfaces*, *libraries*, and *services*.

Interfaces   The *interface* components are "contracts" that define how the different components in the system work together; they are defined by name and by a set of classes. The interfaces cannot be used "as is." The way to work with them is to work with a *service* component that provides their implementation.

Libraries   The *library* components are usually shareable utility classes that do not have their own lifecycle. They are defined by name, a set of classes, and a set of objects (functions). The functions of the libraries are usually accessed via a "factory" pattern and static methods.

Services

The *services* are the most "powerful" components in the infrastructure layer, with complex lifecycle handling, well-defined interaction, and the option to access various APIs provided by the kernel and other services.

Core Services

Some of the services in the system are marked as *core*: If the initialization of any of these services fails during the startup of a node, this startup is stopped.

Lifecycle of the Infrastructure Components

Several lifecycle states are defined for each of the infrastructure components. These states are:

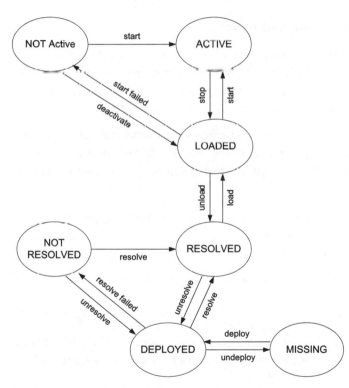

Figure 11.27 Lifecycle of the Infrastructure Components

▶ *Missing*: The component is not part of the system.

▶ *Deployed*: The component is part of the system.

▶ *Resolved:* The component is part of the system and all classes that it needs are available in the system. The component can be loaded.

▶ *Not Resolved:* The component is part of the system, but some classes that it needs to be loaded successfully are not present.

▶ *Loaded:* The component is loaded in the system.

▶ *Active:* The component is started and initialized successfully, and the functions that it provides are available.

▶ *Not Active*: The component is loaded, but not started due to dependency on other non-active components or errors during initialization.

The *active* state is different for the three different infrastructure components. For an *interface*, it means there is a service in an *active* state that provides this interface. For the libraries, the states *loaded* and *active* are one and the same. A service is in *active* state when the system executes and the service successfully finishes its initialization method.

11.5.3 Classloading and Isolation

One of the most important low-level component concepts, which ranges up to the J2EE application layer, is *classloading management*. In this section, we'll look briefly at the main concepts of Java classloading and see how it is extended and used in the SAP Web Application Server.

In Java (J2SE), one can define and implement extensions of the standard Java classloader. The classloaders are responsible for loading the sets of classes into the JVM. Each java object is uniquely identified by its *class* and *classloader*.

When creating a new classloader, you can define a *parent* relation between the classloaders, with the imposed restriction that every classloader has at most one parent.

Reasons for redundant classloaders In general, the reasons for having more than one classloader in the system include:

▶ **Isolation**
A component loaded in one classloader cannot access classes from another component loaded with another classloader, except if a parent-child chain relationship exists.

▶ **Locality**
Different classloaders with no parent-child chain relationship can load a different version of one and the same class having one and the same name. This allows the coexistence of different versions of the same component without a need for refactoring.

▶ Performance

The startup time for a set of components is reduced when they're initialized asynchronously and in different classloaders. Also, special custom-caching mechanisms are available that can accelerate normal Java classloading. If, during runtime, there are many attempts to load a class that does not exist, this will affect performance. Therefore, special "negative" caching is implemented for such cases. Other performance improvements include: closing the *jar* files with timeout so that, during initialization, when many classes are loaded for a short time, the jars are not reopened for every single class; fast search for the appropriate jar file for a particular class and, hence, inefficient searching in many jars is avoided, and so on.

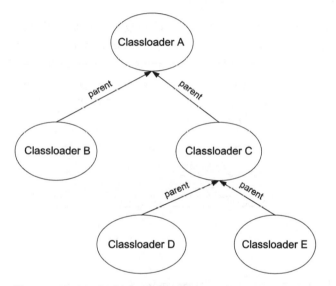

Figure 11.28 Standard Java Classloading

When a Java Object is instantiated, the default algorithm for searching for and defining the class of the object is as follows (we will call *the current classloader* the classloader of the class of the object from which the instantiation is initiated):

1. Check if the class is already loaded and available in the cache of the current classloader.

2. Try to load the class with the parent of the current classloader (recursion!). If no parent exists, go to the next step.

3. Search for and try to define the class in the resource set of the current classloader; usually a set of jar files is available locally on the disc.

Web Application Server Classloading Extension

Classloader
References

An enhanced Java classloading model is available in the SAP Web AS. Here, an additional relation called *reference* allows the definition of classloading references from and to a classloader. By defining 1:1 mapping between the classloader and component in the system, this practically allows the formation of a usage relationship graph among the different components (services, libraries, interfaces, applications), while preserving the isolation among them.

The semantics behind the *loading by reference* (see Figure 11.29) is an extension to the standard classloading function, with an additional attempt to load a class by the referenced classloader. The classloading references do not manifest transitive behavior.

As an example, let's take classloaders *B* and *C* from Figure 11.29, and look at a loading attempt made from *B*. The following will happen: In addition to the steps performed in standard Java classloading—an attempt to load the class by the parent of *B*, which is *A*—there is also an attempt to load the class by the referenced classloader *C* (but not by the parent of *C*, or by the classloaders referenced by *C*!).

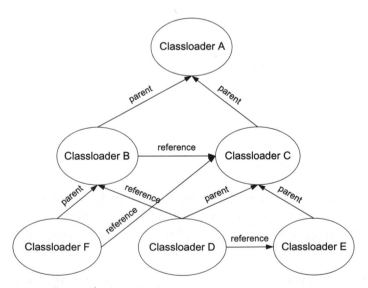

Figure 11.29 Web AS Classloading Extension

The classes of every component in the infrastructure layer are instantiated in a separate classloader. The Java kernel and the API Framework have separate classloaders. We won't discuss the classloading graph of the kernel and infrastructure layers in more detail. Instead, we'll emphasize what is visible from the J2EE application layer, what the classloaders associated during runtime with a deployed J2EE application are, and last, we'll look at how to define references between applications and determine what are these kind of references.

Classloading Structure for J2EE Applications

There are a few simple concepts involved in the classloading organization of a J2EE application:

▶ Every J2EE application, that is, packaged set of J2EE modules (Web modules, EJB modules, resource adapters, and so on), in an Enterprise Application Archive or a standalone J2EE module is loaded into its *own classloader*.[9] Therefore, every component or class in the archive is visible from any other component or class file in the archive, and can be instantiated and used by the same. Consequently, no duplication of classes—different classes with the same name—is allowed within such an archive.

▶ The parent loader of the application is the server "frame" loader, and its parents are the system loaders, giving access to all J2SE classes as well as to classes included in the server class path.

▶ The classloader of the application has a reference to classloaders of all programming APIs, for example, J2EE interfaces like servlet API, EJB API, WebDynpro APIs. These references don't need to be set explicitly by the application developer; they can be set by default in the system.

There are cases where you may need to structure a very big J2EE application in more than one enterprise archive or want to separate part of the application in a separate *library*, so that it is accessible and reusable for the needs of other J2EE applications. In such cases, an explicit reference to this application must be defined. You can do this by describing the reference in the extended J2EE application descriptor (*application-j2ee-engine.xml*); the relevant parts of the DTD of the XML are also included for convenience:

Application References

---

9 The exception to this rule is when standalone resource adapters are deployed: All such adapters are deployed in one common loader and are accessible from all J2EE applications. This requirement originates from the J2EE Connector specification (see the following excerpt):
   – When a standalone resource adapter RAR is deployed, the resource adapter must be made available to all J2EE applications in the application server.
   – When a resource adapter RAR packaged within a J2EE application EAR is deployed, the resource adapter must be made available only to the J2EE application with which it is packaged.

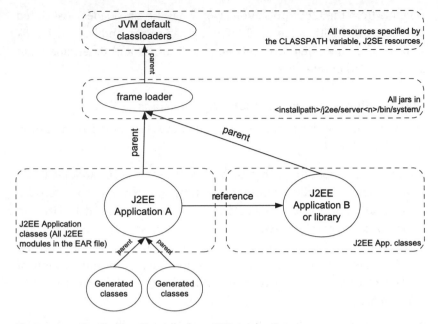

Figure 11.30 Classloading Structure for a J2EE Application

```
<?xml version="1.0" encoding="UTF-8" ?>
<!DOCTYPE application-j2ee-engine [
<!ELEMENT application-j2ee-engine (reference*,
  log-config*)>
<!ELEMENT reference (reference-target)>
<!ATTLIST reference reference-type (hard|weak) #REQUIRED>
<!ELEMENT reference-target (#PCDATA)>
<!ATTLIST reference-target target-
type (application|library|service|interface) #REQUIRED>
]>

<application-j2ee-engine>
  ...
  <reference reference-type="hard">
    <reference-target target-type="application">
      MySharedApplication
    </reference-target>
  </reference>

  <reference reference-type="weak">
    <reference-target target-type="library">
```

```
      sapxmltoolkit
    </reference-target>
  </reference>
  ...
</application-j2ee-engine>
```

The target types for a reference are `application` or `library`. The type of reference and how it relates to the lifecycle of the J2EE applications are discussed in the next section.

In most of the cases where the SAP Development Studio is used, these references are automatically generated. Hence, there is usually no need to manually interact with the descriptor of the J2EE application.

In cases where you want to deploy standalone J2EE modules (for example, resource connectors that are not included in an Enterprise Application Archive), the description of references to other components is slightly different, that is, the *application-j2ee-engine.xml* descriptor is not available, so the references are described in a similar way in the corresponding component descriptor. For more details, see the complete Web AS documentation.

Among the many options available for viewing the actual classloading references at runtime is the *Classloader Viewer*, available in the Visual Administrator Tool. A sample view is shown in Figure 11.31. The viewer displays all references for a given application or library, including those set by default by the server.

Classloader Viewer

Types of Classloading References

Setting a reference between two applications has an impact not only on the classloading visibility, but also on the lifecycle, that is, which application should be initialized, started or stopped first, and so on.

There are two types of reference that a component can set to another component: *weak* and *hard*. Both of these references are unidirectional.

A *weak* reference is present when there is a class use between two components. In this case, the system takes the following actions:

Weak (Soft) References

▶ If a second component exists, a classloading reference is set from the first to the second one.

▶ For successful resolution of the first component, there is the requirement that the second component be resolved successfully, that is, that it has its classloader created successfully.

▶ If the second component is going to be unloaded, the system triggers
the unloading of the first component before that.

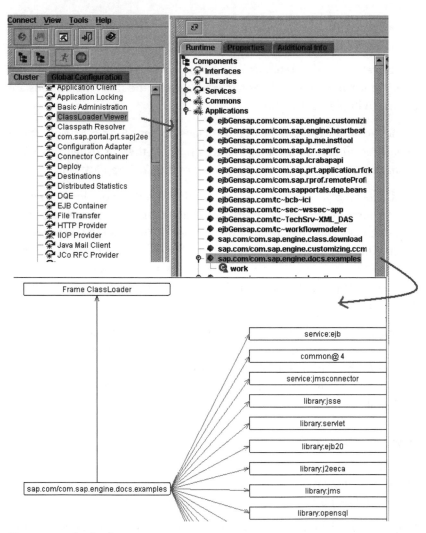

Figure 11.31 Classloader Viewer

Cycles of weak references among the components are allowed only for
infrastructure components. In such cases, there is one classloader for all
components participating in the cycle. Cycles of weak references are not
allowed for J2EE applications.

A *hard* reference is present if there is a functional (object) usage between two components. In this case, the system takes the following actions:

▶ If the second component exists, a classloading reference is set from the first to the second one.

▶ For successful resolution of the first component, there is the requirement that the second component be resolved successfully.

▶ All events connected to a state change of the second component are sent to the first one.

▶ The first component can be started only if the second one is already started.

▶ If the second component is going to be stopped, the system will first stop the first component.

▶ If the second component is going to be unloaded, the system triggers the unloading of the first component before that.

Cycles of hard references among components are not allowed.

11.5.4 Deployment Service and J2EE Containers

An additional "gravity center" is formed by the presence of a special *Deploy Service* in the system. This core service enables the notion of *Application Programming Model Containers*; these are all services that implement high-level programming languages for application development. Such examples are the J2EE Servlet and JSP container, the EJB container, the Connector container, as well as all proprietary SAP programming models, for example, WebDynpro).

The deployment service ensures proper distribution of the deployed components to the registered containers (through a predefined API), synchronization of deployment in a cluster, consistency and the transactional behavior of the deployment (and the enabling of the application), as well as information about the proper deployment of the application as one integrated component among all containers and cluster elements. It also keeps the most important information about an application: the parts it consists of, the path to the classes needed for successful classloading of the application, and so on.

The deployment service uses the messaging protocol provided by the framework to all services for communication in clusters as well as the cluster-wide locking mechanism to ensure application consistency during deployment, and during removal, update, start, or stop operations in the application.

Besides the deployment of J2EE applications or applications that run on top of the available programming models implemented by the different containers, the deployment service also implements the entire deployment logic for any infrastructure components (services and libraries).

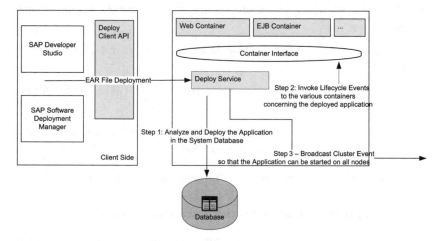

Figure 11.32 Deployment Architecture

12 Supportability of SAP Web Application Server

Supportability is a major factor when assessing a software product. Having a robust and easy to use supportability infrastructure could greatly reduce the total cost of ownership (TCO). In this chapter, we will look at the supportability infrastructure within SAP Web Application Server.

For a product to be supportable, its users must be allowed to operate in an efficient way to ensure the well being of the system. To be able to achieve this goal, they need tools to continually check the status of the system and tools to influence the behavior of the system in order to adjust it to meet specific requirements. Also, occasionally, administrators might encounter situations whereby parts of the system don't respond as expected, or show significant performance degradation. In such cases, tools that enable system administrators and developers to find and collect more details should be readily available to help them resolve the problem.

The aforementioned requirements define four major areas in the field of supportability that we'll cover in this chapter, namely:

▶ Logging (see Section 12.1)

▶ Monitoring (see Section 12.2)

▶ Administration (see Section 12.3)

▶ Performance Analysis (see Section 12.4)

12.1 Logging

Logging is a very popular and straightforward way to provide information about the status of the system. It is used to denote significant events in the lifecycle of the server so that these events can be analyzed in the order in which they happened. The logging infrastructure provided by SAP aims to provide this basic functionality and also meet the different configuration requirements that might appear in the wide range of scenarios executed in the SAP Web Application Server (SAP Web AS).

The log records produced by the system are grouped in problematic areas **Log Messages** (called *categories*) like System/Database, System/Server, System/Security, and so on that helps the user to quickly ascertain the relevance of the respective message. This concept, however, could be expanded in such a way that the category could be defined more precisely, for example, System/Server/Connectivity. Therefore, the problematic areas are structured hierarchically. When the system is running, the user is free to configure the logging infrastructure in a way that best suits his or her needs. Typically, this means assigning a file where the log messages are to be stored, or changing the severity level for a problematic area in order to get more or less information about it. In the hierarchical structure of categories, the more specific problematic areas inherit the configuration of their parents. If we use the previous example, this means that assigning a specific file, or changing the severity for the messages produced by the category System/Server will also have an effect on the messages produced by the category System/Server/Connectivity. In this way, the user would have more flexibility and could manipulate the configuration at different levels of granularity.

Log configuration in SAP Web AS is performed using the *Log Configurator Runtime Control* in the Visual Administrator tool (see Figure 12.1).

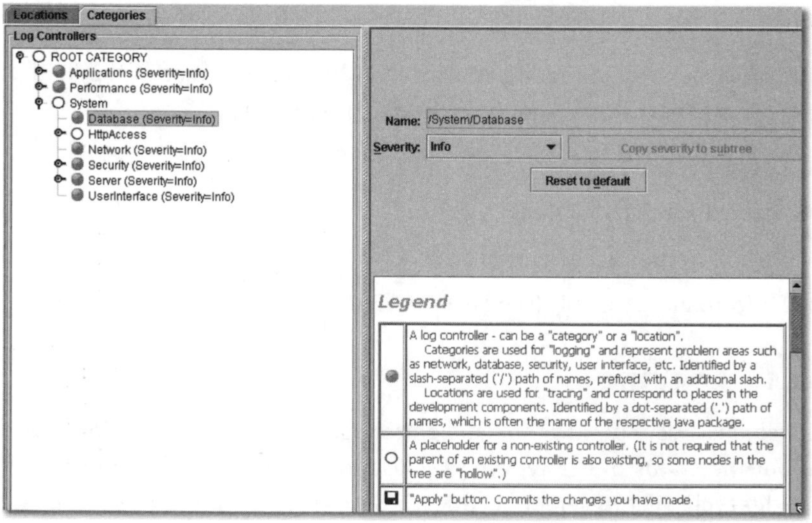

Figure 12.1 Log Configuration in Visual Administrator

Trace Messages   In addition to the log messages, the logging infrastructure enables you to produce additional trace messages that are targeted at more experienced users. These messages are typically switched off. They could be used in extreme situations when a certain errant behavior has been detected. The trace messages usually depict the program flow and are grouped by the software component that produced them. As software components are denoted by the Java packages of which they are made up (for example, *com.sap.engine.services* or *com.sap.portal*) they are also structured in a hierarchical way. Therefore, the user can configure the traces to a greater degree, or at a more fine-grained scale.

Frequently, log and trace messages need to be analyzed together. When a certain problem occurs, typically, the system administrator will detect the problem using the logs and then switch on the traces for more details. The logging infrastructure connects the related log and trace messages using message identificators. These identificators allow the user to verify that a certain trace message belongs to a certain problem area.

Along with the message, each log record contains additional information that helps the user find the context in which the message has been produced. This information includes the name of the application that has been requested, the user that is executing the request, and the session identificator.

The tool that is used to view the log and trace messages is the Log Viewer (see Figure 12.2). There are three variants of the Log Viewer:

Log Viewer

▶ **Log Viewer integrated in the Visual Administrator tool**
This is the full-blown version of the Log Viewer that allows merging of files, sorting, filtering, and searching the contents. It uses the information available in SAP Web AS to automatically detect the relevant files.

▶ **Standalone Log Viewer**
It is decoupled from SAP Web AS and is used whenever SAP Web AS is not available or cannot be started; provides similar functionality to the integrated version, but files to be reviewed have to be added manually.

▶ **Console Log Viewer**
This variant of the tool is started independently of SAP Web AS. It provides quick access to the log file contents.

12.2 Monitoring

12.2.1 JMX Infrastructure

The monitoring infrastructure of SAP Web AS provides the users with an overall picture of the well being of the system. Therefore, it is a critical part of the process of ensuring high availability and high performance of the product.

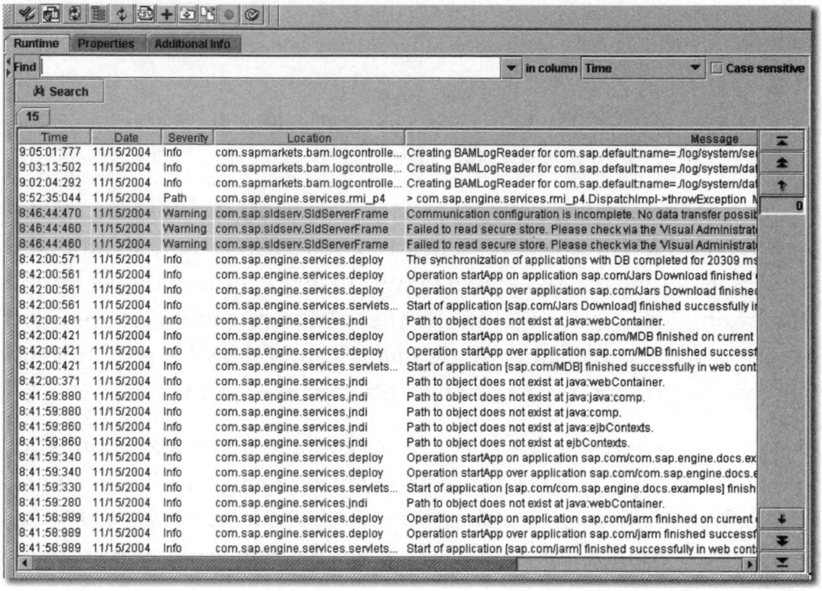

Figure 12.2 Log Viewer Integrated in Visual Administrator

Monitoring of the SAP Web AS Java stack is based on the open standard Java Management Extensions (JMX). On one hand, this ensures a clear logic and an architectural structure built on proven concepts; on the other hand, it allows for easy integration with other existing management solutions. The main concept behind JMX is the separation between the managed or monitored resources and the management system that uses these resources.

JMX Organizational Model

The organizational model defined by the standard specifies three layers, which are highly independent of each other and allow for building flexible and loosely coupled solutions. This is critical when managing huge systems made up of heterogeneous modules.

In the first layer—the *instrumentation layer*—are the managed resources. Their role is to provide management interfaces called *MBeans* through which they expose some management or monitoring information.

In the second agent layer is the JMX agent—the *MBean server*. The MBean server acts as an intermediary for the managed resources and the managed system, therefore preventing any direct communication that could lead to dependencies on class level. The MBean server is also concerned with the lifecycle of the MBeans registered by the resources. Besides the MBean server in the agent layer, a set of additional services are defined. They provide useful functionality such as the ability to define relations between the resources, the loading of classes from remote locations, and timeout events.

In the third layer—the *distributed services layer*—are the clients that retrieve and process the information along with the connectors and protocol adaptors provided by the infrastructure. The clients of the management and monitoring information can vary—from browsers to complex management systems built on proprietary technologies. Depending on the nature of these clients, they use different techniques to connect to the MBean server.

Nevertheless, the means to connect can be sorted in two major groups— connectors and protocol adaptors. *Connectors* are modules that consist of a client part used by the management system and a server part deployed at the MBean server, while protocol adaptors allow for a more generic access to the MBean server by transforming the calls over another protocol like HTTP into JMX calls.

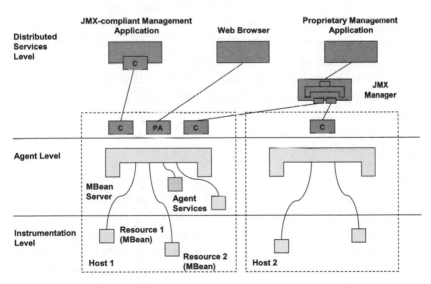

Figure 12.3 JMX Organizational Model

In SAP Web AS, the JMX infrastructure is implemented by a dedicated service called JMX service that also focuses on the distribution of the requests in the cluster and performs security checks on the incoming calls.

12.2.2 Monitors

The monitoring framework in SAP Web AS is a *pluggable* framework that uses the existing JMX infrastructure. It allows different resources to register as providers of monitoring data. The data collected from the resources is then processed by the monitoring framework and displayed in the Visual Administrator tool that comes with the J2EE Engine as well as in CCMS.[1] Typically, a resource that registers and provides monitoring data to the monitoring framework is either a J2EE application or a service that is part of the J2EE Engine.

Monitoring Infrastructure

The monitoring infrastructure builds a tree of monitors—the *Monitor Tree*. A *monitor* is an entity that is concerned with the communication with a single monitored resource and processes data collected from it. A monitor usually represents a small amount of data, that is, it contains a simple type value that tells us about a single aspect of a monitored object. For example, a monitor might represent the name of an object, or the number of successful transactions with an object, but not the object itself. That's why a resource that works with a logical object and wants to provide information about it in the monitoring infrastructure would typically define several monitors representing different aspects of the object and would then group them semantically so that the group represents the whole object. For example, let's use a J2EE application designed to manage the proper functioning of a bank. In this case, the resource that provides monitoring data is the application and the logical object is the bank. The name, the average number of transactions, or the daily cash flow could be different monitors representing the bank.

A monitor is always part of a certain group of monitors describing an object. The objects themselves can be further logically grouped inside the Monitor Tree in entities called *summaries* and the summaries, in turn, can be grouped with other summaries and objects in summaries again. Thus, the hierarchical structure of the tree follows the semantics of the objects being monitored. In the Monitor Tree, the leaves are always *monitors*, the nodes in the first level above the leaves are *objects*, and the nodes in the upper levels are *summaries*. The summaries from the first level below the root are predefined.

---

1 CCMS stands for Computing Center Management System and is a central system collecting and visualizing monitoring data for several application servers including both J2EE and ABAP stacks.

The monitoring infrastructure supports several types of monitors. Some of them represent a simple counter, while others model more complex scenarios such as cache access or session duration. Depending on the type of monitor, you can define thresholds of critical values. When such a critical value is reached, the monitor can signal an alert. The monitors also keep a history of the last 24 hours so that a user can analyze how the system has behaved in the past. History can be configured to be stored persistently, which allows further analysis in a broader scope of time.

Figure 12.4 gives you an idea of what the Monitor Tree looks like.

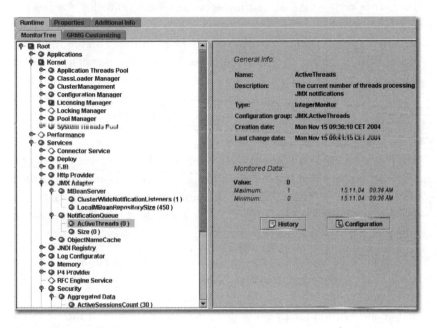

Figure 12.4 Monitor Tree

These are some of the most frequently used parts of the Monitor Tree:

▶ */Root/System*: The monitors below this node provide useful information about the configuration of the system as kernel version, VM parameters, process ID, message and enqueue server configuration (see Chapter 11).

▶ */Root/Kernel/Connections* Manipulator (on dispatcher nodes only): These monitors provide information about the number and the type of connections that have been established to the server.

▶ */Root/Services/http Provider*: This part of the Monitor Tree provides information about the HTTP requests that are processed by the server.

▶ */Root/Services/Memory:* Here, you can see the memory consumption of a server process.

12.2.3 Adding New Content in the Monitoring Framework

As we already mentioned, the monitoring framework is open for new resources to plug in. To do this, they have to fulfill two tasks. The first task is to define the monitors, the objects, and the summaries that have to be created inside the Monitor Tree for them. This is done declaratively via an Extensible Markup Language (XML) file that is packed in the software deliverable archive (SDA) of the resource. The monitoring framework takes care to retrieve the XML file after the deployment of the resource, to parse it, and to install the entities described in the Monitor Tree. The second task is to provide resource MBeans. The *resource MBeans* (also called *runtime MBeans*) are used by the monitors to retrieve the monitoring data at runtime. All the communication between the monitors and the resource MBeans at runtime is done over Java Management Extensions (JMX).

The relation between the resource MBeans and the monitors is one to many. This means that one resource MBean can provide monitoring data to one or more monitors and that one monitor can retrieve its data from one resource MBean only. This is because a monitor typically represents a single attribute of a resource.

The resource MBeans can provide the monitoring data either actively or passively. Providing data actively (this mode is also known as *data pushed by resource*) means that the resource MBean is responsible for initiating a change in the monitor by sending a JMX notification with the updated value. Conversely, passive provision of data (known as *data polled by the monitor*) forces the monitor to periodically check the value of the monitored attribute. In this case, the changes of the value are detected automatically. Which of the two modes a monitor will use is defined in the configuration XML file, which is deployed with the resource.

12.2.4 Accessing Monitoring Data from an External Client

All monitors are registered as MBeans in the MBean server. Therefore, it is possible for third-party tools to retrieve the monitoring data from them over JMX. This allows for easy integration of the SAP Web AS monitoring infrastructure with other existing monitoring solutions.

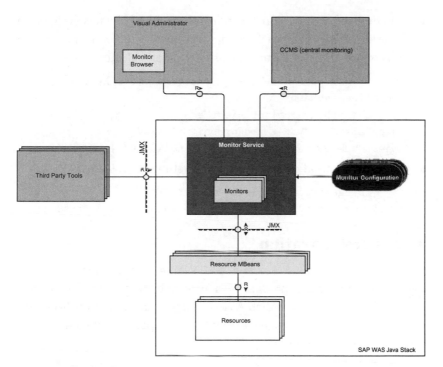

Figure 12.5 Monitoring Infrastructure

A standalone client must execute the following steps in order to retrieve the value of a certain monitor:

▶ Ensure that the client has the JMX implementation provided by SAP in its class path.

▶ Connect to the server—this could be done using the RMI JMX connector in the following way:

```
    Properties pr = new Properties();
    pr.put(Context.INITIAL_CONTEXT_FACTORY,
"com.sap.engine.services.jndi.InitialContextFactoryImpl");
    pr.put(Context.SECURITY_CREDENTIALS, "sap");
//supplies the password
    pr.put(Context.PROVIDER_URL, "localhost:50004");
//supplies host and port
    MBeanServerConnection mbsc = JmxConnectionFactory.
      getMBeanServerConnection(JmxConnectionFactory.
      PROTOCOL_ENGINE_P4, pr); //gets remote connection
                               //using the RMI JMX
                               //connector
```

▶ Build the ObjectName corresponding to the monitor whose value is to be retrieved—the ObjectName has attributes specifying the path in the Monitor Tree, for example, cluster node and cluster name:

```
String pathInTheTree = "/Root/Services/Memory
Info/AllocatedMemory";
    ObjectName monitorObjectName =
ObjectNameFactory.getNameForMonitorPerNode
(ObjectName.quote(pathInTheTree), null, null);
```

▶ Invoke the method of the monitor that returns its value over JMX:

```
    Integer value = (Integer)
mbsc.invoke(monitorObjectName, "getValue", null, null);
```

12.3 Administration

The administration infrastructure of SAP Web AS allows its users to configure and control the product in a way that best suits their needs. Administration of the SAP Web AS Java stack is also based on JMX. This makes the infrastructure highly extensible and open for integration with other management solutions.

12.3.1 Administration Infrastructure

Basic Administration Services

On the server side, there are two administration services that provide different levels of abstraction. The first administration service, which is deployed and started as a core service, is the *basic administration service*. It instruments the kernel and all server components (libraries, interfaces, and services) with MBeans thus displaying management functionality to any internally deployed component or external JMX-enabled tool.

The MBeans registered by the basic administration service can be categorized in two groups:

▶ *Generic MBeans* which expose standard functionality—such as *starting* or *stopping*—depending on the type of the component, *modification of properties*, and so on. These MBeans are registered by default for all deployed components.

▶ *Specific MBeans* which expose component-specific functionality. In order to have such an MBean, a component must register in the framework of the J2EE Engine an object that implements its dedicated management interface.

Both types of MBeans can send JMX notifications when a certain important event occurs. This makes administration more flexible.

The second administration service is the *administration adapter service*. It provides a logical grouping of the administration MBeans in a hierarchical structure and convenient *high-level* interfaces for accessing their attributes and methods. The interfaces provided by the administration adapter service accelerate the building of user interfaces on top of the administration infrastructure.

Administration Adapter Service

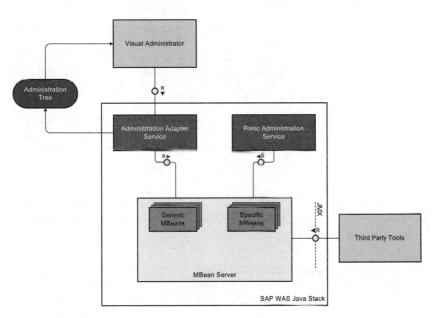

Figure 12.6 Administration Infrastructure

The tool used on the client side for working with the administration infrastructure is the Visual Administrator tool (see Figure 12.6). It uses the interfaces provided by the administration adapter service to retrieve and manipulate the set of MBeans. Following the categorization of the MBeans in the Visual Administrator tool, each component has one *generic* view corresponding to its generic MBean. In addition, services might have a *runtime* view that represents the functionality provided by a specific MBean.

Here are some of the most frequently used parts of Visual Administrator:

▶ **Edition of service properties**: This is the basic customization of service components (see Figure 12.7).

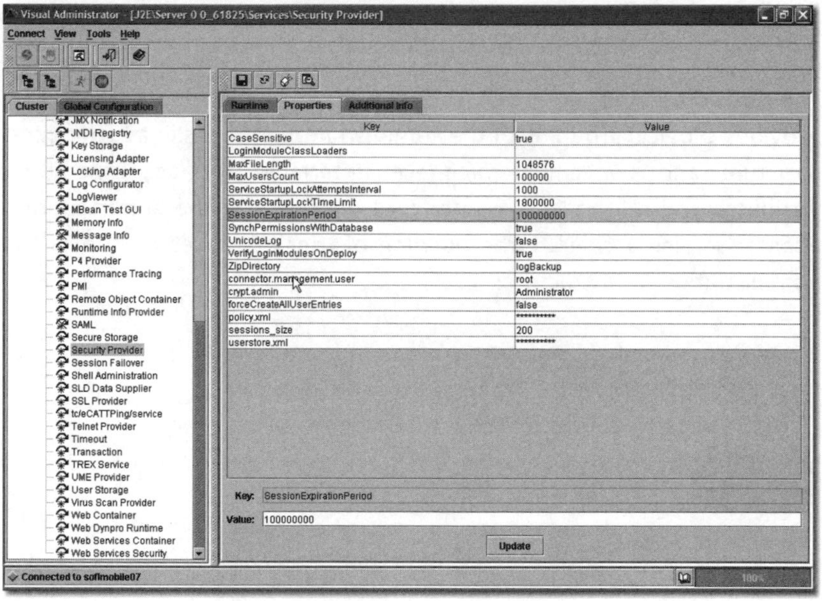

Figure 12.7 Edition of Service Properties in Visual Administrator

▶ **Security Runtime Control**: You can make some security settings here, for example, create a new user and assign it to a certain security group (see Figure 12.8).

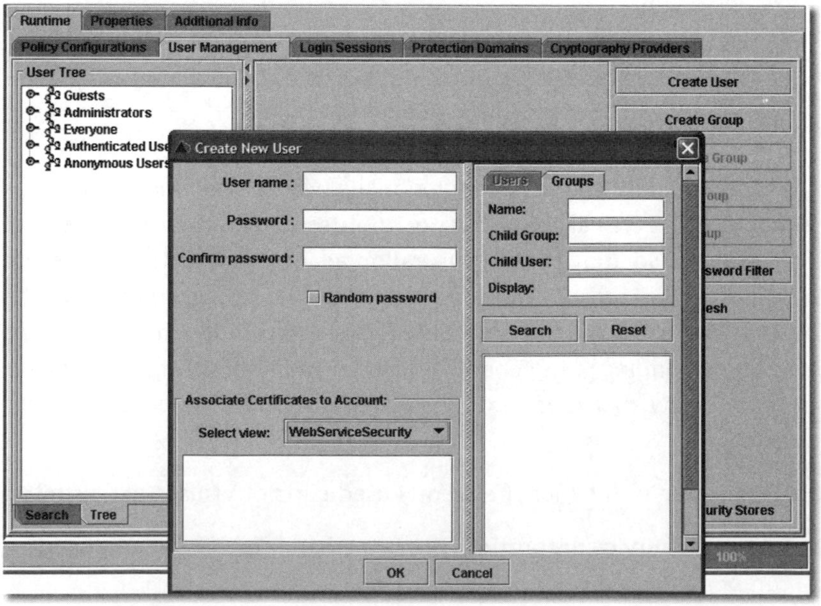

Figure 12.8 Security Administration in Visual Administrator

▶ **HTTP Runtime Control**: In this runtime control, the user can get information about the registered HTTP aliases as well as modify some parameters of the work of the HTTP service as cache usage or keep alive settings (see Figure 12.9).

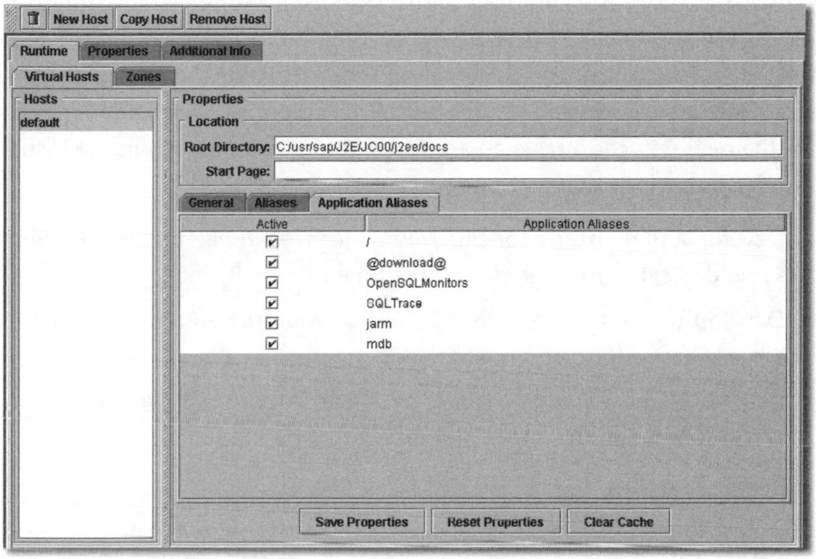

Figure 12.9 HTTP Administration in Visual Administrator

▶ **Starting and stopping of services**: Using this functionality, the user can customize the set of services running on the system (see Figure 12.10).

Figure 12.10 Starting and Stopping of Services in the Visual Administrator

12.3.2 Possibilities to Extend Visual Administrator

Although the Visual Administrator tool comes with lots of preinstalled administrative features, it could be extended even further as it provides a framework in which new user interfaces can be easily plugged into. There are two ways in which the Visual Administrator tool can be extended.

12.3.3 Providing a User Interface for a Newly Installed Service

The service framework of SAP Web AS Java stack allows new services to be developed and deployed. In its deployable archive, any new service can also contain user interface parts. The Visual Administrator tool can detect these user interface parts at runtime and download and plug in their classes so that they appear as runtime views for the respective service. Here are the steps that the service developer must execute in order for the new service to have an arbitrary administration view in the Visual Administrator tool:

▶ Develop and register a specific MBean for the service that will provide some dedicated management functionality.

▶ Develop user interface classes in Swing using the API defined by the Visual Administrator tool framework.

▶ In the *provider.xml*, which is part of the deployable archive for the service, set the main user interface class to **to be loaded**, for example:

```
<runtime-editor>
  my.package.MyClass
</runtime-editor>
```

12.3.4 Adding a New Managed Object in the Administration Tree

Any service or J2EE application deployed in SAP Web AS can add a new managed object in the administration tree. These new objects are displayed with a generic MBean editor that lists the methods and the attributes of the respective MBean. This option is particularly useful when a user interface need not be sophisticated and therefore can be developed with less effort. To add a new node in the administration tree, you must do the following:

▶ Develop an MBean that exposes the functionality which is required to manage the object.

▶ Build a wrapper MBean for the one developed at the first step. In it provide a Properties object specifying the path in the tree where the new managed object will appear and its name, for example:

```
    MyMbean mbean = new MyMBean(…); //here the MBean that
is to be added in the administration tree is built
    Properties p = new Properties();  //define an object
of type Properties to be added to the MBeanInfo of the
```

```
MBean
    p.setProperty("admin.path", "/Cluster/MyPath");
    p.setProperty("admin.displayName", "");
    com.sap.pj.jmx.mbeaninfo.StandardMBeanWrapper wrapper
= new StandardMBeanWrapper(mbean, null, p); //build the wr
apper MBean with an extended MbeanInfo
    mBeanServer. registerMBean(wrapper, wrapperObjectName)
  //register the wrapper MBean in the MBean server
```

12.3.5 Other Administrative Tools

Another useful tool that comes with SAP Web AS Java stack is the Offline Configuration tool. This is an expert tool that is typically used in emergencies. The Offline Configuration tool works directly with the database so it doesn't need a running Web AS to perform its tasks. Some of its most important features include the option to edit the Java settings for the processes running in the cluster and the option to add or remove cluster nodes from the cluster.

Offline
Configuration Tool

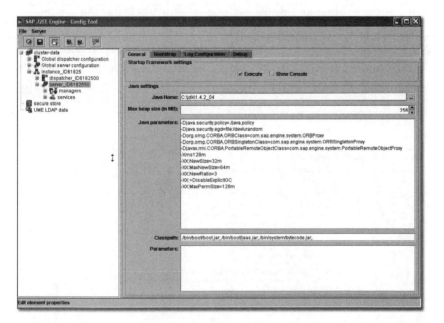

Figure 12.11 Offline Configuration Tool

In the SAP Web AS Java stack, there are also several low-level console-based administration tools that were addressed in Chapter 11.

12.4 Performance Analysis

One of the major topics when integrating or running a system is being able to analyze performance problems. SAP Web AS Java stack provides several techniques to quickly locate bottlenecks. Now, we'll look at three such techniques.

12.4.1 Application Tracing

Application tracing is based on bytecode modification. The main advantage of this approach is that it allows the performance of J2EE applications to be measured at method level without the need for preceding manual instrumentation. What the administrator of the system must do is as simple as restarting the application in modified mode. The bytecode instrumentation is done on the fly when the classes of the application are being loaded. Consequently, for all Java threads executing code inside the application, the stacks of *nested method invocations* are visible. For each of the method invocations, the time in microseconds that it took for execution is measured and displayed. Along with this data, the arguments with which the method was invoked are retrieved. They and their direct or indirect references in the object graph can therefore be accessed by the viewer. In order to better match the runtime information with the code being executed, application tracing provides the possibility for external decompilers to be plugged in and used for displaying the modified classes.

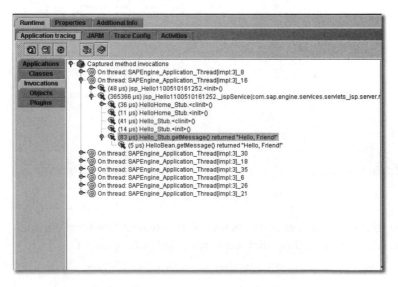

Figure 12.12 Application Tracing Viewer in Visual Administrator

All this information enables the user to work at a very low level when analyzing performance problems in the system.

12.4.2 Single Activity Trace

Another technique that gives performance analysis information at a higher level is the *Single Activity Trace* (SAT). SAT requires manual instrumentation to be performed by the application developers. They are responsible for defining logical components inside the application and triggering events to the SAT API whenever a request goes in or out of the component. Components can be nested and therefore different levels of granularity can be measured. All records written by different components in one request share a common identifier called *passport* that allows their correlation at analysis time.

Most of the applications delivered by SAP are instrumented with this technique so their administrators can, if necessary, switch SAT on and analyze the performance. The information gathered by the applications is written in a trace file using the logging API. The Log Viewer tool recognizes SAT traces and presents them in a special format that reflects the hierarchical structure of the components. When starting SAT, it can be enabled for all requests, or only for those requests that are initiated by a certain user.

The data gathered by SAT contains information about the time spent in the components as well as the number of bytes that were transmitted (see Figure 12.13).

12.4.3 SQL Tracing

SAP Open SQL engine copes with various database management systems and SQL dialects by providing a unified portable solution for all components in the SAP Web AS Java stack that need relational persistence. This is why analyzing the Open SQL layer gives us important information about application behavior. SQL tracing is a technique that uses events from the Open SQL engine to record the SQL statement, duration, application name, and other useful data for each database query that has been executed. It does not require additional instrumentation from the application developer and can be switched on and off dynamically.

The collected information is written to the file system using the logging API and can be subsequently filtered and analyzed via a Web interface (see Figure 12.14).

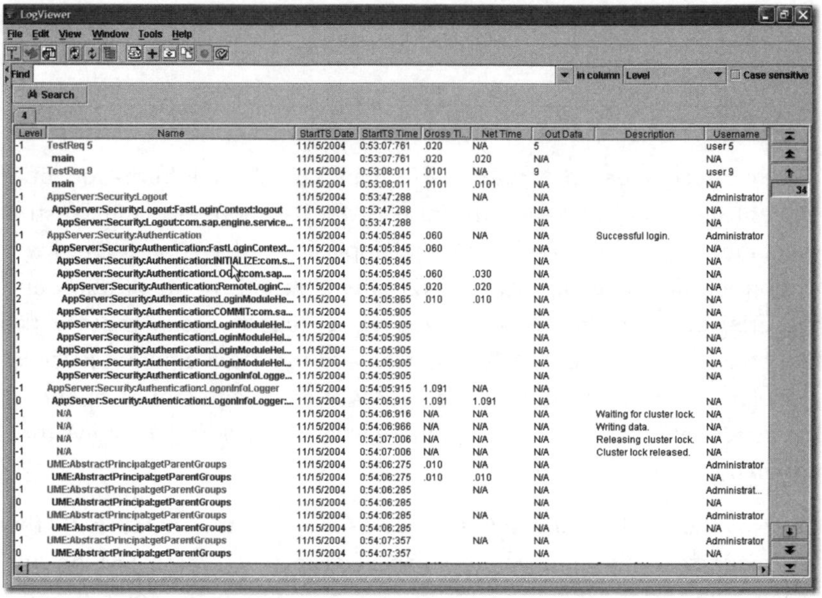

Figure 12.13 SAT Viewer in the Visual Administrator

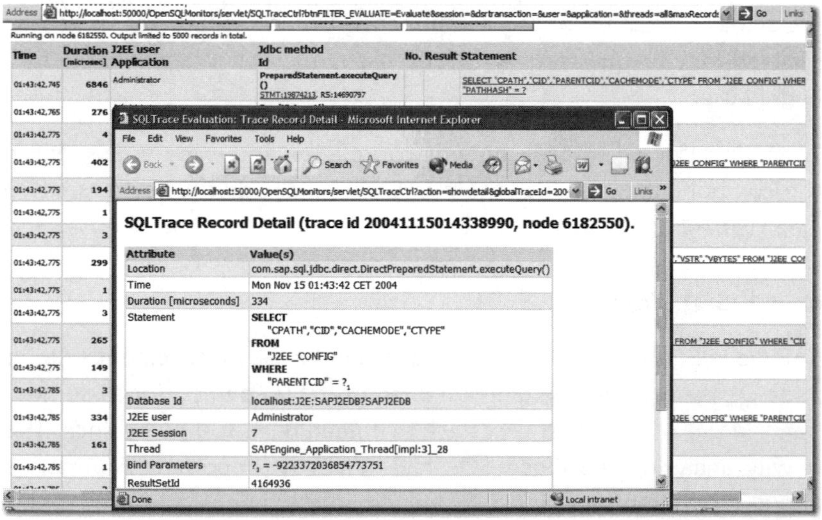

Figure 12.14 SQL Tracing Viewer

The Authors

Alfred Barzewski

Alfred Barzewski (*alfred.barzewski@sap.com*) joined SAP in 1997 as a member of the Product Management group for ABAP Workbench. Initially, he was responsible for Information Development in various areas of the SAP technology. These areas included Remote Communication, Non-SAP Accesses using BAPIs, RFC Programming, and ABAP Development. Most recently, he has focused on Java technologies in the environment of the SAP Web Application Server.

Panayot Dobrikov

For the last five years, Panayot Dobrikov (*panayot.dobrikov@sap.com*) has worked extensively on the design and implementation of the Web Application Server at Prosyst, InQMy, and SAP. Currently, Panayot is the Development Architect for the NetWeaver Foundation and is responsible for the architecture of the SAP Web Application Server Java.

Bertram Ganz

After his position as software trainer, Bertram Ganz (*bertram.ganz@sap.com*) came to SAP in 2002. Since then, he has worked as part of the development team on Web Dynpro Java Runtime. The main focus of his work is on the following topics: knowledge transfer, rollout, and documentation. Bertram regularly publishes articles on Web Dynpro in the context of the SAP Web Application Server.

Wolf Hengevoß

Wolf Hengevoß (*wolf.hengevoss@sap.com*) began his employment in Product Management at SAP in 1999. He has worked in the Basis group on R/3 topics such as Computer-Aided Test Tool and Business Address Services. In the early development stages of the Exchange Infrastructure, he took on topics from the Java environment. Today, his work focuses on the rollout of the Java Development Infrastructure of SAP NetWeaver.

Karl Kessler

Karl Kessler (*karl.kessler@sap.com)* came to SAP in 1992 as a software engineer. After his initial experience with the modeling of the Basis technology, he switched to Product Management for ABAP Workbench, where he was responsible for the rollout of SAP Technology at various conferences. In 2003, he assumed responsibility for Production Management of the NetWeaver Technology Infrastructure, with a focus on SAP Web Application Server Java and ABAP.

Markus Küfer

Markus Küfer (*markus.kuefer@sap.com*) studied Medical Information Technology at the University of Heidelberg. In 2000, he joined SAP and became involved in the technology and application frameworks for Java. When JDO 1.0 was announced, Marcus switched to the SAP JDO implementation team, where he was responsible for object-relational mapping, as well as the integration of JDO in the J2EE Engine at SAP. Currently, Markus is involved in the J2EE kernel development, particularly with the infrastructure of the Configuration Repository. He also represents SAP in the Expert Group for the JDO Specification (JSR 243).

Martin Huvar

Martin Huvar (*martin.huvar@sap.com*) has worked at SAP for over 11 years. After working in the development department, consulting, and different technology departments, he moved to Product Management for various XML and WebService topics. Currently, he is the Product Manager responsible for the Enterprise Service Infrastructure and Web Dynpro at SAP.

Jürgen Opgenorth

Jürgen Opgenorth (*juergen.opgenorth@sap.com*) received his doctorate in Theoretical Mathematics at the Technical University of Aachen (RWTH). After working in software development, he joined SAP in 1998, where he was instrumental in developing the original concept and prototype of the Java Application Server. Later, he joined the InQMy team at SAP. Since 2003, Jürgen has been the Technology Consultant for the SAP Web Application Server Java.

Miroslav Petrov

Miroslav Petrov (*miroslav.petrov@sap.com*) studied Information Technology at the University of Sofia, Bulgaria. In 2000, he began working at SAP Labs Bulgaria. Since 2001, Miroslav has led a development team in the area Java Administration and Monitoring.

Peter Tillert

Peter Tillert (*peter.tillert@sap.com*) joined SAP's Technical Marketing Department in 1989. He was a member of the first SAP R/3 rollout team. Later on, he moved into development and became the Development Architect for Desktop Integration and Business Intelligence. Currently, as part of SAP NetWeaver Product Management, he is the team leader of a group responsible for the Java tools and Runtime services in the SAP Web Application Server.

Yu-Nong Zhang

Yu-Nong Zhang (*y.zhang@sap.com*) received his degree in Technical Information and Business Studies. Then, he worked as a software engineer, before joining SAP in 2001 in the area of Technology Product Management. Today, as part of the NetWeaver Product Management team, he works in the area of Software Lifecycle Management.

Index

The ABAP Developer's Guide to Java

www.sap-press.com

A. Schneider-Neureither (Ed.)

The ABAP Developer's Guide to Java

Leverage your ABAP skills to climb up the Java learning curve

This all-new reference book is an indispensable guide for ABAP developers who need a smooth transition to Java. The authors highlight each fundamental aspect pertaining to the development of business applications in both languages, and the differences as well as similarities are analyzed in detail. This book helps any developer learn techniques to master development tools and objects, application design, application layers and much more. Learn about Beans, OpenSQL for Java, JDBC, Security, and more.

>> www.sap-press.de/777

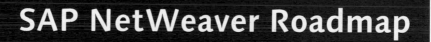

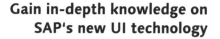